W9-DDE-051

POWER SHIFT

San Francisco

CALIFORNIA

NEV.

Las Vegas

Los Angeles

ARIZONA

San Diego

Phoenix

Albuquerque

NEW MEXICO

Oklahoma City

OK

Fort Wor

TEXAS

THE
SOUTHERN
RIM

Kirkpatrick Sale

POWER SHIFT

*The Rise of the Southern Rim
and Its Challenge to the
Eastern Establishment*

Generously Donated to

The Frederick Douglass Institute
By Professor Jesse Moore

Fall 2000

Vintage Books
A Division of Random House
New York

VINTAGE BOOKS EDITION, August 1976
Copyright © 1975 by Kirkpatrick Sale

All rights reserved under International and Pan-American Copyright
Conventions. Published in the United States by Random House, Inc.,
New York, and simultaneously in Canada by Random House of Canada
Limited, Toronto. Originally published by Random House, Inc., in
1975.

LIBRARY OF CONGRESS CATALOGING IN PUBLICATION DATA
Sale, Kirkpatrick.
   Power shift.

   Includes bibliographical references and index.
   1. United States—Politics and government—1945-
   2. United States—Economic conditions—1945-
   3. Southern States—Politics and government—1951-
   4. Southern States—Economic conditions—1945-
   5. Southwestern States—Politics and government.
   6. Southwestern States—Economic conditions. I. Title.
   [E839.5.S23 1976]   320.9′73′092   76-10327
   ISBN 0-394-72130-6

Manufactured in the United States of America

*This book is dedicated
to the women of tomorrow,
especially
Rebekah and Kalista*

Documentary evidence to support every specific statement of fact in this book is cited in the Notes section beginning on page 313.

Contents

Contents

POWER SHIFT

Introduction

In the Oval Office of the White House, shortly before two o'clock on March 13, 1973, Richard Nixon is nearing the end of a long and rambling conversation with his counsel, John Dean, about ways to deflect the growing Watergate scandals that are just beginning to threaten his Administration. On Capitol Hill, L. Patrick Gray, Nixon's nominee to be head of the Federal Bureau of Investigation, is continuing his testimony to the Senate Judiciary Committee, before whom he has already disclosed damaging secrets that point suspicions directly to the White House; the day before, Nixon issued a proclamation denying permission for his staff members to appear before the various Senate committees, pulling a blanket of "executive privilege" hard around him to withstand the increasingly bitter winds of Watergate. The President is now feeling himself very much the beleaguered hero under attack from a cruel press and a manipulated public, and angrily declares at one point, "Nobody is a friend of ours," later on reflecting more plaintively, "It will remain a crisis among the upper intellectual types, the soft heads, our own, too—Republicans—and the Democrats and the rest." Dean, shrewd to detect and reflect the mood of his superior, soon joins in and begins berating with him "the press . . .

the intellectuals," claiming they would never believe the Watergate burglars were acting alone, "they would have to paint it into something more sinister, more involved, part of a general plan." The President nods, seems to grow morose, and then bursts out with the idea that has been troubling him all along:

"On and on and on. No, I tell you this, it is the last gasp of our hardest opponents. They've just got to have something to squeal about it."

Dean, ever the second banana, begins to chime in, "It is the only thing they have to squeal—" but Nixon, warming to his subject now, won't be interrupted.

"They are going to lie around and squeal. They are having a hard time now. They got the hell kicked out of them in the elections." Then just to make sure Dean appreciates the full dimensions of who this enemy is, Nixon enlarges: "There is a lot of Watergate around in this town, not so much our opponents, even the media, but the basic thing is the Establishment. The Establishment is dying, and so they've got to show that despite the successes we have had in foreign policy and in the election, they've got to show that it is just wrong, just because of this. They are trying to use this as the whole thing."

The basic thing is the Establishment.

Extraordinary. This is a President of the United States talking, and in the normal taxonomy of this country a President is regarded as a key part, if not the very center, of any "Establishment"—yet here is a President who plainly sees himself outside the Establishment, and, more than that, an *enemy* of that Establishment. Clearly, then, Richard Nixon is changing the usual definitions, is in fact pointing to a new conception of what the Establishment is and what its position has become in mid-century America, a conception which he no doubt had never fully articulated but which his highly developed political antennae told him was nonetheless quite real. For Nixon, the Establishment is a distant and a foreign world, the world of New York and Boston and Newport and Grosse Pointe and Winnetka, the world of great wealth, high culture, nurtured traditions, industrial power, and political aristocracies, the world of "the soft heads" and "the media," the "liberal elite" and the "impudent snobs"—"the enemy." Nixon sees himself as standing apart from all of this, obviously a newcomer, an outsider, a challenger, representative of a newer breed of people who, no matter how many deals they make with this Establishment, no matter how many times they rub shoulders with it, will never be a part of that world, for they come from a new place and they hold different values and they serve variant causes. Nixon understands, if only primitively, that there is in fact a new configuration of forces in America, to which he and his Presidency are joined, that stands in opposition to the traditional Establishment and is therefore a new component to be reckoned with in the equations of national power.

Looked at in its broadest terms, the modern Establishment in America enjoyed a virtually undiminished influence from the time of its consolidation after the Civil War right down to the beginning of World War II, roughly the whole seventy-year period from 1870 to 1940. In practically every aspect of life, this country was dominated by a nexus of industrial, financial, political, academic, and cultural centers based in the Northeast, stretching from Chicago to New York, from Boston to Philadelphia, and associated with the names of Mellon, Carnegie, Rockefeller, Morgan, Ford, McCormick, Vanderbilt, and the like. It was this nexus that influenced the selection of Presidential candidates (between 1869 and 1945 only two Presidents were born outside of the Northeast), that controlled the houses of Congress, that determined American foreign policy, that set the economic priorities and directions, that more or less created the cultural and moral standards, that determined who were to be the powerful and the powerless. And such provincial areas as *did* manage to grow up at the same time—the San Francisco Bay Area, say, with its "upstart" A. P. Giannini, founder of the Bank of America, or New Orleans, prosperous through the Mississippi River traffic—were largely contained in their remoter regions and allowed to exert very little economic or political influence on a national scale.

All that began to change with the advent of World War II and its new technologies and priorities. Slowly there grew up a rival nexus, based in the Southern and Western parts of the country that stand in geographical—and to a large degree cultural, economic, and political—opposition to the Northeast, specifically in the *Southern Rim*, the broad band of America that stretches from Southern California through the Southwest and Texas, into the Deep South and down to Florida. Here a truly competitive power base took shape, built upon the unsurpassed population migrations that began to draw millions and millions of people from the older and colder sections of the Northeast to the younger and sunnier sections of the South and Southwest . . . upon an authentic economic revolution that created the giant new postwar industries of defense, aerospace, technology, electronics, agribusiness, and oil-and-gas extraction, all of which were based primarily in the Southern Rim and which grew to rival and in some cases surpass the older industries of the Northeast . . . upon the enormous growth of the federal government and its unprecedented accumulation of wealth, the great part of which went to develop and sustain the new areas and the new government-dependent industries, the new ports and new inland transportation systems, the new military and aerospace bases and the new water and irrigation systems . . . upon the political development of the Southern Rim and its growing influence in almost all national party organizations of whatever stripe, its decisive role in the selection of candidates of both major parties, its control over the major committees and much of the inner workings of Congress, and ultimately, from 1963 to 1974, its occupancy of the Presidency itself. Over the last thirty years, this rival nexus, moving on to the national stage and mounting a head-on challenge to the traditional Establishment, has quite simply shifted the balance of power in America away from the Northeast and toward the Southern Rim.

That this is not some arcane geographical games-playing or a form of paranoia born in Richard Nixon's mind is easy enough to demonstrate. The evidence is abundant and rather wonderfully diverse, manifested, for example, in the takeover of the Republican Party by the new and generally conservative forces from the Southern Rim—Barry Goldwater, Ronald Reagan, Nixon himself—and the consequent displacement of Northeastern liberals, at least for the long decade between 1964 and 1974 . . . in the assaults by Southern Rim tycoons, Clint Murchison, James Ling, Nelson Bunker Hunt, Howard Hughes, and many colorful others, upon the citadels of Wall Street and the giants of Northeastern industry . . . in the shift of major-league sports franchises out of the Northeast to the South and West, and the creation of six new professional leagues by entrepreneurs of that area . . . in the succession to power in the tight and potent world of the U.S. Congress of such men, over the years, as Allen Ellender, Sam Rayburn, Richard Russell, James Eastland, Wright Patman, Wilbur Mills, Chet Holifield, John Stennis, Sam Ervin, Carl Albert, John Rhodes, Howard Baker, Joseph Montoya, every one of them from the Southern Rim . . . in the emergence of new official stock exchanges in places like Miami and Los Angeles, flourishing at a time when the New York exchanges are floundering . . . in the extraordinary rise and growth of new cities like Anaheim, San Diego, Phoenix, Albuquerque, Dallas, Houston, Memphis, Jackson, Atlanta, Jacksonville, Orlando, stretching right across the southern part of the country, cities which have grown from sleepy cowtowns and frontier outposts into major commercial centers, among the most thriving in the land . . . in the relocation of organized crime activities out of the wizened world of the Northeast to the newly hospitable centers of Los Angeles, Las Vegas, Phoenix, New Orleans, Hot Springs, Miami Beach . . . in the extraordinary investment of $55 million by H. Ross Perot, the Texas computer executive, who single-handedly kept the stock brokerages from collapsing in 1971 . . . in the rise within the Democratic Party of figures like George Wallace, Jerry Brown, Lloyd Bentsen, Fred Harris, Jimmy Carter, Robert Strauss, Terry Sanford, Reubin Askew, all of them from the Southern Rim and all among the new figures reshaping that party . . . in the flight of thousands of businesses and hundreds of major corporations out of the big cities of the Northeast into the aggressive new cities of the Southern Rim, draining the Northeast of at least forty of *Fortune*'s top-ranked industrial firms in just the last ten years . . . in the development of serious cultural centers in such places as Los Angeles, Houston, Atlanta, and Miami, each with enterprises to rival those of New York's and to meet or surpass those of most of the rest of the Northeast . . . in the rising personal incomes of the people in the Southern Rim states which have been growing steadily while there has been a decline in the Northeast, and in the last decade the growth rates of the leading sunbelt metropolitan areas have been twice as high as in the leading coldbelt areas . . . and in such small facts as that the West Coast plans to build its own Statue of Liberty . . . that the Federal Reserve Board has established its first new bank in thirty-three years in Miami, Florida . . . that the national headquarters of the American Contract Bridge League is in Memphis . . . that Bergdorf Goodman, the fancy Fifth Avenue department store in New York, is owned by Carter Hawley Hale Stores of Los Angeles . . . and that Hebrew-National Kosher Foods, Inc., the most famous name in all of New York's delicatessen culture, is owned by the Riviana Foods of Houston, Texas. . . . And that's only a start.

And the Northeast under this kind of siege? Well, it has not disappeared, nor does it give any signs of doing so: the very fact that Nixon is no longer in that Oval Office and that he has been replaced by a man from Michigan is evidence enough that considerable power still resides in the Northeast. But one can see plainly that the Establishment is *declining*, and even a Presidential coup cannot disguise that reality. The large urban centers are all decaying and losing population, some like Newark and Buffalo and Detroit and Gary turning into outright sinkholes. . . . The riches of the Northeast are flowing to other sections of the country, producing "a pronounced shift of income" over the next fifteen years toward the Southern and Western regions, according to the Census Bureau, with particularly rapid growths for manufacturing operations in the South and below-average rates for "nearly every major industry in the Middle Atlantic region . . . for the next two decades." . . . The textile firms of New York have picked up and headed for the South, the car makers of Detroit have gone into a disastrous decline, the dairy farms of New England have been deserted and left to lie fallow. . . . The railroad systems have deteriorated so rapidly, with nine major lines in bankruptcy by 1975 and others to follow, that the whole transportation infrastructure of the Northeast is facing collapse and the regional economy is seriously jeopardized. . . . The industrial importance of the Northeast is rapidly diminishing, according to the business-oriented Conference Board, citing figures to show that industries there accounted for 70 percent of all value added in manufacturing as recently as the late 1940s but "by 1971 this share declined to 51 percent" and was dropping with every passing year. . . . The old money markets are no longer capable of supplying the capital needs of the Northeast or of the nation, and the brokerage houses that once served as the glittering jewels of Wall Street have been so badly tarnished that they are going under at the rate of more than fifty a year. . . . And in almost every sphere the conventional stability and dominance of the Establishment is deteriorating. It is surely too soon to say from all of this, as Nixon tells it to Dean, that "the Establishment is dying," but just as surely that hyperbole is pointing toward a truth.

The idea of a "Southern Rim" in American economic and political life is not mere capriciousness, a paranoid's invention. There is a reality to this area, a climatic, historical, and cultural cohesiveness, that serves to set this broad band off from the rest of the country in many ways.

The most obvious unity to the Southern Rim is climatic, and a look at any of those weather maps that the newspapers print helps to show why. No matter what the time of year, there will probably be a dotted line running across the map from around the tip of North Carolina in the East, on out through Memphis and Oklahoma City, swerving down a bit to Albuquerque, and then up through southern Nevada and on to San Francisco. In the winter this is normally the 60-degree line—temperatures south of it running from 60 degrees on up, north of it below 60 degrees—and in the summer it is usually the 80-degree demarcation. It will vary, of course, weather being what it is, but it is remarkable how consistently the temperature line cuts this same pattern.

This seems as appropriate a way as any to start to define the Southern Rim, since it is to a great degree the climate that has given it its spectacular growth. In the area below this line are to be found all of the tropical and semitropical regions of the United States: the Florida beaches, the Deep South savannas, the Louisiana lowlands, the Texas and Oklahoma plains, the Southwestern deserts, the palmy California coast. Here is the zone in which the average annual temperature is above 60 degrees, the average maximum temperature is 74 degrees; there are between 250 and 350 days of sunshine a year, and frost, if it should come, does not descend before November. This is, in short, America's sunbelt.

But there is more than climatic unity to this area. There is also a rough populational cohesion as well, for before the modern migrations this area had a fairly uniform pattern of settlement, the movement sweeping almost due west from the South, spreading a human substratum from the Carolinas to California. The earliest migrations in the eighteenth and nineteenth centuries moved almost exclusively westward from the East Coast, one broad wave sweeping southwest through Georgia and Alabama to the Gulf Coast and on up the Rio Grande, another moving due west through the Tennessee, Arkansas, and Red River valleys across the Texas plains and up against the Rockies. By the early twentieth century both of these waves had tapered off roughly in eastern New Mexico, but then came two final movements that completed the settlements, one pouring down into Florida from the Deep South states from the early 1920s on, and the other, made famous by the Okies, moving westward over the Rockies and into Southern California and the Central Valley in the later 1920s and 1930s. By the time of World War II the entire Rim area enjoyed an unusual homogeneity for "melting-pot America": it was marked not only by Southern—and overwhelmingly Southern *white*—settlement, but by the comparative absence of foreign-born immigration. And even the modern influx, though perhaps a half of it has come from the Northeast, has not changed this fixed character appreciably.

Partly as a result of these migration characteristics, partly as a result of the common heritage they imply, the Southern Rim is also marked by a rough cultural unity. The entire area encompasses almost all the regions that have historically been the principal battlegrounds of the American frontier, from the Tennessee of Davy Crockett to the Texas of Sam Houston to the Arizona of Wyatt Earp, with all that this heritage implies (which, for Frederick Jackson Turner, for example, means "perennial rebirth . . . fluidity of American life . . . new opportunities . . . simplicity . . . primitive existence . . . the meeting point between savagery and civilization"). It also encompasses almost precisely the area unique in this country for its economic dependence upon slave and subservient labor (black, brown, or red), not only the famous plantations of the South and their successors, but the ranches of Texas and the Southwest and the fruit farms of California and Florida. The region includes all of the states of the Southern Confederacy (except Virginia), plus the two territories with greatest Confederate sympathy (Oklahoma and New Mexico), and that implies a cultural heritage that of course goes far beyond the simply military. Finally, the entire region from the Carolina coast to eastern New Mexico and from Oklahoma to Florida is the heartland of the Southern Baptist Convention and its offshoots—it is the most populous church today in every state from North Carolina to Texas—and there are additional strong Baptist representations in Arizona and Southern California as well.

Taken altogether, these characteristics of the Southern Rim define a remarkably consistent geographical area. It hardly seems an accident, in fact, that there is indeed a cartographical line that sets off this area almost precisely: the boundary line which runs along the northern edges of North Carolina, Tennessee, Arkansas, Oklahoma, New Mexico, and Arizona, or, generally, the 37th parallel. Extend this line through Nevada and California to the Pacific, with just the slightest swing upward to embrace San Francisco, and the demarcation is complete. The land south of that line takes in all of thirteen states —North and South Carolina, Georgia, Florida, Tennessee, Alabama, Mississippi, Arkansas, Louisiana, Oklahoma, Texas, New Mexico, and Arizona—and the southern and by far the most populous parts of two more states, Nevada and California. This is the Southern Rim.

Now, traditionalists will have noted that this neat demarcation by the 37th parallel creates some divergences from normal geographical constructs. On the eastern end, for example, it excludes the state of Virginia, despite the fact that it was a part, an important part, of the Confederacy and that in its northern half it has experienced much of the same rapid growth that the true Rim areas have. Still, Virginia is simply different in its basic climate and most of its agriculture from the pattern of the Southern Rim; its historical migrations have been either due west, through the Appalachians into Kentucky and West Virginia, or dead north along the coastlines; and its population growths of recent years have almost all taken place in the Washington environs as part of a suburban belt that relates to Maryland and the North far more than to Norfolk and the South. On the western end, the Rim demarcation includes the mid-California region from the Bay Area on south—despite the fact that San Francisco was an old-line center of wealth, with pretensions to "old aristocracy" and the like, and though much ink has been expended trying to make a dividing line between Los Angeles and the Bay Area. The reason is simple enough: climatologically, topographically, and geologically, this region has much more in common with the south than in contrast to it (the real dividing line in California is not the Tehachapi Mountains but the Mokelumne River), and the area around San Francisco to the south (San Mateo, Santa Clara, and Alameda counties, for example) has been every bit as explosive a growth region as the southern part of the state and shares all its contemporary characteristics. Similarly, the southern tip of Nevada is included in the territory cut by the 37th parallel, again an area that just happens to be of a piece with its southern rather than its northern neighbors: it is related by geography through the Colorado River system to Arizona and Southern California, by its mid-century patterns of growth to the spectacular boom cities like Phoenix and Los Angeles, and by its economy and culture— especially Las Vegas—to the rich world of Southern California, where most of its players come from.

The region that stands in opposition to this Southern Rim should be accorded some definition as well. The Northeast, as used here, encompasses the entire quadrant east of the Mississippi and north of the Mason-Dixon line (and its rough extension westward), taking in the fourteen states of New England and the Great Lakes: Maine, New Hampshire, Vermont, Massachusetts, Rhode Island, Connecticut, New York, New Jersey, Pennsylvania, Ohio, Michigan, Indiana, Wisconsin, and Illinois. This region, too, enjoys a certain cohesion, of climate, geography, culture, settlement, and history, but above all of economics and demography: this is the traditional manufacturing belt of America, the area that since the middle of the nineteenth century has been characterized by a band of heavy industry virtually unbroken from Chicago to Boston; and it is the land of the megalopolis, the vast urban clusters that show up on a population map as a mass of black circles again stretching almost without interval from Chicago along the Great Lakes on to Philadelphia and New York and up to Boston. There are some, to be sure, who would like to divide this quadrant in half, creating some sort of "Midwest" that begins around the Pennsylvania-Ohio border—but there is, alas, no evidence whatsoever that there are real distinctions between the two regions.

There is a broadly metaphorical but rather apt way of describing these rival power bases, the one of the Northeast and the other of the Southern Rim, as the *yankees* and the *cowboys*. Taken loosely, that is meant to suggest the traditional, staid, old-time, button-down, Ivy-League, tight-lipped, patrician, New England-rooted WASP culture on the one hand, and the aggressive, flamboyant, restless, swaggering, newfangled, open-collar, can-do, Southern-rooted Baptist culture of the Southern Rim on the other; on the one hand, let us say, the type represented by David Rockefeller, Charles Percy, Edmund Muskie, James Reston, Kingman Brewster, John Lindsay, Richard Lugar, Henry Ford, Sol Linowitz, Bill Buckley, and Stephen Sondheim, and on the other the type personified by Bebe Rebozo, George Wallace, Lyndon Johnson, Billy Graham, Frank Irwin, C. Arnholt Smith, H. L. Hunt, Strom Thurmond, Sam Yorty, John Wayne, and Johnny Cash.

The terms are meant only in the loosest and most symbolic way, of course—flamboyant operators can be found in the Northeast, staid blue-bloods in the Southern Rim—but it is interesting that they even have an appropriate heritage in this very context. "Cowboy" was the epithet used by the Wall Street people who first ran up against some of the newly powerful Texas entrepreneurs, broad-rimmed hats and tooled-leather boots and all, when they started throwing their weight around in Eastern financial circles in the late 1950s and early 1960s—during the fierce battle, for example, between the Texas millionaires Clint Murchison and Sid Richardson and Pennsylvania's patrician Allen Kirby for control of the Allegheny Corporation and the New York Central Railroad in 1961. "Yankee," the invective which goes back to the days of the Civil War to describe Northerners in general, was naturally the word with which the newcomers responded, at least back home in the boardrooms and bars.

Slowly these words began to have a kind of currency, in financial circles at any rate, and then during the 1960s they came to be used by the New Left—particularly by the theoretician Carl Oglesby—in its attempt to understand and describe the workings of the "power structure" of America. From there they moved gradually into academic and journalistic circles—economist Kenneth Boulding, for example, used "the cowboy economy" to describe the period of rapacious growth after World War II, political writer Milton Viorst analyzed the Northeast as "the Yankee's America," scholar William Domhoff described a "Jewish-Cowboy" financial group behind the Democratic Party. It is doubtful if Richard Nixon ever thought of the world in precisely these terms, as ably as they would have served him, but it just may be that his successor does: shortly after becoming President, Gerald Ford announced that, in settling the economic problems of America, he was not going to "act in cowboy fashion."

Let those simple terms, then, stand for the complicated process that Richard Nixon barely conceptualized that mid-March day in the Oval Office. What he was groping toward, what those labels help to delineate, is an understanding of the emergence of a counterforce based in the cowboy sunbelt states capable of challenging the traditional hegemony of the yankee Northeast, and the unmistakable and irreversible shift of power, for the first time in a century, away from the Eastern Establishment and toward the Southern Rim.

To examine this power shift in all its dimensions, it is necessary to go beyond labels, to explore and examine the whole variegated history of the last three decades of American life, and that is the task of this book. First, to survey the *economic power* upon which the rise of the Southern Rim is based, leading naturally to an examination of how its rapid and rampant growth has created the distinct and in some ways ominous *economic character* of the region; next, to investigate the *political power* of the Southern Rim, especially as it has been manifest on a national scale, and thence to determine how its progress has shaped the particular *political character* of the region; then, to see the changes wrought upon this country as this development culminated in *the cowboy conquest* of the Presidency during the imperious reign of Richard Nixon and his coterie; and finally, to watch how the yankee Establishment responded to this new shift of power and how it worked cal-culatedly to press forward a *yankee counterattack* that would attempt to restore the balance. That whole process is the pattern of the American mid-century; that is the pattern of this book.

This power shift is more than a passing phenomenon; it is a way of comprehending modern America. An under-standing of its sweep and pattern helps to make sense out of the recent past, from World War II to the Vietnam War, from the Kennedy assassination to Watergate, from the rise of Richard Nixon to his resignation. It helps to make order out of the tangled present, to explain the energy crisis and the price of food, the economic chaos of the mid-1970s, the accession to power of Nelson Rockefeller, the kinds of Presidential candi-dates coming forth for the next election. And it helps to illumi-nate the foreseeable future, to suggest the regions that may be benefited, the interests that may be served, the causes that may triumph, not just in the next few years but for as long as this competition will pertain.

1

The Six Pillars: Economic Power

If the Southern Rim were an independent nation, it would have a gross national product bigger than any foreign country in the world except the Soviet Union—it stood at some $312 billion in 1970, is probably closer to $400 billion today—and bigger than that of the United Kingdom, Italy, Sweden, and Norway combined. It would have more cars (43 million) and more telephones (38 million) than any foreign nation (more than the United Kingdom, France, and Germany combined), and more housing units (22 million), more television sets (25 million), and more miles of paved highway (1.1 million) than any nation except the Soviet Union. It would, in short, be a world power on the scale of the present superpowers.

Which is only one way of dramatizing the enormous economic importance of the Southern Rim, an importance all the more remarkable in that it has come about only in the last thirty years, changing the pleasant little backwaters and half-grown cities into an industrial and financial colossus. The explanation of that remarkable growth is that, to an unusual extent, almost all of the general trends in the American economy since 1945 have been more to the benefit of the Southern Rim than any other section of the country.

The first and most important trend was obviously that of the population migrations. From 1945 to 1975, the Southern Rim underwent the most massive population expansion in history, from about 40 million people to nearly 80 million people in just three decades, giving the area today a population greater than all but seven foreign countries. Thanks to a complexity of factors—a hospitable climate, the development of air conditioning, water reclamation projects, available space for commercial and private building, the new technologies of communication and transportation—industries and individuals alike poured into new territories of the Rim. Every single one of the fifteen cowboy states grew during this period, some quite spectacularly—Texas by over 100 percent to become the third largest state, California by 200 percent, to become the largest state of all, Florida by 400 percent, Arizona and Nevada by more than 450 percent—and as a whole they have consistently made up nearly half of the growth that the nation as a whole has undergone. Migrations every year since World War II have poured millions of new people into the area—on average about 650,000 newcomers every year, turning bucolic farmlands into sprawling suburbs and little crossroads cowtowns into gleaming metropolitan centers. The cities have grown unlike any urban areas in the world, 500 and 800 and 1,000 percent in just this thirty-year span—Fort Lauderdale from 18,000 to 150,000, Huntsville from 13,000 to 140,000, Houston from 385,000 to 1,400,000, Phoenix from 65,000 to 755,000, San Jose from 68,000 to 446,000, incredible urban explosions right across the Rim—and today there are actually more cities over 100,000 people in this area than there are in the Northeast. Nor does this development show any signs of slackening, despite the economic downturn, despite the efforts of "no-growth" lobbies: the most recent statistics show that the Southern Rim continues to grow about three times as fast as the whole rest of the country combined, and even modest projections suggest that the region will have 83.7 million people by 1980. According to the demographers, never in the history of the world has a region of such size developed at such a rate for so long a time.

The second decisive economic trend of this period has been the transformations brought about by the sophisticated new technology developed since World War II. In broad terms there has been a shift from the traditional heavy manufacturing long associated with the Industrial Belt of the Northeast to the new technological industries that have grown up in the Southern Rim—aerospace, defense, electronics—and from the dependency upon railroad transportation to the growth of air and highway transportation, both relatively more important in the Southern Rim. Similarly, in the use of natural resources there has been a development away from coal and heavy metals such as iron and steel, the resources of the Northeast, toward oil and natural gas and the light metals such as aluminum and titanium, the products of the Southern Rim. And in agriculture, new technologies have favored large-scale and often corporate farming, advantageous particularly where space is plentiful, growing seasons are long, and the crops are suitable, and that turns out to be the Southern Rim.

Finally, trends in employment patterns over this thirty-year period have also tended to tilt things toward the cowboy economy. The single most important development has been the gradual decrease in blue-collar industrial workers—these the backbone of the Industrial Belt—and the sharp increase in service and government workers—these the ones most important in the newly populated states with expanding governments and in the tourist-and-retirement areas like Florida, Texas, Arizona, and Southern California; especially in the booming new Rim cities, service employment has enormously increased, in fact by more than 70 percent over the last twenty years, as against 6 percent in the older cities of the Northeast. In like nature, the employment shifts brought about by postwar programs of paid retirement, the expansion of Social Security, and union-won benefits for longer vacations and shorter hours have all meant more earlier retirements to the sunnier parts of the land and more emphasis upon climatic amenities as an inducement for resettlement of the labor force.

In a general sense, then, it is clear enough that mid-century trends have been tilting the country southward, but it is in turning to specifics that the process becomes even clearer still, particularly the six specific industries whose development and importance rank them as the six basic pillars of the cowboy economy: agribusiness, defense, advanced technology, oil and natural-gas production, real estate and construction, and tourism and leisure. Inasmuch as each of them has been absolutely crucial in the growth of the Southern Rim and each has had an ineradicable impact on the economy of the nation as a whole, a rather more detailed examination of them is appropriate.

I

AGRIBUSINESS

At the heart of the economic power of the Southern Rim is the activity that, we often forget, remains what the *Wall Street Journal* calls America's "biggest industry"—agriculture, or, as both friends and critics have come to call it, "agribusiness."

Given the vagaries of weather, crops, markets, and customers, agriculture is bound to be cyclical to some degree. But the remarkable thing about American agriculture in the period since World War II is the extent to which its growth has been steady and sure—and, in the early 1970s, almost meteoric. Assets of what the Agriculture Department calls "the farming sector" have risen from $132 billion in 1950 to $310 billion in 1970 and on to nearly $350 billion in 1975.* Farm income has nearly tripled since 1950, outpacing most other sectors of the economy, and farm profits have doubled, from $13.7 billion in 1950 to $32 billion in 1974, with the once-impossible $40 billion mark expected to be reached well before 1980. Exports alone have risen by an unheard-of 150 percent in the last five years, and now provide more than enough cash to pay off all U.S. deficits on oil imports.

Healthy enough, but even more impressive when you figure that all this money is going to fewer and fewer people as the farm population dries up steadily every year. More than three million farms have folded since 1945 and more than sixteen million people have left the business. That has meant many things for the postwar society—crowded cities, lands put up for the developers—but for the remaining farmers it means only one thing: the average income per person has soared from $570 to $4,260 in the last thirty years. Take cotton, for example. There are today fewer than 40,000 cotton farms, compared to

* Figures throughout are in current dollars.

242,000 in 1960, but there's no need to fret for those remaining, since the average farm now makes $300,000 a year, thirty times what it was making in 1960.

At the same time, agriculture has succumbed to the mid-century phenomenon that has characterized the rest of the economy—the corporate takeover. From 1945 to 1970 the size of the average farm, which is one rough index of corporate growth, doubled from 191 acres to 390; by 1969, at the time of the last agriculture survey, these large corporate operations held nearly 40 percent of all the acreage in the country and accounted for 57 percent of all the sales. A state like California is a perfect example of the agribusiness process: in 1950 it had more than 110,000 farms, by 1969 it had only 78,000; nearly four million acres, and three-quarters of the prime irrigated land, were owned by just forty-five top corporations, accounting for the largest slice of California's $4-billion-a-year farm income.

The agriculture industry, in short, has had fewer and fewer people cutting up larger and larger slices of a bigger and bigger pie throughout the last thirty years. The chief beneficiary, it should come as no great surprise, is that region of the country where agriculture has always flourished, where the climate permits the longest growing season, where crops suitable for large-scale corporate cultivation are grown, and where there are the greatest spaces and therefore the biggest farms: the Southern Rim. This last factor is particularly important, since the average Rim farm is four and a half times the national average, and in such states as Arizona and New Mexico ten and fifteen times.

The Corn Belt and popular conception notwithstanding, the Southern Rim is *the* great agriculture belt of the United States. It has more farms than the Corn Belt (over a million, compared to 640,000), more tractors and more farm trucks. All of its states have increased their percentage of the agriculture market in the last thirty years, while the Northeastern quadrant and even the Corn Belt have seen their shares decrease, and the value of its farms have increased from $500 billion in 1959 to more than $820 billion in 1969 and an estimated $950 billion today. The Rim accounted for some $16.5 billion in farm sales at the time of the last agriculture census in 1969, the Corn Belt for only $12.5 billion, and that difference has increased during the farm boom of the last few years; in fact, three Rim states alone—California, Texas, and Florida—account for nearly 20 percent of *all agricultural sales*. And the largest farm-lending banks, which are the real mainstay of the agriculture system, are in the Southern Rim: California's Bank of America, the Security Pacific Bank of Los Angeles, and the Valley National Bank of Phoenix.

Southern Rim farms supply almost all the cotton, fruit, nuts, sugar, and rice produced in this country, and two-thirds of its tobacco and poultry products. California is the leading grower of fruits and vegetables, with Florida second, and between them they supply fully 75 percent of the country's production. Georgia is first in the value of its poultry production, followed by California and Arkansas, and its peanut crop, the largest of any state, goes to make up more than half of the nation's peanut butter (although in spite of its nickname it ranks only fourth in the production of peaches). Texas is first in the number of sheep, which seems reasonable enough considering its wide-open spaces, but it is also first in the number of cattle, outdistancing that traditional cow state, Iowa, by more than 40 percent (5 million head); in fact, despite the much-publicized herds of the Plains and the Great Lakes, the South and West outnumber all of the North by more than 7 million head.

The Southern Rim's strong agricultural position is even more impressive in the light of the changing eating habits of Americans since World War II. Remarkably, the per capita consumption of most food has not increased—for veal, lamb, milk, butter, eggs, and wheat it has even declined—but for three products in particular there has been a steady and comparatively spectacular growth, and they just happen to be the three in which the Rim dominates: beef (annual consumption went from 55 pounds a person in 1940 to 122 pounds in 1975), poultry (from 17 pounds to 50), and frozen foods (from 2 pounds to 24). The eating habits of postwar Americans, in other words, have tended to benefit most the major beef-producing states (Texas, Oklahoma, and California), the poultry states (Georgia, California, Arkansas), and the fruit and vegetable states (California and Florida).

The corporate side of all of this involves not only the large

million-dollar farmers like California's Di Giorgio family and
Walter Knott (of Berry Farm fame), not only the larger billion-
dollar agriculture firms like Anderson-Clayton and Associated
Milk Producers of Texas, but even the multibillion-dollar conglomerates that would seem to have plenty else to do than worry
about seedlings and rainfall, like Greyhound, the Phoenix-based
corporation that owns Armour Meats, and Tenneco, the
Houston-based natural-gas corporation that also happens to
grow, fertilize, package, distribute, and sell food. Dozens of
major corporations, reading the growth patterns in agribusiness,
have attempted to diversify into this area in the last decade,
producing both a greater investment in the agricultural sector
year by year and a steady change in the nature of the industry.
A good deal of the farm-based wealth thereby gets sucked off
into yankee corporate coffers, but much still remains, and the
Rim corporations are every bit as productive: one only has to
go down the roster of such producers as Southdown (Houston:
sugar), Missouri Beef (Plainview, Texas: beef), and Del
Monte (San Francisco: fruits and vegetables); such processors
as Tropicana (Bradenton, Florida: orange juice), Carnation
(San Francisco: dairy products), and Sunkist (California:
fruits); or such giant food retailers as Safeway (Oakland: supermarkets, number one in the land), Coca-Cola (Atlanta:
beverages), and Southland (Dallas: "convenience" stores).

Just now agribusiness, corporations and individuals alike,
is in an unprecedented boom, in part through the legacy of the
Nixon Administration, and there is every indication that it will
continue for half-a-dozen more years at least. Even if there are
leaner times, however, the enormity and centrality of this industry is not likely to decrease, nor the power within it of the
Southern Rim. As one Tenneco executive has said, explaining
why his gas company diversified into agriculture: "People always have to eat, don't they?"

DEFENSE

Of all the mid-century growth industries, none has been
more phenomenal than defense, fed by the apparently inex-
haustible funds from the federal government. All by itself the
military arm of government has created and sustained a whole

spate of new communities and almost single-handedly sponsored dozens of new corporations.

The general phenomenon of America's "military-industrial complex" is so well known by now that it is sometimes forgotten how recent a development it is. The initial blending of the corporation and the Pentagon didn't come until World War II, peacetime research funding for private businesses didn't begin until the late 1940s; the practice of hand-in-glove "negotiated" contracts for corporations to write their own defense tickets didn't emerge until the late 1950s; and the establishment of full military-industrial interlocks didn't come about until Robert McNamara's "systems management" innovations in the early 1960s. Thus it is only in the last ten years or so that the Pentagon has come to play such a major part in the national economy as its operations have branched out from guns and tanks to missiles and nuclear subs.

It is sometimes forgotten, too, now that we have become used to it, just what an enormous impact the defense establishment has. To take just two statistical measures:

—The defense budget has risen from $12 billion in 1945 to $86 billion in 1975 (soon to go over $100 billion), with outlays in the 1960s averaging about $65 billion a year, coming to a grand total in the last thirty years of something like $1.5 *trillion* (which incomprehensible sum amounts to a million dollars multiplied one and a half million times).

—Defense outlays to major corporations—that's leaving aside paying salaries, fighting wars, running the Pentagon, and all the rest—have risen from $15.4 billion in 1960 to $31.6 billion in 1973 (by itself a bigger sum than the entire gross national product of such countries as Switzerland and Belgium), after a peak of $44.6 billion at the height of the Vietnam War; altogether more than $450 billion in prime contracts has been awarded to American businesses since 1960.

The figures are immense, the economic impact equally so, and nowhere greater than in the Southern Rim. This is a region

that was transformed, and brought into modernity, by W
War II, when the defense establishment moved in to take .
vantage of its benign climate, vast open spaces, extensive anu
for the most part protected coastline, abundant and cheap
labor, and nascent shipping and aircraft industries, altogether
pumping in an estimated 60 percent of its $74 billion wartime
expenditures into these fifteen states. And as the defense installations and contractors continued to grow with growing defense
budgets even after the war—$13 billion in 1950, $50 billion in
1960—they continued to build up the substructure of the whole
economy, in practically every state from North Carolina to California. Indeed, if any one industry can be said to be the backbone of the Southern Rim, it is defense.

The decade of its initial postwar impact, from about 1952
through 1962—that is, the period of the Korean War and the
Cold War buildup, but before the Vietnam acceleration—has
been studied in detail by a Brookings Institution economist,
Roger Bolton. According to his findings, the overall contribution of defense to the total income of individual states was
startlingly large—particularly in the Pacific Region (especially
Southern California) and the Mountain Region (primarily Arizona and New Mexico), where it also accounted for 21 and 27
percent, respectively, of the economic growth of those areas,
and in the South Atlantic Region and the Middle South, where
it was responsible for 3 and 10 percent of the growth. At the
same time, he figures a *negative* impact in the Northeast, where
he finds that cuts in defense spending held back the Middle
Atlantic region by 3 percent and the Great Lakes area by a
significant 21 percent. As to individual states, the ones that saw
a gain of 20 percent or more as a result of defense expenditures
were California, Arizona, New Mexico, and Mississippi in the
Rim, only New Hampshire in the Northeast, and Utah, Colorado, and Kansas; such states as Michigan, Wisconsin, and
Indiana actually had negative growth rates.

But in the second decade—the years of Vietnam and the
moondoggle—the effect was even greater. During those years
the balance of Pentagon prime contracts shifted sharply to the
Southern Rim, with the percentages mounting every year, until
by 1970 its states accounted for 44.1 percent of all the money
going to the defense industry, the Northeast only 38.9 percent.

Texas surpassed New York as the number two state behind California, and those two between them accounted for 28 percent of the contracts, more than twice as much as the next two states, New York and Illinois. By 1970, too, the Rim had five of the top ten states in terms of total Department of Defense spending (California, Texas, Georgia, Florida, and North Carolina), four of the top five states in aerospace funding (California, Texas, Florida, and Alabama), and four of the top five states in Atomic Energy Commission grants (New Mexico, California, Tennessee, and Nevada). The number of major defense installations (military bases, missile sites, etc.) in the Southern Rim had grown to 142, more than all the rest of the nation put together, and 82 more than were located in the Northeast. Defense Department payrolls by 1970 were also concentrated in the Rim: military salaries went primarily to California, Texas, Virginia, North Carolina, Florida, and Georgia, in that order, and military and civilian payrolls together amounted to more than $10 billion in the Rim, more than in all the other states combined. And Pentagon research-and-development funds—the seed money that creates new technologies and industries—were concentrated in the Southern Rim, which had 49 percent of the funds as against just 35 percent for the Northeast.

Today the repercussions of military money upon the once-placid Rim are evident everywhere. It is a commonplace that California is a heavily saturated defense area—especially around Los Angeles, where no fewer than seventy firms depend upon Pentagon prime contracts—and that it receives about a quarter of the total defense dollar all by itself; Texas, too, what with the Houston Space Center and major firms like LTV and Convair, has long been identified with the new Washington money. But few realize that even in such states as Louisiana, Georgia, Mississippi, Tennessee, and New Mexico, the defense industry is the single largest employer, an economic presence with enormous ramifications. Take New Mexico, for example. Without defense, it would still probably be a land of Indians and Chicanos—a reversion to which condition those two groups would no doubt welcome—instead of one of the nation's fastest-growing states. It has eight major defense installations (including the White Sands Missile Range, site of the first atomic bomb test), a dozen important research centers (including the Los Alamos and Sandia laboratories), and several dozen corporate defense contractors (including AT&T's Sandia Corporation and United Nuclear). It gets more money from the AEC than any other state and almost as much from the Pentagon, together amounting to some $750 million a year—which works out to about $2,500 for every single family in the state. (The military loves the place so much that even the Navy spends money there—some $11 million a year—even though the state is completely landlocked and there's not even a lake big enough to spit in.) And its industry is dominated by defense work, responsible for half of all employment and by itself the largest manufacturing sector in the state's economy. It seems entirely fitting, if nonetheless gruesome, that one little New Mexico schoolchild after a visit to the Atomic Museum at Kirtland Air Force Base should write to the curator, "You have nice rockets and nice bombs. Thank you."

The industrial aspect of defense spending, though only one part of the total defense cornucopia, has been especially significant in the Southern Rim, inasmuch as it has been largely responsible for building the manufacturing substructure of the region. From 1965, thanks partly to Lyndon Johnson's ascendancy, Southern Rim firms have gotten a greater percentage of Pentagon contracts than any other section of the country, an influx of $15 billion or so a year. One way to see what this means, and how effectively it spreads throughout the full length of the Rim, is to look at the Defense Department's annual procurement tables; in 1967, a peak year for all states, the top two states and their percentage in each product area were as follows:

Airframes: Texas and Georgia (40 percent)
Ammunition: Texas and California (24 percent)
Building supplies: California and Arkansas (52 percent)
Electronic parts: California and Texas (25 percent)
Foods: California and Texas (32 percent)
General equipment: California and Texas (32 percent)
Missile components: California and Florida (32 percent)
Ships: California and Louisiana (32 percent)
Textiles: North and South Carolina (19 percent)

Or, for still another angle, look at the lists of top contractors that the Department of Defense puts out every year. The placements change a bit from year to year, but the top companies remain pretty much the same as on the 1970 list:

1 Lockheed (Burbank, California), with subsidiaries Lockheed-Georgia (Marietta, Georgia) and Ventura Manufacturing (San Antonio, Texas) ....$1,848 million

2 General Dynamics (St. Louis), with aerospace divisions in Fort Worth, Texas; San Diego; and Rochester, New York; electronics divisions in San Diego and Orlando, Florida; and a missile division in Pomona, California ....$1,183 million

3 General Electric (New York), with a defense subsidiary in Santa Barbara, California, and its nuclear laboratories in Pleasanton, California ....$1,000 million

4 American Telephone & Telegraph (New York), whose chief defense work is done by Sandia Corporation, Albuquerque ....$931 million

5 McDonnell-Douglas (St. Louis and Long Beach, California), with defense divisions in Monrovia and Sacramento, California; Tulsa, Oklahoma; Titusville, Florida; and Ann Arbor, Michigan ....$883 million

6 United Aircraft (East Hartford, Connecticut), with a research-and-development division in West Palm Beach, Florida, and test sites in California ......$874 million

7 North American Rockwell (Los Angeles and El Segundo, California*), with defense divisions in Bethany, Oklahoma; Albany, Georgia; and Anaheim, California .... $707 million

* It later became Rockwell International, with headquarters in Pittsburgh, but the defense work continues to be centered in California and the other Rim states.

8 Grumman (Bethpage, New York), with major defense divisions in Savannah, Georgia; Sherman, Texas; and Tulare, California .... $661 million

9 Litton (Beverly Hills, California), with major defense subsidiaries in Pascagoula, Mississippi; and Van Nuys and Woodland Hills, California ....$543 million

10 Hughes Aircraft (Culver City and El Segundo, California; and Tucson, Arizona) ....$496 million

Now it can be seen from this list that there are indeed non-cowboy firms which do very well in the defense business—they are the established giants of American industry, after all, and if the Pentagon wants telephones it pretty well has to go to AT&T, just like the rest of us. The important thing, however, is that fully half of the firms on the list are based in the Rim, two others do most of their defense work in Rim states, and the remaining three have major defense operations there.

And defense contractors, it should be noted, are in a uniquely strong economic position, with advantages not shared by the older, more conventional industries. They depend upon public money, from a Washington fountainhead that just never runs dry, and they are in the happy position of being able to tap it for practically as much as they want. Defense firms just don't work like other firms. Since 1950, for example, 86 percent of their contracts with the Pentagon have been signed without competitive bidding, but simply through secret negotiations between military brass and industrial management, meaning that even firms with high bids can continue to get lucrative jobs, and certain favored contractors—Lockheed and Litton are familiar examples—can go on getting lucrative jobs even when their past performances would argue that they shouldn't be given a contract to put stamps on envelopes. Defense contractors have other gimmicks, too: they are given the use of some $45 billion in plant and equipment in what amounts to a tax-free government loan; they are permitted to exercise cost-plus banditry through the so-called "golden handshake" clauses that provide that the government bails out any company whose costs run over a projected level; and they are permitted by the government to make exorbitant profits as a matter of course, often in excess of 50 percent and sometimes more than 500 percent (when a 20 percent profit would be considered good in most other manufacturing).* All in all, no other business does quite as well as the defense business, and its preponderance in the Southern Rim has almost by itself allowed that region to develop the industrial might that today can challenge the traditional industrial power of the Northeast.

TECHNOLOGY

One part of the defense industry that has been particularly glamorous in recent decades is aerospace and electronics, but that is actually just a part of the whole range of modern scientific and engineering businesses—including computers, calculators, semiconductors, scientific instruments, magnetic recordings, and much else besides—which can broadly be called the technology industry. Given its unquestioned importance now, even more outside of the defense industry than in it, and its assured centrality in any future industrial development, it seems reasonable to regard this as a separate economic pillar.

To take just the aerospace component for a start, this business has expanded from a minor nuts-and-bolts operation after World War II to a $30 billion industry today, with more scientists and engineers than all the universities put together and the largest concentration of research-and-development money of any industry in the nation. In the brief fifteen years of the American space program, federal expenditures quintupled from $900 million to $5 billion, with a peak of $7.2 billion back in 1967, when landing men on the moon was the government's top priority; in all, about $80 billion has been spent by Washington on aerospace development. Most of that money, as any Cronkite-watcher knows, has gone to the Southern Rim, with the

* In 1973 Senator William Proxmire was able to shed some light on Pentagon profits when he discovered that 131 companies were permitted to make "exorbitant rates of return" on net worth—94 of them made 50 percent, 49 made more than 100 percent, 22 made more than 200 percent, three exceeded 500 percent, and one made almost 2,000 percent. Such is the state of a defense-soaked land that these revelations were greeted by the public with stony-faced indifference.

industry's headquarters in Houston, its research arm in California, its rocket center in Huntsville, Alabama, and its launching station in Cape Canaveral, Florida—an aero-arc right across the country. It is the Southern Rim whose firms account for 70 percent of the national aerospace production and whose plants employ more than half of all the country's aerospace workers— 55 percent, as against 27 percent for the Northeast. Only three states in the nation have thirty or more major aerospace plants— California, Texas, and Florida—and there are ten major firms each in Arizona, Oklahoma, Tennessee, Alabama, and North Carolina, a full sweep of the Rim.

But the technology industry is more than just rockets and missiles; it takes in the vast development of sophisticated postwar science in everything from transistors to lasers, all the varied industries that have grown up in the wake of nuclear physics and modern electronics in the last couple of decades. It is somewhat difficult to chart this growth, given the diversity of advanced technology in the national economy, but there are some indices. Research funds for technology, for example, amount today to more than $10 billion a year, out of a total of some $18 billion for all industries; and the manufacturing output of the technology industry, which was practically insignificant in the 1950s, now accounts for some $42 billion a year, more than any other single manufacturing sector—three times as much, for example, as motor-vehicle production. And there is no question but that this industry will be the heart of the nation's future, as American businesses—and lives—become increasingly computerized and electronified; according to several estimates, computer manufacturing will become the nation's largest industry before the next century.

Here, too, the Southern Rim has been the main beneficiary. Sprawling scientific complexes have been established over the whole area, in Los Angeles, Phoenix, Dallas, Fort Lauderdale–Melbourne, Durham–Chapel Hill, concentrations of technological power which have grown up right along with the population in areas where the economic climate was as congenial as the meteorological to new enterprises and innovations. Professional and technical employment in the region has mushroomed in the last thirty years, growing by more than 90 percent (202 percent in California alone), while the Mid-

Atlantic region, for example, though inevitably sharing in the
new sciences, increased by only 41 percent. Today, measured
by state government employment, there are more scientists in
the top four Southern Rim states (California, Florida, North
Carolina, and Texas) than in the top four Northeast states
(New York, Illinois, Pennsylvania, and Michigan); California
alone has an estimated 28,000 natural scientists, twice as many
as Pennsylvania or Illinois, and Texas—long-degraded Texas,
home of cattle, oil, and sagebrush—has more scientists than
Wisconsin and Indiana combined, in fact more than that
famed science-centered state, Massachusetts. Finally, federal
research-and-development funds are highly concentrated in the
Rim area, which absorbed as much as 60 percent at the last
count, and one institution alone—the California Institute of
Technology, the Pasadena laboratory-cum-university—is said
to get more money in grants from Washington than the entire
legislative branch of the federal government, which indicates at
least something about the nation's priorities.

Although the Los Angeles metropolitan area has long had
the largest number of high-technology businesses in the nation
—more than the New York region, more than Boston–Cambridge, more than Chicago–Evanston—the most dramatic proof
of the role of the technology industry is provided by a smaller
25-mile strip farther north, Santa Clara County, California.
There, on land which used to be orange groves just twenty-five
years ago, is located what *Fortune* has called "the densest concentration of innovative industry that exists anywhere in the
world," whose more than 800 scientific companies and 150,000
technical employees have "created an innovative ferment on a
scale without precedent in industrial history." The base of this
phenomenon is Stanford University and the industrial park that
it began to put together in the early 1950s to attract high-technology experts and creative scientific minds; soon such electronic giants as Hewlett-Packard, Fairchild, Lockheed, Sylvania,
and Admiral located in the area, and they in turn began spin-
ning off highly successful smaller operations with those mysterious machine-made names like Syntex, Itek, Zeocon, Rodal,
Litronix, Synetics, and Memorex. Today Santa Clara County
has far surpassed the older technical clusters like Cambridge
and Ann Arbor and is the world capital in the development and

production of semiconductors (transistors, diodes, and the like, fundamental to all modern technology), lasers, and computer disks, the headquarters for the leading firms in medical instruments, microcomputers, magnetic tapes and sophisticated pollution-control devices, the acknowledged leader in all kinds of scientific research and development, the home of at least a hundred technology millionaires, and the center for the kind of advanced research that will stand behind the industrial development of the future.

Santa Clara is especially interesting as a Rim phenomenon in that, with the possible exception of Hollywood, it marks the first time that a major new industry was located largely for climatic and social amenities, with no regard for the old established commercial and trade centers. The brains came because the climate was so congenial, the creative atmosphere so stimulating, the risk-capital entrepreneurs so forthcoming—and the living was easy. A transplanted Bostonian has said of Santa Clara: "I'm continually struck by the fact that things are so informal here, dedicated to accomplishment without the encumbrances of status symbols and hierarchies. Those things still exist, unfortunately, back East, even in the technology area." As with Santa Clara, so with Los Angeles, Phoenix, Florida: modern technology and the Southern Rim seem to be natural partners.

Oil

Because it is now the single source of energy that America depends upon most, industrially and commercially, oil is obviously a major mid-century growth industry—and just as obviously its benefits have been most spectacularly felt in the petroleum province of the country, the Southern Rim.

We tend to forget, what with our gas-geared economy these days, that for most of this century oil was a weak sister to coal. It was not until the 1940s and the unprecedented push in cars and single-family homes that America went on what former Interior Secretary Stewart Udall has called "our post-World War II petroleum binge" and oil (along with natural gas, with which it is found in conjunction) became the dominant source of power. In 1940 gas and oil supplied less than half of U.S. fuel needs, but by 1950 this had grown to 57 percent and thereafter never slackened: in 1960 it stood at 73 percent of the energy market and in 1975 at nearly 78 percent. "King" coal, the Northeast's only energy resource, provides no more than 17 percent of the nation's needs.

In other words, this country—its cars and planes, its utilities and businesses, its farms and homes—now runs on oil. Oil stands behind the threefold increase in the motor-vehicle market, the multibillion-dollar superhighway system, the proliferation of single-family suburbias, and such new and increasingly important industries as petrochemicals, man-made textiles, synthetic rubber, fertilizers, plastics, asphalt, and airplane travel. Oil stands behind more of America's mid-century fortunes than any other product or service, accounting for no fewer than thirty-three oilionaires with net worths of $75 million or more, according to one count in 1968, and for fully a third of all the multimillion-dollar new-money fortunes made in the first fifteen postwar years, including those of the two richest individuals in the world, J. Paul Getty and H. L. Hunt. Oil stands behind a dozen of America's largest corporations, whose assets of more than $100 billion are greater than those of any single industry in the nation, more than twice as large as the runner-up automobile industry; oil's tentacles reach so far into the corporate world that today it accounts for fully 20 percent of all the stocks traded on the New York Stock Exchange. For all the talk about the Nuclear Age, the last thirty years have in fact been the Age of Petroleum—fusion produces less than 1 percent of America's energy—and the next thirty are likely to be, too.

No one needs to be told that during this period it was upon the state of Texas that the oil gods showered most of their manna. From the discovery of the enormous East Texas field in the 1930s, through the opening up of the Permian Basin in the 1950s, down to the offshore Gulf of Mexico finds of the 1960s and '70s, that state has been at the heart of American oil development. All the great names of oil—Getty and Hunt, Sid Richardson and Clint Murchison, D. H. "Dry Hole" Byrd and R. E. "Bob" Smith, John Mecom and Glenn McCarthy, and all the old-timers who bring faraway looks to the eyes of modern oilmen as the evening waxes moister—belong to Texas. That state alone, as of 1970, produced 35 percent of all the petroleum in the country and 40 percent of all the natural gas, at a value of some $6.5 billion a year—so much money that the millions coming into the state from the cattle business, according to Texas historian J. Frank Dobie, "have come to look like tips." In the last thirty years the city of Houston has become not only the oil capital of the country but also without question the energy center of the world.

But Texas is only the heart of the oil business—though of course its braggadocio has made it the most talked-about—and the industry's arteries (or, perhaps better, pipelines) extend in every direction all along the Southern Rim. Next to Texas, the most important oil-producing states are Louisiana, California, Oklahoma, and New Mexico, in that order, and the five of them together account for an astounding total of 82 percent of all the oil produced in the country, 88 percent of all the natural gas. In fact, if you drew a circle with a 500-mile radius and Houston at its center, taking in the major oil areas of all the states from New Mexico to Florida and most of the offshore fields, you would have a Southern Rim energy kingdom that could probably supply this nation with the *totality* of its energy needs, even at accelerated future rates, for the next fifty years. The Rim, in short, is the gas tank of the American car, the furnace of the American home, the turbine of the American generator, and nothing—not the Alaska pipeline or the Rocky Mountain oil shale, not solar energy or geothermal geysers—seems likely to displace its primacy.

Now, naturally all of this means power and money where the oil is, and the infinitude of tales about Texans with four ranches, one for each season, or right- and left-wheel Rolls-Royces so both arms get tanned, are testament to that. It is obvious that the people who own the land, find the wells, and pump the stuff out are going to make money and in some cases considerable money—and these people are, for the most part, Texans, Louisianans, and Californians. But there is a confusing element in the American oil business, for it has an odd mixture of cowboy and yankee to it. The Rockefeller fortunes, after all, are based upon Standard Oil, the Mellon empire upon Gulf, and no amount of divestiture and trust-busting has done much to change that; and the international giants, the "Seven Sisters"

that dominate Middle Eastern production and American markets, are heavily involved with yankee capital even though a
number of their executives and some of their bigger investments
are rooted in cowboy soil. On the other hand, there are also
down-home Texas companies, as cowboy as the Marlboro man,
which now operate overseas in the former yankee provinces and
behave every bit like their yankee counterparts.

The old distinctions—"international" vs. "domestic," "in-
tegrated" vs. "independent"—are simply no help as a way out
of this confusion, but it *is* valuable to draw a distinction between the *old* oil companies, those with their roots in the late
nineteenth and early twentieth centuries, mostly around the oil
strikes of Pennsylvania and Illinois, and the *newer* oil companies, those which grew up after the big Texas strikes of the
1930s, the offshore drillings of the 1950s and '60s, and the
advantageous overseas tax breaks of the 1960s and '70s.

In the first group are the Standard Oil offshoots (Exxon,
Mobil, the Standards of California, Indiana, Ohio, and Kentucky, and small tendrils like Continental and Marathon), plus
other independent giants like Gulf, Texaco, and Shell, and the
Northeastern-based firms like Sun and Cities Service. Many of
these have bought up oil and gas holdings in the Southern Rim,
of course, and have even located division headquarters in Texas
or California, but they are not really cowboy corporations: their
primary province is generally the Middle East, their markets are
as much international as domestic, and their stockholders, their
executives, and their interests tend to be yankee-oriented. To
take just one example, Mobil Oil, though it has four regional
offices and eighteen plants in Texas, a North American headquarters in Houston, some two and a half million acres of U.S.
land, and a domestic production of 400,000 barrels a day, is
still not primarily a Rim company: its American production is
only a quarter of its world-wide gross, its income is more than
60 percent foreign-derived, its stock is owned mostly by yankee
banks (22.7 percent) and Rockefeller interests (1.8 percent),
and its corporate headquarters, the place where the managerial
and money men gather daily, is on Forty-second Street in New
York City. Clearly for Mobil there is considerable interest in
Rim happenings, the positions of the Texas regulatory commissions or the developments of Gulf superports, and it will have

an inevitable effect upon the economy of the Rim, but just as clearly this is not a cowboy corporation.

The second group, containing the newer oil companies and most of the natural gas companies, is by contrast preponderantly Rim-based, though sometimes with outposts elsewhere. There are two different kinds of operators here. The familiar ones are the wildcatters, the so-called independents (who are in reality dependent upon larger corporations for sales, pipelines, and often their very existence, but that's another story), the royalty owners (who are simply landowners who lease out their land and get a percentage of the profits), and various assorted small beasties and roustabouts in between; according to the Liaison Committee of Cooperating Oil and Gas Associations, lobbyists for these people, there are some seven thousand of these independents, more than 90 percent of whom are Southern Rim born and bred. Then there are the much larger new firms which have spread out in recent years on the yankee model, trying to establish vertical monopolies (that means owning everything from the drilling rig to the station pump) and flinging themselves into overseas exploration in areas that the older firms have neglected; most representative here are such companies as Getty, Occidental, Union, Signal (all of Los Angeles), Phillips (Oklahoma), Superior, Tenneco and Tesoro (Texas), all of which are large enough to figure in *Fortune*'s top five hundred industrials but are also of fairly recent vintage. These are firms which, like Getty, have built their dynasties on the offshore drilling operations that became economically significant only in the 1950s, or which, like Union and Occidental, moved into international exploration in the untouched Pacific and neglected North Africa during the 1950s and '60s, when U.S. government tax breaks made it more profitable to find oil overseas than at home.

In fact, it was the irreverent competition from this second group which more than anything else brought on that recent oil panic which went under the name "energy crisis." The instigation was the willingness of the newer oil companies to deal with the Middle Eastern producing companies on the producers' terms just in order to get a share of the riches, an eventuality which exploded the fat-cat monopoly of the old yankee firms and destroyed their happy hold over Middle Eastern oil. For example, in 1973, when all the other oil firms refused to give up a majority share of their Libyan oil finds to the new military government there, it was Occidental, the California upstart, that first agreed to an unheard-of 49–51 split; this started the round of high-pressure renegotiations by the Libyan government and then by other Middle Eastern states which wanted similar lucrative deals, a flurry that eventually ended up with most of the cards in the producers' hand, their eventual boycott of the United States, and the resultant energy panic. With $3 billion in corporate assets, ranking thirty-second among all American firms, Occidental is surely no cowboy David—but its effect upon the yankee Goliaths was very much the same.

It seems hardly accidental that the American energy crisis, causing irreversible losses for the international monopoly in the Middle East and freeing gas and oil prices on domestic supplies, has been the biggest boon to befall the Southern Rim oilers in the last fifteen years. Nothing, of course, not even the final nationalization of the Middle Eastern oil fields, is going to destroy the power of the older oil firms, for they are simply too powerful (even when they get pinched "upstream" at the drilling rig, they'll simply increase their take "downstream" at the service station, which in effect was what the 1973–74 gasoline panic was all about). Nonetheless, their *relative* power has unquestionably diminished in the face of upstart competition and a declared national policy to work toward domestic self-sufficiency, and their monopoly has been shattered: "The big plus that the internationals have had up to now has been access to huge amounts of low-cost crude," one expert pointed out recently in *Fortune*. "That was special, and it's going." At the same time, as *Fortune* goes on to say, looking at the domestic resources, "The essential fact about the oil industry today is that it is possessed of a huge inventory of low-cost oil that is now salable at prices that once were beyond the industry's dreams"; it reckons that the energy panic and succeeding price raises increased the value of domestic oil, in the ground, without a single thing being done to it, by $100 billion. Hardly any wonder that the Texas independent oilers have announced that "we independents are looking at a decade which could be the most exciting and the best in history," or that the president of Diamond Shamrock Oil in Amarillo, Texas, has jubilantly proclaimed that "the United States petroleum industry . . . has been reborn," or that one Midlands oilionaire has recently declared: "I can absolutely guarantee that if I could find ten of the right kind of twenty-year-old men, each of them would make a million dollars by the time he was thirty. That's the future of this business today."

REAL ESTATE

Nothing can be quite as spectacular as the oil boom, but if anything comes close, with perhaps even greater effects on the Southern Rim, it has been the mid-century real-estate boom. Combine an ever-growing population, the extraordinary migrations into the South and West, the insatiable American desire for a home of one's own (and in many cases *two* homes), and you get a buying-and-building spree that is gobbling up 700,000 acres a year and has changed the nature, not to mention the face, of the Southern Rim.

Mid-century Americans seem to have taken to heart that old Will Rogers suggestion, "Buy land, they ain't makin' any more of it," and have produced what is easily the greatest land boom since the Oklahoma Territory opened in 1889. Millions of acres of open land have gone under the plow in the last thirty years in the relentless sweep of "progress," with probably an area bigger than the state of Ohio given over to real-estate development alone. Land prices have gone up every single year since 1945, in the 1970s by 8 percent or so a year, and not even a depressed economy and a downturn in housing starts has slowed that process much; urban Miami Beach in 1974 was going for $450,000 an acre, suburban Palm Springs for $100,000 an acre. A very valuable investment, obviously, and the foundation for some very sizable fortunes.

Building upon this land has been every bit as dramatic, with a relative slowing-down in 1974 and 1975 only after nearly thirty years of headlong prosperity. For complex sociological reasons, American families have tended to split up into smaller groups in recent years, and each of those groups has tended to buy its own housing: since the first enumeration in 1890, the number of families owning homes stayed at about 45 percent up until World War II, but from 1945 on the rate increased significantly and in the last fifteen years nearly 65 percent of all American families have become homeowners. It is perhaps not surprising then that more than 42 million housing units have been built in the United States over these thirty years—but it is still somewhat shocking to realize that this is more units than there were in the country altogether in 1945, or in other words *a doubling of the entire number of housing units within just thirty years.* And the total amount spent on new construction over that period rose no less than 2,000 percent, from $6 billion in 1945 to $94 billion in 1970 and an estimated $135 billion today, while the total economy was growing by only 500 percent.

Real estate and construction, taken together as a single industry, has today become as significant a part of the national economy as, well, automobile manufacturing—except that it is *eight times* more significant, accounting for more than $100 billion worth of the national income in 1970 (and closer to $150 billion by 1975), as against only $13 billion for automobiles. Real estate and construction, in fact, make up 15 percent of the national income just by themselves—more than any other individual segment of the economy, more than retail trade, state and local government, transportation, communication, banking, or medicine.

No area of the country, of course, has been unaffected by the real-estate boom, but inevitably the Southern Rim, because it has most of the available land and got most of the people, benefited most. This was a region only barely touched by urbanization at the end of World War II and it had enormous open areas where, providing water and people could be supplied, unlimited development was possible; the government supplied the water, the climatic tilt supplied the people, and the developers reaped their profits. The South, which had only a quarter of the housing starts in 1945 and scarcely a third even as late as 1960, had almost half of them by 1972; together with the West, it accounted for 70 percent of all housing starts in the country in 1972, a figure which is supposed to grow to 75 percent by 1980, no matter how the housing market fluctuates. The Northeast, in the meantime, beginning to choke in its megalopolitan mess, declined steadily from 41 percent of the nation's housing starts in 1960 to less than 30 in 1972, in spite of the fact that it had a greater absolute population. Two statistics indicate this shift dramatically: New York City had only 49,000 housing starts in 1971, while Atlanta, a city one-fifteenth the size, had 48,000; the fourteen states of the entire Northeastern part of the country had 382,000 new houses that same year, a figure matched by just the seven states of the southeastern Rim (from the Mississippi east).

Every state in the Rim has been touched by this boom, some mightily. A few highpoints:

California. Though there has been some slackening of its growth rate in the last few years, the state is still losing some 75,000 acres a year to the subdividers and developers. One real-estate entrepreneur, typical of many, has bought a parcel of land in the Mojave Desert that is the size of the city of San Francisco—and in spite of the fact that it has no water mains, streets, sewers, or indeed little of anything except cactus, there are 1,000 people already living there. Another developer has a chunk of California up for sale which amounts to 85,000 acres, an area that is four and a half times the size of the entire city of New York.

Arizona. So far this state has had one million lots bought up and subdivided by big developers, and more are being scooped up every year; altogether there may be as many as 500,000 acres currently under development, the most in any state in the union. Typical of the developments there is Sun City, a "retirement community" that Phoenix developer Del Webb threw together in some marginal cotton fields by the Aqua Fria River fifteen years ago; today it has 35,000 people and six shopping centers, its homes sell for up to $100,000, and people are coming in at the rate of four hundred a week.

New Mexico. A state of barely over a million people now, it is undergoing a development onslaught that will provide enough housing for as many as another million in the next ten to fifteen years, an eventuality that neither the citizens, the industries, nor the water table can support, but that seems to be foreordained anyway. There were seventy-seven separate major developments being started at last count, by at least fifty corporate developers, and the area around Albuquerque was already mapped out and subdivided by 1973 in preparation for three times as many people as live there now. Small wonder that a recent campaign by a few concerned New Mexicans plastered a number of billboards with the single word: UNDEVELOP!

Florida. Developers there in the 1970s have been selling 200,000 lots every single year, and though plenty of them are under water, just as in that old con-artist routine, plenty of good green earth is going under the bulldozer, too, and at incredible prices. *Time* magazine recently told this story:

> Near Orlando, Fla., a grove owner sold 30 acres of land 15 miles from Disney World last spring [1973] for $285,-000. Two weeks later a subdivision developer bought it for $525,000. Several months later the developer turned down an offer of $750,000 for the property, upon which he is now constructing apartments.

Miami, which has some 50,000 people pouring into it every year, saw its land prices double each year from 1970 to 1975, and its home prices shoot from an average $16,400 in 1966 to $42,100 in 1973. And even Boca Raton, a tiny enclave of twenty-three square miles just north of Miami, meant to be a quiet and posh retirement spot, had more construction in 1972 than the entire state of Vermont.

And so it goes, right across the Rim.

Naturally such a giant business as this has caught the attention of corporations all over the land, especially those with lots of loose capital, and many a yankee firm has come to cowboy country to make a killing: Republic Steel is a land developer in Alabama, ITT in Florida, Philip Morris in Phoenix and Los Angeles, and Gulf in Texas, California, Arizona, and Florida. But of those corporations whose primary business is land development, the largest ones are native to the Rim: Kassuba Corporation (Florida), the largest apartment builder in the United States; Trammel Crow (Texas), the largest developer of rental housing; Jim Walter (Tampa); General Development Corporation (Miami); GAC (Miami); Gulf States Land and Industries (New Orleans); Major Realty (Florida); McDowell (Memphis); McCulloch (Arizona); John Portman (Atlanta); and countless hundreds of smaller operations. The giants of the construction industry, too, are native to the Rim, which has five of the top ten firms: Bechtel (San Francisco),

Halliburton-Brown & Root (Houston)—these are the top two, twice as big as the nearest competitors—Daniel International (Greenville, South Carolina), Fluor (Los Angeles), and Mc-Dermott (New Orleans).

An enormous industry, then, this real-estate and construction industry, with an enormous impact on the cowboy economy. Even the recession years, though hard on parts of the real-estate business all across the country, have affected the Rim areas the least—for even if they ain't makin' any more land, they are making more people, and more of them keep moving to the Southern Rim, and buying places to live in.

Leisure

Americans spend more money for food than anything else, and that seems reasonable enough, but, according to the National Resources Review Commission, their next biggest expenditure is on tourism. Add to that the amount spent on other leisure-time activities and all the paraphernalia associated with them and it seems fair to assume that the populace is spending even more on having a good time than on eating.

This peculiar state of affairs is of rather recent origin, dating roughly from the early 1960s. Owing to a mixture of such things as increased vacation time, shorter work hours, earlier retirement, more credit, more affluence, more boredom, and the construction of the far-flung interstate highway system, the leisure industry—by which oxymoron we may understand all the businesses making money on tourism, sports, recreation, and entertainment—has been an extraordinary growth industry over the last fifteen years, whose income has increased by more than 100 percent in the 1960s and is expected to increase another 100 percent in the 1970s, depression or not. There is enough Puritanism left in our hedonistic society to make the idea of such an industry seem somewhat frivolous, but the fact is that today it is a very big business indeed.

The tourist component, for example, which took in some $23 billion in 1960, had more than doubled to $50 billion by 1970 and by 1975 earned an estimated $88 billion, a nearly fourfold increase in just fifteen years. The recreation component —that's at-home, in-city fun-and-games, as distinct from tourism—amounted to $18 billion in 1960, $39 billion in 1970, and something around $55 billion in 1975, a threefold increase. Spectator sports have become a big business during this period —revenues have tripled from 1960 to 1975, up to more than $1 billion a year, with some 64 percent of the population watching sports events in 1974—and participant sports are even bigger— that's a $10-billion-a-year industry these days, thanks to the fact that the number of golfers, for example, has tripled since 1950, the number of tennis players grown tenfold, with something like thirty million people between them as of 1975. And the perfect ostentatious symbol for it all, the "recreation vehicle," or "Rec-V," as it's called around the Rim—the expensive land yacht designed to make the outdoors like your living room —is wholly the product of this era; virtually unknown before World War II, the recreation vehicle grew with the Southern Rim, with only 83,000 of them sold as late as 1961, but 740,000 of them in 1972 and an estimated 7 million were on the road in 1975, all for the weekend pursuit of, as the ads put it, "the Rec-V life."

The multibillion-dollar leisure industry is spread nation-wide, but its obvious focus is in the region where there is the most space, the best climate, the most spectacular natural sights, the largest unspoiled preserves, the longest stretches of federal forests and parks, the most miles of beaches, the greatest number of lodgings and campsites, and the preponderance of specially built tourist attractions—and statistically this means the Southern Rim.

As a measure of the importance of tourism to the Southern Rim, all you have to do is think of the Disney fantasylands at either end of it (Anaheim, California, and Orlando, Florida), the dude ranches and "fat farms" of the Southwest, the convention centers of Dallas and Houston, and such cities as Miami Beach, Las Vegas, and New Orleans, which would probably be lonely towns today were there no tourists. Tourism is the largest single industry in Nevada and Florida, the third largest in Louisiana and California, the fourth largest in Arizona and New Mexico, and it is growing in all of those states. Florida gets 25 million visitors a year, far more than any other state—that's as if a city the size of Chicago moved en masse into the state eight times a year—and they bring in between $5- and $6-billion

when they come; California, second in popularity, gets more
than 8 million tourists, spending over $3.5 billion. Certain
cities along the Rim more or less live on tourism—Miami
Beach, for example, which earns $600 million a year from tour-
ists, Las Vegas ($600 million), New Orleans ($400 million),
Phoenix ($350 million), Orlando ($300 million), and even
little Gatlinburg, Tennessee, in the Great Smoky Mountains,
home base of the most popular national park in the country
($100 million). Among them, California, Florida, and Texas
account for 21,000 hotels, motels, and campsites, which is
about a quarter of the total in the nation, and more than all of
those found in New York, Illinois, New Jersey, Pennsylvania,
Ohio, and all of New England added together.

Since it's figured that about 11 million people go to see
a place like Disney World every year, it's probably unnecessary
to describe what such so-called "theme parks" are like. Today
they are the hot center of the tourist industry, and their growth
shows how important tourism has become. As many as 16
million people visited theme parks in 1964, just ten years later
this had climbed to 55 million, and by 1976 there figure to be
73 million people enticed to these supertraps. The Walt Disney
people, of course, based in Burbank, California, rake in most of
the money—total revenues in 1973 came to $385 million—but
they are closely followed by the Six Flags organization (Six
Flags Over Texas, Six Flags Over Georgia, etc.), which has the
largest number of parks and attractions of any company, by the
Sea World outfit (based in San Diego, with outposts in Orlando
and, for some reason, Cleveland), and by the Hardwicke companies, based in Miami, who do wildlife parks. Great clusters of
these theme parks have grown up all across the Southern Rim—
around Disney World in Orlando, for example, and between
Dallas and Fort Worth in Texas—but the Los Angeles area
takes the prize: there, within a radius of twenty miles, you can
find—and visit, should dementia set in—Disneyland, Japanese
Village, Movieland Wax Museums, Lion Country Safari,
Knott's Berry Farm, Marineland of the Pacific, and even the old
Queen Mary, and that's just counting the big attractions.

Beyond tourism, there are other parts of the leisure industry in which the Southern Rim figures prominently. A few:

Games and toys. The Mattel corporation of Hawthorne,

California, is by far the largest manufacturer, even with its recent financial troubles, but it is joined by enough other Southern California firms (Wham-O, maker of Frisbees, is probably the best known) to make Los Angeles the largest toy manufacturer in the country, outdistancing the old leader, New York, by $16 million a year, surpassing Chicago by $76 million. And it should come as no surprise that the new and phenomenally successful "video games"—computer-run amusements like "Pong"—were invented and are produced in the Santa Clara technology complex.

Entertainment. This complicated part of the leisure world, encompassing television, movies, records, music, and the like, is by nature both so widespread and so local that no one area can be said to dominate. Still, the Southern Rim does have its industry capitals: Hollywood, of course, is still the leader in movie production and employment (New York is second and Dallas, surprisingly enough, is third) and accounts for some 65 percent of all TV production; Las Vegas is "the show business capital of the world," according to *Parade* magazine, paying out some $500 million a year just to support its live-entertainment industry; Nashville is the center of the rapidly growing country-music business, with forty-three recording studios and a gross of $250 million a year; Macon, Georgia, of all places, is the capital of the new white rock music, the base of Capricorn Records, the leader in this field; and Los Angeles is the center of record and tape manufacturing, with twice as many people employed as second-ranking Newark, twice as many studios as second-ranking New York. Radio and television networks are predominantly based in New York—though the upstart challengers, like the Hughes Network and Wometco Enterprises, are Rim-based—but it is interesting that the Southern Rim has 43 percent of all the radio and TV stations in the country (California, Texas, and Florida rank as the top three), and that little North Carolina has more stations than New York State.

Motel chains. By far the most successful company in this booming business—motel income doubled in the ten years after 1958, then quadrupled again between 1968 and 1975—is Holiday Inns, based in Memphis, Tennessee, and run by a Bible-toting Southern Baptist named Kemmons Wilson; it is about as large all by itself as the next four motel firms combined. And though yankee firms like Sheraton and Howard Johnson play significant roles, the industry is dominated by such cowboy firms as Ramada Inns (based in Phoenix), Hilton (headquarters in Los Angeles), Travellodge (Los Angeles), and Hyatt (Los Angeles). By the mid-1970s the western part of the United States accounted for 48 percent of all new room construction, highest in the nation, rivaled by the South Atlantic region with 27 percent.

Sports. Nothing dramatizes the pull of the Southern Rim like the highly successful expansion of professional sports into the booming cowboy cities—ask any fan of the Brooklyn Dodgers, whose team is now three thousand miles away in Los Angeles, has been, in fact, since 1957. During the period that professional sports have changed from a happy pastime to a bountiful business, they have moved steadily into the nether reaches of the country. The National Football League, for example, a Northeastern enclave for many years, merged with the upstart American Football League, financed largely by cowboy money, and moved out from yankeeland all across the Rim— San Francisco, Oakland, Los Angeles, San Diego, Dallas, Houston, New Orleans, Atlanta, Tampa, and Miami, with Memphis and Phoenix likely to be; basketball, baseball, and even, *mirabile dictu,* hockey franchises have expanded in the same pattern. Perfectly fitting, then, that in both 1973 and 1974 the world-champion baseball team was located in Oakland, California, the world-champion football team in Miami, Florida.

And if the Rimsters have their way, there will be no end to this expansion. Lamar Hunt, for example, son of oilman H. L. Hunt and part owner of the Dallas Cowboys, has determined that the once-genteel sport of tennis should be a fast-buck profession and has launched the World Champion Tennis Organization in Austin, Texas, signing up almost all the important international tennis stars to lucrative contracts and almost single-handedly breaking the long-standing dominance of amateur tennis; his operation has become such a television success that the networks now consider it worthwhile to spray-paint the trees around the Austin courts to give them a more springlike look for the viewers. Gary Davidson, a Southern California lawyer and acknowledged hustler, has had a similar success, having challenged the old-line professional leagues with such rivals as the American Basketball Association, the World Hockey Association, and the World Football League, all of them somewhat shaky still but strong enough to have struck consternation in the established teams. And now there's even a fellow out in Newport Beach, California, who is trying to start up a World Professional Golf League, whatever that may be.

Leisure, in short, has become a crucial and integral part of the Southern Rim way of life, and thanks to that a mammoth industry. Just drop in on Tuscaloosa, Alabama, or Austin, Texas, some Saturday during the fall when the football team is in action, or the Orange Bowl in Miami when the Dolphins are at play, and you can see it. Or the auto track at Daytona on the day of the Daytona 500, or in Charlotte, North Carolina, when they're running the World 600. Or the gilt-plush new Grand Ole Opry house in Nashville, the Astrodome in Houston, the Omni complex in Atlanta, the Los Angeles Civic Center. Or visit Yosemite Park some summer night, when campers jam so close together that the wilderness looks like Coney Island. Or fly over New Orleans at 10 o'clock some September night, when the lights are on and people are waiting to play on tennis courts throughout the city. Or, for a clincher, go take a look sometime at the parking lot of the Motorola plant in Phoenix: on a Wednesday it looks like any factory anywhere in the country —on Friday afternoon before the weekend it looks like the front lot of a Rec-V supersalesman.

II

These, then, are the six pillars of the Southern Rim economic establishment—agribusiness, defense, technology, oil, real estate, and leisure—and very substantial pillars they turn out to be. They are of such dimensions, in fact, that by themselves they could sustain any region in the world and allow it to compete economically with the developed industrial nations— and surpass most of them. But the full picture of the Southern Rim's economy doesn't stop there, and to these pillars we should add a few smaller industries, entablatures really, which on a lesser scale are important in the Rim's development.

Transportation. With its extensive coastline—two-thirds of the continental total—and abundant harbors, its early identification with the aircraft industry, and its wide-open spaces, the Southern Rim has naturally been a prime area in all kinds of transportation. In shipping, it has the four largest ports after the old established port of New York (New Orleans, Houston, San Francisco, Los Angeles–Long Beach), and taken altogether its docks handle fully 60 percent of the nation's shipping, a percentage that is rising every year; its Gulf Coast waterway system is the largest in the country and handles more freight than either the Atlantic or Pacific systems. In air transportation, the Rim, which grew up with the plane, has more than 40 percent of the nation's public airports, including the much ballyhooed Dallas–Fort Worth jetport, the largest in the country, and it has half of the ten most successful airlines in the land: Delta (based in Atlanta), the top income-earner in the industry; Flying Tiger (Los Angeles), the leading freight line and fastest-growing air company of all; Braniff (Dallas); Western (Los Angeles); and National (Miami). In railroad transportation, the Rim's stature is abundantly clear, since the Northeast has no fewer than nine rail companies in bankruptcy and a number of others only a few steps away, while the South and West by contrast are bulging with successful railroads, including the Southern Pacific Railroad (San Francisco), first in revenues, assets, and income of all railroad companies—in fact, leaving aside the bankrupt Penn Central, the largest transportation company of any kind in the land. And in land transportation, the Rim has the two largest bus companies (Greyhound, based in Phoenix, and Trailways, part of Holiday Inns), the two largest trucking companies (Consolidated Freightways, of San Francisco, and Maclean Trucking, in North Carolina, which is also the fastest-growing truck company), and the largest truck-leasing outfit (Ryder, of Miami); trucks, in fact, are very important in the Rim, whose fifteen states happen to have over half of all the trucks in the country.

Banking. Of course nothing can quite match Wall Street and the nineteenth-century-vintage banks of New York for financial clout, but in recent years the Southern Rim banking industry has proved particularly aggressive and successful, and in some cases it has even surpassed its yankee counterpart. Of the twenty-five largest commercial banks, only nine are in the Rim—but one of them is California's Bank of America, by far the largest bank not only in the country but in the world, with assets of some $60 billion in 1974, and one of them is the National Bank of North Carolina, the fastest-growing and most profitable bank in the country. The Southern Rim also has the largest interstate bank organization (Western Bancorporation, in Los Angeles); the largest international banking consortium (Security Pacific and Wells Fargo, of California, plus National Bank of Detroit), which outranks even the Rothschild banks and the Manufacturers Hanover combine; four of the top ten diversified financial companies (Ahmanson, Western Financial, and First Charter Financial of Los Angeles, and Transamerica, of San Francisco); and all but one of the nation's fastest-growing banks (one each in Texas, Oklahoma, Tennessee, Puerto Rico, and North Carolina, and four in Florida; the yankee exception is the Republic Bank of New York). And the Los Angeles area has now become the second-ranking financial center in the nation, after New York but well ahead of Chicago, and Los Angeles and San Francisco combined represent assets that are now three-quarters of those of the New York colossus.

One interesting key to Rim banking prosperity in recent years has been the creation of what are called bank holding companies, which are simply supercorporations allowed (among other things) to buy up smaller banks throughout a state or region and hence able to compile significant assets and handle major loans that would otherwise go to older and larger Northeastern banks. Though begun in the 1950s, it was not until the mid-1960s that holding companies began to expand on a large scale—even, thanks to the innovative hustling of California's Union Bank, moving into nonbanking areas—and to rival the financial empires of the yankee giants. As a result, where in 1963 there had been only 16 banks with more than a billion dollars of assets outside of the established money markets of New York, Chicago, and San Francisco, by 1973 there were 66 and the number is growing. And as *Forbes* magazine has pointed out, with a bit of yankee huffing, this holding-company challenge has worked: "These outlanders are cutting into loan volume and reducing correspondent balances of the big guys."

Odds and ends. The Southern Rim has a few other primacies worth noting. There is the timber industry, for example, for which the Southern Rim grows more commercial forest land than all the rest of the country put together, cuts half again as much lumber as the Northwest, and handles some 45 percent of all the cut boards in the land. There is the related industry of furniture manufacturing, heavily concentrated in the Carolinas and Georgia, where wood is abundant and labor cheap. There is textile production, also based in the Southeast, which has 70 percent of all textile workers and 50 percent of all the textile plants in the nation, including Burlington Mills (North Carolina), the largest textile manufacturer in the world, and seven others of the top ten producers. There is the related apparel industry, with 35 percent of its workers in the Southeast and its leading firms stretched across the Rim from Levi-Strauss in California through Farah in Texas to Hanes and Blue Bell in North Carolina; as to wholesale apparel centers, New York City ranks number one and has ever since the first bustle was made, but not far behind, second and third in sales, are the growing complexes of Los Angeles and Dallas. There is the petrochemical industry, obviously located in conjunction with petroleum resources in Louisiana and Texas, making the Gulf Coast by far the largest petrochemical concentration in the world. And, just to round everything out, the Southern Rim has the largest lease underwriter in the world (ITEL, San Francisco), the largest soft-drink company in the world (Coca-Cola, Atlanta), the largest title insurer (TI Corp, Los Angeles), the largest cigarette manufacturer (R. J. Reynolds, Winston-Salem), the largest leasing company (U.S. Leasing, San Francisco), and the largest credit-service firm (Retail Credit, Atlanta). Nothing in all of that on which to build an empire, but good indications nonetheless of the relative strength of the Rim economy.

III

With all of this, what if the Southern Rim were—to bring us back to the beginning—an independent country? It would have to have a capital, of course, and its capital would have to express both the newness of this economic rise and its centrality, the dynamism of growth and the substantiality of power. The logical choice is Houston.

Houston sits in the very center of the Southern Rim, the

pluperfect mid-century metropolis, the fastest-growing city in the nation in population, employment, and personal income, a center of every pillar of the Rim economy. It is the undisputed capital of the petroleum industry, the headquarters of several hundred oil companies, the number one city in refining, oil-field equipment, gas transmission, and petrochemicals; it calls itself "Space City, U.S.A.," the site of the Manned Spacecraft Center and the new space-shuttle project; it is the home of the nation's first Space Science Department (at Rice University), ranks ninth among national science centers, third in the manufacture of scientific instruments; it lies at the heart of the Southeast agribusiness area as the leading producer of agricultural chemicals and fertilizers, a center for cattle and livestock marketing, with more than 50 percent of its port's exports in agricultural commodities; it is the third-ranking city in construction, surpassing even Chicago, with $670 million a year being built nowadays, the tallest skyscrapers of the Southwest, the farthest-flung suburbs; and it is a major tourist attraction (Space Center, Astrodome, Astroworld), convention center (with the largest single-story convention hall in the world), sports capital (professional teams in football, basketball, baseball, hockey, tennis), and recreation playground (245 parks, Lake Houston and the Gulf of Mexico, seventy miles of beaches within an hour's drive).

The characteristic of Houston that makes it so choice as a capital is that it is so totally a *functional* city. Its downtown business area is made up almost entirely of high-rise office buildings and large department stores, with a few smaller restaurants to refuel the denizens of both, but nobody *lives* there, as they do in other urban downtowns. Houston central is just a place to drive into, work or shop, eat lunch, and drive home, a vast utilitarian island, almost totally devoid of character, which would only get in the way—a conglomeration of sleek undistinguished skyscraper boxes, the Texasthetic brought to its finest peak. Surrounding it, in concentric circles as far as the eye can see, for more than five hundred square miles, is suburbia, some of it fairly tacky, some supremely elegant, here and there broken by a high-rise office building or condominium or shopping center (there are no zoning laws in Houston, making it unique among America's large cities, but appropriately so), the whole thing apparently built upon the rough democratic principle of one-man-one-house. And connecting the two are the supermodern, metal-studded highways, six and eight and sometimes ten sweeping lanes, the arteries upon which all social and commercial life depend, said to be the finest urban freeway system in the country.

And the spirit which infuses all this is, as it has been since the founding of Houston, the making of money. The business of Houston, as its functional character would suggest, is business. In a downtown bookstore, fully a quarter of the display space is given over to business books, one full panel of *You Too Can Be a Millionaire* but shelves of somber textbooks, too (they're *serious* about their business in Houston). . . . After completing his five terms in office, Houston Mayor Louis Welch moved up to the next highest rung on the political ladder, to where the real power lies, as head of the Chamber of Commerce. . . . The business section of the *Houston Post* is one of the finest in the nation, far more extensive than that of the *Washington Post* and a rival to the *New York Times,* with one whole page each day devoted to the latest in gas and oil. . . . Downtown Houston begins to fade right after 5 o'clock, is left only to the convention visitors by dinnertime, and rolls up the sidewalks around 9: you don't mix business with pleasure, apparently, in a place where business *is* pleasure. . . . No fewer than 550 of the nation's million-dollar corporations have decided to put their regional or national headquarters in Houston, and, as long as the girders and glass walls hold out, the city will keep on adding them at the rate of some thirty-five a year. . . . A Houston businessman describing to a radio announcer how many seconds he saw a flying saucer one night, says, "It was as big as life and there I was counting, one, money, two, money, three, money—" . . . On a freeway leading from the downtown into the suburbs, an electric sign of the type that registers time or weather in other cities gives the Dow-Jones Industrial Average. . . . A radio commercial sums it up: "Business is more than a profession. In Houston it's a way of life."

A fitting capital, indeed.

2

The Growth Culture: Economic Character

In 1940 San Diego was a small city, more like an overgrown town, with a population of just over 200,000, basking in the Southwest sun, cooled by the breezes from the Pacific Ocean, partaking more of the somnolent style of its immediate southern neighbor, Mexico, than of the awakening bustle of its northern companion, Los Angeles. Thirty-five years later, San Diego is a major metropolis, the twelfth largest city in the country and second largest in California, capital of a metropolitan area with more than a million and a half people, still basking in the Southwest sun but cooled now by the ever-present air conditioner, long shed of apathy and lethargy, now a major manufacturing and distribution center, home base of the U.S. Pacific fleet, and an economic hub of such activity that it can out-Los Angeles practically any city in the country.

And what accounts for this remarkable development? Put simply, an economy built upon money from Washington and a culture devoted unreservedly to growth.

The money from Washington began with World War II, when San Diego was inundated with Naval personnel, ships, shipbuilders, airplane manufacturers, and munitions factories, and overnight became a major military center; since then it has been blessed by the fact that American wars have been fought largely in Asia and the Defense Department has deemed it necessary to establish no fewer than twenty-one Naval installations in the area. Navy and Marine payrolls as early as 1950 brought in more than $100 million to the town; today they come to more than $700 million a year, making the Navy what the *San Diego Union* calls "an important part of the basic economy." Aerospace is, and since the war has always been, the largest manufacturing employer in the city, responsible for more than $100 million a year during the 1950s, close to $1 billion a year in the 1960s, and a comfortable $700 million a year in the 1970s. Shipbuilding comes in a poor second to that, but even so grew from a $6 million business in 1945 to around $100 million today. Add to these sums the federal money that goes for welfare payments, agricultural subsidies, transportation grants, and pension benefits for the thousands of Naval personnel who have retired in the area, and it can be calculated that Washington pumps something like $2 billion a year into the San Diego economy, more than a third of the city's total income.

All of this money feeds the San Diego culture of growth, which for the last three decades, and especially the last fifteen years, has produced a boom period of freeway construction, real-estate expansion, land development, business advancement, and financial growth—along with which has gone fast-buck marketing, rampant wheeler-dealing, fraudulent stock schemes, land-sale scandals, and the ascension of organized crime to a position of power extending from the leading banks right into city government. Sound exaggerated? Take the word of the *San Diego Tribune,* usually an uncritical town booster, that San Diego has become the "West Coast distributor of flimflam men and holder of the national record for suede shoes per capita." Or of a local investment manager, a transplant from the East Coast: "The place is a lodestone for shady types. I don't know whether it's being close to the Mexican border, the sunshine, or what, but it seems to be a town where nobody gets terribly upset if you pull a fast one. My friends in Boston and Chicago just shake their heads. They can't believe it." Or take a look at the recent economic record of the town's leading businesses, characterized by the *Wall Street Journal* simply as "a wave of scandals and failures." Prominent among these have been the

Royal Inns motel chain, the town's largest, which went bankrupt under flashy suede-shoe management; U.S. Financial, Inc., the area's largest home builder, which collapsed after the Securities and Exchange Commission accused it of fraud, resulting in the largest Chapter 11 bankruptcy proceedings on record; and the most spectacular of all, the U.S. National Bank, which turned out to have been bilked of some $400 million and collapsed in 1973 in the largest bank failure to that time in American history.

Then there's the unsavory nature of some of the town's leading citizens. John Alessio, for example, a man named "Mr. San Diego" in 1964 and awarded an honorary doctorate by San Diego University—he was a bookmaker for thirty-eight years, a companion of known gangsters, the business partner of convicted drug traffickers, and recently spent two years in jail for skimming $1.2 million from his race-track operations and forgetting to tell the Internal Revenue Service about it. Or John Donnelley, a prominent attorney and Democratic Party bigwig —he has been friends and partners with leading figures in organized crime for the past twenty-five years, a manager of a Las Vegas casino during a time that the FBI says it was used for illegal skimming operations, and a conduit for illegal campaign contributions to San Diego city officials. Or Congressman Bob Wilson, the city's senior representative in Washington, fittingly enough the only advertising man in the House—he has been for many years the paradigm of the Southern California redneck, has been cited twice for unethical campaign activities, has been caught lying on his Congressional attendance record, and was one of the major engineers for the deal by which ITT was supposed to have paid $400,000 to the Republican Party so that the 1972 GOP convention could be held in San Diego. Nor should one overlook the interesting venture in northern San Diego County, the Rancho La Costa Country Club and resort community, an enterprise begun with some of San Diego's most prominent civic leaders along with a half-dozen of the more eminent names in organized crime—including Moe Dalitz (an old-time rumrunner and gambling czar who had fled his Las Vegas casino to avoid a federal skimming probe), Allen Dorfman (a Teamster Union wheeler-dealer convicted of conspiracy and fraud), and Allard Roen (a convicted stock swindler); given this patronage, it is not surprising that La Costa soon developed the reputation, as one Justice Department attorney put it, as "the West Coast R & R center for all sorts of hoods from throughout the country."*

But the foremost example of the San Diegan growth culture, Exhibit Number One, is the well-known Conrad Arnholt Smith, "Mr. San Diego of the Century" according to the local paper, the very symbol of cowboy success and the way it is reached. Smith started as a poor boy, dropped out of high school, worked as a grocery clerk and bank teller, hustled his way up to become vice-president of a little local bank, U.S. National, while still in his thirties, and then seems to have swindled it out from under the president while the latter lay on his deathbed. Upon that small foundation, Smith, growing right along with his city, wheeled-and-dealed his way to a $215 million conglomerate empire, which by the 1960s owned tuna fleets, a cannery, an airline, hotels, real-estate developments, taxicabs in eight Southwestern cities, farms, private clubs, insurance companies, and a major-league (more or less) baseball team, in addition to hundreds of interlocking subsidiaries of less determinate function. He had also worked his way into the world of politics, placing confederates at several levels of the city and state governments, and, and best of all, befriending a young Congressman named Richard Nixon, for whom he was an ardent million-dollar fund-raiser right from the beginning and with whom he shared such intimate moments as the agonized night of watching election returns in 1968. Alas, however, this Horatio Alger story had a particularly San Diegan flavor: Smith was simply a high-level con man, running one of the most massive bank frauds in history, churning depositors' money through his fronts and dummy corporations, skimming millions for himself and his friends, making deals with organized-crime figures up and down the Coast. For a long while, of course, none of this was known, Smith being quite ingenious with his entrepreneurial tricks and enjoying the protection of a Presidential ally in Wash-

---

* Funny-coincidence watchers will have noted that it was at La Costa that the Teamsters, who have invested some $50 million in the place, met to endorse Nixon in 1972, where Teamsters President Frank Fitzsimmons cemented certain deals with known mobsters in 1972, and where Nixon aides Ehrlichman, Dean, and Haldeman met to plan the Watergate cover-up in 1973.

ington, but so odious were the operations, so enormous were the frauds, so notorious were the allies, that eventually the empire came unstuck. In 1973 four federal suits were brought against C. Arnholt Smith: the SEC charged him with "egregious fraud" in systematically looting $100 million from his conglomerate; the U.S. Controller of the Currency sued his bank for lending out three times the legal limit to various Smith-owned enterprises; the IRS sued him for $23 million in back taxes owed for the single year 1969, the largest individual tax lien for one year's income in U.S. history; and a federal grand jury indicted him for criminal fraud, charging that he had manipulated the bank's records, let out no fewer than ninety-seven phony loans, and diverted $170 million from legitimate bank deposits into his own pockets. And then on top of all that the poor man was found guilty of making illegal campaign gifts to Republicans in both 1970 and 1972. Whether and for how long Arnie Smith will go to jail is still unknown, but his fraudulent empire has collapsed, his nefarious fortune has been decimated, his reputation has been irretrievably tarnished, and Mr. San Diego of the Century is no longer thought of, even there where much is excused, as the town's leading citizen.

Is San Diego too extreme, too bizarre, to be considered in any way representative of the cowboy culture? Perhaps yes, perhaps the proximity to Mexico or the excessive sun *does* account for much, but still it serves as a striking example of the process that has taken place to one degree or another in so many other cities of the Southern Rim in the last three decades, a process which blends vast new sources of federal money and the experience of unrestrained and speedy growth into an economic culture that, for whatever else you want to say about it, is decidedly different from what goes on in most of the rest of the country. It is those new sources and that swift growth which together form the essential character of the Southern Rim economy.

I

Traditionally in this country the financial support for business, especially new enterprises or corporations of any size, has come from the banking and stock-market communities of Eastern capital, centered on Wall Street—for, in the Willy Sutton maxim, that's where the money was. But beginning in World War II, and accelerating in every year since then, there has grown up an alternative source of capital supply, for the first time in the nation's history: the federal government.

There is no question that the single greatest economic phenomenon of mid-century America has been the expansion of the federal government; as the *Wall Street Journal* has pointed out, whereas private corporations have not enlarged their share of the national wealth much over the last thirty years, "in percentage of national income, the main postwar growth industry has been government." Today the role of the federal government in the private economy supersedes that of any group of corporations or any financial center, even that of all of them put together: manufacturing concerns, for example, spent only $32 billion in 1970; all businesses large and small, $102 billion; but Washington spent $197 billion. Or, to take just business income, it is reckoned that American corporations raised $55.5 billion from private external sources in 1972 but got nearly $100 billion in direct government purchases that same year and an estimated $180 billion more in indirect government subsidies. Thus the role of New York as a capital center, though by no means minimal, has been overshadowed by Washington: although New York is the seat of perhaps $200 billion worth of assets and the source of perhaps $30 billion a year in capital backing, Washington is the home of almost limitless assets in tax monies and national properties and the source of something like $300 billion a year for private businesses. No longer, therefore, need new or expanding businesses look to the old financial centers for money to operate with now that this new financial center has such resources. Federal budget expenditures, which never amounted to more than $15 billion a year before World War II, have now climbed to over $300 billion, rising much faster than the Gross National Product as a whole. Federal civilian employment has increased from 2 million to 3 million, payrolls from $613 million to $3 billion. Federal debt has risen from $259 billion in 1945 to $371 billion in 1970 and nearly $500 billion in 1975. Reckoned by federal budgets alone, and not counting cumulative trickle-down effects of government expenditures, the economy has been bolstered by Washington to the tune of more than $3.5 *trillion* in the last thirty years.

Now, for all the enormity of this federal role in recent years, it is somewhat startling to realize that it is concentrated in a limited number of areas—and only slightly less so to discover that so many of those areas are ones we have already identified as pillars of the Southern Rim. Of the ten basic domestic items in the federal budget, five of them relate directly to the Rim economy—defense, space and technology, natural resources (oil), housing, and agriculture; another—transportation—is important for several aspects of the leisure industry; four—education, health, veterans' benefits, social welfare—are outlays in which the Rim participates at a level generally above its populational share. In other words, half of the federal budget by category, and more than half by financial expenditure, go to support those industries which are heavily involved in the Southern Rim.

Let us take as an example the federal budget for 1970, roughly a midpoint in the period of sharp budgetary growth. More than half of that $197 billion budget was given over to areas in which the Southern Rim economic pillars are to be found:

Agriculture	$ 6.2 billion
Defense	80.3
Space	3.7
National resources	2.6
Housing	3.0
Commerce and transportation	9.3
	$105.1 billion

An additional 37 percent of the budget—$73 billion—went for general welfare services, of which the Southern Rim received about 40 percent, though it contained only 35 percent of the population. The remainder of the budget went for governmental operations—and here again the Rim enjoyed a slight edge, with 40 percent of the federal employment in its borders—and for interest payments.

An even clearer picture of the federal role in business support comes when we narrow the focus from *total* federal expenditures to specific federal *subsidies*—direct cash payments, tax breaks, credit benefits, regulatory price fixing, and benefits-in-kind—for those constitute the most valuable and direct capitalization of industry and show most clearly the way that Washington aids what it likes to call "the private sector." According to the staff of the Joint Economic Committee of the Congress, which has made the most careful study to date, federal subsidies amount, at a conservative estimate, to some $63 billion a year, excluding the regulatory subsidies for transportation and broadcasting that add on another $20 billion or so, and the numerous defense procurement subsidies, which are estimated to amount to at least $16 billion—in all, some $100 billion paid out by the federal government to private businesses and individuals every year, over and above the straight purchase of goods or services. Not even Wall Street, assuming it was mad enough to go giving away money, could match that sum.

And the recipients of these subsidies? Again, using the figures for 1970, which strike a fair average, they were the areas of the Southern Rim's special economic interests:

Agribusiness. As for most of the last thirty years, direct subsidies were a major source of corporate farm income, amounting to some $5.2 billion in 1970;* to this should be added food subsidies of $1.6 billion and a myriad of other payments such as housing subsidies for farm labor, export benefits and import protections, water-reclamation projects, farm-

---

* Direct cash subsidies for many crops were formally abandoned in 1973, because Nixon Administration policies in other directions had forced prices up to the point where they were temporarily unnecessary; the government, however, still guarantees a basic $20,000 a year to any farmer whose income is threatened and is still committed to a system of commodity price supports, which is a kind of subsidy system at the selling rather than the growing end. As a measure of the importance of Rim agribusiness in these former subsidies, here is a list of the top five beneficiaries, and their amounts, for the years 1967–70:

J. G. Bosell (California)	$15.7 million
Giffen, Inc. (California)	$13.3
South Lake Farms (California)	$5.7
Hawaiian Commerce and Sugar Company (Hawaii)	$5.1
U.S. Sugar Corporation (Florida)	$5.0

credit loans, and the hidden but very real benefits of government acquiescence in a system of racial exploitation by which farmers are able to use cheap black and Chicano labor. All told, according to a Brookings Institution study,........$9 billion.

Defense. The forms of subsidies to defense contractors are so numerous that it has taken two Congressional subcommittees to try to sort them out and even they couldn't untangle it all. At the very least, however, the government allows some $4.7 billion a year in so-called "progress payments," an estimated $10 billion in padded profits, and $1.3 billion a year through use of government property and equipment, a total of . . . $16 billion.

Technology. Although the aerospace component here provides some overlap with the defense segment, taking technology benefits alone, the government provides $6.5 billion a year in research-and-development funds, a tax break on those funds of some $500 million, subsidized technological education at another $500 million a year, and private benefits and patents from publicly financed research of roughly $750 million; the total is ....$8.2 billion.

Oil. Everyone is by now familiar with the famous subsidies to the oil industry, somewhat more glaring than most because they go so quickly and obviously into the pockets of the rich; they include depletion allowances ($1.5 billion a year), foreign tax benefits ($2.5 billion), drilling cost allowances (340 million), and import quotas ($5.7 billion),* for a total of ....$10.3 billion.

Real estate. Direct housing subsidies amounted to some $8.4 billion, through direct payments to the poor, tax breaks which encourage home ownership, and various federal mortgage guarantees. Tax subsidies through capital-gains depreciations on property and on land speculation add another estimated $7.4 billion at least, together amounting to ....$15.8 billion.

---

* Though the import quotas were formally dropped in 1974 because other government policies made such protection of the domestic industry unnecessary, over the fourteen years they were in effect, they are estimated to have provided between $70- and $100-billion for the oil corporations. At present there are still in force numerous license-free arrangements which continue to safeguard domestic prices and certain government pricing tactics which have added almost $9 billion a year to oil-industry profits since quotas were dropped.

Leisure. Direct federal subsidies here go largely for high-way building ($3.5 billion), airlines and airports ($467 million), and federal parkland and recreation expenditures ($330 million), but there are also regulatory subsidies to the airlines, half of whose operations are for pleasure travel rather than business ($1.5 billion). To this there must be added at least some part of the federal expenditures for retirement benefits, and, calculated at the percentage that consumers of all ages spend on leisure, this amounts to $1.8 billion, making a total of . . . . $7.6 billion.

TOTAL $69.0 billion

The amount of federal subsidies, then, to the economic areas in which the Southern Rim plays the predominant role comes to something like $70 billion a year. Add to this, as a final fillip, some proportion of the general subsidies (capital-gains tax breaks, for example, and investment tax credits) that go to all kinds of businesses—say, conservatively, just a third of the $19.3 billion estimated here—and the total exceeds $75 billion.

Now, there is no one-to-one correlation between federal handouts and Southern Rim pockets—the tax breaks for the oil companies, for example, go equally to the New York giants and the Dallas cowboys, and real-estate subsidies are shared throughout the country wherever homes are being bought. Moreover, given the geographically diffuse, if not precisely democratic, nature of the federal government, in which each of the fifty states is supposed to share in the national bounty, it is certain that federal money has played an important part in the economies of every region across the land. Nonetheless, it is obvious that the Southern Rim has been helped proportionally more than the rest of the country not only because it started so far behind, but also because federal supports have gone in such profusion to those industries in which it tends to predominate. All home builders may get tax breaks, but if it turns out that most of those homes are being built in the Southern Rim, it is that region's economy that benefits most; all defense industries may take a slice of the federal budget, but, as we have seen, those industries tend more and more to be concentrated in the Southern Rim. In short, the kinds of industries that grew up in the Rim were those which benefited most from the expansion of federal power over the last three decades and which owe their relative position in the national economy in large part to federal funds.

Thus it can be said that the basis for the Southern Rim's sweeping economic development—the cement under the pillars, if you will—is the huge federal treasury, a source of capital unlike that of any known previously in the world. This is not to suggest, of course, that traditional financing is unheard of along the Rim—in fact a great deal of borrowing is still done through normal stock flotations, and a great deal of money, say for real-estate ventures or oil exploration, is still obtained from private financial institutions, including the prominent banks associated with yankee capital. It *is* to suggest, however, that in addition to this usual source of capital the Southern Rim has been able to find another and even more fruitful reservoir and that the enormity of this reservoir has been responsible for the sudden and extraordinary economic resurgence of the last few decades. Washington rather than Wall Street is at the core of cowboy growth.*

* The issue of yankee money in cowboy corporations is one of some importance, since there have been those who hold that if a corporation is owned by people in New York, it is a part of the yankee power complex no matter where it may be located. The question of corporate ownership is complicated, but for our purposes only three points need be stressed. First, corporate ownership is not the same as economic impact: generally a company has more overall effect where its plants are located than where its stockholders are located. If a New York-based group owns a mine in Arizona, a percentage of the profits therefrom will certainly be going back to New York—but an even greater percentage of the profits, and virtually all other money, will stay right there in Arizona, in the form of plant and equipment, reinvestment and expansion, salaries for labor and management, exploration, maintenance and the like; that money, moreover, is creating a ripple effect in the local economy, generating what economists figure to be two dollars in disposable personal income for every dollar invested. Second, corporate ownership is not the same thing as corporate control: most large corporations are owned by thousands of stockholders, and even the largest individual holders rarely have more than 5 percent, enough to make their voice heard but not necessarily to make them dominant; even when banks, through their trust departments, gather sizable portions of a company's stock—10 or 15 percent would be considered a lot—they generally do not try to interfere with the corporate management, in only a few cases

It should be noted that the *where* of capital supply has a good deal to do with the *how*. Generally speaking, bankers and brokers make their capital available on strictly economic grounds, calculating everything as best they can on a neat profit-and-loss ledger; generally speaking, Washington's politicians make their capital available on political grounds, calculating votes and campaign payoffs and vague notions of national interest. Thus the cowboy corporation is somewhat more concerned with political approaches than economic ones, with influencing legislators, contributing to campaign committees, building lobbies in Washington, extending favors to regulators and bureaucrats, accumulating credits and bringing pressures, all the vast mingle-mangle that is the stuff of politics. It is this that Herbert S. Denenberg, the former insurance commissioner of Pennsylvania, had in mind when he told a Senate committee in 1974 of the "fundamental disease" of Washington: "the power of the special interests that is strong enough to make puppets of too many of our legislators, our executive branch, and our judges."

A case in point—only one among many. The Associated Milk Producers, Inc., of San Antonio, Texas, is a very well-run organization, the largest dairy cooperative in the country, an efficient marketer for some forty thousand farmers in Texas, Oklahoma, Kansas, Arkansas, Tennessee, and New Mexico,

---

do they try to influence the selection of that management, and only in very rare instances will they ever vote that stock against management wishes. Finally, corporate control is most likely to be exercised by managers, on the spot where the operations are, than by either the multiplicity of owners or even the board of directors, off in remote cities: in general, it seems, it is the group that makes day-to-day decisions, that allocates day-to-day finances, that especially controls day-to-day information, that will hold power in any operation. Even if it is a corporate board in some distant city that ultimately authorizes, say, a new plant expansion, it is bound to be making its decision on the basis of information provided by the local management, and the carrying out of that decision will depend on the management; Norton Simon, the California industrialist who has spent thirty years at the upper levels of corporate life, has asserted flatly that "most company managements run their business without the benefit of independent viewpoints."

In sum, the weight of the evidence suggests that the presence of yankee capital, even considerable yankee ownership, does not affect the role of a cowboy company based in the Southern Rim or greatly lessen the importance of that company to the cowboy economy.

and a corporation ably handling billions of dollars a year. But the milk business, like agribusiness in general, depends upon federal supports, and no amount of efficiency in operation would benefit it nearly as much as a few decisions made in Washington. Hence AMPI has made it a practice over the years to give quite generously to Congressional lawmakers, especially those on agricultural committees, and to Presidential candidates, regardless of party, and it has thought it wise to establish for itself a team of political lobbyists who try to ensure that such generosity is properly repaid. And for the most part this method has worked very well indeed: in 1970, after a $100,000 cash donation to Richard Nixon, the President revised import quota restrictions in its favor; in 1971, after a $60,000 retainer paid to Presidential crony Murray Chotiner and a pledge of $2 million to Nixon's reelection, the Administration granted high milk-price supports worth tens of millions of dollars. Of course there are certain risks involved, because there are a few laws here and there which might be—and in this case were—transgressed, resulting in unpleasant publicity and the payment of several thousand dollars in fines; yet the lesson from such transgression is only that the mode of operation should be perfected and, if possible, kept entirely under covers—not that the fundamental method of maneuvering should be abandoned. For the political process, clearly, is essential to the economic.

II

All of which—the huge federal presence and its rapid appearance in this once-laggard region—leads to the second essential feature of the Southern Rim economy: its pell-mell growth. As money and people poured into virgin areas, deserts sprouted with suburbs overnight, downtown slums were replaced by corporate high-rises, whole new cities were carved out of lakeside camps and mountain hideaways, empty ocean fronts were soon lined solidly with beach houses, industrial parks suddenly appeared on the fringes of cities and sleek landscaped factories grew up around the airports, five-and-dimes turned into posh department stores, greasy spoons into night clubs, sleepy banks into holding companies, real-estate back rooms into glass-walled office buildings, and out-of-the-way cities became the linchpins of sophisticated economies. All this had to have its effect: across the Southern Rim, growth became the catchword, progress the raison d'être.

We are no longer in the realm of figures here but of attitudes, and in a growth economy there are few pessimists. Maybe not everyone can share the enthusiasm of this editorial from the *Los Angeles Times*—

> Los Angeles' double-barrelled growth—a constantly widening fringe of suburbs and the trend toward higher buildings and the use of vacant land overpassed in early booms —brings problems peculiar to the city and to the West, problems of water, finance, transport, and planning. But a youthful, dynamic city faces these problems with confidence. In its surge to greatness, Los Angeles moves eagerly into the tumultuous decades in which it expects to make the megalopolis the center of the future's terrestrial paradise.

—but there are enough believers in heaven-on-earth in this and other cities across the Rim to provide an unremitting source of new ideas, new businesses, new finances, and new population. "There ain't *nothin'* we can't do," is how an Atlanta Chamber of Commerce executive puts it, adopting a bit of folksiness for a Northern visitor, "and that's includin' the things we ain't even tried yet." "We've got a growth *attitude* here," says the vice-president of a Phoenix bank.

> We feel that it's *good* to grow, you have to take chances along the way, but there's a lot of opportunity out here— and I think that's a lot different from the what-I'd-call regressive attitudes of the East, careful and kinda prissy. We're a *new* society here, young people, a whole *lot* of money, I'd say millions in discretionary capital, always looking for investment. Fact is, we're even first in bankruptcy—but that only means that there's a lot of opportunity out here, a lot of risk, people are always willing to try things, and if one thing doesn't work they'll turn right around and try another.

A real-estate operator in the booming Ozark Mountain region puts it bluntly: "If the devil came here and brought business and money to the town, I wouldn't complain." More reflectively, a California scientist who moved out to Southern California after years in New England says:

> Their incomparable vitality is euphoric; it is born from an assumption of success which exists because so far their failures are quite dwarfed by their victories. In contrast with the mood or whatever place they left, they revel here in a conviction that anything is worth trying; they assume it will work, because everything else seems to be working.

Which is the essence, really, of the growth mentality.

One of the important economic consequences of this growth mentality has been the generation of venture capital, an important though much smaller companion of governmental capital, in all sections of the Rim.

Though of course there are no strict geographical limitations on the adventurous investor, to a remarkable degree the Southern Rim has fostered individuals and financial institutions which are willing to take more than the usual risks in the confidence of reaping more than the usual rewards—and the oil rigs in the deserts and the factories added on to backyard garages attest to their success so far. The stories are heard all across the Rim. A young entrepreneur in Texas in 1961 sought capital for his information-processing machine, turned immediately to Dallas businessmen—"There is a spirit here that allows people with good ideas to be given a chance," he said later—got the capital and turned it into the multibillion-dollar Recognition Equipment Corporation. A young technician in Santa Clara County in the early 1960s, hoping to manufacture sophisticated telephone equipment, got venture capital from a local engineer-turned-businessman, built up his Vidar Corporation into a thriving business, and sold it for $27 million within a half a dozen years. An insurance executive in Oklahoma in 1964 took a fling with an extra $100,000, invested in a pair of Louisiana brothers starting a computer business in Texas, and today has a healthy piece of the $100-million-a-year University Computing Company.

And so it goes: growth is infectious. A California technology executive with plenty of experience in raising venture capital sums it up:

We raised money from all over the country. But we found more willingness to consider high-risk situations here. In the East and Midwest, people kept asking us how we expected to compete against big companies. Around here it's accepted that a small company with good ideas and good people can do it. Local financial men know the vulnerabilities of big companies, because so many people have made it competing with them.

That David-Goliath attitude, and the growth dynamic that it reflects, has also been responsible in recent years for another and even more spectacular Rim phenomenon, the audacious assault by a number of young entrepreneurs upon the giants of corporate power through the modern slingshot, the conglomerate.

A creation of the heady stock-market days of the mid-1960s, the conglomerate was nothing more than the cowboy growth philosophy at work in the fields of business ownership, a system of joining one company after another into an enormous corporate machine always growing bigger and more powerful, or at least—all the stock market cared about—*appearing* to; the basic idea, in the words of Tex Thornton, one of the most successful of the cowboy conglomerate builders, was:

> We grow not just to stay in business but to have a virile, stimulating atmosphere. Growth is associated with progress, the means to accomplish more things. Profit is only one of the motives. A strong motive is a deep pioneering spirit.

Though the conglomerate movement eventually inspired entrepreneurs in every corner of the country—often Jewish, often young, usually outsiders like the cowboys themselves—its wellsprings were in the Southern Rim and to a remarkable degree its most spectacular practitioners were products of that "pioneering spirit" along the Rim. People like Jimmy Ling, Oklahoma-born-and-bred, a high school dropout in Louisiana and a scratch-together electrician in Dallas, Texas, who built a $2,000 savings into a million-dollar electronics firm and then into a $3.7 billion conglomerate known as LTV, fourteenth largest corporation in the country by 1969; Tex Thornton and Roy Ash, the one a Texan and the other a Californian, who moved together through the Howard Hughes empire in Texas, left to take over a small California defense firm called Litton Industries, and turned it into a $2-billion-a-year conglomerate ranking among the top fifty industrial corporations in the country; Eugene Klein, a California wheeler-dealer and one-time used-car salesman who put together a dozen separate businesses into the National General Corporation, a billion-dollar-a-year business at its height; and other lesser-known operators like the Florida-based James Crosby, head of Resorts International, Burt Kleiner, a mod Los Angeles stockbroker who put together deals for just about every West Coast conglomerate of the 1960s, and Norton Simon, the California entrepreneur. To a remarkable degree, too, their targets were old-line Establishmentarian firms, usually Eastern, whose officers were staid and careful people who did not appreciate the idea of growth-for-growth's-sake; it was, as economist Michael Tanzer has observed, "a fight between two wings of American capital: large established wealth, such as that represented by the Rockefellers, Morgans, DuPonts, Fords, and other leading families of the tiny economic elite, and smaller but growing 'upstart' wealth." The upstarts did not always win, of course, and after a few years many even gave up trying the more audacious takeovers, but their record was nonetheless impressive: Ling's LTV, for example, took over Chicago-based Wilson & Co. and then Pittsburgh's venerable Jones & Laughlin steel company; Litton acquired Stouffer Foods; Hunt Foods bought the McCall Corporation of New York; Occidental Petroleum purchased Ohio's Island Creek Coal Company; National General bought out Grosset & Dunlap, and so on and on. Such a reordering of the economic order had never taken place on such a scale before.

The conglomerate assault began to falter in the stock-market crash of 1970–71, when the realities of economics began to catch up with the illusions of growth, and many of the earlier high-flyers have been forced to go through major reorganizations and diversifications. But the pattern that the conglomerators had established continued—and still continues—to operate in a major way on the American corporate scene; in the estimation of economist Richard Barber, the conglomerate "gives every promise of becoming the dominant form of American business in the last third of the century."

III

Much of what the Southern Rim's pell-mell growth has wrought has been decidedly positive—even if, as in the case of conglomerates, somewhat chaotic—but there is another side to that development, an unquestionably darker side.

In any rapidly developing economy the moral niceties of the past tend to get trampled underfoot. Where fortunes, or at least unaccustomed riches, are made quickly and often, they supply their own reason-for-being, their own justification—and their own morality. It is not so much that a whirlwind economy causes people to lose their ethics or forget their honesty as that it sweeps them at least temporarily above and beyond such proprieties, less inclined to give the cutting of corners and the fudging of agreements and the padding of accounts the same opprobrious weight. Considerations of what's right tend to take second place to considerations of what works; ethical tenets that once were taken for granted can seem unnecessary impedimenta, outmoded, inconvenient, superfluous. Cautious and high-collared ways of doing business give way to the rough and tumble, corporate presidents and bank directors start to look for the angles and the loopholes, and in their wake fast operators and wheeler-dealers appear, supplanting the slow ledger-balancing businessmen, coming to seem, in a time of flush prosperity, appropriate if not exactly honorable. To such an atmosphere the con man is attracted, and the swindlers—and not far behind, the gambler and the gangster.

Such a society can grow up anywhere, at almost any time. In the last quarter of the nineteenth century, that society was to be found in the Northeast, where a culture of rapid growth produced the economic amorality and political chicanery of the robber barons, the corruptions of the big-city machines, the war profiteering of J. P. Morgan, the brutal strike-breaking of Andrew Carnegie, the whole stinking swill of nineteenth-century capitalism out of which the current Northeastern Establishment has risen. In the middle of the twentieth century, that society was to be found in the Southern Rim. But this Southern Rim society had some special characteristics as well, which go to reinforce and to exaggerate the normal evils of rapid economic growth. It is a society which is still close to the frontier traditions, those traditions which, in Frederick Jackson Turner's words, breed a "scorn of older society, impatience of its restraints and its ideas, and indifference to its lessons," whose "tendency is anti-social" and whose spirit is "antipathy to control" . . . a society in flux, formed of successive waves of restless immigrants, who are without particular roots or allegiances or traditions and in fact often are on the move in order to break free from just such ties . . . a society which acts as a magnet for people frankly in search of climatic hedonism and economic opportunism . . . a society swirling into new urban and suburban configurations which sprawl carelessly and unplanned without much in the way of cohesion or community, emphasizing atomized lives built upon single-family homes and single-minded jobs . . . a society of new wealth, first-generation riches, heedless often of social trappings, wrapped up in material showiness, with all of the I'm-all-right-Jack arrogance of those who see themselves as "self-made" and heaven-blessed . . . and hence a society where restraints are likely to be slack, the moral bonds unfirm, and sanctions against ethical abuse far fewer and less often applied to.

No way has yet been found to measure the ethical quotient of a society, of course, and generalities deserve to be treated with suspicion. But for a start it is possible to indicate that the Southern Rim at the very least produces more than its share of fraud and flim-flam, of business scandals and illegalities, of outright violence and criminality.

Think for a moment of the recent colossal frauds of American business: the largest bank failure in U.S. history—U.S. National Bank, San Diego; the largest stock swindle—Four Seasons Nursing Centers, Oklahoma City; the largest insurance fraud—Equity Funding, Los Angeles; the biggest commodity-options fraud—Goldstein-Samuelson (and West Coast colleagues), Los Angeles. Or the more scandalous flim-flams of recent years: Home-Stake Production (Tulsa), the Baptist Foundation of America (Los Angeles), the Sharpstown Bank (Texas), Commutrix (Fort Lauderdale), Seabord Corporation (Los Angeles), State Fire and Casualty (Miami), Alabama Equity (Birmingham), Geo-Tek (San Francisco). Or the great names of American fraud: Bobby Baker, the South Carolina boy who hooked up with a Texas politician, established an arm-twisting business throughout the defense industry, and spread shady investments in Florida, Nevada, California, and the Caribbean; Alexander Guterma, the Florida-based manipulator who built an empire of worthless companies, joined forces with operators in New Orleans and gangland gamblers in Las Vegas, and bilked upwards of $10 million from unwary investors; William Penn Patrick, a North Carolina-born cosmetics salesman who built a $150 million empire in California and the Southwest called Holiday Magic, Inc., upon an illegal "pyramid sales" scheme and, according to the government, managed to swindle a cool $250 million; Billie Sol Estes, the fast-talking Texan who made millions by selling nonexistent fertilizer tanks in Texas and Oklahoma and was brought down only when he tried too openly to bribe high officials in Washington; and such lesser lights as Allen Lefferdink, Michael Arthur Strauss, "Dr." Noe, Luke Lea, S. Mort Zimmerman, Frank Blosser, Stewart Hopps, all of them products of the cowboy economy.

Perhaps it is too great an honor—other areas from San Diego to Little Rock might rival the claim—but southern Florida has been nominated by one of the *Wall Street Journal*'s long-time investigators into business frauds as "the Con Man's Capital":

> Securities swindlers clearly have established Fort Lauder-dale–Miami as their capital. The climate is beautiful. The advance fee racket [by which a phony money broker collects fees in advance for promises of finding cash loans] has made it easier to work from one location. Since most organized swindlers were born and bred far from the country's Eastern financial centers, they succeed best when dealing with Wall Street from a distance. South Florida also offers the swindlers proximity to most of the offshore havens they use. . . . And at least until 1972, the law enforcement agencies in Florida, even those representing the federal government, lacked the keenness for securities law prosecution that a crook might encounter in New York or Boston.

What is true for Fort Lauderdale–Miami is true for many other shady spots along the sunny belt: the Southern Rim climate, moral as well as meteorological, seems to be hospitable to the swindler.

One example cannot, of course, constitute proof, but the classic case of the Baptist Foundation of America is certainly suggestive. The BFA was established in Los Angeles in 1966 by one T. Sherron Jackson, a Texan by birth and breeding, a Baptist minister, a religious author, a pastor of a suburban California church, and, according to the House of Representatives' Select Committee on Crime, which takes an interest in people of this sort, a mover behind "one of the largest phony securities operations ever to come to light in the American business community." The stated purpose of the BFA was "creating support required for hospitals, education and other significant institutions" so as to forestall dreaded federal interference in these matters; its stated overseers were a board of apparently reputable Rimsters (six from California, three from Arkansas, two from Texas, one each from Mississippi and Nevada); and its stated assets for its noble goals were listed at $20 million. With that $20 million, however, there were certain small problems: $660,000 of it was said to be the value of a small Texas bank on which the BFA had put a down payment of only $29,000 and didn't even own; $100,000 was held in shares of a totally worthless corporation created out of whole cloth by *another* stock-fraud artist in Florida; $1 million was purported to be in stock of a New Jersey defense firm, Datacomp, which had been driven into bankruptcy by representatives of organized crime; nearly $3 million was credited for a hotel in Del Mar, California, which turned out to be a run-down wreck on which the BFA didn't even own a mortgage; $1.3 million was listed for the value of land in Tennessee which was sold to Jackson by a man he knew to be a convicted swindler and which, of course, was nonexistent; and $9 million was said to be based in two mining claims in California which happened to be worth, according to the tax assessor, all of $1,600. Behind the BFA's listed $20 million, in other words, was less than $10,000 in real assets, but that is a discrepancy which does not stand in the way of a real manipulator. With this façade and a lot of fast talking, Jackson and his friends managed to go on and bilk $800,000 out of a Toledo bank, $700,000 out of a Las Vegas hoodlum, $3 million out of an Oklahoma life-insurance company, and approximately $20 million more out of various individuals and corporations primarily in Florida and California, the two states that always turn out to be most fertile ground for con artists. Of course such venal fraudulence, even wrapped in holy cloth, cannot last for long, and eventually the BFA tripped over its own tangled machinations, falling apart in late 1971 with Jackson and his cronies in the arms of the law, forced to pay their debt to society. That society being the Rim society, however, on April 19, 1974, Jackson was smote by Los Angeles federal judge Harry Pregerson with a sentence of eighteen months in prison, six of his codefendants were let off with probations; nothing was said about returning any money.

The generality to which this example points, the congeniality of fraudulence along the Rim, is confirmed by the actions of the Securities and Exchange Commission, the Washington watchdog which, despite inadequate staff and creaking machinery, manages eventually to nail most of the more outrageous swindles. In recent years the SEC has been taking criminal action against cowboy corporations in a disproportionate number of cases: although the Southern Rim has only about 35 percent of the nation's population and business enterprises, it is regularly responsible for close to 50 percent of the criminal cases. (In a fairly typical six-month period, June 1974 to December 1974, court enforcement actions by the SEC involved 180 cases of domestic business illegality, 83 of them against cowboy businesses: 35 in California, 14 in Texas, 13 in Georgia, 10 in Florida, 5 in Arizona, and the rest in Nevada, Tennessee, and North Carolina.) That is a pretty serious indictment of the business practices of the region by itself, but just as revealing is the magnitude of the Southern Rim's schemes of fraudulence, by far the largest in the land, as for example, Equity Funding (a $400 million fraud), Holiday Magic ($250 million), Goldstein–Samuelson ($100 million), and Geo-Tek ($30 million). Such enormous sums that they make the swindlers of the past look like pikers; even Charles Ponzi, the granddaddy of all the con men, whose ingenious schemes are copied to this very day, never made more than $10 million.

Still further to the generality, it is extraordinary how often the names of cowboy corporations keep cropping up as scandals in the business world are uncovered. Of the eighteen major

companies found by early 1975 to have committed serious illegalities in their 1972 campaign donations to Richard Nixon,
eleven of them, 61 percent, were from the Southern Rim, and at
least three of them—Phillips Petroleum, Northrop, and Braniff
Airways—were discovered to have kept multimillion-dollar illegal slush funds for upwards of a decade. Of the score of Bell
Telephone subsidiaries around the land, two have been tainted
by scandal in recent years: Southwestern Bell, acknowledged by
its own officers to have kept an illegal political slush fund for a
decade and to have made gifts to various state utility regulators
to get its rates increased; and Southern Bell, charged by the
SEC with having made illegal corporate donations in the 1972
elections. Of the dozen ports whose officials and shippers were
named in connection with the great grain-shipping scandals of
1975, and convicted of bribery, theft, fraud, obstruction of
justice and the like, the overwhelming majority were in the
Southern Rim, and the centers of the whole corrupt operation
were New Orleans and Houston. The empire of Texas billionaire H. L. Hunt, which was being contested by two sets of the
old man's children for years even before his death in 1974, is
involved in potentially the biggest business scandal in years—
"the likes of which will surely rival Watergate" in the words of
Parade magazine—made up of equal parts of wiretapping, obstruction of justice, embezzlement, dummy corporations, kickbacks, payoffs, and cover-ups, which so far has involved the
names of all ten Hunt children, three Hunt employees, two
private detectives, former Justice Department officials Will
Wilson and Richard Kleindienst, Texas Congressman George
Mahon and his nephew Eldon, and Mississippi Senator James
Eastland. And that's just a start.

Finally, it does not seem an accident that the industries
which are the economic pillars of the Rim are historically the
ones most open to fraud and chicanery. Land buying, to take a
notorious instance, seems to be a God-given province for shady
operators, with frauds so common in states like Florida and
Arizona that entire state bureaucracies have to be given over to
curbing the flagrant abuses; the Arizona attorney general figures
that dishonest promoters there bilked at least $500 million out
of the public in the 1965–75 decade, and the Florida attorney
general in 1975 was prosecuting a $1 billion swindle in his state

that federal investigators estimate to be "the biggest fraud in the history of the country." So gross have the practices become that the federal government was forced to set up a special Interstate Land Office, which in less than two years received some 20,000 complaints, managed to catch about 125 unscrupulous land companies, and returned about $4 million in ill-gotten monies to consumers. The home-building industry, for another scandal-riddled example, is rife with unscrupulous operators, shoddy builders, and fast-talking agents who have created what one former SEC official has called a "national scandal" and have prompted governmental reaction across the country, from the SEC task force in Los Angeles which filed against no fewer than ten promoters in 1972 and 1973, to the Florida Condominium Commission which studied the whole real-estate explosion and concluded, balefully and unhelpfully, that it represented "an opportunity for greed and efficiency by sharp developers." Agribusiness, too, unlikely as it may seem, has been an easy area for law-skirting operations, both on the growing end, where abuses range from the exploitation of migrant workers in the Southeast to the importation of illegal aliens in the Southwest, and on the marketing end, where price fixing and other illegalities have been charged in recent years against the sugar industry, the lettuce growers, the meat packagers, and the milk co-ops. And finally the oil industry, where field-level abuses have been commonplace since the days of the first Texas gushers (slanted drilling, "hot" oil, claim jumping) and to which have been added such recent board-level abuses— all of them documented by federal agencies—as rigged bidding, falsified reporting, antitrust violations, interlocking directorates, and price fixing. In fact, the extent to which oil companies could go in their chicanery was fully demonstrated during the "energy crisis" of 1972–73 when, not content with getting more money than ever before in their history, they were investigated (by the Government Accounting Office, the Federal Energy Administration, and the Federal Power Commission) for price fixing, fraud, forgery, and other illegalities which cheated hapless customers by at least $3 *billion*. (The defense industry might be added here, except that it is in the happy position of having all its corner cutting, price fixing, influence peddling, and fraudulent operating sanctioned by the Defense Department.)

Turning from the specific world of business to the wider societal setting, the incidence of crime should also help to give some indication of the Southern Rim's ethical quotient. The way in which the region has developed has tended to create a society where, for example, values are in constant flux, cultures are repeatedly in conflict, material goals are predominant, community ties are fragile, and frontier values are ingrained— and it just so happens, according to Donald R. Taft, perhaps the leading social criminologist in America, that these are exactly the specific attributes which "normally" produce a high incidence of crime. The presumption is more than borne out by the statistics which, though notoriously unreliable in this area, repeatedly show the same general pattern of violence and criminality. In 1970, an average year, the Southern Rim had a murder rate far above the national average (10.9 per 100,000 people, vs. 7.8 nationally), and the top ten states in murder percentages were Georgia, South Carolina, Florida, Alaska, Louisiana, Alabama, Texas, Mississippi, North Carolina, and Arkansas; burglary rates, to take a different kind of measure, were also higher in the Southern Rim—about a hundred more incidents per 100,000 people than the national average—with the leading states being California, Nevada, Michigan, Florida, Arizona, Hawaii, Washington, New York, Colorado, and New Mexico. City statistics show the same pattern: for 1974, by the FBI's accounting, 20 of the top 25 cities in overall crime rates were in the Southern Rim, and pretty neatly distributed over the whole area, too (Phoenix, Daytona Beach, Las Vegas, Fort Lauderdale, San Francisco, Fresno, West Palm Beach, Albuquerque, Stockton, Miami, Los Angeles, Sarasota, Gainesville, Bakersfield, Santa Cruz, Santa Rosa, Modesto, Orlando, Tucson, Baton Rouge); Southern Rim cities made up 21 of the top 25 for burglary rates, 18 of 25 for rape, 17 of 25 for aggravated assault, 18 of 25 for larceny, and 20 of 25 for murder.

And if such figures remain too remote and imperfect, perhaps another index can be found in the spectacular incidents of individual violence of the last dozen years. Of the grisly mass murders of recent years, only one—Richard Speck's in Chicago —took place outside the Rim; the others—notably the Manson killings, the murders of the California migrant workers, the University of Texas tower shootings, the Santa Cruz murders, the New Orleans motel shootings, and the Houston homosexual slayings—were all committed in the turbulent Rim. And of the notable political assassinations in recent years, two have taken place in the Northeast—Malcolm X in New York (1965) and the attempt on George Wallace in Maryland (1972)—but the rest were in the Southern Rim: Medgar Evers in Mississippi (1963), John Kennedy in Dallas (1963), Schwerner-Goodman-Chaney in Mississippi (1964), Viola Liuzzo and Jonathan Daniel in Alabama (1965), Martin Luther King in Tennessee (1968), Bobby Kennedy in Los Angeles (1968). (Put on a more statistical basis, the Southern Rim throughout American history has accounted for 63 "political assassinations and assaults," as defined by the 1969 National Crime Commission, the Northeast for only 7.)

No irrevocable conclusions can be drawn from these instances, but in cumulation they do seem to point to aspects of the social character and of the economic morality of the region to which they are endemic.

IV

But it doesn't stop there. The growth culture is also open to penetration by other sources of capital which fit in nicely with its ethical slackness, sources which, though in no sense rivals to the flow from Washington, have played important roles in cowboy development. Specifically, the high-flying pension funds and organized crime itself.

Pension funds today control an estimated $170 billion worth of assets, amounting to what the *New York Times* has called "the fastest-rising mountain of investment capital in the country." This awesome sum of money is all the more important because over the last thirty years of their existence the pension funds have been essentially uncontrolled, permitted to invest when and where they wanted to, with very little regard for the ultimate customer, the retired worker who hopes to live on the fund's profits. To be sure, not all of them, probably not most, are loosely managed or ethically fuzzy—but enough of a scandal was created in recent years by improper investments and unpaid benefits to force the Congress in the summer of 1974 to place the funds under some governmental supervision. And the fact that the largest pension fund of all is known to play both immoral and illegal games suggests, at any rate, certain troubling thoughts about the rest of them.

This fund, probably the most powerful in the country, is the notorious Teamsters Pension Fund, officially a retirement cache for members of the International Brotherhood of Teamsters which is said to contain assets of $1.5 billion. Though its investments range from Massachusetts to Mexico, its primary economic impact has been in the Southern Rim, where it has invested heavily in real-estate development (especially in Florida and Southern California) and hotel-casino operations (chiefly in Las Vegas); of the more than $700 million which it is known to have dealt out over the last decade or so, at least $540 million, or three-quarters, has gone into cowboy enterprises.

What's particularly important about the Teamster money is that it is capital that no other source would probably have supplied and without which certain lucrative Rim developments would never have taken place. The incredible explosion of Las Vegas, for example. What ordinary bank or pension fund would want to invest in such a peculiar institution as a gambling casino, a highly speculative and unstable venture, involving thoroughly unsavory characters from the ranks of organized crime, in which the profits are regularly skimmed off the top for foreign bank accounts, and outsiders are discouraged from poking their noses into how the management is run? Very few. But the Teamsters Fund has had no qualms whatsoever: in the last fifteen years it has put more than $225 million into Nevada casinos and has been chiefly responsible for building fully a third of the luxury "carpet joints" in Las Vegas. In fact, without the Teamster money there might be no big-time Las Vegas; reporter Ed Reid, a long-time Vegas-watcher, says simply, "The Teamsters' pension fund generally provides the big guns and the ammunition necessary to justify . . . the continued existence of Las Vegas." Whether that existence should really continue, given the nature of the city's business and its intimacy with crime, may be open to some dispute, but there is no question that gambling in Las Vegas today is a $500-million-a-year business that simply did not exist fifteen years ago, the centerpiece of the multibillion-dollar development of southern Nevada.*

Or, for a humbler example, take little Deming, New Mexico, a town of some ten thousand people tucked in the southwestern corner of the state about thirty miles from the Mexican border, a place that you might call God-forsaken were there any signs that He had been there in the first place. No one seemed interested in developing the town until 1959, when the city fathers of Deming, trying to fall in behind the march of progress that was changing other parts of New Mexico, issued $4.5 million in new bonds with the hope of attracting light industry into the area; the idea was that out-of-state corporations, wanting to take advantage of the area's cheap labor, would hurry down to Deming, buy up the bonds, and thus supply the city with enough capital so that in return it could build them tax-free factories to work in. For some time there were no takers, but then the Teamsters Pension Fund stepped in and bought up $2,628,000 worth of bonds and arranged for an Indiana toymaker, the Auburn Rubber Company, to move down. Auburn hired 300 workers, Deming built them a plant, the Teamsters came down and organized it, the Fund poured in another $4 million, and the town began to grow; in 1971 another out-of-state firm with Teamster backing, Gaylur Products, moved in, employing 40 workers.

Now you might wonder why the Teamsters should express such generosity to this unprepossessing New Mexico town, and in trying to unravel that we come to another important feature of the Pension Fund. For it looks very much as if the operations there were really established so that Teamster officials and their friends could pull off what the underworld knows as a "scam" and a "skim." Auburn, the scam victim, was milked of all its liquid assets and went bankrupt in 1969, owing the Teamsters more than $5 million—which would have upset the Fund man-

---

* Teamster money was not quite the only kind willing to play by the strange rules of Las Vegas investment. Two huge Texas insurance companies—Gulf Life Insurance, bought by Troy Post from the Murchison family in the 1960s, and American National Insurance Company, owned by the Moody family and with a history of dealings with criminal types —have also invested heavily in the gambling enterprises there.

agers except for the fact that they knew for seven years that the business was failing, kept pumping additional millions into it, and were presumably taking the money out the back door and lining their own pockets with it; the Fund lost out on $5 million, the drivers who are supposed to get their pensions suffered, but a few individuals made themselves wealthy. Gaylur, the skim company, took over the abandoned Auburn building and got another $1.4 million loan from the Fund, and *this* money, according to an indictment by a federal grand jury (February 20, 1974), went straight into the Chicago underworld with the blessings of the Fund managers. Of course the real beneficiaries of all this (at least until arrested) seem to have been the friends of the Teamsters Fund, but the town of Deming, too, has had its benefits—three hundred families received salaries for a decade, a two-story union hall and a modern factory were built, the airport facilities were expanded, and other legitimate businesses have since moved in. It's no Las Vegas, for sure, but development is development.

Lest the Deming episode seem unusual, it is necessary to point out that the Teamsters Pension Fund has consistently provided a cozy front and an easy siphon for organized crime interests. It was the source of the $50 million which built San Diego's notorious La Costa Country Club, that retirement haven for the mob; it put $1.2 million into La Mesa Bowl, a Los Angeles bowling alley owned by the Matranga family of the San Diego Mafia; it gave $2.5 million to Andrew Lococo, a Los Angeles restaurateur and two-time convict the Justice Department calls a top figure in the California Mafia; it has invested $7 million in the Savannah Inn, in Georgia, run by Lou "The Tailor" Rosanova, one of the FBI's "Top 300" Mob leaders— and the list could go on and on. In the words of one federal investigator—words echoed by virtually everyone who has looked into the Fund—"that outfit is a wholly-owned subsidiary of Organized Crime, Inc., and they'll never change."

And where do the Teamsters and the criminals seem to do the bulk of their business together? In the areas where new capital is always welcome, where real estate offers easy legitimate entry and a certain anonymity, and where the hecticness of growth obviates most probing questions: the Southern Rim. As crime specialist Ovid Demaris has noted, "The infusion of

Teamster money in underworld projects has been overwhelming, not only in Las Vegas but also in Palm Springs, Los Angeles, Orange County, San Diego County, Tucson, Phoenix, Dallas, Houston, New Orleans, Orlando, Fort Lauderdale, Miami, the Bahamas, and throughout the Caribbean"—and that leaves out the recorded investments in New Mexico, North Carolina, Alabama, and Georgia. The managers of the Pension Fund, like the vacationers and the aerospace executives, apparently love the sunbelt.

Which brings us very neatly to organized crime itself.

Crime writers like to make much of Meyer Lansky's statement, "We're bigger than U.S. Steel," but in fact organized crime by all estimates is at least ten times bigger than U.S. Steel—indeed, were it a cohesive corporation, it would easily rank as the largest firm in the nation, with annual revenues double those of the current leader, Exxon. To be sure, the estimates are very chancy, since those who know aren't telling and those who tell are probably exaggerating, but from a number of different sources a rough indication is that the total annual intake of organized crime is something around $80 billion —at least $30 billion of it from gambling, legitimate and not, another $15 billion or so from loan-sharking, $10 billion from stolen securities, $10 billion more from legitimate businesses such as motels and real estate, some $8 billion from drugs, and the remaining couple of billion from other smaller activities such as prostitution, pornography, smuggling, and hijacking. Poor U.S. Steel, by contrast, pulls in only around $8 billion a year.

And, of course, that $80 billion is a very special kind of money, since most of it comes in loose cash and has to find an outlet quickly and secretly; the crime czar, after all, can't very well spend his heroin-sale income on new cars and yachts or the tax men will show up asking embarrassing questions. In order for it to be useful in any sense, this money has to be made somehow legitimate and untraceable, either through laundering in certain banks that are friendly to the mobsters or through investment in certain legitimate businesses that will take ready sums without inquiring too carefully as to their source. This combination of enormous sums, available in cash, and in need of quick reconversion is what makes organized crime so important as a source of investment capital; in the view of one expert, Eugene Rossides, a former Assistant Secretary of the Treasury, "Organized crime is literally a competitor to commercial banking because it has huge sources of capital illegally obtained."

Both the size of the criminal coffers and their role in legitimate enterprise have expanded considerably in the last few decades, beginning sometime during the late 1940s when a few money mavens like Meyer Lansky figured out the wisdom and the mechanism of turning ill-gotten gains into respectable-looking investments. Organized crime, too, is another mid-century growth industry—and, as we should expect, that growth has taken place to a significant degree in the Southern Rim.

At the end of World War II, the strength of organized crime was in the big cities of the Northeast—Boston, New York, Cleveland, Detroit, Chicago—where it had first developed among the Italian and Jewish out-classes, and there were only a few outposts—the Carlos Marcello organization in New Orleans, the Trafficantes in Tampa, Sam Maceo in Galveston—in the Southern Rim. But as the population moved out, so did the mob, and since the new areas were regarded as open territory, all kinds of gangland figures were allowed to move in easily, setting up their own organizations, their own rules, and their own rackets. Gambling centers which had been dusty outposts in the 1930s suddenly began blossoming across the Rim in the 1950s: Miami Beach, Florida; Phoenix City, Alabama; Biloxi, Mississippi; Gretna, Louisiana; Beaumont, Texas; Gardena, California; and the blossomingest place of all, the place where it all was legal, Las Vegas, Nevada. Smuggling—especially of heroin, in which the trade grew steadily more lucrative after the opening up of Asia's Golden Triangle in 1948—tilted to the South, taking advantage of the enormous Rim coastline and the porous Mexican border, along which whole networks of "Latin connections" and "Mexican connections" were developed; by 1950 or so Miami had surpassed New York as the leading entrepôt for smuggled drugs. Loan-sharks found natural waters, supplying cash to the marginal operators that migrated to the growth areas, floating various new enterprises that seemed too adventurous for legitimate lenders, providing all-important front money for backwoods wildcatters in Texas and Louisiana or for corporate farmers overextended at the local banks. And everywhere in the booming Rim, millions of dollars were placed in legitimate investments, chiefly in those high-risk operations where venture capital is hard to come by—oil exploration, for example, and land speculation—and in those large-scale businesses where sizable amounts of capital are necessary—corporate farming, for example, technological manufacturing, and, above all, real-estate development. So swiftly did this invasion of the Rim take place, and so successfully, that when the Kefauver Committee began its frontal examination of organized crime in 1950, fully half the cities it held hearings in were in the Southern Rim, and pride of place went to Miami Beach.

In the wake of the sensational Kefauver hearings, several Northern cities took steps to eliminate the grosser forms of criminal corruption and to beef up their organized-crime squads —a commendable procedure which, however, had the effect of sending the slipperiest mobsters southward to the cities where much less was being done and where the local sheriffs could more often than not be bought. Meyer Lansky was arrested in New York in 1952, served ninety days, and upon release promptly bought a home a few miles north of Miami and proceeded to expand his operations throughout Florida and the Caribbean; New York Mafioso Joseph Bonnano bought a retirement house in Tempe, Arizona; Moe Dalitz moved from Cleveland out to the Desert Inn in Las Vegas; New York syndicate leader Jimmy Alo moved down from New York to Miami Beach; and Detroit mobsters Joseph Zerilli and Bill Tocco bought up a couple of ranches in Arizona. A clutch of mobsters from Cleveland, Chicago, Detroit, and Milwaukee, the heat on at home, began turning up in Las Vegas, and set in motion the scheme of giving the sawdust casinos some red-carpet respectability—with luxury hotels, Hollywood entertainment, golf courses—that turned the gambling joints into multibillion-dollar businesses. Other of their criminal confreres joined in the real-estate boom: "It was Mob money," one historian has noted, "that bought the land and financed the hotels along the Miami Beach Gold Coast and in Las Vegas, that financed the welter of condominiums that have sprung up in the Florida Everglades, the deserts of the Southwest, in Palm Springs and all across Southern California."

The 1960s saw more of the same, except that now a vengeful Attorney General named Robert Kennedy set out to destroy the more prominent criminal organizations (as well as the outfits, like the Teamsters Fund, that played with them) and an awakened J. Edgar Hoover finally conceded that yes, maybe there was such a thing as organized crime but it consisted entirely of Italian Mafiosi. The effect of this was to focus federal attention on the more notorious criminal leaders, especially the Italian families of the big cities of the Northeast who had always attracted headlines with their feuds and slayings, and to divert investigations away from the quieter overlords of the rest of the country who went right ahead with their white-collar thievery, gambling skims, and legitimate investments. By the end of the decade many of the old Mafia families in the Northeast were in disarray, their traditions revealed and their operations exposed by informers, their bosses tied up in courts or jails, their *capos* now old and sick, their younger chieftains feuding in the streets, their turfs being invaded by black and Spanish minorities.

Today the extent of organized crime's operations in the Southern Rim is clearly vast—indeed of incalculable proportions. Unfortunately, because it is strictly incalculable we must rely on tidbits, clues which suggest the totality. Such as: A junior-grade "Dixie Mafia" operating in Georgia and Alabama is said to do $20 million worth of stolen-car business a year. . . . The New Mexico Crime Prevention Council has reported that its state "is part of a region which is organized" by criminal overlords with their eyes on the $60-million-a-year race-track business. . . . According to an official report commissioned by Florida Governor Claude Kirk in 1967, organized crime owns 45 hotels and 25 restaurants in the city of Miami alone. . . . The two largest seizures of counterfeit money in American history have taken place in California ($8 million in 1974) and Tennessee ($6.1 million in 1973), and law officials estimate that organized crime's biggest operations today are in the South and Southern California. . . . The New Orleans Crime Commission estimates that $1.1 billion is collected by organized criminals in that city every year, the enormity of which is indicated by the fact that Chicago, popularly thought of as Gangland, U.S.A., collects only twice as much, although its population is five times greater. . . . One Mafia family is known to control $400 million worth of Southern California real estate. . . . Meyer Lansky is said by the federal government to get as much as $7 million a year in skim money from just one of his casinos in Las Vegas, and the man is thought to have a finger in several dozen such operations. . . . A leading Detroit Mafioso owns or controls five separate businesses in Tucson, Arizona, including a ranch, a motel, a printing company, and a riding stable. . . . Samuel Cohen, the owner of the garish Eden Roc and six other luxury hotels in Miami Beach, took part in a $2 million skim from a Nevada casino, according to a federal indictment in 1971. . . . Mexico and Latin America have replaced Europe and Asia as the primary source and conduit for heroin and other narcotics smuggling, with Florida and the Southwest today accounting for 90 percent of the illegal drug traffic in the United States and little Tucson, Arizona, gaining prominence as the marijuana capital of the United States. . . . And in Arizona the attorney general has confessed that his state "is now a center . . . for mobsters," many of them participating in the multimillion-dollar land-sale frauds, and that "organized crime is not a bogeyman but a real live problem here."

Only tidbits, but the conclusion to which they point seems clear enough: the growth culture of the Southern Rim has proved warmly hospitable to the penetration of organized crime, the financial wherewithal as well as the basic operations, and this process has been both a result and a determinant of its moral climate.

San Diego, in retrospect, does not look like such an aberration: it partakes, legitimately as it were, of the economic character of the region of which it is a part. That character, shaped by the greatest source of capital yet known to the world and perhaps the most rapid deployment of capital yet witnessed in the world, is variegated and complex, of dark strains and light, but surely in manifold respects distinct from that of the rest of the country. And in the same way that it has been instrumental in affecting the economic style of the nation for the past thirty years, so does it bid fair to do over the next thirty. An eventuality that might make us all wary.

3

From Right to Left: Political Power

Is it only a coincidence that in 1973, before the whole yankee shake-up, the chairmen of the Democratic Party, the Republican Party, the American Party, and the unnamed Wallace-ite movement were all from the Southern Rim? Undoubtedly so, for what conspiracy of worldly intent or godly chance could contrive such a circumstance? And yet there it was: the Democratic Party chairman was Robert Strauss, a wealthy Dallas lawyer; the Republican Party chairman was George Bush, scion of a yankee family but a Texan for the last three decades; the American Party, descendant of George Wallace's 1968 party, was led by Thomas J. Anderson with headquarters in Pigeon Forge, Tennessee (though there was a rival branch of the party, known as the American Independent Party, led by William Shearer of California); and the national Wallace-ite organization was guided by Charles Snider, of Montgomery, Alabama, and Hall Timanus, a Houston lawyer. (Not only that: the head of the Young Democrats was Delesseps Morrison, Jr., of New Orleans, and the head of the Young Republicans was Richard Smith, of Fort Lauderdale.)

Yes, surely a coincidence. But it does point to a phenomenon about which there is nothing coincidental, and that is the political emergence of the Southern Rim in the last few decades (and most especially in the last dozen years) and its growing role in national politics. This region, which used to consist of an insular and taken-for-granted Democratic South, an impotent Democratic Southwest, and a mishmash California, is now a turbulent and contested area, a two- and three-party battle-ground in elections both local and national, and the site of a renascent Republican Party, a rejuvenated Democratic Party, and the only serious third-party challenger in sixty years. It is an area which, thanks to the democratic instincts of the Found-ing Fathers, has gained electoral votes with every succeeding census, rising from 161 votes in 1948 to 184 in 1972 (at the same time that the Northeast has declined in votes from 235 to 218), and which today accounts for 68 percent of the 270 votes necessary to win an election, a percentage which is certain to grow as the population migrations continue. It is an area which similarly has steadily increased its representation and impor-tance in the House of Representatives, adding 22 new seats in the last three decades (while the Northeast has lost 17 seats) for a total of 154, or 35 percent of the total membership. And it is an area that has supplied four of the last six Presidential candidates, the last two elected Presidents, much of the leader-ship of the Congress over the last two decades, and the basic strength for all the conservative movements of whatever party flag.

It is of obvious significance, then, the political emergence of the Southern Rim. Let us look at its influence across the political spectrum, reading from Right to Left.

I

It may seem today that the Far Right is as important in American politics as, say, the Mugwumps or the Prohibitionists. Certainly nothing on the scene today commands the attention given the McCarthy witch hunts of the early 1950s or the John Birch Society of the early 1960s; and certainly, too, the more militaristic elements like the Minutemen, the blatant fascists like the Nazis, and the rabid racists like the Ku Klux Klan seem to have lost both fervor and following, at least for the time being. But the Far Right is nonetheless alive and, as usual, kicking. The John Birch Society is said to have more members today than at the height of its notoriety (as late as 1970, when George Gallup last asked, some eight million Americans declared themselves strongly in favor of the Birchers), and Birch Society members sit in the halls of Congress and repeatedly stand for public office in at least a dozen states. The gospel demagogues of the Right have more radio outlets (and a growing number of television outlets) today than at any time in their history, and they report increasing attendance at their various anti-Communist "revival" meetings. And the millions who flocked to the star-spangled banners of Americanism in the 1960s, though still only a fringe, continue to write their letters to the editor, censor books at the high school library, harass newsdealers who sell *Playboy*, and come forth from time to time for one of their pro-American Legion demonstrations or Support Richard Nixon committees.

The Far Right can be found anywhere in the country, of course, for political madness knows no geography, and there is scarcely a large city today, whatever its location, that does not have a few right-wing groups, a Citizens Against Fluoridation Committee, a chapter of the Birch Society, an affiliate of the Christian Crusade. But it is in the Southern Rim, from the reactionaries of Orange County to the rednecks of South Carolina, that the Far Right has its greatest strength, and, with a few important exceptions, where the main rightist organizations are located. As witness here, there is no less an authority than Texas oilman H. L. Hunt, whose fortunes and ideas alike derived from the Mesozoic Era, who wrote in a message to Richard Nixon, "It is a well-known fact that this southern area encompasses a segment of the population that is more truly and typically American, with most of the citizenry untouched by the isms and alien philosophies that have found acceptance in other sections of the country."

Southern California, as the media have taught us, is of course the pluperfect paradise of the Far Right. Now in fairness one should point out that the area actually contains plenty of liberals (Hollywood and Beverly Hills have always been centers of liberal Democratic money) and even a number of radicals (the left wing of the Communist Party is based in Los Angeles, as are several offshoots of the Students for a Democratic Society); John Tunney, as liberal as the California Democrats turn out, carried Southern California in his 1970 election, and four of the seventeen Los Angeles congressmen are decidedly liberal Democrats. But that's really just the fuzz on the peach: most of the region falls into a range somewhere between Birchism and fanaticism. "Southern California is the lotus land not only for the [John Birch] society but for ultraconservatism in general," William Turner has written in his comprehensive *Power on the Right*, and he calls Orange County, its geographical center, "the most solidly conservative area of them all," not simply a hotbed of Birchite activity but pervaded by "a kind of state-of-mind Birchism," which sounds a most uncomfortable disease indeed. Another analyst, George Thayer, has observed that a person "can lead a complete 'right-wing life' in Southern California, cut off from all other political points of view," surrounded by avowedly rightist organizations, newspapers, radio stations, bookstores, churches, banks, restaurants, colleges, and even grocery stores (the special features of the Hughes supermarkets is that they have racks full of Birch Society literature).

But Southern California is only an exaggerated part of it; the same kind of thing exists in other areas of the Southern Rim, where similar social and economic conditions have wrought similar politics. Without being too schematic about it, it is easiest to demonstrate the affinity of the Far Right with the Southern Rim—and vice versa—by briefly examining the geographical base of major rightist organizations.

Violent. Of the avowedly violent organizations on the Far Right, many have gone into a decline in recent years, and those with any strength are only locally based. The Ku Klux Klan—in fact, two of them, one with headquarters in Georgia, the other in Alabama—has lost most of the following that it gathered in the days after "The Decision" in 1954, and its peckerwood image does not rest well with the more sophisticated and urban rightists of the South; still, together they claim organized and functioning "klaverns" in Texas, Arkansas, Louisiana, Mississippi, Alabama, Georgia, Florida, the Carolinas, and Virginia. The Minutemen, based in Missouri, have suffered an even worse deterioration, and it seems probable that as a national organization they are defunct. Some of its former members have turned to local paramilitary organizations, at least four of which, all in Southern California, have been mentioned in the press from time to time (their need for secrecy, naturally, makes them somewhat difficult to keep track of): the Secret Army Organization, based in San Diego; the Christian Defense League, in Lancaster; the Sons of Liberty, in Los Angeles; and the U.S. Rangers, in Los Angeles and Orange County. And these are not harmless organizations, either: the Secret Army Organization ran a campaign of terror in Southern California in 1971–72 which consisted of firebombings, shootings, beatings, and repeated death threats and bomb scares.

Racist. One other segment of the Far Right whose ranks seem to be dwindling, yet which always surfaces when it senses a crisis is composed of the quasi-fascist groups openly professing racial hatred. The American Nazi Party (now called the National Socialist White Peoples' Party) is the best known of these, though today it probably consists of no more than a mad hard core of several dozen or so at its headquarters in Arlington, Virginia, and two small outposts in Los Angeles and San Francisco; there is also a National Socialist League, for *homosexual* Nazis, based in Los Angeles. Somewhat to the right of the Nazis is the Christian National Party of old-time hatemonger Gerald L. K. Smith, who has a headquarters, a magazine, and a publishing company in Southern California, and who has also established in recent years a tourism-cum-indoctrination center around an illuminated seven-story statue of Jesus Christ in Eureka Springs, Arkansas, where every year he puts on performances of the anti-Semitic Passion Play from Oberammergau. Then there are the two well-known organizations that have tried to rally the redneck crowd against integration in particular and Afro-American progress in general, the National States Rights Party, based in Georgia and claiming chapters throughout the South, and the Citizens Councils (*not* "White" Citizens Councils, for they would regard that as redundant), with a headquarters in Alabama and branches in several Southern states and, recently, in Southern California as well.

Religious. The Far Right groups that combine rabid anti-Communism, varying degrees of anti-Semitism and racism, and a hard-driving religious fundamentalism are naturally based in the part of the country where the most stiff-necked and pulpit-pounding traditions adhere. The fundamentalist capital of the land is probably Tulsa, Oklahoma, the headquarters of both Oral Roberts, reputed to make $15 million a year on his diatribes and successful enough to have established Oral Roberts University in his own honor, and of Billy James Hargis and his Christian Crusade, even more virulent and political, but, at $1 million a year, somewhat less lucrative, though prosperous enough to endow *his* own school, the American Christian College. (The Fundamentalist college gimmick, in fact, is a standard device of the Rimster Right. In addition to these two schools, there is Pepperdine College in Los Angeles, the incubator of the farthest of Southern California's Far Right; the University of Plano, near Dallas, run by Robert Morris, out of the Senate Internal Security Subcommittee by New Jersey rightist politics, and funded by oilionaires of the likes of H. L. Hunt; Bob Jones University of Greenville, South Carolina, a preacher production line that has come out against evolution, jazz, playing cards, the UN, the Peace Corps, sex, chess, and virtually anything printed since 1900 except U.S. dollars, of which it is said to have more than 30 million; and Harding College of Searcy, Arkansas, "the academic center of the right wing," according to one watchdog group, and the "largest producer of radical right propaganda" in the country, according to another. Who needs Harvard?) Other rightist Protestants in this same tradition stretch across the Rim: Fred Schwarz, an Australian who after a world-wide search found the most congenial home for his Christian Anti-Communist Crusade in Long Beach, California, and who sends traveling "American Schools Against Communism" all around the country; William Bright, head of Campus Crusade for Christ in San Bernardino, California, a $15-million-a-year operation with three thousand full-time staff members; C. W. Burpo, who covers the Southwest, mostly through radio broadcasts, from his base in Phoenix; Oren F. Potito, of St. Petersburg, Florida, head of something called the Church of Jesus Christ-Christian, which also has an outpost in Lancaster, California; and—lest we forget—the most prominent and sophisticated of all, the Reverend Billy Graham, whose home and headquarters is in North Carolina, and whose subtle brand of nationalism and superpatriotism once took him right into the bosom of the Nixon White House.

Now, to be fair, there are at least three important right-wing fundamentalist organizations outside the Rim: the Church League of America operated by a Major Edgar Bundy out of Wheaton, Illinois; a Cardinal Mindszenty Foundation, with headquarters in St. Louis; and, most successful of all, the American Council of Christian Churches complex, run by one Carl McIntire out of southern New Jersey. But it says something about even these groups that when the Reverend McIntire was forced to give up part of his New Jersey base, he immediately moved to Cape Canaveral, Florida, where he relocated his disaccredited Shelton College and his Freedom Center Hotel right alongside his "charitable" Carl McIntire Foundation, and set up plans for a 26-story, 20-acre replica of the Temple of Solomon. And he was helped in the whole venture by a North Carolina textile firm that sold him the whole 300-acre complex on generous terms.

Political. The largest political organization on the Far Right today, as it has been for the last dozen years, is the John Birch Society, based in the heart of yankeedom, Belmont, Massachusetts, and with considerable support in several yankee cities and in some suburban areas in southern New Jersey and the Ohio River area. That said, however, the rest of the story of the Birch Society is almost all Southern Rim. Its founder, Robert Welch, was born and brought up in North Carolina, and of the six outsiders who own shares in his magazine, *American Opinion*, five are Rimsters: a North Carolina minister, a South Carolina textile manufacturer, a Texas oilman, a California politician, and a California businessman. Its main electoral strength has come in California and Georgia (the only states to have elected Birchers to the U.S. Congress), Florida, Alabama, Alaska, and Wisconsin, and its most prominent spokesmen in mainstream politics have been Los Angeles Congressman John Rousselot, a former PR man for the society and once its West Coast leader, and former Louisiana Congressman John Rarick. Most significant of all, the membership strength of the Birch Society is predominantly Rimian: Florida, especially in the suburban areas; Texas, where Houston alone is said to have no fewer than fifty-five chapters, and where Dallas, Amarillo, and San Antonio are recognized hotbeds; Arizona, where "Phoenix . . . has emerged as a new citadel of Birchism," according to investigators from the Anti-Defamation League; and of course Southern California, "the strongest Birch area in the nation" according to these same experts, the place in which Robert Welch once admitted he had chosen "to concentrate practically from the beginning," and where at least 20 percent of the national membership is located; in addition, there are said to be pockets of Birchite strength in Birmingham, Atlanta, and Memphis.

The second largest political group on the Far Right is the Liberty Lobby, which, as a lobby, is of course based in Washington, D.C., but which has as its guiding light Willis Carto, a Californian grown infamous in the last twenty years for his anti-Semitism and neo-Nazism, and which has as its political representatives Curtis B. Dall, a Southerner, and W. E. Hicks, a Texan. There's no way to judge the geographical distribution of the Liberty Lobby, since the secretive Carto does not let out such information, but we do know that its major affiliates are located in California—its Noontide Press in Los Angeles, and its *American Mercury* in Torrance; that its finances have gone to support Max Rafferty in California, George Wallace in Alabama, and Senator Edward Gurney in Florida, among others; and that its annual awards in recent years have gone to a Texan, a South Dakotan, a Louisianan, a South Carolinian, a Californian, and a Mississippian.

There are other Washington-based lobby groups within the Far Right—though generally without the blatant anti-Semitism —which range from such single-issue outfits as the National Right to Work Committee and the Friends of Rhodesian Independence to broader and more influential organizations like the Americans for Constitutional Action and the American Security Council. By their nature these lobbies have to deal with mainstream politicians of all states and regions, but even so, their cowboy coloration is unmistakable. Those groups which release ratings of how well they think Congress has been performing always give top honors to the politicians of the Rim; those which raise and channel money for political campaigns usually concentrate on Rim states; most of the organizations have boards of directors with an unusually high percentage of Rim representatives; and the majority of them seem to depend heavily for their financing on the rightists of the Rim.

Take as only one example the Americans for Constitutional Action. The group was begun in Memphis by Tennessee businessman Robert B. Snowden and a retired admiral, Ben Moreel, a yankee who now lives in California, and it moved to the capital in 1959. In 1972, when it listed its organizational chart, it had 23 nonstaff members on its board of directors, of which 14 were from the Southern Rim, including Max Rafferty, Patrick Frawley, and the big cowboy himself, John Wayne (and only four from the Northeast). It has only three ongoing statewide chapters, located in Georgia, Alabama, and Texas. The senators to which it has given its highest cumulative ratings (as of 1973) were Jesse Helms of North Carolina, Dewey Bartlett of Oklahoma, Barry Goldwater of Arizona, Carl Curtis of Nebraska, John Tower of Texas, and Strom Thurmond of South Carolina. Its financial ledgers are not completely open, but what is on file indicates that something like half its support comes from Rimsters, including Patrick Frawley, Henry Salvatori, and Walter Knott of California, Frank de Ganahl of Arizona, Roy Cullen of Texas, and Bruce Alger, a former Texas congressman now living in Florida. And of those politicians it chooses to spend this money on ($80,000–100,000 a year), half of them —in the 1970 elections, 77 out of 157—come from the fifteen Rim states.

These groups by no means exhaust the political side of the American Far Right, though they seem to be the most influential. Of all the other organizations which can be identified in the literature, roughly two-thirds are located in the Southern Rim. They range from a Liberty Amendment Committee, in Los Angeles, which is working to get state passage of a new constitutional amendment which, roughly, would repeal the federal government and its taxing powers (predictably enough, they have so far succeeded in Texas, Nevada, Louisiana, Georgia, Mississippi, South Carolina, and Wyoming), to Let Freedom Ring, Inc., of Sarasota, Florida, which arranges telephone numbers in various cities where one can call in and hear a taped message of rightist inspiration. And, you can be sure, every other kind of bizarre principle is represented in between.*

One of the principal media of the rightists, both religious and political, is the radio, as anyone who has driven across the country can attest, and here we can get a fair indication of where rightist support exists geographically. It may seem fantastic—no, it *is* fantastic—but there are estimated to be ten thousand programs broadcast by rightists of all stripes every week in this country, and a map of the stations which play them indicates that there are six major clusters—around the cities of Seattle, San Francisco, Los Angeles–San Diego, Dallas–Fort Worth, Atlanta, Columbia, and Chicago—and that the general spread runs right across the Southern Rim, with additional representation in Virginia, Indiana, and Pennsylvania; the area between the Rockies and the Mississippi is practically barren, as is most of New England and New York. Most of the radio pitchmen, too, are located in the Rim (the most successful being Dan Smoot in Texas, Billy James Hargis in Oklahoma,

---

* Of the political groups of any standing, duration, or national composition generally listed in various catalogues of the Far Right, excluding those named above or wholly controlled by them and leaving aside the various lobbying groups based in Washington, eight are located in the Northeast (American-African Affairs Association, Association of American Physicians and Surgeons, Foundation for Economic Education, Individuals for a Rational Society, Intercollegiate Studies Institute, National Tax Strike Coalition, New England Rally for God, Family and Country, Society for Individual Liberty, World Youth Crusade for Freedom); three are in Colorado (Committee to Restore the Constitution, the Freedom School, and the Libertarian Party); one is in Washington state (Citizens Committee for the Right to Keep and Bear Arms); one in Virginia (the American Nazi Party); and twenty are in the Southern Rim (American Center for Education, American Independent Party, American Party, American Viewpoint, Americanism Education League, Campus Studies Institute, Center for American Studies, Christian Nationalist Party, Citizens Councils, Conservative Action League, Conservative Society of America, Information Council of the Americas, Institute for Humane Studies, Let Freedom Ring, Liberty Amendment Committee, National Committee to Legalize Gold, National Education Program, National States Rights Party, United States Industrial Council, We, the People). (See *Key Influences in the American Right*, by Ferdinand V. Solara, National Information Center, Springfield, Massachusetts; *National Directory of Rightist Groups*, by the Alert Americans Association; and *Power on the Right*, by William W. Turner, Ramparts, 1971.)

R. K. Scott in North Carolina, and Howard Kershner in California).

Now there is one other group that is often identified with the Far Right, but which shares very little of the character of the groups in the above spectrum and in fact scorns and has denounced a great many of them: the *"National Review* crowd," centered around the indefatigable William Buckley, and its satrapies like the Young Americans for Freedom. It is a conservative crowd, to be sure, but *Republican* conservative, everyday conservative, and perfectly happy to work within the Republican Party; not like the Birch Society, for example, which regards the Republican Party as the tool of the Communist conspiracy and has tried in several states to destroy Republican organizations it regards as too "liberal." It is a carping crowd, full of criticisms of Things As They Are, but it does not argue that the nation's leaders, even the liberal ones, are evil men intent on high treason, but rather are misguided souls in need of enlightenment and wisdom, to be found, most probably, in the pages of the *National Review.* The Buckley people generally argue in favor of American imperial control around the world; the Far Right, though wildly militaristic, tends to be more isolationist. The Buckleyites usually favor moderation or reform of governmental programs they don't like; the Far Right wants their instant abolition. The Buckleyites would never condone racism or anti-Semitism; the Far Right in almost all guises supports some of both. The Buckleyites, like Buckley himself, tend to be academically oriented, bookish, erudite, and given to writing; the Far Right is non-scholarly, earthy, practical, and given to speechifying, in the tents and on the airwaves. All of which makes it hardly surprising that the *National Review* crowd is based in New York, rooted in the Ivy League, infused with yankee patrician types, and comfortably cozy with Eastern capital (some Buckley family money does come from oil, but the *National Review* supporters and advertisers are predominantly Wall Street types). Or that, next to the Rockefellers, the Buckleyites are the Far Right's most favored targets of hatred.

One of the reasons for the importance of the Far Right in America, despite its clear oddities, is that it has at its disposal an incredible amount of money; had the Far Left but half as much, no doubt the revolution would already have taken place. Careful studies of a decade ago estimated that between $20- and $30-million was spent on Far Right activities, and this has surely increased since, not just because of inflation but because the Rim fortunes have increased and the Rim influence has grown.

There's no possible way to isolate all the financial sources of the Far Right, but one can draw certain broad outlines.

Oil money, it is no secret, has always played a large part; as Robert Engler says succinctly in his definitive *The Politics of Oil*, "The extreme right . . . has depended heavily upon the fears and finances of oilmen." Defense money, similarly, tends to be scattered around the Far Right, particularly in Southern California, and, naturally, among groups like the American Security Council and the Liberty Lobby which continually press for greater armaments for Fortress America. Agribusiness, traditionally tied to the conservatism of the countryside, is an important source of right-wing money in such agriculturally important states as California, Texas, and Florida—most often for the organizations of the political preachers. Southern manufacturing, especially in the textile and tobacco industries, is another financial fountain for the rightists, particularly, of course, for those groups that work to prevent union organizing.

As to individuals, a few of the bigger moneymen turn up often enough with enough different organizations to provide at least a rough donors' roster. No one should doubt that there are some powerful and well-fixed yankee benefactors—the Pew family (Sun Oil) of Pittsburgh, for example, various DuPonts, the Alfred P. Sloan family, and a Chicago group which includes Robert Wood of Sears, A. C. Nielsen, Avery Brundage, and James S. Kemper of Kemper Insurance—but they do seem to be less numerous, certainly less notorious, than the political philanthropists of the Rim. There's Walter B. Knott, for example, of the tourist-trap Knott's Berry Farm in Orange County, Holmes Tuttle, Southern California's used-car king, Houston oilman Hugh Roy Cullen, New Orleans medical entrepreneur Alton Ochsner, and South Carolina textile manufacturers (and Birch supporters) Roger Milliken and A. F. Heinsohn; there's James Copley of the McKinley-era *San Diego Union*, Texas lawyer

Peter O'Donnell, and Ed Ball, the DuPont family's long-time operative in Florida. There's Henry Salvatori, a Los Angeles millionaire who made his money in oil tools and exploration and then merged with Litton Industries, who has been a major supporter of Fred Schwarz's Christian Anti-Communist Crusade, the American Security Council, and Americans for Constitutional Action, and who has funded and advised any number of California campaigns (*for* loyalty oaths and Sam Yorty, *against* obscenity and Nelson Rockefeller) as well as the two rajahs of the Right, Barry Goldwater and Ronald Reagan; and, just in case his message wasn't getting across, Salvatori a few years ago decided to establish a $1 million Research Institute on Communist Strategy and Propaganda at the University of Southern California. And there's the even more famous Texas multibillionaire, Haroldson Lafayette Hunt, reckoned to be one of the half-dozen richest individuals in the world until his death in 1974, who gave most of his propaganda money to his own Life Line Foundation (which puts out a magazine, pamphlets, and radio broadcasts on some one hundred stations with over a million listeners, mostly in the South and Southwest), but had something left over for his friend Dan Smoot, for Texas-based rightist groups like Youth Freedom Speakers and a Public Service Educational Institute, and for every conservative politician who came down the right-hand edge of the pike (George Wallace, Douglas MacArthur, Joseph McCarthy, General Edwin Walker, and various local mossbacks); Hunt was even magnanimous enough to have given money to such dangerous people as Barry Goldwater, Lyndon Johnson, and Richard Nixon, despite his stated belief that the United States is run by a "Communist government."*

But even Hunt seems to have been a penny pincher compared to the most notorious moneyman of all—"the most visible, resourceful, and possibly wealthiest" of the "men of wealth and power" on the Far Right, according to William Turner's study, *Power on the Right*—Patrick J. Frawley, Jr. Frawley was

* It should not go without note that Hunt was also once a supporter of Gerald Ford. In Miami Beach in 1968, when Nixon was searching for a Vice-Presidential candidate, Hunt went around plugging the cause of the congressman from Michigan—but no one paid either of them any mind.

born in Nicaragua, where his father, an Irishman, was a successful small businessman, then migrated to California to seek his fortune after World War II. He found it in a backyard garage, where he met a man who had perfected a leakless ballpoint pen, and with a borrowed $40,000 he proceeded to launch the Paper-Mate Pen Company, which he turned into a $26-million-a-year business in just five years. Frawley sold that business and went off on a conglomerate-buying spree during the 1960s that brought him Eversharp, both Schick electric shavers ("dry Schick") and Schick safety razors ("wet Schick"), and Technicolor—all told, a $200-million-a-year empire by 1970; forced by the Justice Department and various competitors to divest himself of some part of this empire, he reduced his holdings to "dry Schick," an investment company, and a mini-conglomerate called Frawley Enterprises, but all that does well enough to bring in more than $100 million a year these days.

Healthy enough, at any rate, for Frawley to spend vast sums supporting an amazing array of Far Right groups, of which these seem to be only a sampling: Schwarz's Christian Crusade (to which he is said to be the largest donor), the American Security Council (of which he is "clearly the driving force," according to one watchdog group), Moral Re-Armament, Young Americans for Freedom, Americans for Constitutional Action, Freedoms Foundation, the Information Council of the Americas, the Hoover Institution at Stanford University, the super-Catholic Cardinal Mindszenty Foundation, the super-Jewish American Jewish League Against Communism, and the super-ecumenical Up With People! Frawley has also put a few million into establishing a Twin Circle company that propagandizes for the Right with various magazines (sample article: "Mini Skirts and the Rise in Crime"), books (sample title: *Danger on the Left*), campus conferences (sample number: "Communism on Trial," featuring Herbert Philbrick and Phillip Abbot Luce), and a radio and television series (sample commentators: Daniel Lyons, a right-wing Jesuit, and Tom Davis, former Birch Society official); and a few more million have gone into establishing a chain of clinics and a laboratory devoted to curing alcoholism and smoking, not with the "left-wing approach" of treating such addiction as a mental problem but "the conservative approach" of regarding it as a physical problem which can be cured by some still-undiscovered drug. With all that generosity, Frawley has still had enough money left over to be the biggest financial angel of the resurgent right wing in California politics in the 1960s and 1970s, having been one of the earliest and largest contributors to the campaigns of Ronald Reagan, Sam Yorty, Max Rafferty, and George Murphy (Murphy, it will be remembered, got into trouble by being on the take from Frawley's Technicolor company).

All of which seems to justify the judgment of Washington's Institute for American Democracy, a group that oversees the activities of the Far Right, that Frawley stands "at the center of an ideological apparatus of unprecedented scope."

Very well heeled, then, this Far Right—in fact, not a whit poorer than the major political parties themselves. It is that fact that makes the Far Right a very real power on the national scene, whatever its ups and downs from time to time, whatever the fortunes of its national heroes. It is entrenched in well-funded academic, religious, propagandist, and political institutions, it has coffers ready to be emptied for conservative candidates at all levels of government, and it has the wherewithal to embark on political and social crusades whenever it feels the nation to be threatened in one way or another. Like the shotgun in the closet, it makes the Southern Rim a perpetual threat in American politics.

II

George Corley Wallace, a poor boy from Clayton, Alabama, is a racist, a demagogue, a crude, vindictive, repressive, power-hungry bigot, a tiny man whose body is half useless now and confined to a wheelchair, the governor of a nationally insignificant state which ranks forty-eighth in per capita income and offers only nine electoral votes, and there's no reason in the world that he should be anything more than a local oddity on a level with Georgia's Lester Maddox or Mississippi's Ross Barnett. Except for one thing: George Corley Wallace enunciates the fears and grievances of a considerable segment of the American people, most particularly the rootless and the dispossessed of the Southern Rim but also those elsewhere similarly buffeted by swift and perplexing change, and at a time when no one else, certainly none of the major party leaders, seems able to. This quite considerable achievement has made him the center of a potent political movement and, for the time being at least, a figure of national importance.

What Wallace speaks to is that same part of the Southern Rim that listens to the appeals from the Far Right. He plumbs to, rubs, and inflames the fears of those uneasy with the present and wistful for the past—or, at least, some imagined past—the uncertain few who see themselves as the little against the big, the white against the black, the uneducated against the intellectual, the powerless against the powerful, the frightened against the secure, the looked-down-on against the lookers-down. Racism is a part of it, though somewhat muted in recent days and spoken of largely in such code words as "bussing," "federal interference," and "law 'n' order," but more potent still is a broader *adversarianism*, a being-against. Wallace has no real policies, plans, or platforms, and no one expects them of him; it is sufficient that he is *agin* and gathers unto him others who are *agin*, agin the blacks, the intellectuals, the bureaucrats, the students, the journalists, the liberals, the outsiders, the Communists, the *changers*, above all, *agin* the yankee Establishment: when he berates the "pointy-headed professors," "the filthy rich in Wall Street," the "briefcase totin' bureaucrats," the "federal judges playing God," and the "socialist, beatnik crowd running the government" . . . when he says, "We're sick and tired of the average citizen being taxed to death while those billionaires like the Rockefellers and the Fords and the Mellons go without paying taxes" . . . when he excoriates the two major parties for having "moved away from the people" and says "there's not a dime's worth of difference in any of 'em, national Democrats or national Republicans" . . . then George Wallace is sounding that cowboys-against-the-yankees chord that resonates so richly throughout the Southern Rim.

Alabama is, and always has been, the base of Wallace's operations, the home of his staff, and the source of much of his money, and as he has gained in national prominence his strength has spread out through the South and on into Southern California. In his first national campaign in 1968, for example, Wallace got his financial backing—outside of the $5 and $10 contributions in the mail and a neat rake-off from selling campaign supplies—from a collection of Rimster moneymen: Bill France, millionaire race-track owner in Alabama; Roger Milliken, the South Carolina textile titan and Birch Society supporter; Edward Ball, the DuPont satrap in Florida; Leander Perez, the repugnant patron of Plaquemines Parish, Louisiana; Henry L. Seale, a Dallas millionaire who supported Wallace because "he's like us on the nigger situation"; H. L. Hunt, who gave at least $250,000 secretly in cash; "Colonel" Harland B. Sanders of Kentucky fried-chicken fame; and, good for at least $30,000, the most conservative cowboy in Newport Beach, California, John Wayne. He also got a considerable part of his campaign staff and precinct workers from the wilder elements of the Southern Rim's racist Right, as in California, where two rival state committees formed, one led by the secretary-treasurer of the California Citizens Council, the other by a long-time associate of fascist Gerald L. K. Smith; in Georgia, where the campaign head was Roy Harris, a super-segregationist of long standing and then head of the Citizens Councils of America; in Louisiana, where the campaign was run by Leander Perez, famous the country over for his cruel racial dementia; and in Texas, where the state chairman was an avowed member of the Birch Society. Among others who urged and worked for Wallace's victory were the Minutemen, the National States Rights Party, the Citizens Councils, Hargis's Christian Crusade, Gerald L.K. Smith, Kent Courtney, Willis Carto and his Liberty Lobby (which started a Youth for Wallace organization), and the KKK (Alabama's own Robert Shelton, head of the United Klans of America, told his followers, "We must make him President"). And ultimately, Wallace got most of his electoral support that year from the Southern Rim, winning five Southern states—Arkansas, Louisiana, Mississippi, Alabama, and Georgia—with between 39 and 66 percent of the vote, scoring well enough to beat the Democratic candidate in three others—Tennessee, and the Carolinas—with 31 to 34 percent, and finishing a strong third in four others—Virginia, Florida, Texas, and Oklahoma—with between 19 and 29 percent; in the Southwest he pulled only moderately, with 7 to 13 percent of the vote, presumably undercut by the support for the area's favorite son, Richard Nixon.

Wallace, a Southern phenomenon, could probably be expected to score well in the South, but what is significant about the 1968 campaign—and this represents a new importance of the Southern Rim in national affairs—is that he had such an impact on the rest of the country. It was Wallace's national appeal that got him onto the ballot in every state of the union, an extraordinary feat given the legal thicket erected by the two-party system, and his American Party became the first significant third-party movement since Teddy Roosevelt's Bull Moose Party in 1912, and the first *right-wing* third party since the Know-Nothings of the 1850s. It was Wallace's obvious success with his favorite issues of "law 'n' order" and bussing that persuaded major-party candidates Nixon and Humphrey to shift to those issues as the campaign went on, echoing the Wallace line to the point where the Alabama governor could boast, "Before it was over it sounded as if both national parties' speeches were written in Clayton, Alabama." It was Wallace's drawing power among the skilled workers and marginal suburbanites of the North and Border States that ultimately energized the moderates of both parties, the liberal alarmists of press and television, and the leaders of organized labor into launching a late but vigorous stop-Wallace movement in the weeks before Election Day. And it was Wallace's striking ballot-box success despite this movement—of his 9.9 million votes, 44 percent came from areas outside the Rim, especially Illinois, Indiana, Michigan, Pennsylvania, Maryland, and Virginia—that suddenly shifted the whole political balance of power and set up the Alabama governor as a force for the two national parties to reckon with in 1972.

Obviously the Democratic Party, whose registered voters Wallace had taken, both North and South, was worried about Wallace's new stature as a potential power broker for the 1972 convention, and, if thwarted in this, his threat as an independent candidate again. Even more worried, however, was the Republican Party, which had nearly lost the 1968 election when the anti-Democratic vote bypassed the GOP for Wallace and which could count on winning the 1972 race with ease only if Wallace was not running and it could hold on to that disgruntled-Democrat vote. This worry—translated, as was so much else in the Nixon White House, into paranoia—led to the formulation of a full-scale operation against George Wallace over the next four years.

First, the Nixon forces tried to defeat Wallace's bid for reelection as Alabama's governor in 1970, using a scheme devised by the Alabama construction millionaire and former Postmaster General Winton Blount; Nixon's top aide, H. R. "Bob" Haldeman, and his lawyer, Herbert Kalmbach, secretly funneled $400,000 to Wallace's opponent, Albert Brewer, and distorted the race enough so that Brewer almost pulled it off, losing only after a runoff election. Next, Nixon had his henchmen try to destroy Wallace's American Party, and in the fall of 1971 the Nixon operators in California went so far as to enlist Nazi Party help in convincing American Party voters to re-register and thus, it was hoped, wither the party's registration strength and keep it off the 1972 ballot. Finally Nixon went to work on Wallace's income taxes—standard practice for the White House in those days—and managed to discover that George's brother Gerald seemed to be fudging on his declarations from the two brothers' law firm and maybe even using the firm to cover political kickbacks; the IRS investigation continued until the spring of 1972, when, after Nixon and Wallace had a long talk on a private plane ride in May, Wallace announced that he would not be running on a third-party ticket in 1972 and the IRS case was suddenly dropped.

Despite such shenanigans, however, Wallace roared into the 1972 primaries with unexpected strength. After he took the Florida primary with 42 percent of the vote—helped inadvertently, as we now know, by the Nixon Administration's sabotage of the other Democrats—and then added four other wins (including Michigan and Maryland) in six other places, he seemed to have gained an unshakable place as a national figure, the lightning rod of rightist discontent. Until the afternoon of May 15, when an assassin's bullet sent the Alabama governor, paralyzed, into the hospital, ending simultaneously that year's Wallace-ite campaign and the worries of the White House. Now, there is no evidence to link this particular deed with the Nixon coterie, who proved that they were capable of practically everything short of that, but it is interesting that Richard Nixon himself was sufficiently alarmed by the possibility of such links that he immediately ordered his close aides to check on the

political background of the assassin and apparently told the FBI
to go slow on its investigation until such a check was made.
(One can even speculate, reasonably if without foundation, that
it was a fear that the Democrats had tumbled onto such a link
which made urgent the break-ins at the Democratic Headquarters, for which the first reconnaissance was made on the afternoon of the assassination and for which the first attempt was
made just eleven days after the assassination attempt.) In any
event, with Wallace gone, the Nixon campaign was without
right-flank worries, and on Election Day it proceeded to absorb almost the entire Wallace electorate. (The American Party
ran on its own in 1972, with California's Birchite Representative John Schmitz as its Presidential candidate, but it was not
supported by Wallace himself nor taken seriously by the national media and it ended up a disreputable—1.3 percent—
third.)

Remarkably enough, Wallace's influence on a national
scale shows no sign of diminishing despite the assassination
attempt. He is accorded a position of power and respectability
by press and politician alike. He has run ahead of all Democratic candidates in various preelection polls for 1976, and—in
what must be one of the most extraordinary examples of American forgiveness, or brainwashing—he is regarded by some 55
percent of the public as neither a demagogue nor a racist. He
has been overtly wooed by such Republicans as Richard Nixon
and Gerald Ford, such Democrats as Henry Jackson and Teddy
Kennedy—the last of whom actually gave Wallace a "Spirit of
America" award in 1973, exactly ten years after his older
brother had to order federal troops into Tuscaloosa to push this
same man aside in order to open up the University of Alabama
to Afro-American citizens of that state.

Whatever role Wallace may play in the 1976 elections, the
fact that he has a real constituency makes him a formidable
power broker, even more formidable now that the Democratic
Party has abandoned its winner-take-all primaries for propor-
tional representation, enabling Wallace to pick up Northern
delegates to go along with his Southern support. The Republicans know this: Nixon while President went out of his way to
heap effulgent praise on Wallace in public, but urged him to

avoid a third-party ticket in private. The Democrats know this: they have given Wallace lieutenants positions on all the councils of the party, and Democratic strategists frankly conceded that, in the words of one, "We can't win a Presidential election without getting back his voters."

And even if Wallace himself should retire from the scene, it seems likely that "his voters" will remain a constituency with which all future politicians will have to contend. Wallace-ism, in short, seems powerful enough to survive George Wallace.

III

The Republican Party, formed a century ago to transform the South, has finally had to admit defeat; it is the South that has transformed the Republican Party. In fact the most far-reaching change in any political party in recent times has come about from the single fact of the Republicans opening themselves to the new and increasingly powerful forces of the South and the Southwest, and thereby relegating the previously dominant powers of the Northeast to a diminished position. Theodore White, the conservative chronicler of American campaigns, has gone so far as to call this "one of the most fascinating stories of Western civilization," which seems a bit much, but it is certainly, in the words of political reporters Stephen Hess and David Broder, "the greatest political revolution in the country." And whatever jockeying may now come about as a result of a Ford–Rockefeller Administration serving in the interests of yankee readjustment, whatever realignments occur behind a Ford–Rockefeller campaign in 1976, the Republican Party will never again be the sole property of the Northern industrialists.

The movement of the Southern Rim into the Republican Party began as early as the 1950s, when the first period of cowboy growth spawned a new generation of Republican politicians—Nixon, Goldwater, William Knowland, John Rhodes in Arizona, William Cramer in Florida, James Quillen in Tennessee, John Minor Wisdom in Louisiana—but it had no national impact until the selection of Richard Nixon as the Presidential candidate in 1960. Nixon was without question a cowboy politician—poor California boy, small-town breeding, cow-college education, ambitious, hustling—and especially so in contrast to

the wealthy, Boston-bred, Harvard-trained yankee the Democrats put up, but in 1960 he was not his own man and didn't
control his own party. Nixon had to run in the shadow of the
Eastern Republicans' hand-picked President, Dwight Eisenhower, he had to work in a Republican organization dominated
by New York and Washington pols, and he had to let his campaign be managed by old-time Eastern professionals like Leonard Hall and Clifford Folger (only Robert Finch, his old friend
from California, was around to represent the Rim). So little did
Nixon control at that time, in fact, that he was an easy prey for
the East's premier power, Nelson Rockefeller, who made him
subscribe to a Rockefeller-written platform (Barry Goldwater
called it the "Munich of the Republican Party") and a Rockefeller-backed Vice-President, Massachusetts' Henry Cabot
Lodge (thence known, on the Far Right, as Henry Sabotage).
Even with all that, though, Nixon showed that the Republican
Party was able to make considerable progress along the Southern Rim: Nixon won California, Arizona, Oklahoma, Florida,
and Tennessee, came within .2 percent in New Mexico and
Arkansas, .4 percent in Louisiana, and .5 percent in Texas (or
better: Texas Republicans charged that the Lyndon Johnson
machine stole 100,000 votes there, a charge unproved but not
unlikely), and he actually scored better than Eisenhower had
before him in Alabama, Georgia, Mississippi, and South Carolina. Clearly 1960 signaled that a new power alignment was
shaping up.

And it burst full force upon the Republican Party in 1964,
in the person of Barry Goldwater.

"For an unbroken twenty years," wrote Theodore White
after the 1964 campaign, "the Establishment of the East Coast
had dominated the conventions of the Republican Party," and
then suddenly, in 1964, came "the *défi* proper, an outright
challenge, a taunting enmity which never, even in their wars
with Taft, had they experienced before." It was a movement
within the party of the young against the old, Right against Left,
outs against ins, "citizens" against "regulars," activists against
pols, ideologues against compromisers, but, above all, it was a
movement of cowboy against yankee, and felt to be exactly
that (though not in those terms) by both sides in the struggle.

Those that rallied behind the Arizona senator were the new and heretofore unchampioned forces of the South and Southwest, along with conservatives everywhere in the country, comprising what Goldwater himself saw, with just a touch of irony, as "sort of the Western Establishment"; those that were marshaled against him were the patricians of the East, whose followings made the battle lines clear with denunciations of the Goldwaterites as "yahoos" and "rednecks" and "extremists" and "kooks."

The Eastern Establishment, in a rare display of party divisiveness, did everything it could to stop Goldwater. First Nelson Rockefeller himself strode forth, with the traditional yankee forces in tow—Wall Street lawyers like Thomas Dewey and Roswell Perkins, New York media-men like William Paley of CBS, Ivy League intellectuals like Henry Kissinger—and slugged it out with Goldwater in the primaries, only to go down finally, appropriately, in California. Then other Northeastern heroes entered the ring—Henry Cabot Lodge, Michigan Governor George Romney, Pennsylvania Governor William Scranton, even, God save the mark, Harold Stassen—and an enfeebled Dwight Eisenhower was tottered forth as a second to them all. Millions of dollars were spent, all available arms were twisted, old-line party bosses were energized, columnists and magazines were mobilized, political brains throughout the Northeast were picked. Nothing helped. White, with hindsight, wrote:

> The Easterners were almost unaware of how the country was changing. They knew professionally that great rival banks were growing up in the West and Far West, that great new industries were surging with a power they could not control. They could spot population shifts, for that was their business. But they could not grasp that, in the world of politics, faces and forces change far faster than in the world of business.

In short, Goldwater was riding the crest of history.

By the time of the convention Goldwater was in control. His organization, working long and carefully since the last convention, had put together a solid block of delegate votes, mostly from the Southeast and the Southwest but with important admixtures from the Ohio Valley states, and it could not be chipped away. New York and Pennsylvania, of course, were gone, and certain favorite-son states, too, but the South was solid, Arizona locked up, California secure through the primary vote, and Kansas, Alaska, Illinois, and even Ohio seemed safe enough. On July 15, fittingly enough in San Francisco, and at the Cow Palace, one of the most stunning takeovers in modern politics, probably even more sweeping than that of the McGovern forces eight years later, was ratified: Barry Morris Goldwater was nominated as the Republican candidate for President of the United States. The yankee patriarchs were knocked right out of the party—only temporarily, perhaps, but with enough momentum to keep them off balance for the next decade and enough sting to keep them from forgetting, ever, who had administered the blow.

That the yankees realized the significance of this takeover —what the columnists were calling a coup d'état—is evident from their reaction. Rockefeller addressed the convention not in the conciliatory role of healer of party splits, as is customary for the loser, but in the castigatory role of spokesman for the enlightened East, denouncing the convention for its "extremism." He thereupon turned on his heel, retired to New York, and refused to aid his party's Presidential candidate. He was followed by many Easterners—Scranton, Romney, New York Senators Kenneth Keating and Jacob Javits, Massachusetts Governor John Volpe among them—who spent most of the fall trying to discourage Eastern money and Eastern support, and who decided to make hand-sitting their major contribution to the campaign. And before the campaign was over, the Northeast had produced two further defections: the traditionally Republican press (papers as varied as the *New York Herald Tribune*, the *Cleveland Plain Dealer*, the *Indianapolis Times*, the *Philadelphia Bulletin*, and the *Detroit Free Press* refused to endorse Goldwater) and the Buckleyite conservatives, who gave only a grudging and somewhat aloof endorsement and virtually no tactical or strategic support at all.

Goldwater, even if he had not planned it that way, was thus left dependent almost solely upon his Southern Rim base and leaning heavily on a battle plan which his followers described as the Southern Strategy (i.e., against civil-rights progress and federal intervention; for defense expenditures and private enterprise). His campaign team was built around what reporters called the "Arizona mafia"—a trio of Phoenix lawyers, Dean Burch, Richard Kleindienst, and Denison Kitchel, the last of whom, the campaign director, was a secret member of the John Birch Society—and a clutch of bright young men in the South of new money and old politics—John Grenier (Alabama), Peter O'Donnell (Texas), Bo Callaway (Georgia), Drake Edens (South Carolina), and Wirt Yerger and Fred LaRue (Mississippi).* His most successful alliances were established with Rim Republicans like California's rising political star, Ronald Reagan, Arizona's three-term governor, Paul Fannin, Oklahoma Governor Henry Bellmon, Texas Senator John Tower, and South Carolina Senator (only newly converted from the Democrats) Strom Thurmond. And his financial base was preeminently Southern Rimian—Walt Disney, Henry Salvatori, John Wayne, and cowboy-turned-realtor Gene Autry in California, the Kleberg family of the King Ranch and D. D. Harrington (whose daughter was married to Goldwater's brother Robert) in Texas, the Maytag family of National Airlines in Florida—and the whole thing apparently under the control of the ubiquitous Roger Milliken, "quietly but firmly supervising and directing just about everything," according to one insider. There was, to be sure, conservative money from elsewhere in the country—the Pews and the Mellons of Pennsylvania, for example, and perhaps half a million funneled through New York fund-raisers Jeremiah Millbank and William Middendorf—but the Southern tilt to this campaign was unmistakable: California became the main source of Republican money for the first time in a national campaign, surpassing New York by 40 percent, and according to the party's own quotas, the biggest money-giving states were California, Arizona, Nevada, New Mexico, all of the South except North Carolina, Tennessee, and Florida, plus Indiana, Wisconsin, Idaho, and Montana. As summed up somewhat cautiously by the Citizens' Research

---

* It seems unfair to slight one New Yorker, F. Clifton White, who played a crucial part in the preconvention Goldwater organization and without whom there might have been no Goldwater boom at all; but he *was* slighted, by Goldwater himself, and after the convention reduced to a minor role while the Rimster crowd moved to the fore.

Foundation, which keeps an eye on election expenditures, "In geographic terms there were indications in 1964 of increased financial support in the South and Southwest and decreases in parts of the North and East."

The cowboy nature of Goldwater's support would have been much clearer that year if it hadn't run head-on into another cowboy base. Goldwater had always wanted to run for President against John Kennedy, a man whom he saw as his ideological as well as geographic opposite, and against whom he thought a clear-cut campaign would be very successful, or at least instructive; that, however, having been denied him by an assassin's bullets, Goldwater had to do battle with a Southwesterner who also had old lines of support to the Southern Rim, and who also embodied a good deal of its style and philosophy. The campaign therefore lost all its clarity, and through the subsequent blur the public was treated to such gross distortions as Lyndon Johnson posing as a man of peace who would never send American boys off to Asian wars, or as a champion of the rights of Afro-Americans in the South, or as a defender of the First Amendment who would not tolerate threats to the rights of political demonstrators; Goldwater, a plain blunt conservative, was made to seem a wild man, psychologically imbalanced, capable of annihilating the planet, ready to throw civil-rights activists into concentration camps. That, on top of a supremely bungled campaign and a loss of fire in the candidate's own heart, spelled disaster of enormous proportions for Goldwater in the election.

Still, one couldn't deny the new presence of the Republican Party in the Southern Rim and its success in breaking into Democratic strongholds. Goldwater won in Arizona, Mississippi, Alabama, Georgia, and South Carolina (with percentages from 50.4 percent to 87.1 percent), and came close, despite the Johnson landslide, in Idaho (49.1 percent) and Florida (48.9 percent); according to analysts, he also won a majority of the *white* vote in Arkansas, Tennessee, North Carolina, and Virginia, though this was not enough to outweigh the growing black votes combined with the traditional Democratic vote. Goldwater did poorest in New England and the Middle Atlantic States, taking only 35 percent of the Northeast vote in all; his strongest showings (despite disaster areas in Texas and California) came in the South and West, with 43 percent all together.

Nor could one deny the new presence of the Southern Rim in the Republican Party. Though the Goldwater appointees were pretty much run out of the Republican National Committee in the wake of the election—Arizonan Dean Burch, for example, was replaced as party chairman by Ohioan Ray Bliss —the party solons saw that the power of the Goldwater movement was based on new populational and financial clusters that had better be catered to. Goldwaterites were given full voice in the Republican Coordinating Committee which was set up to plan for the 1968 elections; Southern Republicans of all stripes were given at least limited help in establishing new and serious state-wide organizations for the first time, and party machinery was established to continue tapping the new financial wells that the 1964 campaign had uncovered. Nor was the success of the Goldwaterite Southern Strategy lost upon the party leaders, though it did seem advisable to have its overtly racist form subtly modified to make it acceptable to the somewhat more sophisticated urban Republicans of the "New South." And when the 1966 midterm elections confirmed Republican strength all along the Southern Rim—governors in California, Arizona, New Mexico, Nevada, Oklahoma, Arkansas, Florida, and even Georgia (though this last was forced into the state legislature and handed over to the Democrats), senators in South Carolina, Tennessee, and Texas, and a total of 40 representatives where a decade before there had been only 27—then it was proven to Republicans the country over that there was a new region to reckon with.

None of this was lost upon one dimly remembered politician who immediately began girding up for his second try at the nomination. Richard Nixon, the Republicans' perpetual pop-up doll, decided that his run for the Presidency would be built on the capturing of the Southern Rim.

Nixon's move to New York, where he lived from 1963 through the 1968 election, was for him a psychological wrench of major proportions. He was in the heart of the Eastern Establishment now—he had tried once before, after graduating from Duke Law School, but no one would give him a job then—but he was still not *of* it. He was a politician of national stature, a statesman even, and yet he was snubbed by both Democratic aristocrats like Averell Harriman and Republican grandees like Rockefeller and Douglas Dillon. He was making lots of money, and he had a chauffeur and an apartment on Fifth Avenue, and he was even able to invest in Florida real estate just like the other people at the Links Club, and yet he was not accepted in the circles of wealth. His law partner John Mitchell once said, "In California he always looked up at the chairmen of the boards of the Eastern Establishment, and now he was dealing with them," but still he didn't feel any more *comfortable* with them, in fact his stoop-shouldered awkwardness was probably even harsher in contrast, and there is no evidence that he made friends with a single Establishmentarian patriarch during his whole five years in the city. Instead, the best he could do in the way of comrades were the younger members of his own law firm and a few backroom types like John Mitchell and Leonard Garment, hardly yankee Establishmentarians, any of them. It seems little wonder that Richard Nixon paid regular visits to a psychiatrically oriented doctor; he must have been as comfortable in New York as a frog in a snakepit. ("You can be alone there," he once said, "easier than any other place in the world.")

All of which surely reinforced Nixon's political perception that the Northeast was not going to be behind him no matter what he did, and that both for the nomination and the election he might just as well write off the whole place. Hence for the two years leading up to the 1968 convention he concentrated on sewing up the Southern Rim, functioning, as political reporters Hess and Broder said at the time, "as the surrogate Goldwater." First and most important, he wooed and won Goldwater himself, a task made easier by the fact that he had been practically the only major Republican of the Northeast to give unblinking support to the 1964 ticket. Then next door in New Mexico he made overtures to the new Republican governor, David Cargo, and moved on to Texas to win over Goldwaterites John Tower and Peter O'Donnell by arguing that he alone could be a "mainstream" winner in 1968. Next into the South and the assiduous courtship of such new Republican powers as Clarke Reed and Fred LaRue of Mississippi, Bo Callaway of Georgia, Bill Murfin of Florida, promising them new horizons in the Republican

Party, acceding to their regionalist demands, dangling before them the bauble of national power. And finally into South Carolina for abject overtures to Strom Thurmond, symbol of Southern racism for twenty years, to whom, in one of the most important meetings of his career, he made solemn vows of super-hawkery, continued anti-Communist dedication, and unwavering opposition to bussing, "forced integration," and "Federal interference." All this behind him, by the time Nixon came into the 1968 convention—held, suitably enough, in rococonutty Miami Beach, Florida—he had a potential of 436 Southern Rim delegates toward the 667 necessary for the nomination, and needed only the allegiance of the Border States and the Rockies to put him over the top.

Into the cozy Nixon calculations, however, rode another cowboy, California's right-wing darling Ronald Reagan, who proceeded to warble the most romantic serenades to the Southern delegations, slowly wooing away earlier Nixon supporters, weakening others. Nixon was in a sweat: the South was the key to his victory. First he dispatched prime ally Strom Thurmond to visit all the wavering delegations—Thurmond, mule-stubborn, colt-frisky, pig-ignorant, and a powerful and persuasive man—and reinforce the notion that a vote for Reagan would only block Nixon and permit archenemy Nelson Rockefeller to grab off the nomination. Then Nixon himself, more unctuous than usual, held a secret meeting with the Southern delegates en masse, assuring them that he was *against* bussing, pornography, Communists, the Supreme Court, and open housing laws (yes, he'd supported one open housing bill, but that was out of a desire for "party unity," not genuine conviction), and *for* law 'n' order, more missiles, the Vietnam War, local control, and "freedom of choice" schools; if it'd been ham 'n' hominy, the delegates couldn't have liked it more. Lastly, Nixon made it known that his Vice-President would be someone acceptable to the South, and he let Strom Thurmond believe that he would have veto power in the selection of that person. It was quite a performance, but as Nixon biographer Gary Wills was later to observe:

If Nixon gave more, and more flamboyantly, to the South, that was because the whole convention hinged on the

South. Others he could soothe or try to placate; those
delegates he had to serve.

And the South, which had never been courted this way before at
a Republican convention, and sensing that there might be even
grander courtships with its man in the White House, held firm.

Nixon won the nomination by twenty-five votes. Strom
Thurmond was there to hold his hand on high when he came to
accept it.

Nixon immediately made good on his Vice-Presidential
pledge. Rockefeller, Lindsay, Romney, and other such yankee
types were out (only an institution with true Northeastern my-
opia like the *New York Times*, which announced on its front
page that Lindsay was the Vice-Presidential choice, could believe that Nixon was going to spend the next four months, or
years, with a tall, erect, blue-eyed, good-looking, self-assured
yankee by his side). Reagan, Howard Baker, and John Tower
were all considered, but they seemed a little too glamorous for
Nixon to be comfortable with. Robert Finch, by then California's lieutenant governor and a long-time friend, was finally
selected and offered the job, but he declined, fearing charges of
nepotism. Finally Nixon consulted his own private polls, which
showed clearly that he scored best among the public with no
running mate at all. He did his best to oblige: he picked Spiro
Agnew. Though no Southerner, Agnew had shown as governor
of Maryland that he was quite happy to sic federal troops on
ghetto uprisings and to tongue-lash black leaders with all the
fervor of a plantation boss, and that was good enough for Thurmond and the Southern kingmakers, who gave their assent. "It
shows," said the Louisiana party chairman, "the South *did* have
veto power."

The campaign was more of the same. Nixon had a much
broader appeal than Goldwater—partly because he was mar-
ginally to Goldwater's left, partly because he had learned to
disguise his beliefs under twaddleous camouflage, and partly
because he had not estranged the whole Bos-Wash channel—
but he stood on a similar pedestal of power. His campaign staff
was heavily interlaced with the cowboy types Nixon found congenial: Robert Finch, "closest of all to the candidate" in Teddy
White's estimation, whose "function ran beyond any title";

H. R. Haldeman, scion of a wealthy Southern California family, a Los Angeles-based ad-man who had run the 1962 gubernatorial campaign in California and now served as "chief of staff"; and inside advisers Herbert Klein, on leave from James Copley's antediluvian *San Diego Union*, Murray Chotiner, the old California wheeler-dealer, and Richard Kleindienst, the only important holdover from the Goldwater crew. There was of course a leavening of people from the New York crowd that Nixon had been working with, people like Leonard Garment, Peter Flanigan, Raymond Price, and particularly the campaign manager himself, John Mitchell; but it is indicative that Mitchell was only the third choice for the job, after it had been resigned by Gaylord Parkinson, a California doctor whose wife was ill, and Henry Bellmon, who chose instead to run for senator in Oklahoma. On the financial side, under the direction of Midwesterner Maurice Stans (who had held the same post in Nixon's 1962 campaign), the money was rolling in from the entire business world, yankee and cowboy alike, but the early money, the large amounts that come before the convention and matter most, was from those Southern Rim sources that had always backed Nixon: oilmen, real-estate operators, defense contractors, corporate farmers, and textile manufacturers, plus the usual Nixon cronies like C. Arnholt Smith, Bebe Rebozo, Howard Hughes, Henry Salvatori, John Wayne, and the lads of Newport Beach's extremely rich and conservative Lincoln Club, who have claimed that their money single-handedly got Nixon into the Presidency in 1968. What is publicly known about the donations for 1968 indicates that the major defense contractors gave at least $1.1 million (Litton Industries listed $156,000), petroleum companies donated $345,000, John M. King of Texas listed $77,500, New Mexico's Robert O. Anderson was down for $100,000, and the technology industry gave $387,000.*

The campaign itself was similarly tilted. Not having a

---

* Campaign financing is shrouded in secrecy, and what is known about it is only the tip of the iceberg; big donors can always give in cash, or under the table, or through intermediaries, or through dummy fronts, or before disclosure is required, so the amounts listed by the political committees and in the press for each giver must be taken only as approximations.

Democratic cowboy to worry about this time around, the Republicans could make a flat-out appeal to the Southern Rim and count on winning a good proportion of its 176 electoral votes, a base that would provide two-thirds of the total needed for election and, with the Rockies and Plains States, put Nixon within 43 votes of victory. Of course, as it turned out, there was a strong competing Rimster in the person of George Wallace, and this figured to cut into the Nixon bid in several Southern states, but it didn't change by a whit Nixon's basic Southern Strategy (which was in fact a Cowboy Strategy, aimed equally at the conservative and anti-black vote of the Southwest). That strategy, as the liberal-Republican Ripon Society later analyzed it, was "to give as many positive signals to the potential Wallace voter and avoid giving negative signals to everyone else." Hence on the one hand, Nixon kept talking about "law 'n' order" (dropping the "and justice" he had used before), railed against federal bureaucrats, argued against bussing, and promised "strength" in Vietnam, all patented Wallace positions; on the other, he ran a campaign which, like the candidate himself, was mechanical, cautious, contrived, and passionless, uniquely vacuous at a moment in the nation's history that cried out for substantiality. And it worked—barely, but it worked.

Nixon won the Rockies and Plains States, as expected, and did unusually well in the Great Lakes region, picking up Illinois, Indiana, and Ohio. He lost all of the important New England and Mid-Atlantic States except New Jersey, where Wallace siphoned off normally Democratic votes. The margin of victory came in the Southern Rim: though he lost five states there to Wallace and Texas to Humphrey (by 1.2 percent), he won all the rest, giving him a packet of 113 electoral votes, which proved to be almost exactly the difference between his vote and Humphrey's. Once again the evidence was clear of how vital the Southern Rim had become in the fortunes of the Republican Party, for if Hubert Humphrey had taken these states, which were after all traditional Democratic strongholds, he would have been elected President. Moreover, it was this region which gave the Republicans most of their congressional victories in a year when the party did none too well: of the six new Senate Republicans, three came from the Southern Rim

(Arizona, Oklahoma, and Florida); and of the four new House Republicans, all came from the Rim (Texas, North Carolina, and two from New Mexico). As the Nixon campaign's house theoretician, Kevin Phillips, wrote of this election:

> Few Northeasterners realize the new prominence of the South and West or appreciate that a new political era is in the making. . . . The political center of power in the United States is shifting away from the Northeast, and the Sun Belt is the principal beneficiary.

Of course the 1972 elections were a poor proof of that thesis, inasmuch as the Democratic Party was pretty effectively sabotaged in both the primary and general elections by the savage and illegal machinations of the Nixon coterie. Still, it is important to note that campaign machinery and strategy, even including these machinations, were even more firmly in the hands of Rimsters than four years before. Mitchell and Stans still played important roles, but H. R. Haldeman was the single most important figure—it was he who had the idea of setting up a "Committee for the Reelection of the President" separate from the regular party machinery and to make the President all but invisible during the campaigning—and he was flanked by a clutch of key Rimsters: Presidential Assistant John Ehrlichman (Tacoma-born, brought up and educated in California), Press Secretary Ronald Ziegler (Southern California), erstwhile Treasury Secretary John Connally (Texas), White House aides Dwight Chapin (California) and Frederick LaRue (Mississippi), chief fund-raiser Herbert Kalmbach (California), and Deputy Campaign Manager Frederick Malek (California). The "November Group" of political ad-men recruited for high-powered PR work was run by two Los Angeles advertising executives, Peter Dailey and Phillip Joanov.

It is also important to observe that so much of the money that came into this campaign was given by the industries that provide the Rim's economic pillars, and that among the major contributors were such old familiars as Howard Hughes, Arnholt Smith, Roy Ash, and Lewis Maytag, plus dozens of new donors like motel magnate Marion Isabell in Arizona, shipbuilder

E. W. Brown, Jr., in Texas, entertainment entrepreneur Taft Schreiber in California, textile tycoon Eugene Barwick in Georgia, oil-pipe manufacturers John and Charles Williams in Oklahoma, and hospital supplier Jack Massey in Tennessee. Altogether a larger outpouring of Rim money than ever before in Republican Party history.

The strategy of the campaign was simple. As Nixon himself said in private before the race, "We come in with forty-three percent of the vote"—his 1968 percentage—but "with the Establishment [that view of the Northeast again] giving us nothing but a kick in the butt, the press kicking the bejeezus out of us, the intellectuals against us," so the only place to find the eight additional percentage points was in the South or the West. With Wallace out of the race by May, and his 13.5 percent of the vote likely to go to Nixon, the task was absurdly easy. Little wonder that Nixon hardly budged from the White House during the whole campaign.

In the event, the victory was greater than that, but that was mostly because George McGovern failed to stick with his natural constituency (the young, women, blacks, intellectuals, liberals, and the Northeast) and attempted to blur his own positions to attract more conservative Democrats. But it wouldn't have mattered. Even if McGovern had taken all of those states where he ran strongest (Connecticut, Massachusetts, Rhode Island, New York, Michigan, the District of Columbia, Illinois, Minnesota, South Dakota, Oregon, and California), he still would not have surpassed the Nixon-plus-Wallace combination in the rest of the country. Nixon, as planned, picked up the Wallace vote almost completely, particularly in such Rim states as California (a combined total of 54.6 percent in 1968, compared to a Nixon vote of 55 in 1973), New Mexico (59.7 to 61), Arkansas (69.7 to 69), Mississippi (77 to 78), Georgia (73 to 75), South Carolina (70.3 to 71), and North Carolina (70.8 to 70). It was all he needed. And if anything more were needed to prove Republican strength in the Rim, Nixon need only observe that of his best states—the ones he took by more than 60 percent—fourteen were in the Southern Rim, only five in the Northeast. Perfectly reasonable, then, that it was this that stuck in his mind in going over the election results: "Just think of the shift in the South," he said triumphantly.

On the congressional side, similar Rim strength was evident, though the Presidential coattails were notably short that year. The Republicans had exactly the same strength in the Congress in 1972 that they had in 1968, thanks only to the fact that their losses in the rest of the country were made up for by their gains within the Rim. In the House, the GOP gained seats in fifteen Rim states while it lost seats in fifteen states in the rest of the country; in the Senate it gained new seats in New Mexico, Oklahoma, Tennessee, North Carolina, Connecticut, Maryland, and Ohio, while losing in Maine, Delaware, Illinois, Kentucky, Iowa, South Dakota, Colorado, and California. In other words, though Republican strength had generally eroded in all sections of the country since the last election, it remained firm in the Southern Rim (the only exception being California, and that had to do with suicidal Republican infighting).

One careful survey of the 1972 results underlined the phenomenon of new Republican strength along the Southern Rim. Political scientist Walter De Vries, a respected electoral expert, went into North Carolina to examine the results there, and the *Wall Street Journal* summarized his survey:

It shows the 1972 results were not just an aberration traceable to the McGovern candidacy but a well-established, long-term trend as the South becomes more urban, more white-collar, better educated.

Straight-ticket Republicans, the survey found, were the largest single voting bloc in 1972, better than one out of three North Carolina voters. Nearly one out of three voters split their ticket in state and local races, favoring Republican candidates more often than Democrats. Only one out of four Tarheel voters went straight Democratic. Nearly twice as many 18-to-21 year olds voted straight Republican as straight Democratic.

"And," De Vries reported, "the same thing is happening in other Southern states."

Or, to put it more schematically, here's the history of the Republicans in the Southern Rim over the last fifteen years, including the 1974 post-Watergate debacle:

REPUBLICAN SHARE OF RIM SEATS 1960–75

Election year	House		Senate	
1960	21 of 137—15 percent		3 of 30—10 percent	
1962	25 of 146—17	"	4 of 30—13	"
1964	31 of 146—21	"	5 of 30—17	"
1966	40 of 146—27	"	6 of 30—20	"
1968	44 of 146—30	"	8 of 30—27	"
1970	44 of 146—30	"	8 of 30—27	"
1972	53 of 154—34	"	11 of 30—37	"
1974	43 of 154—28	"	11 of 30—37	"

The message, you can be sure, was not lost upon the Republicans. After the 1972 elections George Bush, a Texan, was made chairman of the Republican National Committee; Lyn Nofziger, from California, became deputy chairman; David K. Wilson, from Tennessee, was put in charge of the National Finance Committee; and Harry Dent, from South Carolina, was made chief counsel. "The big figures of the Eastern Republican establishment, who were so prominent under Ike," reported columnist Clayton Fritchey, "have all been sidelined by Nixon" —to the point, in fact, where Northeastern Republicans started complaining to reporters about a "Southern Mafia" at the Republican National Committee. No doubt others had come to the conclusion that had been apparent all along to Republican theorist Kevin Phillips: the sunbelt states were "the leading national base of the Republican Party."

IV

Impressive gains, then, by the Republicans, suggesting serious realignments and much infighting as the Southern Rim begins to throw its considerable new weight around in national politics. But though this *relative* shift is important, the fact is that the Southern Rim has always been, and is still today, a palpable and potent force within the Democratic Party. Despite the Republican assault, which expresses itself largely on the Presidential level, there is a lot of territory still occupied by the Democrats: in 1972, after a dozen years of Republican challenge, the Democrats held 19 of the 30 Senate seats from the Southern Rim, 101 of 154 House seats, 11 of 15 governorships. Moreover, as we shall see shortly in considering the Congress, many of the Rim's Democrats in both House and Senate have long years of service and considerable power, well beyond their numbers.

Of course, Democratic strength in the Southern Rim has been traditional. Arizona, New Mexico, and Nevada elected Democratic officials, state and national, for most of their brief tenure as states; Texas and Oklahoma were traditionally Democratic despite an occasional Republican maverick; Florida, Tennessee, and North Carolina remained Democratic strongholds even with a growing suburban Republican vote (and a bizarre Republican tradition in East Tennessee); and the "Solid South" of course knew no more of Republicans than Eskimos did of palm nuts. California alone had a strong Republican presence, though often of such a "nonpartisan" and liberal stripe that it did nothing to diminish Democratic strength, and in the last twenty years the Democrats have generally been in command of the state legislature. But despite all this Democratic control, there wasn't very much in the way of Democratic *power*, for the populations in these states were small, their electoral votes minimal and taken for granted, their *uitland* policies disregarded in party councils, and their leading figures more often than not either laughable or unpalatable. True, the Deep South did have some power in Congress during the New Deal period and in some instances a veto power over certain national candidates and platforms, but the South was certainly not the center of ideas, money, personnel, or votes for the Democrats— and Harry Truman proved in 1948 that you could even let the racist South go off by itself and still pull out a victory.

All that began to change gradually with the populational and economic shifts to the Southern Rim, drawing new blood and new cash into the Democratic Party—still the party to go to, when possible—and with the rise in seniority of congressmen from Southern constituencies. Southern Rimsters gradually became *important*, on a national level, a development symbolized in 1953 by the election of Lyndon Baines Johnson as party leader in the Senate, joining party leader Sam Rayburn in the

House and thereby giving Texas the two top Democratic positions in Congress. At the same time a coterie of Southern Rimsters moved to congressional eminence—men like Richard Russell, Carl Hayden, Robert Kerr, Albert Gore, George Smathers, and Estes Kefauver in the Senate, Mendel Rivers, Chet Holifield, Wilbur Mills, and Wright Patman in the House. State leaders like Terry Sanford in North Carolina, Ernest Hollings in South Carolina, LeRoy Collins in Florida, Allan Shivers in Texas, and Jesse Unruh in California began to play national roles within the party. Southern Rim money—the Kerr-McGee empire in Oklahoma, the Murchison family in Texas, the Sterns family in Louisiana, the Reynolds tobacco fortunes in North Carolina—started to be felt in Democratic circles. And a few important Rimster independents—men like Tennessee-born Abe Fortas, California lawyers Fred Dutton and Eugene Wyman, Texas oil guardian Robert B. Anderson—began having their voices heard in Democratic Party councils.

No better indication of this growing power could be provided than the 1960 election. Kennedy, knowing he was in trouble on his Southern flank, selected a Texan to be his Vice-Presidential candidate—only the fourth time since the Civil War that the Democrats chose a man from the Southern Rim—and that alone may have been the stroke which took him into the White House. But in addition, he wooed the Southern Rim with certain back-room guarantees, never made public but known to have to do with increases in cotton support levels, reassignment of defense contracts, holding off on civil-rights legislation until the second session of Congress, and "fair" Southern representation in federal appointments. And he sealed the whole thing with a shrewd phone call to Coretta King, whose husband had been thrown in jail in Georgia during the campaign, which did a lot toward shifting the traditionally Republican black vote over to the Democrats and handing them a strong black percentage throughout the South. At election time Kennedy carried all of the Southern states but six, despite his much-made-of Catholic handicap in a Baptist region, and this gave him the margin of victory; had those 81 electoral votes or even half of them gone to the Republicans, Richard Nixon would have been President eight years earlier.

But it was not until 1963 that the Southern Rim came to

dominate the Democratic Party—and thereby hangs a tale, the terrible, tragic, tangled tale of Dallas, Texas, November 22, 1963.

Even today the full story of that day is unknown, but enough has been uncovered by a small band of amateur sleuths and researchers to prove at the very minimum that the Warren Report was not justified in its bland conclusion that Lee Harvey Oswald was the sole assassin of President Kennedy. Serious questions still remain about all the central details—the direction and number of the gunshots, the nature and location of the wounds, the background and politics of both Oswald and *his* assassin, Jack Ruby, the procedures of the Warren Commission in gathering and presenting evidence; even larger questions remain about the nature of the conspiracy behind it. It is not possible yet to answer all these questions, and it may never be, but it is possible to suggest the combination of forces involved in the assassination and to indicate who benefited from its achievement.

Let us take a broad perspective, not worrying about the details, in the form of a before-and-after analysis.

Before November 22, 1963, there was evidence that the third year of the Kennedy regime was causing problems for a lot of people.

Robert Kennedy as Attorney General was apparently serious in his efforts to go after organized crime, having launched an official Organized Crime Drive with special Justice Department teams to investigate mobsters in a number of selected cities and a special "get-Hoffa" unit headed by top operative Walter Sheridan. He had publicly promised as late as September 1963 that he would step up his war on the underworld, and he mentioned as his chief targets Hoffa, Chicago Mafioso Sam Giancana, and New Orleans boss Carlos Marcello. Two men were particularly unhappy about all this. One was Carlos Marcello himself, who had already taken all he wanted to from the Kennedy Administration: he had been humiliatingly deported to Guatemala in 1962, and though he smuggled himself back and got a court to protect him here, he is reported to have told his Mafia confederates, "Don't worry about that little Bobby son-of-a-bitch! He's going to be taken care of!"—asserting that the

way to do it would be to go after his brother first.* The other
unhappy soul was Meyer Lansky, who already had enough
problems on his hands, having seen his lucrative gambling
operation kicked out of Cuba in 1960 and having been frustrated in establishing another Caribbean base partly by John
Kennedy's *Alianza* policies. He reportedly put up $1 million for
the assassination of Fidel Castro and, more conventionally, was
working to establish his influence in the Caribbean through
Bobby Baker, secretary to the Senate Democrats, a maneuver
that was ended in October of 1963 when Baker was forced to
resign, caught in a scandal involving Lansky's cronies Ed Lev-
inson in Las Vegas and Benjamin Sieglebaum in Miami Beach.

Also in 1963, John Kennedy was beginning to soften his
hawkish foreign policy and establish better relations with Cuba,
North Vietnam, Russia, and China, all of which disturbed
American right-wing interests, anti-Castro Cubans, the military-industrial complex, and the militant side of the CIA. He
established a détente with the Russians in June, signed a test-
ban treaty in August (the first major agreement between the two
countries since the war), ordered a complete review of Southeast Asian policy in November, and approved diplomat Roger
Hilsman's trial balloon speech on détente with China scheduled
for December. On Vietnam, Kennedy, belatedly disillusioned,
was planning a phased withdrawal of troops, which was announced to the country on October 2, confirmed in a secret
National Security Action Memorandum on October 11, and
actually begun with a return of 220 "nontechnical personnel"
on December 3; his approval of, or acquiescence in, the overthrow of the Diem regime on November 1 was designed to
further this policy by establishing a government that could do
the fighting on its own. On Cuba, Kennedy was moving away
from his quarantine policy, allowed Adlai Stevenson to hold out

* Marcello's empire at one time extended as far as Dallas, Texas, a city
where he assuredly still had influence, and if he wanted an operative
there a logical one would have been Jack Ruby, a product of the Chicago
Mafia ("errand boy" for Al Capone and a friend of Chicago murderers
and gamblers), a close friend of various Las Vegas and ex-Cuban gamblers, probably including the Lansky brothers themselves, and reported
by several criminals to be the key man in Dallas for smoothing gambling
and smuggling operations with the local police.

an olive branch in a United Nations speech on October 7, encouraged informal U.S.–Cuban contacts through UN aide William Attwood, ended tacit support for raids from Florida on Russian ships bound for Cuba, and clamped down on anti-Castro Cubans training and gunrunning in the United States (arrests were made in Florida on April 1, May 5, and October 1, and at Lacombe, Louisiana, on July 31). And, perhaps most significantly, Kennedy was moving to establish greater White House control over the CIA following its Bay of Pigs fiasco and his embarrassment over its use of Yale professor Frederick Barghoorn as a Russian spy, which almost scuttled the test-ban treaty; in fact, he is reported at one point to have vowed "to splinter the CIA in a thousand pieces and scatter it to the winds."

All of this movement toward international adjustment of course made much of the business community very nervous indeed, signaling as it did the possibility of an end to the imperial arrangements that for so many years had guaranteed the profits of the multinational corporations, the international oil companies, and the armament industry. The defense people in particular had cause to worry, especially after indications from Secretary of Defense McNamara on November 18 that armaments might even be cut to "a lower level than today," leading *Business Week* to assert flatly that "a major cut in defense spending is in the works." And the oil interests simply had to add this problem to existing threats at home from a Kennedy Administration that was looking into "tax reform" and antitrust regulation for the oil industry, refusing to approve various proposed mergers, considering a revision of the import quota system, and on the verge of uncovering a "political scandal" in the operation of import allocations.

The Far Right, too, could be expected to react to these shifting currents. The anti-Castro guerrillas operating in Florida and Louisiana, already feeling betrayed by Kennedy's halfheartedness at the Bay of Pigs, were incensed by his new moves to quash their underground movement; in Florida a flyer, printed up by someone in Texas, was widely distributed to the Cuban community that year calling for "an inspired act of God [to] place in the White House within weeks a Texan known to be the friend of all Latin Americans." Nowhere was the Far

Right more vociferous than in Texas, where H. L. Hunt (who had spent thousands on a vicious anti-Catholic attack on Kennedy in 1960) was broadcasting daily against Kennedy policies, where in October a Dallas congressman offered to name a hundred ways in which Kennedy was furthering Communism, where in October rightists demonstrated against United Nations Day and spit on Adlai Stevenson, and where "Wanted for Treason" handbills with Kennedy's picture were distributed in the days before his visit by an associate of Dallas's right-wing hero, General Edwin Walker.

Finally, on a more mundane level, it should be noted that the political fortunes of Vice-President Lyndon Johnson, and his Texas ally John Connally, were at a dangerously low ebb at this same time. Johnson was threatened by two Senate investigations: one into the awarding of TFX contracts to General Dynamics's Convair division in Fort Worth, which had already caused the resignation of his protégé Fred Korth as Secretary of the Navy in October; the other into the dealings of his former right-hand man, Bobby Baker, which involved shady and illegal business with Texas millionaires, Las Vegas gamblers, Florida realtors, organized crime, and defense contractors from coast to coast. And he knew that they spelled trouble, for he complained in private that fall that the Kennedy people were trying to smear him and force him out of office. Moreover, his hold on that office was shaky anyway, since it depended upon his control of the Texas Democratic machine and that was beginning to slip; John Connally, a part of that machine as governor of Texas, was in the middle of a bloodily divisive battle with the liberal Democrats down home, and faced a very difficult reelection against a young Republican whom he had only narrowly beaten the year before. . . .

After November 22, 1963, everything changed.

Organized crime did not, to be sure, get back its lucrative Cuban playground, but it was able to move into the Bahamas and Haiti without worrying about whether Washington was going to encourage any do-gooding liberals there—a belief which was confirmed when the United States granted $2.6 million to the corrupt Haitian regime in 1964, when Thomas Mann, a planner of the Bay of Pigs, was made Assistant Secretary of State for Latin America in 1964, and when U.S. Marines were dispatched into the Dominican Republic to stop a "Communist takeover" in 1965. Moreover, though Bobby Kennedy was to be Attorney General for another year, he no longer had the fervor for the job or the standing with the President—"Bobby Kennedy is just another lawyer now," as Jimmy Hoffa gloated when he heard of the assassination. The campaign against organized crime lost its steam, the bright young prosecutors Kennedy had collected went off to other jobs, the FBI gave up looking for gangsters and moved, when at all, only against the aging and decaying Mafiosi of the North. Carlos Marcello remained secure as the crime boss of New Orleans.

Internationally, Lyndon Johnson wrought an almost complete reversal of the growing Kennedy détente. He canceled the withdrawal program in Vietnam, moved to an expanded military involvement there, ordered studies of escalation as early as the spring of 1964, and within nine months had engineered a Gulf of Tonkin resolution permitting him to wage a full-scale war in Southeast Asia for the next four years. All friendly soundings toward Cuba were stopped and the CIA was permitted to activate its two bases in Florida where anti-Castro Cubans were trained and from which small-scale raids were in fact staged right up until 1968, when it was finally agreed that one Vietnam was enough; the CIA was even allowed to contract with General Dynamics for a special high-speed boat to be used for Cuban raids. Similarly all dovish signals to China were squelched and CIA operations there expanded, involving U-2 overflights of Chinese territory (the Chinese claim to have shot down nineteen planes between 1964 and 1969) and border raids from Laos. Relations with Russia were frozen, no further détente being sought until the Glassboro meetings in 1967. And the CIA was back in business, its black operations in Southeast Asia and Latin America once again secure, its director, Californian John McCone, once again in the intimate Presidential councils.

Corporate America greeted all this with considerable joy, setting off an unprecedented boom period with steadily rising stock prices for the next twenty-four months. The defense industry immediately reaped its rewards—LTV and Collins Radio, two Dallas firms, were given new multibillion-dollar contracts within five months of the assassination—and within two years prime defense contracts had risen from $24.4 billion to $31.7 billion, reaching $37.2 billion before Johnson was through. (Texas's share of all that, incidentally, rose from 5.3 percent, or $1.3 billion, to 11 percent, or $4.1 billion.) The oil industry, now with an old Texas friend in the White House, could be sure that such areas as the South China Sea and Indonesia were secure for new exploration and development and that there would be no more talk of changing depletion allowances or import quotas; it even felt free to go ahead with a series of at least eight questionable mergers during the Johnson years which significantly limited competition, without much in the way of complaint from the antitrust people.

The anti-Castro elements and the super-hawks on Vietnam were pleased with the initial Johnsonian militarism; the anti-Catholic Bible Birchers were glad to have a Baptist back in the White House; and the anti-Communist conspiratorial outfits were bolstered by the popular belief that Oswald was a Communist or a Castro agent, a belief first broadcast to the nation by the Dallas constabulary on the day of the assassination and subsequently adopted, despite much evidence to the contrary, by the Warren Commission itself.* Over the next three years

* Oswald was certainly not a member of the American Communist Party (even the Warren Commission had no trouble proving that) and no evidence has been uncovered that he had any relationship whatsoever with the Cuban government. He did engage in a flurry of leftist activities in 1963, just before his attempt to go to Cuba, but their superficial nature —his Fair Play for Cuba Committee in New Orleans, for example, had no office or members and listed its address as the building where *anti*-Castro Cubans were headquartered (Warren Report, page 408)—suggests that they were probably an attempt to establish credentials to convince the Cuban government that they should give him a visa. (It did not.) Indeed, if Oswald were a genuine Marxist, as he once claimed, it is difficult to understand why he was met upon his return from Russia by the secretary-general of a rabidly anti-Communist group called the American Friends of the Anti-Bolshevik Nations (WR, 713); why he and his family were taken in and aided during 1962 and 1963 by the outspoken right-wing White Russian community of Dallas, mostly in the oil business (WR, 280–84, 400–4, 713–25); why he made private contacts with anti-Castro Cubans in New Orleans (WR, 728–30); why he was employed by well-known rightists in both Dallas and New Orleans (WR, 400–4, 737–40); why he attended and apparently addressed a number of anti-Castro meetings in Dallas (Volume 11, Warren Hearings, page 424, 26 WH 738, 19 WH 534); and why he had a barrelful of

there was an enormous proliferation of rightist organizations and an expansion of their membership—the Birch Society, for example, *doubled* its membership between 1963 and 1966, quadrupled its income—and the popularity of Far Right views contributed to the rise and eventual nomination of Barry Goldwater just one year later.

And what of Lyndon Johnson himself? No longer a shaky Vice-President but a lauded President, he suddenly held all the marbles. His Texas machine was no longer threatened, and Connally in fact was elevated by an assassin's bullet to one of the most popular figures in Texas, easily winning reelection in 1964. The Senate investigation into his state's TFX scandal,

---

"Freedom for Cuba" leaflets in his belongings at the time of the assassination (7 WH 548).

One possible explanation for Oswald's checkered political background may be that he was in fact an agent of the U.S. government, perhaps hoping to enter Cuba (as others before him had done) as a spy; evidence pointing toward this includes the facts that his mother believed him to be a government agent (1 WH 142, WH 326); he served in Japan at a base from which U-2 spying flights originated (WR 683–4); he had a "secret clearance" given to people who work in intelligence (18 WH 232, 298); he was given an unusually speedy "hardship discharge" from the Marines shortly before his entry into Russia on the basis of documents dated *after* he was shipped out of his unit for discharge (8 WH 257, 26 WH 711, 19 WH 658, WR 688–9); he was not charged with any crime, investigated, or followed upon his return to the United States, despite his attempts to renounce his citizenship and his threat to spill secrets to the Russians (WR 713–15); he was given a new passport in 1963 in a single day, despite the fact that the Passport Office was run by Frances Knight, an outspoken anti-Communist, to whom the information on Oswald's "leftist" background was presumably available (WR 773–6); and he went out of his way to contact the FBI in New Orleans in August 1963, may have contacted an FBI agent in Dallas in April (based on the similarity of 17 WH 733 and 20 WH 511 reports, which must have come from a Dallas source, not Washington [17 WH 809–10]), and had the Dallas FBI agent's name and phone number in his address book (Exhibit 18, 16 WH 64). Despite this evidence, the Warren Commission satisfied itself that Oswald was not an agent by directly asking and receiving denials from the FBI and the CIA, two organizations known more for their deceptions and untruths than their willingness to expose their agents; the Commission forgot to ask the Office of Naval Intelligence, which was the much more likely government agency inasmuch as Oswald had been a Marine and it was known to have an extensive file on Oswald (26 WH 130, 145).

scheduled to have resumed in December, was shelved entirely and not heard of again for another six years, when Johnson was out of the White House. The Bobby Baker investigation, shifted away from pesky Senator John J. Williams of Delaware to Senator Everett Jordan of North Carolina, a wealthy textile manufacturer and an old Johnson crony, was curtailed; the FBI, for example, immediately stopped sending information to the committee, and three members of that committee later charged that the full story never came out because the Democrats "prevented the investigation from proceeding." In the end Baker was given a gentle reprimand by the committee, his shenanigans remained buried at least through the 1964 elections, and it was not until *three years later*, when most people had forgotten who Bobby Baker was, that the federal government finally sent up an indictment.

No doubt the truth about the assassination of Jack Kennedy will be a long time coming, if ever, but there is an old legal principle that can stand us in temporary stead in the meantime: *cui bono*—to whose advantage?—the idea that probable responsibility for an act lies with those with something to gain. *Cui bono* Dallas? A confluence of forces including organized crime (especially its Southern branch), the defense industry (especially its Texas components), the oil industry (especially the newer and Texas-based elements), the Far Right (especially the Texas and Floridian branches), and beyond doubt Lyndon Johnson, the thirty-sixth President of the United States. Or, to put it in three words, the Southern Rim.

"The President always controls the machinery of his own party," writes Sam Houston Johnson of his brother, "unless he's politically naive or indifferent, and you certainly couldn't say that about Lyndon." Indeed, it would be accurate to say that the President, in this case anyway, *was* the machinery of his own party—at least there was none discernible elsewhere, certainly not at the Democratic National Committee, nor any rivals to challenge him until his last year in office. Hence the measure of Southern Rim power in the Democratic Party from 1963 on was more or less the extent of Southern Rim power in the White House.

And it was considerable.

First the flamboyant, coarse, bullying, drawling President himself, Texas from Stetson to boots, a fitting blend of the Southwest's bowlegged swagger and the Southeast's down-home charm—famous, indeed, for alternating between just these two personas—a man of little culture or education but enormous drive and raw intelligence, new to wealth and the lifelong companion of others similarly blessed, easy with power—especially behind the scenes, and with those who understood his freewheeling use of it, awkward in the face of style, especially in public, and with those who scorned his lack of it. "He had triumphed over one area of Washington," David Halberstam observes, "the doers, the movers, men of the South and West, shrewd insiders, but he had always failed in another area, the taste-makers, so much more Eastern, more effete, judging him on qualities to which he could never aspire, all the insecurities confirmed." Not a mossback, nor a true redneck in the tradition of George Wallace, nor even a raw conservative in the style of Goldwater—he had too much of the New Dealer, too little of the ideologue, for that—he was nonetheless an accurate product of his culture, an anti-Communist and interventionist hawk, a believer in the military-industrial complex (and the more complex the better), a defender of private and corporate capitalism built upon the base of governmental finances, a wheeler-dealer of legendary proportions, a hill-country provincial with more or less benign prejudices (including racial) that could be put aside for practical purposes, a partisan fiercely loyal to his friends, his party, his state, and his region. In his way, an authentic cowboy President.

Around him, more of the same, at least where it counted. Because of the nature of his ascendancy and of his desire for "continuity," Johnson was forced to keep a fairly even mix between Austin and Boston in his Cabinet, and in most of his major public appointments he scrupulously tried to avoid the image of cronyism politics. ("I needed an appointee for the Federal Power Commission," he once complained, "and because I'm a Texan I had to get a fellow who couldn't spell oil. I finally found someone, a solicitor for the railroads from Illinois.") Of his fifteen Cabinet appointments, only four were from the Southern Rim, eight from the Northeast, two from Border States, and one was a mixture (John Gardner, born, brought up, and educated in Southern California, but a foundation man in New York for twenty years). Still, by the end of his tenure Johnson had juggled things so that he had a Cabinet of six people from the Southern Rim (Attorney General, Postmaster General, Secretaries of State, Interior, Commerce, and Transportation), four from the Northeast (Treasury, HEW, HUD, and Labor), and two from elsewhere (Agriculture and Defense).

Even then, the Cabinet make-up was not a true index of power, since not only was Johnson practically a one-man executive branch but the people he depended on most and gave most authority to were those around him in the White House. And though a few of the White House intimates were Kennedy holdovers (McGeorge Bundy and Walt Rostow in particular), most of those closest to Johnson's heart, and ear, were of the cowboy contingent: Walter Jenkins, Jack Valenti, Horace Busby, Bill Moyers, Marvin Watson, Jake Jacobsen, Harry McPherson, and George Christian, White House powers all, and every one a Texan. Behind them were a group of unofficial advisers of probably equal influence, and though it included such men as Missourian Clark Clifford and New Englander Thomas Corcoran, the umbra of this shadow Cabinet was decidedly Rimian: Robert B. Anderson, the Texan whose business was promoting gas and oil interests, "the most important man in Johnson's shadow cabinet," according to Johnson biographer Robert Sherrill, and the one he summoned first upon assuming the Presidency; Abe Fortas, born and raised in Tennessee, for years a Washington lawyer with a special interest in Johnson's Texas affairs, including the court case that won him his first contested election as a senator in 1948; A. W. Moursund, a close friend of Johnson's from his earliest Texas days and the man put in charge of Johnson's multimillion-dollar financial holdings; Lady Bird Johnson, also a thoroughgoing Texan and a woman of strength and undoubted influence; and, in the penumbra, other Texans such as John Connally, Homer Thornberry (whom Johnson made a federal judge), William S. White (the superconservative columnist), George Brown (of the Brown & Root construction firm), and his brother Sam Houston Johnson.

The Johnson Presidency, naturally enough, was a cowboy

Presidency, its apparent motto being, What's good for the Southern Rim is good for the country. Lyndon Johnson liked to make much of the various pieces of legislation he pushed through to launch his War on Poverty, and indeed the accomplishment should not be scorned—but the fact is that all of the federal outlays for poverty during his regime averaged only $13 billion a year (and that includes Social Security, veterans' pensions, railroad retirement payments, and other New Deal benefits), while the federal outlays for just research and development in defense and aerospace *alone* averaged exactly as much. Despite all the orchestrated hullabaloo over domestic legislation, the real mark of the Johnson Presidency, the important economic impact, was in defense and aerospace. Defense expenditures, as we have seen, soared dramatically, defense contracts tripled in value, boondoggles like the antiballistic missile system, the McNamara Line, and the supersonic transport were begun, and it was the California–Texas–Georgia complex that got most of the business. It was during Johnson's years that prime contractors from the Southern Rim increased their take from $9.5 billion to $16.5 billion, surpassing the Northeast for the first time, and the two most important awards during the entire period were the multibillion-dollar C-5A contract for Lockheed's Marietta, Georgia, plant and the enlarged TFX contract at General Dynamics's Fort Worth, Texas, plant. (The TFX is a particularly good symbol of Johnson's cowboy politics: the plane could have been built cheaper and better, according to the Pentagon, by Boeing, in its Kansas and Washington plants, so Johnson and his Texas cronies lobbied to get the contract awarded to General Dynamics in Texas; by 1966 it was running about $6 million per plane over the original estimate, so Johnson merely reduced the order, giving the company more money for fewer planes; it turned out by 1966 to have a totally unworkable design—the wings kept falling off—so Johnson gave it top priority; and when it was finally sent into combat and proved to be totally unworkable, grounded within the first few months, no one seemed to care much, since the whole thing had effectively spread more than $6 billion of federal money around the land, much of it ending up in Texas pockets.) So full was the defense cornucopia, in fact, that it proved to have benefits for industries not even in the defense business, a good share of them Rimian. The most notorious example was the consortium that was put together to do all the American construction work in Vietnam and Southeast Asia, a combination of one firm from the Northeast (Raymond International of New York), one from the Northwest (Borrison-Knudson of Boise, Idaho), and two from the Southern Rim (Brown & Root of Houston, Texas, and J. A. Jones Construction Company of Charlotte, North Carolina); this little combine was given the largest wartime contract ever awarded, and it ended up with federal funds at somewhere near the *billion*-dollar mark.

Other examples of Johnson's favoritism toward his native region are found throughout his tenure. When he pushed through the first comprehensive aid-to-education bill, it just so happened that its pocketbook was tilted to the Southern Rim, which consistently took about 45 percent of all the funds—North Carolina, for example, with 5 million residents, got nearly $100 million a year in federal grants from the Office of Education; Indiana, with about the same number, got just over $50 million; Alabama, with almost 3.5 million people, got $80 million; Washington, with the same number of people, got $47 million. When he finally got approval for a Department of Transportation for the federal government, he designed it not to cope with the wracking problems of mass transit in the nation—primarily a Northeastern agony—which were left to fester in the overstuffed corridors of HUD, but to help the airline, railroad, highway, trucking, and shipping industries, where the Southern Rim is unusually well represented—and then, just to underscore the point, he put Alan Boyd, a Floridian, in charge. When he figured it was time for a World's Fair, he had it set in San Antonio, Texas, and let an old friend and angel, H. B. Zachary of San Antonio, do the construction work; when work had to be done on the underwater Mohole project, he gave it to Brown & Root; when regional development projects came up, he saw that the money went to the $1 billion Appalachian project, whose prime effects were on the Southern and Border States, and the Four Corners project (Arizona, New Mexico, Utah, and Colorado).

It was during the Johnson years, also, and inevitably, that

Southern Rim money came into the Democratic Party in a major way—and not just for the 1964 election, either, when all kinds of businessmen switched over to the Democrats. Texas, of course, was a steady source of funds, for Johnson had always had close ties with the business barons of his native state, independent oilionaires like Sid Richardson, Jubal Parten, and John Mecom, with defense industrialists like James Ling of LTV and Erik Jonsson of Texas Instruments, with corporate construction men like George and Herman Brown and H. B. Zachary, and with agribillionaires like the Klebergs of the King Ranch and William Clayton of Anderson, Clayton. But now, significantly, other areas of the Southern Rim began to be heard from. Among the members of the Democratic financial establishment during this period were real-estate operators Ben Swig, Walter Shorenstein, Joe Shane, and Louis and Mark Boyer, Hollywood mogul Lew Wasserman, San Francisco shipping company president George Killion, in California; Kenneth S. Adams, head of Phillips Oil, in Oklahoma; Walter G. Helis, an oil and shipping millionaire, in Louisiana; C. H. Murphy, an independent oilman, and Wilton Stephens, executive of the Arkansas-Louisiana Gas Company, in Arkansas; LeRoy Percy, a wealthy agribusinessman, in Mississippi; Ed Mauldin, another Southern agribusinessman, in Alabama; the Woodruff family, of the Coca-Cola Company, Mills B. Lane, a banker, and the Talmadge family, into everything, in Georgia; Jim Walter, a multimillionaire real-estate developer and builder, in Florida; and the Jordan family, textile manufacturers, in North Carolina.

Johnson, despite holding the Presidency for the Democrats in the 1964 elections—it seems now as if any warm body to the left of Caligula could have done as much—did nothing much for the party as a whole while he was in office. In 1964 the Democrats added 37 new representatives and one new senator, not much of a landslide year; in 1966 it lost 48 seats in the House and 4 in the Senate, losses beyond the usual midterm adjustment; in 1968 it lost 4 more House seats and 7 more Senate seats, ending up with about 15 percent less power in the Congress than when it started. Not that it mattered all that much, since the Democratic Party kept control over both houses and the Southern Rim kept its relative power within the party. But it is not uncharitable to say that given the way things were

going in 1968 and the turmoil Johnson was creating in the
Democratic Party, ultimately nothing helped its fortunes like his
leaving it.

The 1968 convention brought to a halt the Johnsonian era
in the Democratic Party and a lessening of Southern Rim
strength at the national level. Johnson might have picked another cowboy to be his successor—from time to time he toyed
with the idea of pushing John Connally—but no obvious national figure had surfaced from the Southern Rim while Johnson
was astride the Democratic Party, and anyway Hubert Humphrey had shown over the preceding four years that he was
willing to abandon his previous yankee liberalism in support of
Johnson's cowboy policies, and that seemed good enough.
Moreover, since this loyalty—especially the slavishness on
Vietnam—had cost Humphrey most of his old-time Northeastern support already, and since the core of Humphrey's Democratic Party strength was therefore in the more hawkish areas of
the Southern Rim, he seemed a safe enough candidate.

At the convention itself, Humphrey acknowledged his odd
new position as the repository of cowboy hopes transferred
from the Johnson account by his very careful solicitation of the
Rim's 757 votes, 58 percent of those needed for the nomination. True, he came in with a core of strength from his home
state of Minnesota and several bastions of the Northeast, but he
desperately needed the Southern Rim support if he was to beat
back the various peacenik challenges. What else but his realization of this could account for his repeated genuflections to the
Rim delegations, his unmodified hawkery on Vietnam, his refusal to criticize the Chicago police, his willingness to seat a
segregated Georgia delegation, his support for the unit rule over
Northern objections? Time after time Humphrey placated the
Southerners—and even then it took the threat of a Teddy Kennedy peacenik boom on the party's left wing, and repeated
phone calls to Southern governors from chief arm-twister Lyndon Johnson himself, to keep the Southern Rim in line. But it
was absolutely necessary, and it worked: the baton was duti-
fully passed on to the chosen successor.

At campaign time, however, Humphrey seemed to have
forgotten the lesson of the convention. Aside from a ritual repe-

tition of the Wallace law-'n'-order line, he refused to take the route that Nixon was taking so successfully: he told Texas oilmen that he could not guarantee to keep the depletion allowance; he told audiences North and South that he could not promise to let up on civil-rights laws or open-housing enforcement; and he made certain dovish noises on Vietnam that suggested he wasn't willing to decimate the place. No Cowboy Strategy for Hubert Humphrey—and it may have cost him the election. Humphrey did worse in the Southern Rim than any Democrat in history, winning only the state of Texas, thanks to Johnson's manipulations, and that by just 1.2 percent.

Nor, even after its defeat, did the Democratic Party want to have much to do with the Southern Rim. Humphrey, titular head, did try out Oklahoma Senator Fred Harris for a year as party chairman, but that choice did not suit the regulars, and in 1970 the party went back to Kennedyite Larry O'Brien, tried and true. None of the major party commissions for the 1972 convention was given over to Rimsters, nor did they occupy more than their exact national proportion (9 of 28 seats) on the crucial McGovern Commission on party reform. It was as if the party wanted to turn its back on the region that spawned the man who had given them all their troubles. Even the two cowboys who rose to contend the 1972 Presidential nomination were treated more or less as pariahs: Wilbur Mills, the Arkansas congressman who was disregarded by all except a handful of large special interests, and George Wallace, whom few regarded as a genuine Democratic possibility—or indeed as a genuine Democrat. Most Democrats gravitated instead toward Edmund Muskie of Maine or George McGovern of South Dakota, possibly John Lindsay or Shirley Chisholm of New York, Scoop Jackson of Washington, or even Humphrey himself—but not, most emphatically not, to another Rimster like the last one.

All this behind it, the Southern Rim was less of a kingmaker at the 1972 convention than it had been at others past, but the fight over the 271 delegate votes from California was nonetheless crucial. That one hung on the question of whether all of California's votes would go to McGovern, since he had won a winner-take-all primary, or whether they should be split up proportionately among the contenders, as the McGovern Commission reform rules had suggested and the convention's

Credential Committee had ruled. The McGovern forces put all their energy into manipulating a floor fight on the question of the California votes, more than on any other issue of the convention. And, at the expense of the delegations from South Carolina and Alabama (as well as of racial and sexual principles the McGovernites once made so much of), they got the delegates to approve their stand and send all of California's delegate votes their way. That gave McGovern the votes he needed for the nomination.

The McGovern campaign, if that's the word for it, was not particularly responsive to the Southern Rim Democrats, and vice versa. The old mossback Democrats went in droves to Richard Nixon, who didn't mix with such things as welfare, bussing, and defense cuts; the younger urban Democrats generally stayed at home, unenthusiastic about McGovern's brand of politics. But such was the importance of the Southern Rim by this point that the Democrats found themselves willy-nilly dependent on cowboy support. Among the chief advisers to McGovern were two important Californians, Rick Stearns and Frank Mankiewicz, and among the chief sources of money—pried open by fund-raiser Henry Kimmelman, who himself had heavy Caribbean and Florida investments, and Morris Dees, an Alabama lawyer—were James Kerr (a California-based aerospace executive), Max Palevsky (head of his own California technology firm, which later merged with Xerox), Harold Willens (Los Angeles realtor), Ruth Handler (of Mattel Toys, in Hawthorne, California), Wiley Fairchild (Mississippi contractor), Louis Wolfson (Florida-based financier), and Jubal Parten (the Houston oilman). It is interesting to note than even though the Democrats were running a decidedly un-Rimian candidate, they still depended to some degree upon Rimian money, indicating that the cowboy moneymen, though not necessarily dominant, had come to occupy an important place in the party and had achieved a rough parity with the yankee moneymen in just thirty years.

In the wake of the disastrous 1972 election, though, the Southern Rimsters began to move back into positions of greater power and influence in Democratic Party councils. The operation began with a move by Lyndon Johnson himself and a passel of Rimster politicians (ex-Governor David Hall of Oklahoma, Senator Dale Bumpers of Arkansas, Governor Robert McNair of South Carolina) who were determined to get rid of the McGovern-Northeastern influence in the party, and with the support of conservative state chairpeople, they installed Robert Strauss as Democratic national chairman in 1973. Strauss, a Dallas lawyer and director of the Strauss Broadcasting Company, with a string of radio stations from Tucson to Atlanta, had learned the party machinery well as party treasurer from 1970 on, and he immediately took control of the organization and began mending the fences—especially the cowboy fences—that had been kicked over by the McGovernites. He smoothed the way for Terry Sanford, a former governor of North Carolina and then president of Duke University, to take over the party's potentially powerful Charter Commission, and as head of the Association of Democratic State Chairmen installed first Robert Vance, of Alabama, and later Donald Fowler, of South Carolina.

The new types of Southern Rim Democrats now in control of the Democratic Party may be significant, because they are changing the coloration of the party. Men like Sanford and Vance, and other leading Democrats like Florida Governor Reubin Askew, Georgia Governor George Busbee, Arkansas Senator Dale Bumpers, Oklahoma Governor David Boren, Texas Senator Lloyd Bentsen, California Governor Jerry Brown, are conservatives by any objective measure, but they are far different from the "good ol' boys" who once held sway in the Democratic Party, and they know how to direct their appeals and policies to the new populations of the booming areas. Which is not to deny that there is still considerable power in the hands of the more traditional back-room pols, the reactionary and race-baiting officials long common in the Democratic Party, but just to recognize that the major trend in the party seems now to be inspired by the realization that sweeping economic and populational changes have indeed been wrought.

The Democratic Party, it seems clear, has no intention of abandoning such a valuable area as the Southern Rim, no matter how many inroads the Republicans may make. In fact, as Gary Wills saw it after attending the Democrats' "mini-convention" in 1974, party strategy is based on the principle that "the

party desperately needs to regain the South": "Democrats have
spent all the years since 1948 trying to make the South join the
rest of the country. Maybe their only hope is to give in and join
the South."

V

Although it would no doubt surprise Will Rogers—who
once remarked that Congress is the place where they put fellers
when they want to keep them out of trouble—there is another
locus of political power in this country outside the parties and
their various men in the White House. Its importance has certainly diminished during the last several decades of a growing
"imperial Presidency," and it stands in general low repute with
most of the public—in January 1974, for example, only 21
percent of the citizens could be found to give Congress a good
word—and yet there is no question that many of the decisions
that affect the national bearing most centrally are made by the
U.S. Congress.

It is no secret that Southerners hold a disproportionate
share of the legislative might in Congress—even after the much-
publicized reorganization after the 1974 elections—but it is not
generally realized just how extensive that share is and, when
teamed up with their colleagues from the Southwest, how powerful they really are.

One way to measure this cowboy clout is to see how many
Rimsters are in control of congressional committees, since
those positions provide the most obvious muscle power in Congress. There is some fluctuation from year to year, but in general the period from 1950 on has been dominated by the Southern Rim. The Ninety-third Congress in 1973 was fairly typical:
of the 17 standing committees of the Senate, 9 were in the
hands of Rimsters, including *all* the important ones (Appropriations—John McClellan, Arkansas; Armed Services—John Stennis, Mississippi; Banking—John Sparkman, Alabama; Finance
—Russell Long, Louisiana; Judiciary—James Eastland, Mississippi; Rules—Howard Cannon, Nevada); by contrast, only 2
committees, Labor and Veterans Affairs, were run by Northeasterners. In the House, 9 of the 21 standing committees were
controlled by Rimsters, including all but one of the important

ones (Appropriations—George Mahon, Texas; Armed Services—F. Edward Hébert, Louisiana; Banking—Wright Patman, Texas; Ways and Means—Wilbur Mills, Arkansas; the other one was the Judiciary Committee); only 7 were led by yankees. In other words, the Southern Rim, making up 30 percent of the Senate, controlled 53 percent of the committees, and making up 35 percent of the House, controlled 43 percent of the committees. (Of the joint Senate–House committees, which have chairpeople from both Houses, 11 of 18 were from the Southern Rim.)

Even after the unusual shake-ups in the Ninety-fourth Congress, brought about by the resignation of many old-line legislators and the election of many liberal newcomers in the wake of Watergate, the Southern Rim hadn't lost much power. In the Senate's new line-up of 18 committees, 7 were controlled by cowboys, and again all the important ones except Banking and Budget, more than any other regional group. In the House, despite all the talk about turning out the Southern mossbacks, Rimsters were still in control of 9 of the 22 committees (Appropriations—Mahon; Government Operations—Jack Brooks, Texas; Interior—James Haley, Florida; Post Office—David Henderson, North Carolina; Public Works—Robert Jones, Alabama; Science and Astronautics—Olin Teague, Texas; Standards—John Flynt, Georgia; Veterans—Ray Roberts, Texas; Small Business—Joe Evins, Tennessee); yankees controlled only 7 committees—and for the first time in fifty years no New Yorkers were among them.

Another measure of congressional power is party leadership. Although these positions do not always mean congressional control—Lyndon Johnson and Sam Rayburn used them to amass considerable influence, but not everyone can—they are inherently among the important legislative jobs. In the Senate, as of 1974, though neither of the party leaders was from the Rim, the president pro tem was from Mississippi (Eastland), the Democratic Campaign Committee chairman—the man that distributes party funds to candidates—was from Texas (Lloyd Bentsen), the Republican Campaign Committee chairman was from Tennessee (William Brock), and the Republican Policy Committee was run by another Texan (John Tower). In the House, both parties were directed by Rimsters (Carl Albert of

Oklahoma as Speaker, John Rhodes of Arizona as Minority Leader), the Majority Whip was from California (John Mc-Fall), the Democratic Caucus chairman was from Texas (Olin Teague, later replaced by Californian Phillip Burton), the Republican Campaign Committee chairman was from California (Bob Wilson), and the head of the Republican Research Committee was from Florida (Lou Frey).

Of course, position doesn't automatically equal power. Some congressional chairpeople are nullities, some have become part of the core establishment of the Congress—and a considerable number of this latter group turn out to be from the Southern Rim. James Eastland, for example, who's been in the Senate for more than three decades, is "one of the Senate's most powerful members," in the opinion of the *New York Times*—he was given a unique inside connection with the Nixon White House through a special "little red phone" that went directly to the President. Russell Long is another recognized superpower, now that he's come out of a bout of alcoholism and morbidity, and as the rejuvenated major-domo of Senate money matters he has become influential enough to challenge the House, which takes some doing, and the Constitution, which takes even more, by originating financial legislation in his own Finance Committee despite the Founding Fathers' provisions that the House alone had this power. John Stennis, another "senority Southerner," is the recognized wizard of the Senate on all matters military and according to the *Times* "is the single most influential member of Congress on intelligence matters" as well. Carl Albert, for all his self-effacing shyness and reluctance to be compared to Speaker Sam, is still the most powerful man in the House; his influence on the Democratic Caucus has given him effective control over most committee assignments, and his manipulation of the Rules Committee has made him, according to *Time*, "the first Speaker in almost 40 years with absolute control of the House's legislative agenda." And Phillip Burton, the energetic representative from San Francisco, who has emerged in recent years as a champion of the liberals and a friend of the conservatives, was the man who worked with Albert to reorganize the House committees in 1974, the main effect of which was to draw new powers to the Democratic

Caucus, which he just happens to head; he figures to be in line for the Speakership when Albert steps down.

Beyond all that, however, there are many legislators without major titles who nonetheless are known to influence congressional votes, to be important in behind-the-scenes maneuvering, and a disproportionate number of these are Rimsters. There's Joe Waggoner, for example, the Democratic representative from Plain Dealing, Louisiana. He's chairman of nothing, and yet he is one of the most important congressmen around, "a potent power broker" according to the *Wall Street Journal*, and "the leader of conservative Southern Democrats," a body that runs to maybe eighty or so in the House, and that's a hefty power bloc. There's Barry Goldwater, the Arizonan now become almost an elder statesman, also chairman of nothing but the acknowledged leader of the rightists in both chambers and the man to whom the Congress—and the nation—looked as being the conscience of the cowboys during the two-year Nixon finale. There's Paul Rogers, a little-known Florida Democrat who ranks way down at sixth on the House Commerce Committee but happens to be a persuasive politician, with twenty years of service, the chairman of the Public Health and Environment Subcommittee, and, according to one observer, "perhaps the single most powerful Congressman in matters pertaining to health." There's Wilbur Mills, of Arkansas, deposed now from his chairmanship of Ways and Means, but still second-in-command of that committee and the most knowledgeable tax legislator in either chamber, and if he ever swears off the sauce he is certain to retain considerable influence. There's Howard Baker, from Tennessee, vaulted by TV to eminence in Republican councils, and Dewey Bartlett, from Oklahoma, recognized as the official mouthpiece for the oil industry, and Morris Udall, from Arizona, one of the two or three leaders of the liberal camp, and Robert L. F. Sikes, from Florida, in charge of spending for military construction and thereby an important man to know. And there's a crop of newer Rimsters who were exposed to the nation through the House Judiciary Committee's impeachment hearings but already rising stars within the chamber, such as South Carolina's eloquent James Mann and California's lawyerly Charles Wiggins.

Now it must be pointed out that many of the congressional patriarchs are getting on in years and for all their power cannot be expected to survive forever. This, however, is not likely to diminish the importance of the Southern Rim. In the first place, behind these men stand others of nearly similar seniority who will most probably inherit their chairs: eliminate all the Rimsters of the age of seventy or more in the Senate (as of 1975), and there would still be 7 Rimsters with seniority among the top 20; similarly in the House, there would still be 13 among the top 22. And in the second place, since House membership must reflect the nation's population distribution, more and more representatives will come from the rapidly growing areas of the Southern Rim; an indication of how that progress has already swung power to the leading states of that area can be put schematically:

HOUSE MEMBERSHIP 1940–1980

	1940	1950	1960	1970	1980
Southern Rim	132	139	146	154	167
Florida	6	8	12	15	17
Texas	21	22	23	24	26
Arizona	2	2	3	4	6
California	23	30	38	43	48
Northeast	207	202	196	190	183

Thus it can be seen that by 1980 the power of the Southern Rim in Congress will have grown by more than 25 percent over its 1940 level and can only increase in the years thereafter if the population trends continue.

A Congress with Southern Rim power is not indifferent to Southern Rim interests. As we have already seen, the decisions of Washington have for decades now benefited the industries of the Southern Rim, particularly its six economic pillars, and it is obviously no accident that those favors have been granted during a period of considerable cowboy clout. Rimsters in Congress have always supported militaristic policies—Vietnam, ABM, defense appropriations—that put more money into their own backyards; they have always seen to it that their home states got more than their share of defense contracts and military installations; they have protected every phase of the oil and gas industry, from the famous depletion allowances down to pipeline safety; they have regularly promoted the growth of the construction industry, especially in highway building and, in recent years, suburban housing; they have seen to it that supports of every description were placed under agribusiness, whenever and wherever needed; they have pushed through, sometimes quite shamelessly, tax shelters for investments in real estate, media, oil drilling, cattle, and land; they have been among the foremost friends of the aerospace and air-transport industry, providing federal money for everything from speedometers to solvency.

The Southern Rim does not always hold sway, of course. When other sections of the country gang up, or when some particular issue galvanizes the yankee powers, or when the interests of Rim constituencies are not clear, Congress has enacted legislation inimical to the congressional cowboys. The civil-rights and welfare legislation of the mid-sixties, for example, was generally opposed by Southern Rim politicians, but the confluence of forces at that time made passage of some kinds of new laws inevitable, and in the end it was only a few of the most Paleozoic senators who put up ritual protest. It was an indication of Rim power, however, that even much of this legislation was watered down or underfinanced, as with the Voting Rights Act of 1965, which failed to provide for sufficient enforcement in many Southern districts, and the "Great Society" measures of 1967–68 whose effective funds were progressively slashed year by year.

More often than not, the Rim power in Congress is telling. The evidence is everywhere: Mendel Rivers, from 1930 to 1970 the representative from Charleston, South Carolina, and for many of those years a power on the House Armed Services Committee, managed to get one defense installation after another put into his hometown, ending up with an Army depot, a Marine Corps air base, a Marine boot camp, two Navy hospitals, a Navy shipyard, a Navy base, a Navy supply center, a Navy weapons center, a Navy submarine base, a Polaris missile base, two Air Force bases, and a federal housing development. However strategic Charleston, South Carolina, may have been, it wasn't strategic enough to risk dipping the eastern edge of the state into the ocean. . . . Confronted by oil companies whose profits rose by anywhere from 100 to 300 percent during the energy scare of 1974, Southern Rim congressmen—led by Russell Long (Louisiana), Dewey Bartlett (Oklahoma), Paul Fannin (Arizona), and John Tower (Texas), plus Clifford Hansen (Wyoming)—managed to forestall any moves to increase oil industry taxes, even to bring them in line with other corporations, and worked in committee, conferences, and corridors to continue its $9-billion-plus tax windfalls, leading yankee voices like the *New York Times* to protest, accurately: "Even though oil prices and profits have been climbing almost vertically, Congress appears reluctant to take back any of the tax breaks from that industry". . . . On behalf of the agribusiness and real-estate giants of Arizona, Congress was happy to enact the biggest regional boondoggle since TVA and the largest water reclamation bill ever, the Colorado River Reclamation Act of 1967, expressly for the purpose of getting federal funds to divert Colorado waters into the desert acreage Central Arizona Project. . . . James Eastland and the Mississippi delegation got word in the spring of 1974 that the Department of Agriculture had forced the chicken-farming folks of their state to kill twenty-two million chickens because of pesticide contamination, so they immediately got to work with their Southern Rim brethren to indemnify the poor fellows: Eastland and eight other Rimsters pushed a Senate bill from Talmadge's Agriculture Committee, the entire Mississippi delegation and twenty other Rimsters swept a House version through Tennessee Congressman Ed Jones's poultry subcommittee; Rimsters led and won votes in both houses, and within a week or so some $8–10 million was on its way to the chicken farmers of Mississippi. It turned out that 95 percent of the funds would end up in the hands of five large poultry corporations. . . . Whose voices were raised in protest when Wisconsin Senator William Proxmire tried to lower real-estate closing costs, a saving of $14 billion a year for home buyers and an unpleasant gouge into the real-estate industry? Why, Senator William Brock of Tennessee and Alan Cranston of California, a Republican conservative and a Democratic liberal reaching across the meaningless gulf of labels to join hands where it really counts. And who in the House rose to beat back similar efforts by Leonor Sullivan of Missouri? Why, Congressman Robert Stephens of Georgia, joined by a bunch of Rimster representatives from California to Florida. . . . A land-use bill which tried to place some restrictions on headlong suburban sprawl and threatened the bulldozer operations of the Rim developers was defeated in 1974 by a cowboy coalition of Southern Rim representatives, lobbyists from real estate, construction, leisure, and agribusiness industries, and rightist groups like the Liberty Lobby and the American Conservative Union. As if to show that the Southern Rim is not without its contradictions, the fight *for* the bill was led by Representative Morris Udall of Arizona, the fight *against* it was led by Representative Sam Steiger, also of Arizona. . . . Of little notice but of vital importance, an offshore oil bill was ushered through Congress in 1974, for the first time allowing the coastal states to share in the revenues made from offshore drilling and giving them millions of federal dollars besides for any inconvenience they might suffer, a measure to the particular benefit of California, Louisiana, Texas, Mississippi, and Florida, in whose waters most of the drilling is now going on, and of eventual benefit to the Carolinas, Georgia, and Delaware, off whose shores additional reserves are located. . . . When Congress passed the 1974 housing bill giving $11.3 billion dollars in aid to cities for the 1975–80 period, 47 cities in all parts of the country were selected, but only 15 of them were favored with authorized *increases* in federal funds over that period: New York and Chicago (up 45 and 50 percent), San Juan (up 100 percent), and no fewer than 12 Rim cities, with Miami, Memphis, Dallas, Fort Worth, and Phoenix each getting raises of more than 300 percent, while the funds for such cities as Boston, Bridgeport, Denver, Hartford, Pittsburgh got slashed in half. . . . When the time came for the Senate to undertake the tricky and risky investigation of Watergate and the 1972 Presidential campaign, Southern Rim power became manifest: the chairman and vice chairman were both from the Southern Rim (North Carolina and Tennessee), as were three of the five members (Florida, Georgia, New Mexico), plus one from a Rimlike state (Hawaii) who had been a protégé of both Sam Rayburn and Lyndon Johnson. It should not have come as any surprise to yankee-cowboy watchers that the strongest, almost shameless defender of Richard Nixon was Edward Gurney from Florida, while the only one to express true indignation and to press the investigation at least as far as it went was Lowell Weicker of Connecticut. . . .

And so it has gone, so it goes. Cowboy power in Congress begets cowboy legislation; cowboy legislation enhances cowboy power.

Across the greatest part of the political spectrum, then, from the fringes of the Far Right to the directorates of the Democratic Party, and around the arenas of power, from the corridors of Congress to the pinnacle of the Presidency, the Southern Rim has come to play a significant, and in many instances dominant, role. That fact is of historic proportions. There have been only four major political power shifts in U.S. history: the first with the consolidation of federal control at the turn of the eighteenth century, the second with the introduction of Jacksonian democracy in the early nineteenth century, the third with the expansion of Northern industrialism after the Civil War, and the fourth with the establishment of Rooseveltian welfarism in the 1930s. The rise of the Southern Rim marks a fifth.

4

The Three Rs:
Political Character

Richard Gordon Kleindienst is a totally political animal. Political, that is, in a totally cowboy way.

Born in the small town of Winslow, Arizona, on the edge of the Painted Desert, the only son of a Santa Fe Railroad brakeman, he was the top debater through all four years of Winslow High School. He matched this reputation at the University of Arizona for three years until he was interrupted by World War II and went off to serve three years as an Air Force navigator; after the war, with the GI Bill paying the way, he shrewdly chose to transfer to Harvard, from which he graduated Phi Beta Kappa in 1947 (today he doesn't even bother to list his attendance at unprestigious Arizona in his official biography). He earned a degree from Harvard Law School three years later and went back to Arizona, where presumably the competition would not be too tough, to be a politician.

Kleindienst was elected to the Arizona House of Representatives in 1952, became chairman of the Maricopa County (Phoenix) Young Republicans in 1954, chairman of the Arizona Young Republican League in 1955, campaign manager for Paul Fannin's successful race for governor in 1960, and himself an unsuccessful candidate for governor in 1964. It was during this last campaign that Kleindienst was inevitably forced to enunciate his policies: he spoke of Cuba as a "Communist menace" (presumably to the people of Arizona), he denounced the "communists or leftists in the Supreme Court," and he opposed federal aid to education on the grounds that it betokened a "federal takeover"—sounding for all the world like Robert Welch. It was also during this campaign that Kleindienst became known as a hard and vindictive campaigner, not dirty necessarily but with a ruthlessness that gave him a reputation, in the words of an editorial in one small Phoenix paper, as "a political son-of-a-bitch."

In 1964 Kleindienst, a long-time sidekick of fellow Arizonan Barry Goldwater, became director of his Presidential campaign, even though his own politics have been described as being "somewhat to the right of Goldwater." Certainly he had no particular loyalty to Goldwater, for it was not long after the 1964 defeat that he switched his allegiance to Richard Nixon, probably the first Goldwaterite to do so. In 1968 he was rewarded for this allegiance by being named general counsel of the GOP National Committee and the field manager of Nixon's campaign, his general mode of operation earning him the nickname the "Genghis Khan of Miami" at the convention, and his general political stance earning him the job of plotting and carrying out the Southern Strategy in the campaign. With Nixon's election he was made Deputy Attorney General, second in command at the Justice Department behind John Mitchell, a very powerful position to which he brought—as he confessed to Mitchell's predecessor, Attorney General Ramsey Clark—total ignorance.

Learned or not, at the Department of Justice Kleindienst was in an advantageous position from which to carry out some of his most deeply held political ideas.

He immediately created and led a new federal campaign against the Left, publicly denouncing "these radical, revolutionary, anarchistic kids" and stating bluntly that "if people demonstrated in a manner to interfere with others, they should be rounded up and put in a detention camp." It is not recorded whether the Deputy Attorney General did in fact oversee the construction of such camps, but he *did* create a special "campus rebellion" task force, increase FBI infiltration and harassment of political groups, unleash a special "Litigation Section" to use grand juries as a weapon against political dissent, and establish a supersecret intelligence unit to monitor all left-wing activity in the country.

Kleindienst stepped up the use of force against political demonstrations. Before even taking office he personally took charge of the police and military operations against demonstrators at the 1969 Inaugural ceremonies, taking a near-bloodthirsty delight in the use of troops:

> We had a dispute about where the security troops should be stationed. I wanted them hidden in nearby alleys, offices, and basements, but Clark wouldn't listen. He said troops that close might appear repressive and cause a backlash. But after President Nixon was sworn in, *I* took over. I was up in the command center in the Justice Department, and when I heard there were militants on 12th and 14th Streets along the parade route I ordered out a few hundred more troops, and that cooled them off. You've got to crack down.

And from then on it was the same: find a group of citizens demonstrating for the redress of grievances, and you've got to crack down. It was under the Kleindienst aegis that there took place the largest mass arrest in American history, of some thirteen thousand people protesting Nixon and his system on May Day 1971, and all but a handful of these arrests, the courts were to decide, were illegal. But illegality never troubled Kleindienst:

> There is enough play at the joints of our criminal law— enough flexibility—so that if we really felt that we had to pick up the leaders of a violent uprising we could. We would find some things to charge them with, and we would be able to hold them that way for a while.

Kleindienst helped design and was in charge of Operation Intercept, a federal program in 1969 created to harass the entire nation of Mexico so that it would move against its marijuana growers and stop North American youths from tripping out.

Mexican President Gustavo Diaz Ordaz called it a "bureaucratic blunder"; everyone else called it blackmail, an extraordinary attempt to have the browner people solve the problems
of the whiter. The program was eventually halted, after causing
complete chaos in legitimate border traffic for several months,
but not before it provided Kleindienst with at least one contact:
Gordon Liddy, the later Watergater, whom Kleindienst assigned
to go "from town to town along the United States–Mexico border to inform the business community we were quite concerned
about so-called Operation Intercept."

Kleindienst helped to fulfill the "Southern Strategy" promises of the Nixon campaign. He played a large part in the selection of two Southerners for the Supreme Court—Harrold Carswell and Clement Haynsworth—both of whom were rejected by
the Senate on the basis of their racist records. He fired a black
member of the U.S. Parole Board so that Arkansas Senator
John McClellan could install his own man. He helped to slow
down the pace of enforcement of the voting-rights and desegregation laws in the South. And he thwarted black advancement
within the Justice Department ("The new people," complained
Roger Wilkins, director of the Civil Rights Section, who resigned upon seeing Kleindienst in action, "don't have the faint-
est idea of how to talk to black men").

As Deputy Attorney General, Kleindienst also found time
to amass quite a remarkable record of service to Richard Nixon
and the Nixonian idea of justice. Over the strong objections of
the antitrust division, he personally approved (after Mitchell
had disqualified himself) the merger of two drug firms, Warner-
Lambert and Parke, Davis, perhaps because the largest stockholder in Warner-Lambert, whose holdings were increased by
$18 million with this merger, was an old friend and campaign
contributor of Nixon's, Elmer Bobst. He personally authorized
immunity for one Frank Sharp, the Texas wheeler-dealer who
had engineered a $50 million stock fraud with the help of vari-
ous state politicians, thereby letting him off with a three-year
suspended sentence and a piddling $5,000 fine but making him
eligible to start telling tales about high-ranking Texas Democrats and effectively miring them in scandal for the next two
years. He personally approved and exonerated the conduct of
the U.S. attorney for San Diego, Harry Steward, after Steward

had squelched investigations into corrupt campaign practices by companies and cronies of C. Arnholt Smith over the vigorous objections of the Justice Department's own investigators. And he personally oversaw the Justice Department's settlement of antitrust suits against the International Telephone and Telegraph Corporation—one highly favorable to the ITT conglomerate, which he knew had donated some $400,000 to the Republican Party and which he knew had won Nixon's complete support. But of course: *Kleindienst* means "little servant."

It seemed only fitting, with this kind of service behind him, that on June 8, 1972, when John Mitchell was forced to resign, Richard Kleindienst became the Attorney General of the United States, the first in the history of the country from the state of Arizona. Only fitting, too, that he continued in his new post with the same brand of politics. One indication of it was that under Kleindienst the Justice Department carried out repressive trials against the Gainesville Veterans Against the War (ending in acquittals), the Harrisburg "conspiracy" (ending in acquittals and reversals), Daniel Ellsberg and Anthony Russo (ending in dismissal), and the Camden 28 (ending in acquittals); it oversaw the mass arrests of 1,000 demonstrators at the Democratic Convention in Miami; and its narcotics agents engaged in a series of raids on and murders of innocent victims. Another indication was that he cavalierly and without explanation ordered the end to a fruitful investigation by the FBI of a million-dollar Teamsters-Mafia scheme in California to defraud the Teamsters Pension Fund, and just as blithely dismissed a tax case against Morris Shenker, called by *Life* the "foremost mob attorney," although Justice Department investigators had been gathering evidence against him for years. Still another indication was the imperious philosophy enunciated to a Senate committee in April 1973 that the President was a supreme authority, capable of extending his "executive privilege" to all two and a half million employees of the federal government down to the lowliest letter-sorter and keeping private any information about his activities (including criminal ones) if he wanted to; and if Congress didn't like it, its only recourse was to "cut off our funds, abolish most of what we can do, or impeach the President."

Certainly when it came to Watergate, Kleindienst acted as

if he believed the President was supreme, ranking well above the legal system of which he was in theory the chief guardian. In charge of the original investigation, he promised the most thorough job since the Kennedy assassination, and yet saw to it that his own investigators were kept ignorant of information which he had had from the beginning about the involvement of top White House and campaign people, that Gordon Liddy and Howard Hunt were not formally linked to the case until four months after the break-in, that the trial of the original Watergate burglars was postponed until after the election, that high-ranking officials were treated with kid gloves and interrogated outside of the grand jury's presence, that Nixon was kept informed of secret grand jury information, and that his entire department, from FBI to prosecutors, made such a botchery of the whole thing that it was not until March 1973, nine months after the break-in, that the true story began to come out. When it finally did, Kleindienst felt himself implicated up to his curly hair by his connections with all concerned, and he submitted his resignation, right along with Haldeman and Ehrlichman, accepted by Nixon on April 30, 1973. Such was Kleindienst's aplomb, however, that even after all this he could sit casually before the Ervin Watergate committee, calmly smoking cigarettes, fiddling with a pack of matches from Caesar's Palace in Las Vegas, occasionally slinging one leg over the arm of his chair, and look the assembled senators in the eye and tell them, "Our criminal justice system works."

Perhaps he meant that it works for former Attorneys General. For Kleindienst somehow escaped all obloquy in the Watergate scandal and went on to set up a Washington law practice as if nothing had happened. Even when it came out that Kleindienst had lied to the Senate Judiciary Committee, under oath, back in March 1972 when he denied that White House pressure had been put upon him in the ITT case, even then no real harm was visited upon him. Special Prosecutor Leon Jaworski, a Texan, presented him before Judge George Hart, a Virginian, whereupon Kleindienst pleaded guilty to a minor "criminal information" rather than to the obvious charge of perjury and was given a wrist-tap sentence of one month in jail and a fine of $100, both suspended; Judge Hart went so far as to call him a "man of highest integrity." And this for a man who was the first Attorney General of the United States, the highest legal officer of the land, ever to plead guilty to a criminal offense.

Richard Kleindienst is a revealing example of the political character of a cowboy to the manner born. He shows, in one degree or another, the attributes that seem to be inherent in so much of the area: a political conservatism, a belief in the superiority of his culture, and a hard line against expression and dissent, or, in other words, what one is tempted to call the Three Rs: rightism, racism, and repression. Plus a remarkable ethical blindness and a self-serving notion of legality, which finds echoes in the unusual affinity of the Southern Rim—in its political life as in the economic—with scandal, shadiness, and corruption somewhat beyond the norm. Pass from this one man, then, to the area of which he is a part, and see these attributes writ large.

I

To say that rightism sinks its deepest roots and enjoys its greatest efflorescence in the Southern Rim is to make a political, perhaps a sociological—but not a moral—observation. The reasons for it have to do with the particular history of the region and especially the nature of its recent growth, not with any special infirmity of its citizens.

At bottom is probably the religious fundamentalism of so much of the area, especially the region extending from eastern New Mexico to the Atlantic Coast, which is the land of the Southern Baptist Convention, the largest Protestant denomination in the country and by all accounts the most hidebound and conservative. The apocalyptic nature of Baptist fundamentalism, its good-and-evil simplism, its intolerance, antimodernism, insularity, emotionalism, and xenophobia—all these fit very smoothly indeed into the politics of the Right, even if the devils change to Communists and the saviors are earthly. It is no accident that it is precisely in this area that, as we have seen, the peculiar blending of anti-Communism and revivalism takes place—Fred Schwarz, Billy James Hargis, Harding College, and all.

There is also something about the still-potent frontier experience of most of the Southern Rim that produces a rapport with the Right. The attachment to the *land*, especially the emphasis upon property and its inviolability, to be defended with the shotgun if necessary, this basic tenet of the frontier underlies all conservative thought, and it is no less ardent among the current quarter-acre home owners of the Southern Rim than among their log-cabin forerunners. A propensity for force, too, the gun culture that pervades the entire region, South and West, finds its political manifestation in the Cold War posture of the Right, the emphasis upon defense spending, armaments, military solutions. It is an oversimplification, but in this case might does make Right.

Beyond this there is the impact, which we noted in the economic sphere, of a growth so rapid that it warps the patterns of the past, distends and destroys settled communities, and brings on the disturbing, churning influence of urbanization (or, perhaps worse, suburbanization). As sociologist David Riesman has written:

> In many communities, notably in the South and Southwest, extremely rapid urbanization and industrialization (often based on or growing out of defense activities) have disrupted the already fragile social structure so that there is no old elite sufficiently in charge of affairs. . . . The fluid social structure in many expanding communities creates anxiety and bewilderment as well as opening opportunities for aggressive political activism among the newly awakened and the newly rich.

Yes, the newly rich. Peculiarly, they tend to move toward the Right, sometimes all the way Right, as in the case of Patrick Frawley and H. L. Hunt, sometimes only to crusty Republicanism, as with Roy Ash and Arnholt Smith. As with the nouveaux of the late nineteenth century, who were notoriously reactionary, so the nouveaux of the middle twentieth century: they try to freeze the world at the point where they have reached their success, resisting advances by other people, other kinds, protesting anything that threatens their wordly goods (taxes, governments, unions). Far more than the families of established wealth, who have grudgingly adjusted to the inevitability of taxes, the painlessness of charity, the *oblige* of *noblesse*, the families of nouveau wealth still tend to protest the pulls at their purse strings and are not too concerned with the sophistication of that protest.

Then add to this chaotic growth the migrations that have recently swept into the Southern Rim, composed in large part of what the sociologists are pleased to call the "discontented classes," people unhappy with their small-town, imprisoned existence, rootless and unfulfilled, in search of comforting material lives in the sun and salaries of the Southern Rim—"the discontented classes have come," in the words of a pair of (possibly biased) Eastern sociologists, "not to the large civilizing cities, but to the new or expanding industrial frontiers . . . Jacksonville or the Gulf Coast, Houston or San Diego." And they are also in search of a comforting political justification for their lives, which they do not find in the general postulations of American liberalism, with its intellectualism, its wracking guilt, its uneasy welfarism, so they turn to the comforting postulations of conservatism and the simplicities of the Far Right. Many of those, too, in this migratory wave are the elderly, of all segments the most prone to disorientation and insecurity—such is the way America has designed its family structure—and for them the holistic systems of the Right are especially appealing, thus accounting in part for the virulence of rightism in such retirement centers as Miami, St. Petersburg, Phoenix, and San Diego.

Finally, the geographical paranoia that has infected so much of the migratory populations of the Rim in the past has its most explicit outlet in the Far Right's denunciations of the wicked Northeast. An underlying distrust of the "Liberal Eastern Establishment" is central to almost all the dogmas of the Far Right, and it takes in Republicans as well as Democrats, Washington bureaucrats as well as Wall Street bankers, the New Deal and the Federal Reserve System, the New York-based Council on Foreign Relations and the Rockefeller family, the Ivy League State Department and the *New York Times*. It is what conservative historian Peter Viereck has called "the revolt of radical Populist lunatic fringes against the eastern, educated, Anglicized elite," what liberal sociologists David Riesman and

Nathan Glazer see as a reaction to the threat of "the older educated classes of the East, with their culture and refinement." For the John Birch Society this vision of the conspiracy of the East may be strictly political, but for the Birchers of, say, Southern California it is deeply psychological as well, expressive of the envy-contempt of yankee power that is found throughout cowboy country.

There are a number of ways to demonstrate the conservative nature of the Southern Rim as translated into politics. One could, for example, examine the character of its newspapers: on average they tend to be more conservative and hidebound than papers elsewhere, and—with a few exceptions like the *Chicago Tribune* and the *Manchester Union-Leader*—most of the rabidly right-wing papers are published in Rim cities: the *San Diego Union*, the *Los Angeles Herald Examiner*, the *Phoenix Gazette*, the *Dallas Morning News*, the *New Orleans Times-Picayune*, the *Jackson Clarion-Ledger*, the *Memphis Commercial Appeal*, the *Charleston News and Courier*. Or one could pore over the findings of the Gallup Poll which consistently show the South and West to be farther right on political issues than the East—as, for a couple of examples, a 1970 poll asking about immediate withdrawal from Vietnam (16 percent in the South were in favor, 17 percent in the West, 23 percent in the East) or a 1970 sample about whether there should be more conservatives on the Supreme Court (53 percent of the South favored it, 50 percent in the West, only 42 percent in the East). Or one could chart the progress of the Equal Rights Amendment through the various state legislatures around the country; after three years of pressure following the Senate approval in 1972, 34 states had ratified the amendment—13 of them in the Northeast, 17 in the rest of the country, and only 4 in the Southern Rim (California, New Mexico, Tennessee, and Texas —and Tennessee subsequently voted to rescind its ratification); typical of the Rim states where the measure was defeated was Georgia, where the leader of the opposition denounced it as "stinking of communism."

But the most revealing way to examine Rimian rightism is to look at the U.S. Congress, for there politics so clearly crosses party boundaries that its geocultural character is obvious. Not that every individual selected from the Southern Rim has to be a consummate conservative: one thinks of distinguished (though by no means flaming) liberals of the recent past like Estes Kefauver of Tennessee, Lister Hill of Alabama, Fred Harris of Oklahoma, Ralph Yarborough of Texas, William Fulbright of Arkansas, or of a few from the present, like John Tunney and Don Edwards of California, Morris Udall of Arizona, Barbara Jordan of Texas, Claude Pepper of Florida. But it is certainly true that most of those representing the Southern Rim, today as in the past, are conservatives, and usually *conservative* conservatives, regardless of party, age, education, career, or constituency.

Take a look at recent congressional issues. Who led the fight against a consumer protection agency? Senators Sam Ervin of North Carolina and James Allen of Alabama. Who fought down efforts to establish stronger pesticide controls? Representative Jamie Whitten of Mississippi. Who stopped reform action against strip-miners? Representative Craig Hosmer of California. Who spoke against federal money for abortion clinics? Senator Dewey Bartlett of Oklahoma. Who protected the billboard lobby from unwanted regulations? Representative Jim Wright of Texas. Who worked to squelch any congressional control over the CIA? Representative Edward Hébert of Louisiana. Who organized the opposition to a land-use bill? Sam Steiger of Arizona. Who led the battle against the bill to limit Presidential war-making powers? Senators John Tower of Texas and Paul Fannin of Arizona. And it is the same pattern in every congressional session, on every controversial bill, in every important vote.

Or take a look at the key Senate votes of recent years. In every major roll call the Southern Rim politicians have made up the largest geographical bloc on the conservative side, usually accounting for more than half of the votes themselves. In the important vote to end the bombing of Cambodia (May 31, 1973), the Senate managed to find just 19 people who could oppose it—and 8 of them were Rimsters (3 Democrats, 5 Republicans). On bussing (May 15, 1974), 45 senators went on record in opposition—24 of them from the Southern Rim (15 Democrats, 9 Republicans). On campaign financing (April 10, 1974), 30 senators voted against any new restrictions, 19 of them from the Southern Rim (10 Democrats, 9 Republicans).

On legislation to create a consumer affairs bureau (September 18, 1974), 36 senators stood in opposition—21 of them from the Southern Rim (11 Democrats, 10 Republicans). Consistently, the same results: the Southern Rim produces the bulk of the conservative votes, *regardless of party*—in fact, almost in defiance of party lines.

Another and perhaps broader way to observe the same pattern is to look at those ratings on key votes that the conservative and liberal Congress-watchers put out every year. Americans for Constitutional Action, a group whose principles are about as far to the Right as it is possible to get before running smack into Birchism or Nazism, issued a roughly typical rating of Congress in the spring of 1974, a cumulative appraisal of all the legislators sitting in the Ninety-third Congress. In its opinion, only 31 senators deserved a rating of better than 60 percent conservative; and of those, 17 were from the Southern Rim (as against 4 from the Rockies, 3 from the Plains, 3 from the Border, and 4 from the Northeast). The highest-ranking conservative senators for the ACA were Jesse Helms of North Carolina, Dewey Bartlett of Oklahoma, Barry Goldwater of Arizona, John Tower of Texas, and Strom Thurmond of South Carolina; the only states with *both* senators strongly conservative were Arizona, Georgia, Mississippi, North Carolina, Oklahoma, Tennessee, Nebraska, and Virginia. Similarly, among the ACA ratings of the House, the Southern Rim had 83 of the 184 people (45 percent) who scored over 60 percent and 8 of the 15 delegations which had a majority of conservatives ranked over 60 percent (Alabama, Arizona, Colorado, Florida, Indiana, Arkansas, Mississippi, Nebraska, New Hampshire, New Mexico, North Carolina, Ohio, South Carolina, Tennessee, and Virginia).

A slightly different rating is put out periodically by the American Security Council, a cold-warring group, which rates legislators on their general hawkishness. In the 1974 listings, only 22 senators were deemed sufficiently militaristic to win a perfect 100 percent rating, a full 15 of them from the Southern Rim states (Alabama, Arizona, Florida, Mississippi, New Mexico, North Carolina, Oklahoma, South Carolina, Tennessee, and Texas), only 2 from the Northeast; likewise, 22 senators were thought to be so wimpy as to get a zero rating, 10 of them from the Northeast and not one of them from the Southern Rim. In the House, 96 representatives were given perfect scores, 44 of them from the Southern Rim (including South Carolina, the only state to have *all* its members with 100 percent), as against 32 from the Northeast.

Or, taken from the other end, the ratings of the Americans for Democratic Action, a major liberal group, show that almost none of the people with a strongly liberal record come from the Southern Rim. In its 1974 ratings there was not a single Rim senator outside of California to whom it could give a liberal score of better than 60 percent. Its highest-ranking senators were from the Northeast and the Plains States, its lowest from the Southern Rim (Alabama, Arizona, Mississippi, North Carolina, South Carolina, and Texas). Similarly, in the House, almost half of its lowest-ranking selections—96 of 201—came from the Southern Rim, and of those that earned a flat-bottom zero rating, exactly half came from the Rim; in fact there were *only 10 members* out of the 148 representatives from the Southern Rim that the ADA could rate above 90 percent (7 from California, 2 from Texas, 1 from Georgia—and three of them are Afro-Americans).

All such ratings are, of course, only suggestive, but their unanimity in this case is particularly striking. In the halls of Congress, the politicians of the Southern Rim represent the core of the rightist bloc. Such a unanimity cannot be accidental, and it argues that the region from which these politicians come has to have some kind of common political culture.

II

The subject is always ugly, but another aspect of the Southern Rim's political character that cannot be ignored is its racism. For while it is perfectly true that racism is a national sickness, infecting all states and all races within those states, the fact is that no region of the country has a history of enslavement, maltreatment, degradation, murder, and genocidal destruction of darker races to match that of the South with regard to Afro-Americans, and of the Southwest with regard to Mexican-Americans and Indian-Americans.

History informs culture, and clearly the inhuman system of

slavery and the bloody massacres of the frontier, though each long past, helped to mold the nature of the Rim. Although neither slavery nor genocide could survive long into the twentieth century, new imperatives continued to feed the region's racism: economically, the need for cheap, primarily agrarian labor, which the South satisfied with impoverished blacks, the Southwest with imported Mexicans and detribalized Indians; politically, the need for scapegoats and underlings against which white officialdom could operate, again supplied by the black, brown, and red. Even with the post-World War II migrations into the Southern Rim, racial attitudes were not much modified —though usually made more genteel—since the rootless and ambitious newcomers were precisely those more concerned with economic advancement than racial equalization; as political analyst Kevin Phillips puts it in his careful way:

> Most of them have risen to such [middle-class] status only in the last generation, and their elected officials predictably embody a popular political impulse which deplores further social (minority group) unheaval and favors consolidation of the last thirty years' gains. Increasingly important throughout the nation, this new middle-class group is most powerful in the Sun Belt.

Much has changed in recent years, of course, and to dismiss the quite extraordinary progress toward racial balance and harmony in the last twenty years is to dismiss reality. Restaurants, schools, swimming pools, barbershops, playing fields, universities, and employers have all nominally ended discrimination. Blacks and Chicanos have slowly been added to the voting rolls, and their votes are at times crucial enough to require homages from even racist politicians. The booming urbanization of the entire region has drawn many of the rural poor into the cities, resulting in a gradual homogenization of racial attitudes as well as more concentrated political clout for some minority groups able to elect their own local officials. And growing industrialization, the desire to attract Northern industries, television exposure to the national culture, and a realization that de jure integration has not resulted in a total collapse have all meant a lessening of racism in the last two decades.

And yet. And yet racism is not wiped away so easily, history is not so neatly exorcised from contemporary culture. The Southern Rim, even if only because a product of its past, is more prone to racism than the rest of the nation, and the racism is there more virulent.

Objective measures of regional racism are, of course, almost impossible to come by, but there are some suggestive findings. The Equal Employment Opportunity Commission, for example, reported in May 1974 on black progress in employment during the 1960s: "The figures showed that the underrepresentation of blacks in white-collar jobs was greater in the South and Southwest." The Department of Housing and Urban Development, which catalogues complaints about violations of the various civil-rights acts, issues figures which consistently show that well over half and sometimes close to two-thirds of all complaints in the nation come from the fifteen states of the Southern Rim—even though they have less than half the black population and even though states like Mississippi and South Carolina, as might be imagined, do little to encourage complaints. The Council on Municipal Performance, a New York research group, catalogued American cities on the basis of housing segregation in 1974 and found that the five worst cities were Dallas, Chicago, Houston, Atlanta, and Los Angeles. And the list of states which have the greatest numbers below the federally established "low-income level"—a fairly good indication of the treatment and regard for minorities—show that the only places acknowledging more than 15 percent in distress were Alabama, Arizona, Arkansas, Florida, Georgia, Kentucky, Louisiana, Mississippi, New Mexico, North and South Carolina, Oklahoma, South Dakota, Tennessee, Texas, Virginia, and West Virginia.

But statistical evidence of Rimian racism is hardly necessary. One has only to remember George Wallace, and the nine million votes he won in the Southern Rim . . . or the men who make up the cowboy congressional delegations, men like Eastland and Stennis and Thurmond, whose names are enshrined in the pantheon of bigotry . . . or the State of Arizona's refusal to let Navajo Indians have even the right to vote until 1972, and then only when forced to by the federal government . . . or the gross anti-Semitism of some of the New Orleans men's clubs and Mardi Gras "krewes," blatant enough to cause the temporary migrations of Jews out of the city at carnival time . . . or the violent resistance of California farmers and agribusiness interests to the organizing of Chicano farm workers by Cesar Chavez and his group, an economic war that has overt racial overtones . . . or the public remarks by the controller of the State of Texas who called one of his critics "that nigger woman" —in 1973 . . . or the Far Right racist groups along the Rim, from the Liberty Lobby ("Black Revolution Is Red Revolution") to Billy James Hargis ("God ordained segregation") to Gerald L. K. Smith ("Negroes [are] a child race")—and that's without even mentioning all the white-sheet and swastika-armband groups . . . or the employment of an estimated three million "illegals"—the euphemism for what used to be called "wetbacks"—in the states of Arizona and New Mexico, aliens unlawfully hired and maintained in the nearest thing to outright servitude . . . or the killing of black students, not eons ago but just within the last decade, at Southern University, South Carolina State, Jackson State, North Carolina Agricultural and Technical University, and Texas Southern University . . . or the impoverished black mill hands of the Milliken textile factories in North Carolina, the migrant laborers picking the oranges of Florida, the hardscrabble masses of Plaquemines Parish in Louisiana, the exploited poor of the squalid border towns of Texas, the mud-stuck Indians in the crumbling pueblos of New Mexico, the blank-eyed truckloads of dollar-a-day Chicanos in the Imperial Valley in California.

At a different level, one has only to remember the career of Lyndon Johnson. His entire congressional service of twenty-two years was marked by its unanimity with the rest of the racist Southern delegations of the time: he voted at least a dozen times against attempts to remove the poll tax which prevented blacks from voting in the South; he denounced civil-rights legislation as "a farce and a sham" and "an effort to set up a police state"; he voted for the importation of cheap Mexican labor into the United States despite high unemployment among American Chicanos in the Southwest; and as Senate leader he continually displayed what *New Yorker* analyst Richard Rovere called "wizardry in beating back the civil-rights bloc." Becoming Vice-President, he changed not a whit: as presiding officer of the Senate, he ruled with the Southerners against attempts to end filibusters which throttled civil-rights legislation, and as head of the U.S. Commission on Equal Employment, charged with promoting minority hiring in firms doing business with the government, he refused to take any action against a single one of the eight hundred corporations of the Southwest which had been found to have not a single Chicano among their six hundred thousand employees. As President, Johnson evolved a reputation as a friend of civil rights, but in fact the 1964 Civil Rights Act was a creation of his predecessor and passed as a memorial to him; the 1965 Voting Rights Act (which merely reaffirmed a constitutional right, anyway) was enforced by Johnson in barely a tenth of the counties available; the 1966 civil-rights bill was such a farce that it died in committee; the Great Society "inner-city" programs were allowed to wither for lack of funds; and all the while the President kept his underlying belief that, as he told a black audience one day in Cleveland, "Equality is given." A racism tempered by expediency, yes, but racism nonetheless.

Of the other cowboy President, the best that can be said is that his "I can't be a racist" ranks about on a par with his "I am not a crook." Of course much of what Richard Nixon did as President that was apparently racist could have a political explanation instead: perhaps having the Justice Department go slow on civil-rights enforcement, ordering HUD to ignore guidelines on school desegregation, selecting racist Southerners for the Supreme Court, accepting the idea of "benign neglect" of twenty-two million Afro-Americans—perhaps these were designed simply to win Southern white votes and fulfill the Southern Strategy. But what is one to make of Nixon's pre-Presidential record—his signing of a lease with a restrictive covenant against "anyone of negro blood, or any person of the semitic race" when he was a U.S. senator in Washington in 1951; his statement questioning not only the method and wisdom of the 1954 *Brown v. Board* desegregation decision but its *legality*; his public stand, while still Vice-President, against "total integration"? What is to be made of his selection for the sensitive post as head of the Presidential Task Force on Model Cities of Edward Banfield, absolutely notorious in academic circles for his racist opinions of the poor ("improvident, irresponsible . . . unable or unwilling either to control impulses or to put forth any effort at self-improvement," etc.)? What of Nixon's incredible admission when, asked about his Supreme Court nomination, "Would you have nominated Judge Carswell if you had known that he was a racist?" he replied, without even a blush, "Yes, I would." And what of the repeated epithets out of the President's own mouth, as revealed in the White House transcripts, exposing a mind continually categorizing people by race and nationality, usually in the ugliest terms. No, the racism of Nixon went deeper than politics: he too was part of the cowboy heritage.

III

It is bizarre but not at all fanciful to see football as the objective correlative of the third major characteristic of the Southern Rim: repression. No other sport is inherently so rigid, so autocratic, so brutal, so anti-individualistic. No other sport combines one-man rule on and off the field, systematic and sanctioned violence, automatonism as a clear virtue, established and elaborate plays and patterns, and the orderliness of a set field of play and an inflexible clock. No other sport surrounds itself with such patriotism and piety, such spectacle and militarism, such mechanization and organization. And no other sport is so beloved in, associated with, and characteristic of, the Southern Rim, all the way from the Rose Bowl in the west to the Orange Bowl in the east.

Repression is particularly hard to come to grips with because in this country it is so mercurial. It can appear in blatant form, as in the attempt by federal agents to infiltrate, harass, jail, and destroy dissident groups, or it can be much more subtle, as in the gradual erosion of personal privacy by various organs of government. It can be obviously illegal, and frowned upon, as in the attempt by one political party to sabotage the campaigns of its opponents, or it can be to all appearances legal, and approved, as in the passage and enforcement of laws which permit "no-knock" arrests, police frisks on whim, and "use immunity" jailings. It can be concrete and observable, as with the increasingly large and mechanized police forces of the land, or it can be intangible and hidden, as with that superpatriotism which denies the questioning of and deviance from national authority. But whatever form it takes, when so many of them coincide—as all of these have in the last decade under two cowboy Presidents—there can be no doubting the reality of it.

The repressive use of force is, like racism, interwoven into the history of the Southern Rim. More than any other region, this area has been marked by violence, usually sanctioned violence, carving out its territory by force and coercion, building its economy upon compulsion and servitude, governing its towns and provinces by the whip and the gun, just as much in the smaller piny-woods towns of the Southeast as in the fabled *High Noon* cities of the Southwest. The traditions of authoritarianism, too, are inherent here: in the magisterial family life of the plantations and the frontier farms, the pantokratorial fundamentalism of the religions, the benevolent paternalism of the one-man cow towns and the one-man states (Huey Long's Louisiana, Leland Stanford's California), the paternalistic and anti-union corporations in the textile, lumber, and food-processing industries, and the despotism of every kind of agricultural production from slavery to indenture to migrant labor.

And again, little has changed with the admixture of the mid-century migrations. The new settlers, having pulled up stakes and turned their lives around, have proved to be precisely the ones who most want order and stability, who seek the kind of serenity that social and political authoritarianism bring. Conformity is a familiar malady of all suburbs, but the Southern Rim cities, so often little more than concentric suburban sprawls without either a physical or a cultural center, so new that they lack the cohesion of tradition and the comfort of convention, are particularly prone to such rigidification. Often they seek to create cohesion and unification, where there is no natural reason for it, through the artifice of uniform architecture (in Irvine, California, home owners must select paint for their houses from a list of twenty-five approved colors), or the economic interdependence of risk investment (in Coral Springs, Florida, a "cooperative" community, each home owner has a financial stake in the houses, gardens, schools, children, and lives of all the rest), or an exaggerated allegiance to pretended social norms (in Houston, it was the unwillingness of parents to even admit the existence of homosexuality that kept the

Henley/Corll murders hidden for so long). Often, too, these cities are the first to cry law 'n' order, to institute local vigilantism, to provide new police riot tanks before buying books for the school library, all in the search for an authoritarian stability that will secure the blessings of prosperity for themselves and their progeny. All of this is the product of, the climate of, repression.

Police loom large in the mythos as well as the ethos of the Southern Rim. The Southern sheriff, the Texas Ranger, the frontier marshal, the Los Angeles cop, all achieved fame because they were in reality preeminent powers in their domains, unmatched in fable or in fact by any other region of the land: what do we know of the Maine sheriff or the Michigan state trooper? Now statistics show that the actual number of police in the Southern Rim is almost exactly consistent with its population—having 35 percent of the national population in 1970, it had 34 percent of the police, and that seems fair enough—but the importance with which they are imbued and the roles they are permitted to play give them a stature in their society beyond their numbers. What this can lead to was dramatically demonstrated in the civil-rights struggles of the late 1950s and early 1960s, when police were repeatedly given both popular license and official sanction to brutalize people seeking to change the existing forms of racist repression. The statements, postures, and sometimes the orders of such elected officials as John Patterson in Alabama, Ross Barnett in Mississippi, Farris Bryant in Florida, Lester Maddox in Georgia, Orval Faubus in Arkansas—the litany will bring back sad memories for anyone who lived through those days—produced police violence across much of the South for a dozen years as the police billy club was chosen as the popular instrument to halt progress.

Prisons, too, loom large in the Southern Rim. The fifteen Rim states have 45 percent of all the state and local prison guards in the country, 42 percent of all the state and federal prisoners, and almost *twice as many* local jails as in the entire rest of the nation. Moreover, in the days when the death penalty was being carried out routinely, these Southern Rim prisons were the most violent: between 1940 and 1967 (the date of the last execution), an amazing 63 percent (1,395 of 2,192) of all the hangings, shootings, and electrocutions were performed in the Rim states, top marks going to Georgia, Texas, and California. And, ominously, as prison repression today begins to take more sophisticated forms, the Rim still takes the lead, with California's Neuropsychiatric Institute at UCLA developing the most advanced techniques in lobotomy, psychosurgery, chemoneurology, and "behavior modification" at one end, and North Carolina's new Federal Center for Correction Research carrying them out upon "members of minority groups [and] high security risks" in the prison population at the other end. True enough, the Southern Rim has more crime, and perhaps needs more prisons. Yet any society which seems to depend so much upon prisons, building them more often and staffing them better and stuffing them fuller and making them harsher, betrays something.

In the last ten years, under the guidance of two Southern Rim Presidents, repression has stalked a national path. This cannot be a coincidence. Something in the background and heritage of Lyndon Johnson and Richard Nixon led them, each in his own way, to feel the need for, plan, create, and supervise the most far-reaching and intricate systems of political and military repression this country has ever known.

Different as the two men were in superficials, their root natures were quite similar. Political scientist James David Barber, in his exhaustive study of Presidential personalities, determined that both of them displayed what he calls an "active-negative" character, which is marked by hard personal struggle for success, compulsive activity, and deep aggressive instincts, a lust for power and centralization, a tendency to intolerance and paranoia, and a sense of being above the limitations of the law or accountability to the public. In other words, repressive.

The manifestations of this character during the years between 1963 and 1974 are too numerous to catalogue, but it is worthwhile to recall at least the outlines. Under Johnson, the federal government used twenty-six investigative agencies to spy on the political activities of its citizens. The Defense Department and the U.S. Army kept a watch on civilian demonstrations, and without a shred of constitutional justification, amassed a file on eighteen million civilian citizens. The Justice Department began a campaign of judicial harassment and intimidation of antiwar protesters, prosecuted more than two thousand draft-resistance cases, and began a program of arming and coordinating local police forces. The CIA from 1964 on was used to spy on, control, disrupt, destroy, and entrap various radical and student organizations around the country—as well as checking on certain respectable politicians and jurists—in complete violation of the charter under which it was established and the Constitution under which it is supposed to operate. The FBI was first used as an all-out political weapon to spy and amass files on a variety of political enemies in the established parties and out—including Barry Goldwater, Spiro Agnew, Bobby Kennedy, and Martin Luther King and other civil-rights leaders—and the White House secretly gathered such a collection of files that J. Edgar Hoover was forced to complain that his agents were overworked. The Internal Revenue Service established special units to check on and harass political organizations. And armed troops were sent to quell rebellions in dozens of cities, including Chicago, Detroit, Jackson, Newark, Wilmington, Tampa, and the capital itself—more than fifty-eight thousand troops, the most ever mobilized for domestic control, in 1968 alone.

Under Nixon, all programs were continued, and more added on. The Justice Department established new units to collect all government surveillance information and to originate and prosecute hundreds of new political cases. The FBI enlarged its Cointelpro operation of harassment, surveillance, provocation, and entrapment of black and left-wing organizations, and assigned agents and informers to every single college campus and every known black organization in the land; according to the FBI's own report, "some Cointelpro activities involved isolated instances of practices that can only be considered abhorrent in a free society." The Department of Health, Education, and Welfare (among other agencies) funded extensive "behavior modification" programs (drug therapy, brain surgery, implanted transmitters) which a Senate report found to be operated in violation of "the constitutional rights of the subjects" and to "pose substantial threats to our freedoms." The Immigration and Naturalization Service got into the act with a series of dragnet raids in 1972 and 1973, sweeping up "illegal aliens" in such cities as Los Angeles, Dallas, Denver, New

York, and Chicago, arresting and summarily deporting altogether more than thirty thousand people. The White House established its own office to collect and monitor intelligence reports and political files on the citizenry, a venture that was eventually expanded into a top-level "domestic intelligence" operation—the "Huston Plan" of 1970—which provided for illegal burglaries, buggings, wiretaps, mail-openings, informers, and other police-state tactics by a variety of federal agencies; this plan, despite Nixon's claim and the stories of Hoover's refusal to go along, was in fact never rescinded, and its essential operations were continued for the next four years. The White House also carried out other supralegal forms of repression which ranged from the activities of the "plumbers unit" and wiretapping of aides and newspeople to the electoral sabotage of the Democrats and the Watergate burglary—and even more besides, though so far unknown: according to Howard Hunt, "The Watergate bugging is only one of a number of highly illegal conspiracies engaged in by one or more of the defendants at the behest of senior White House officials" but which are "as yet undisclosed."

Quite a record. "Tyranny was not yet a fact," the *New York Times* observed later, "but the drift toward tyranny, toward curtailing and impairing essential freedoms, was well under way."

Nor was it all confined to secret bureaus and hidden deeds. In both Administrations there were open attempts to cow and control the press, official policies of deception and deceit, unconstitutional acts of international warfare, undisguised efforts to fill judiciary positions with political allies and beholden supporters. In both Administrations there was a public disregard for the opinions and even the laws of Congress, expansion and concentration of power in personal and White House agencies, emphasis upon pomp and ceremony surrounding the person of the President, sanctioned demands for patriotism and expressions of loyalty to the President. Does it all sound ominously familiar, with echoes from Europe of the 1930s? The *New York Times* found it "was redolent of a police state"; Senator Sam Ervin said he detected aspects of "the Gestapo mentality"; and Columbia University historian Herbert S. Levine, who has spent a lifetime on the study of fascism, said bluntly, "Hitler's use of the German Government . . . differed only in degree from Nixon's use of the executive branch. There is no discernible difference in kind."

In both Administrations, too, a reign of indiscriminate terror—there is no other phrase for it—was visited upon the people of Southeast Asia. Never before in history has such an extraordinary military attack been waged, month after month for the greater part of ten years, a relentless bombardment of military and civilian targets in Vietnam, Laos, and Cambodia, a campaign of mass murder organized by the CIA to kill some twenty thousand civilians, a systematic defoliation and destruction of millions of acres of South Vietnam, a day-and-night war waged with the most sophisticated weapons, the most lethal ammunition, by what was supposed to be the world's most powerful army—and all this directed not at a mighty superpower bent on world mastery or a military giant threatening America's shores, but a tiny, poor, faraway, economically underdeveloped country that had been betrayed and maltreated by the colonial nations of the world for most of the past half-century. Lyndon Johnson and Richard Nixon oversaw, justified, defended, and applauded a war which killed at least 2 million people in Indochina, left nearly that many wounded, drove at least 10 million people from their homes, and destroyed some 6.4 million acres. During one single month—November 1972—when the United States was following a stated policy of *restricted* bombing, Richard Nixon authorized the dropping of one hundred thousand tons of bombs on Indochina—25 percent more than Hitler had dropped on Britain in the entire five-year course of World War II. William Shirer, certainly no rabble-rouser, drew the obvious conclusion: "Though Richard Nixon does not yet have the dictatorial power of Adolf Hitler—at least not yet—he has shown in Vietnam that he has the awesome means, unrestrained by any hand, and the disposition to be just as savage in his determination to massacre and destroy the innocent people of any small nation which refuses to bow to his dictates and which is powerless to retaliate."

Perhaps the conditions of the nation, the conditions of the world, would have drawn such a response from any occupant of the Presidency over the last dozen years, perhaps the individuals were not fully masters of their times. Perhaps. But more likely the character of their heritage, which spoke very powerfully in the soul of both men, propelled them down these paths of repressive response.

IV

Watergate was a window onto America. It allowed us to see the condition of political morality as it had developed over the last thirty years, the level to which the foremost elected leaders of the nation had sunk, the extent to which public tolerance could be stretched and moral outrage blunted. Such a condition of ethical rot is not a sudden disease to which the body politic succumbs overnight, nor the result of a single Administration, however venal, nor a single man, however evil. It takes rather a long time to corrupt a nation. A headlong drive for international power and imperial sway begun at a time when most of the world lay in ashes; a long period of anti-Communist paranoia, made up of witch hunts and red scares and political purges, where ends are thought to justify means; the development of an ever-engorging economy which needs constantly to be inflated with the world's resources so that it does not go flat; an unprecedented concentration of riches which resulted in a material culture manufacturing the unneeded to be sold by the unprincipled to the unwary; a growth of corporations, cities, and institutions of all kinds to a size where they are unreachable, unresponsive, alienating; a political system similarly out of reach, dominated by back rooms and front money, cynically rejected where it is not simply shrugged at, so little responsive to the citizenry that each year fewer and fewer people bother to go through the motions of casting ballots—these are the processes that, in time and in conjunction, will corrupt a nation.

Can it be only a coincidence that these processes were concurrent with the emergence of the Southern Rim on the national scene? That the heedless growth philosophy of the new industries and the new cities of the Rim has gradually become the growth philosophy of the country at large? That the last two elected Presidents, who brought political morality to its dimmest point in generations, were from the Southern Rim? That the culmination of the cowboys' place in the economic life of the nation so far has coincided with the culmination of the cowboys' influence in its political life so far—and that this has also been the high point of political corruption? A coincidence —or may there not be something in the political character of the Southern Rim that would help to explain this, too?

The kind of culture that produced the particular *economic* morality of the Southern Rim that we have previously explored obviously shapes the *political* morality of the region as well. Again, the point is not that political corruption is an affliction found only in cowboy country—the sorry records of New Jersey and Maryland, Chicago and New York City, easily belie that— but that the history of the Rim's development seems to give it a greater propensity for this affliction and a more brazen disregard for its improprieties. It is the region that more than any other has depended for its rapid growth upon the favors and finances of the federal government—for water, roads, harbors, canals, military installations, and much else—which have been dispensed largely upon the basis of political influence and therefore are uncommonly open to political finagling and chicanery. It is the region whose major industries are especially dependent upon federal contracts—particularly in defense, aerospace, and technology—and federal subsidies or tax breaks—particularly oil, real estate, and agribusiness—and are therefore especially inclined to political pressuring of all kinds, legal and illegal. It is the region that has had to develop its political traditions and political leaders almost overnight—in the last twenty years, remember, California has been asked to supply 20 new people of congressional caliber, Florida 9, and that is only at the national level—and this headlong pace has sometimes produced as many weak and self-serving politicians as reliable and public-spirited ones: cream rises to the top, but so does scum. It is the region whose cities have been built up in the last fifteen years precisely through the cooperation/collusion of the business and political communities—the Dallas Citizens Charter Association, for example, a group of the city's top businessmen, has ruled that city since the late 1930s and never made any bones about it, and Atlanta, Jacksonville, Memphis, New Orleans, Phoenix, and other Rim metropolises all have similar arrangements— which has meant dozens of new skylines, to be sure, but has also meant a blurring of the distinctions between citizens and consumers, between public good and private gain, between civic charity and outright bribery. It is a region that has been a one-party province to a degree unusual in this country, with the result that an unusual number of its representatives have been immune from meaningful voter referendums and the exposés of rival candidates, and hence have been able to use their offices pretty much as they themselves see fit, a condition clearly lending itself to malfeasance. And it is the region where organized crime, making its most recent inroads and finding its most lucrative prospects, has spread its stain of corruption throughout the political fabric—Miami, New Orleans, Las Vegas, and Southern California come particularly to mind—not with any greater ugliness than it has done in the big cities of the Northeast but with greater subtlety, greater riches, and, so far at least, greater immunity.

The catalogue of political corruption on the state level alone in this region in just the last few years is revealing. In Texas, the Sharpstown scandal—a $50 million stock-fraud scheme engineered by real-estate developer Frank Sharp through his Sharpstown Bank and Houston insurance company —managed to involve, and bring to an end, the political careers of the governor, lieutenant governor, state treasurer, speaker of the Texas House, two of his aides, the chairman of the House Appropriations Committee, another House member, the Democratic Party state chairman, and two former state attorneys general. In Florida, taking just 1973 and 1974, the lieutenant governor was censured by the House of Representatives for using public employees for his own personal gain; the state treasurer was indicted for influence peddling and perjury; the commissioner of education was forced to resign when indicted on a $70,000 kickback and bribery scheme; the controller was indicted for bribery extortion, and tax evasion in connection with the granting of bank charters, and a half-dozen officials of the city of Miami and North Miami were forced to stand trial on charges, as the *New York Times* put it, of "widespread corruption in the courts and local governments of Miami and Dade County." In California, the lieutenant governor ended a career that was heading him toward the leadership of the country's most populous state when he lied to a Senate committee

about having offered a bribe on behalf of the notorious ITT
corporation; the former mayor of the largest city has been accused in federal grand jury proceedings of profiteering and
accepting illegitimate kickbacks while in office. In Louisiana,
a special legislative committee found that the building of the
New Orleans Superdome involved political favoritism, public
deception, theft, bribery, falsification, and simple corruption by
state officials and contractors under two separate gubernatorial
regimes. In Oklahoma, the 1970–74 governor and a Texas
business associate were found guilty of bribery and extortion on
a $10 million investment scheme; five other state officials have
been indicted for giving kickbacks on state contracts with the
governor's approval; and the state treasurer and highway commissioner both spent a year under nine federal indictments for
extortion and misuse of funds until, suddenly, mysteriously, the
Oklahoma attorney dropped the case. ("There have been so
many scandals in the state," Bill Moyers reported in *Newsweek*
in 1974, "that the wags say it's news when an incumbent isn't
indicted.") In Alabama, where the publisher of the *Montgomery Advertiser* says "Watergate doesn't hold a candle to the way
Wallace runs this state," there have been exposures of the involvement of George Wallace and his brother Gerald, plus various other state officials, in scandals of kickbacks and bribery in
the asphalt business, engineering contracts, highway construction, and liquor selling; Wallace himself has used state funds
and personnel for his personal campaigning, has taken an illegitimate $30,000 tax write-off on personal papers, and has appar-
ently pocketed—or at least never accounted for—the $200,000
left over from his 1972 campaign. In Arizona two state legislators were involved in an insurance scandal, in Louisiana the
attorney general was jailed, in Georgia the state's leading black
politician was found guilty of filing false income-tax statements. . . .

Yes, yes, New Jersey and Maryland: corruption does exist
elsewhere. But the record here is overwhelming, the pattern
unmistakable. And there are other ways to limn the portrait,
too. . . . Along the 3,000-mile border with Canada, touching
upon thirteen states, there has never been a major case of corruption in the history of the United States Immigration Service;
but along the 1,600-mile border with Mexico, touching on four

states, scandal is endemic and has been for years—things got so
bad that by 1973 the Department of Justice, which oversees the
Immigration Service, was forced to acknowledge "widespread
corruption" among the American border officials, who were
found to be engaged in smuggling aliens, importing illegal drugs
and armaments, selling false immigration papers, and plying
various other forms of illegality, including bribery, entrapment,
brutality, extortion, prostitution, and general corruption while
on the federal payroll. When the Mexicans refer to the border
area as *Poso del Mondo*—asshole of the world—they do
not mean the southern side alone. . . . Of the six impeachment
votes issued by committees of the U.S. House of Representatives in the twentieth century, four have been directed to honored officials from the Southern Rim: two judges from
Florida, one judge from California, and one President from
California. . . . The only member of the United States Supreme
Court in its 200-year history ever to resign in the face of public
scandal, and thereby escape impeachment charges, was Abe
Fortas, from Tennessee—appointed by Lyndon Johnson, from
Texas—who acknowledged accepting money from a foundation
run by Florida financier Louis Wolfson, while sitting on the bench.
The emolument was particularly odious because Wolfson was
then under investigation (and later convicted) for stock fraud, he
was a known friend and business associate of various members of
the Florida criminal underworld, and the money represented the
first installment in a cozy and totally unprecedented $20,000-a-
year-for-life arrangement with a sitting Justice. It was, according to Yale Law School Professor Alexander Bickel, "very
probably the gravest known lapse in the personal ethics of a
Justice of the Supreme Court in the history of the institution."
. . . The State of California did not invent the art of the political
smear, but it has perfected it and sent it across the land—as
Washington Post reporter Lou Cannon has summarized it, "A
unique combination of circumstances, operating almost since
the birth of California, frequently has produced a political climate of 'anything goes' in this vast nation-state." . . . The highest
point of political corruption yet experienced by this country, the
criminal complexus known as Watergate, was conceived, directed, committed, and covered up by a creepy-crawly lot, almost all of whom came from the Southern Rim. At the top, of

course, Richard Nixon, a Californian; next in line, Bob Halde-
man (California) and John Ehrlichman (California); under
them, Dwight Chapin, Lawrence Higby, Gordon Strachan, Herbert Porter (all California) and Harry Dent (South Carolina);
then the operatives at the Committee for the Reelection of the
President, Jeb Magruder (New York-California), Frederick
LaRue (Mississippi), Frederick Malek (California), Clark
Macgregor (California), Robert Mardian (California), and
Murray Chotiner (California); the on-the-road saboteurs for
CRP, Donald Segretti (California), Kenneth Reitz (Tennes-
see), Robert Benz (Florida), George Hearing (Florida), Her-
bert Kalmbach (California), and Bernard Barker, Virgilio
Gonzales, Eugenio Martinez, Frank Sturgis, Felipe de Diego
(all from Florida), with funds supplied by Kalmbach, Robert
H. Allen (Texas), and William Lietke (Texas). There were
miscreants from other parts of the country as well—John
Mitchell, Maurice Stans, Charles Colson, John Dean, Howard
Hunt, Gordon Liddy and James McCord most prominently—
but the main planners and main operatives were clearly selected
from the cowboy crew that Richard Nixon felt most congenial
with. Of all the Nixonians who were indicted or convicted for
Watergate and related crimes as of the beginning of 1975, fully
two-thirds of them (28 out of 38) are from the Southern Rim,
and that leaves aside the one who is free of any indictment save
that rendered upon his body by his conscience. They might all
accurately say, with Jeb Magruder, "Somewhere between my
ambitions and my ideals, I lost my ethical compass." . . . And,
lastly, the rest of the Nixonian record, overshadowed by Watergate but in many ways as vile: the illegal and unconstitutional
air and ground war against the neutral nations of Cambodia and
Laos for the greater part of the period between 1969 and 1973,
carried on under an elaborate cloak of secrecy personally ordered by Nixon, involving falsification of military records up
and down the military chain of command and repeated lies to
the Pentagon, the public, the Congress, and the world; the use
of the CIA under Nixon's personal directives to subvert and
overthrow the legitimate Chilean government of Salvador Al-
lende Gossens, and the subsequent lies to cover up this involvement by everyone from Nixon on down; the extensive criminal

frauds and kickback scandals in the Federal Housing Agency (resulting in "one of the biggest white collar prosecutions in history," according to the *Washington Post*), the Small Business Administration, and the Immigration Service, which alone would be enough to mark the Nixon regime as the most corrupt since Harding's; the blatant and repeated political hirings and firings in HUD, the General Services Administration, the National Highway Traffic Safety Administration, the Office of Economic Opportunity, the Law Enforcement Assistance Administration, and other government agencies, all against civil service regulations; the impoundment of funds authorized by Congress, even after such impoundments were found illegal by various federal courts; the acceptance by Nixon of "other emoluments" while in office, in direct violation of the Constitution, including jewelry and other gifts from foreign heads of state and government, improvements to his personal estates in San Clemente and Key Biscayne paid for by the government, and certain tax breaks on his personal papers which were fraudulently obtained. Quite incredible, really, this catalogue. Small wonder, then, that Nixon could face the nation and say, "I am suggesting that the House follow the Constitution—if they do, I will," the first time that a President has publicly established his relationship to the Constitution on a conditional basis.

But it is not the mere *fact* of corruption that is necessarily so striking in the cowboy populace, it is the *attitude* toward it. There is usually a lassitude, if not complete indifference, by both the perpetrators and the public, to most revelations of unethical activity and political shadiness. Of course there is always *some* outrage, from a paper here, a pulpit there, but the ease and frequency with which malodorous acts are justified or ignored in the communtiy at large suggests that there may really be a different standard at work.

There is, let's face it, an indifference, a cowboy cavalierness, to certain political goings-on that would raise at least eyebrows, if not Cain, elsewhere. It seems to be epitomized by the lovely conversation secretly recorded in 1954 between Clifford Jones, at the time the lieutenant governor of Nevada, and an investigator for a local newspaper who posed as a gambler looking for a license:

> JONES: You have a record?
> INVESTIGATOR: Nothing recent. A few things when I was younger, a little narcotics, bootlegging, murder, manslaughter.
> JONES: Anything recently?
> INVESTIGATOR: Not in the past 11 years.
> JONES: You're all right.

This is the ethical mentality we came to recognize most recently in the responses to Watergate by defenders of Richard Nixon all along the Southern Rim: it's always been that way, no one was really harmed, his only crime was getting caught, he has a right to, they all do it anyway. We saw it when the folks in Louisiana greeted with blank indifference the admission by Governor Edwin Edwards in January 1974 that he made regular gambling trips to Las Vegas and had even been known to lose up to $8,000 a shot, an open invitation for the criminal elements of Nevada. When the people of Arizona reacted with complete apathy to an Arizona Senate committee which decided in early 1974 to exclude two categories of people from provisions of a new campaign-reform bill: the state legislators themselves, and "people in the business of gambling." When Californians ignored the fact that Jerry Brown, when running for governor in 1974, took a healthy campaign contribution from the Gallo wine family at the same time that he was supposed to be supporting a boycott of the Gallo wineries, all the citizens apparently accepting his explanation that "it would not be a viable campaign strategy to reject a contribution from someone just because you disagree with them." When the people of New Mexico expressed neither public outcry nor private indignation at the disclosure that Governor Bruce King, while in office from 1970 to 1974, received $6 million in regular installments from a huge real-estate company to which he had sold some of his vast land holdings in the state, then went and granted permission for this company to develop property in an area where the water table was proven to be dangerously low. When the Re-

publican Women's Club of California rose and cheered wildly
on national television at the appearance of Spiro Agnew, known
then to be under investigation for his myriad slimy deals with
his Maryland friends—and when just a few months later, after
Agnew had pleaded guilty and resigned, they rose and cheered
wildly at the appearance of Ed Reinecke, under indictment for
lying about his part in the brazen $400,000 bribery from ITT to
the Republican Party. When the *New York Times* reported that
the millionaire members of the Lincoln Club in Newport Beach,
California, "appeared to find nothing shocking, or even ethically
questionable, in the disclosures of political espionage, bugging
and burglary" by the President's campaign committee, and
when one of them, Robert F. Beaver, a wealthy construction-
company president, could say, "Political espionage is as American as apple pie, and I have yet to see where the American
people have been hurt in any way." When an independent
Southern oilman, asked if he had any regrets over his $30,000
contribution to the 1972 Nixon campaign, replied, "Watergate
is the most ridiculous, overblown incident in American history.
Anyone who understands American politics knows that. The
use of illegal methods is common in this country." When a
wealthy Los Angeles businessman, Z. Wayne Griffin, took it
upon himself to send out fund-raising letters in the summer of
1974, even after Nixon had resigned in disgrace, asking for half
a million dollars to be donated to Bob Haldeman for his cover-
up trial and adding, "There is little doubt that history will reveal
Bob and most of his associates as dedicated young American
patriots victimized by a massive twist of political persecution."
When South Carolina lawyer J. Fred Buzhardt shrugged off
Watergate with the comment, "Would you rather have a competent scoundrel or an honest boob in office?" When Richard
Nixon could look us all in the eye and say, "I am not a crook."

But for moral obtuseness, there is no place like Texas. It's
as if that state, in the middle of the Southern Rim, partakes of
knavery and deceit with the aplomb of the land-robbing rancher
and the slave-holding aristocrat combined. And in that state no
one typifies amoral smoothness better than its most famous
politician today, the man who nearly became President of the
United States, John Connally. How Connally has been able to
advance his career so successfully after all the things he's been

involved in is a genuine mystery, explainable only as a monument to the moral blindness, or forgetfulness, of the citizens of Texas—and of Richard Nixon.

Connally began his career as a wheeler-dealer on behalf of multimillionaire oilman Sid Richardson, during which his most notable service was in a neat little deal by which Texas oilmen paid $1 million to Robert Anderson just before he became Secretary of the Treasury and architect of the national oil-import program. An early lackey of the Texas Democratic machine, Connally went on to be elected governor of Texas in 1962—and then was elected again in 1964 despite the disclosure that he was receiving between $75,000 and $100,000 a year from the Richardson estate while serving as governor and passing on legislation affecting the oil industry. (Of course, that only happened to be a violation of the Texas Constitution—"nor shall [the governor] practice any profession, or receive compensation, reward, fee, or the promise thereof for the same"—but that fact went almost completely unnoticed in that charitable state.) A fair sample of Connally's moral stance as governor was his position on awarding $500 million a year in architectural contracts for the state university system, as reported by University of Texas regent Frank Erwin: "Since architectural contracts are not let on a competitive-bid basis, they simply constitute valuable gifts that are awarded by the state government . . . to competent architects who have been friendly to him and his Administration"—and in Texas, everyone seemed to think that made perfect sense. In 1971 Connally went on to the national stage in a big way, as Nixon's Treasury Secretary, but he kept his down-home ethics: during his eighteen months in office he managed somehow to award no fewer than eight precious bank charters to various cronies in Texas; he intervened with the Justice Department to get them to lay off his friend Jake Jacobsen, whose only transgression was that he had defrauded a bank out of some $800,000; and he was twice offered bribes to support higher milk prices without reporting the briber either time, as required by law. In 1973 Connally moved right into the Nixon White House, as a Presidential adviser, and showed no compunction whatsoever about simultaneously continuing to represent his various law clients and to serve on the boards of various companies, almost all of which had million-dollar stakes in federal decisions. Shortly after leaving Nixon's service, having learned nothing and forgotten nothing, Connally declared that "there isn't a Republican . . . anywhere in the nation who has to hang his head in shame because of Watergate"—though at that time there had already been fourteen indictments or convictions against the Nixon crews—and then went on to argue that the Supreme Court was not, after all, "the ultimate arbiter of all disputes" and that "there are times when the President of the United States would be right in not obeying a decision of the Supreme Court." An extraordinary statement for anyone, least of all a member of the bar, to make, but in Texas they're not quite as finicky about laws and judges as the Founding Fathers were. Finally—perhaps one should say, inevitably—John Connally was himself indicted on five counts of bribery, perjury, and obstruction of justice and charged with taking a $10,000 bribe in the milk scandal; though eventually found not guilty, Connally was at least temporarily wiped out of the 1976 Presidential sweepstakes and his reputation for the time being tarnished throughtout the land. Everywhere, that is, except Texas, where most of the citizens said all along that Big John just couldn't have been guilty—not because his character is too noble, or his sense of ethics too acute, but because the bribe was too small.

V

"It could probably be shown by facts and figures," Mark Twain wrote eighty years ago, "that there's no distinctly native American criminal class except Congress"—and things have changed little since then. It is on the congressional level that the greatest pressures toward corruption are exerted and the greatest opportunities for corruption are presented, and the possibilities of chicanery and improbity short of outright corruption are well-nigh infinite. Nor is there any restriction upon congressional behavior, as Princeton historian James H. Banner has pointed out:

Congress is governed by no ethics regulation.

No law forbids a member of either house from holding a position with a law firm which may be doing business with the government. No law forbids Congressmen [sic] from accepting free rides on a company plane to visit a distant military installation. No law requires members of Congress to disclose their finances, nor are House and Senate rules governing such disclosures effective or complete. Who wishes a body so unconcerned about its own actual or potential conflicts of interest and about the ethical standards of its members to gain greater authority over us?

All of this, as might be imagined, provides fertile territory for the members from the Southern Rim, and it is they who are so often involved in improprieties, conflicts of interest, pork-barrel scheming, campaign chicanery, and outright corruption. In part this is obviously because it is the Rimian politicians who have the preponderant power in Congress and hence are the ones the favor-seekers will seek out first. In part, too, it is because so many of them have been secure in their seats for so long that they fear no retribution from their constituents no matter what moral lapses they may be guilty of. But in part it must also be that to some degree they reflect the ethical standards of their communities, the political cultures whence they spring.

Conflicts of interest are so common in the U.S. Congress that the conflicts no longer interest, but still the ethical quotient they reveal says something about the nation's highest legislative body. About the senators we know practically nothing, since they are not required to disclose their financial holdings; about the representatives we can tell somewhat more, since they are. As of the 1972 tally, 266 House members had outside financial interests in defense corporations, 55 in real-estate firms, 42 in oil and gas companies, 31 in agribusinesses, and more than a sixth kept up affiliations with their law firms, all of which presumably have clients interested in federal legislation. Not all of these double-hatted legislators were Rimsters, of course, but a disproportionate number—39 percent, to be exact—were. Most interesting were the conflicts connected with the banks, since the House, after all, has a special constitutional responsibility for initiating and overseeing most financial legislation. Yet at least 104 members of that body in 1974 owned up to having outside banking interests, and almost half of them—48 out of

104—were from the Southern Rim; of the 37 members who acknowledged being bank directors, 16 were Rimsters; and of the 15 who were on House committees directly responsible for drafting bank legislation 8 were Rimsters. You'd think that all of this would at least be cause for a certain amount of shame and embarrassment among the legislators, but the cowboy establishment of Congress long ago decreed that representing private interests while serving on the public payroll was perfectly acceptable. "Why, if everyone abstained on grounds of personal interest," Oklahoma's Senator Robert Kerr used to say when someone noted how his legislation always seemed to benefit his Kerr-McGee Oil Company, "I doubt if you could get a quorum in the United States Senate on any subject." As for himself, he would add, without apology, "Hell, I'm in everything."

Let us take a look at the ethical records of a few of the Southern Rim stalwarts in Congress—not the lesser fry, whose pecadilloes may be reprehensible yet relatively less important, but the bigger fish, those who have a major influence upon the laws of the nation.

Russell Long, the Louisiana Democrat, is chairman of the Senate Finance Committee and oversees legislation which, among other things, determines the financial future of the oil and gas industry; he is also a millionaire oilman. He quite brazenly proclaims himself "the darling of the oil industry" and almost as brazenly helps to funnel gas and oil dollars to the campaigns of senators he happens to like. In his successful effort to become the Senate Whip in 1965, he had the benefit of a bottomless treasure chest from his down-home oil friends and passed out oil money to wavering colleagues in an open effort to get their support, commenting to the press, "Shucks, that's the name of the game." Asked once if his private oil holdings and public oil legislating represented a conflict of interest, he replied, "If you have financial interests completely parallel to your state, then you have no problem." Presumably, the 933,000 people in Louisiana who live below the official poverty level were overjoyed to learn that they had interests parallel to their millionaire senator.

Long's non-oil career is equally slippery. He has had a number of dealings with probably the only other organized force in Louisiana that can rival the Long machine, the crime empire of Carlos Marcello. Marcello henchmen have taken credit for helping Long with his 1965 Whip election, claiming to have bought seven votes with money from Marcello and the Teamsters, and one of the Louisiana Mafiosi has admitted being a money carrier from Marcello to Long. Long was also instrumental in getting the Department of Transportation to push through construction of a section of the Dixie Highway on land owned by the Regent Development Corporation of Louisiana, whose vice-president and secretary-treasurer, according to the New Orleans Metropolitan Crime Commission, just happen to be old-time associates of Carlos Marcello. Long took an abnormally vivid interest in the Jimmy Hoffa case, as well—one that coincided with Marcello's—and Long's friends and associates went to great lengths to threaten and cajole key witnesses to get the testimony against Hoffa reversed, though to no avail; and when these same friends were faced with a federal grand jury investigation in Louisiana to see if some of their great lengths were criminal, Long is reported to have become a wild man in the offices of the Justice Department in his attempts to have it stopped.

So far, Long's record has no formal blemish, though that may speak more for his power than his perspicacity. Twice formal indictments were voted against Long by a federal grand jury in Baltimore accusing him and two other legislators of forty-five "overt acts" in connection with a bribery-kickback scheme during the construction of the Rayburn House Office Building in Washington, and twice the U.S. attorneys in Baltimore—first a Democrat, then a Republican—recommended his indictment to the Justice Department. The Justice Department at the time, though, was being run by the old watchdog of the Southern Strategy, John Mitchell, and it twice denied the recommendations, no reasons given. Strangely enough, former Senator Daniel Brewster of Maryland was also indicted in the same case for the same offenses, and this one Mitchell approved—possibly reflecting the fact that Brewster had been a one-term senator with no chairmanships and was no longer even in office.

John Sparkman, the Alabama Democrat who heads the Senate Banking Committee, has been a consistent champion of banking interests and is sometimes even known to send bills through his committee that were written by the bank lobbies—

and he saw nothing wrong in accepting $16,000 from the banking industry's campaign committee in 1972 (more than five times what any other politician got), or $10,000 from other banking groups around the country, or $11,200 in honoraria from banking groups to whom he gave speeches. Nor did he see anything wrong back in 1962 when he was one of the few people to be offered stock in a new District of Columbia bank at a preferred rate while just about everyone in town was trying to get a piece; he took the offer, and then allowed the bank itself to secure the loan which he took out to pay for the stock, a piece of business that was not only immoral but flatly illegal. Nor did he see anything wrong when in 1973 he sponsored a bill to give the Continental Investment Corporation a special three-year hiatus before having to change its lucrative brokerage-mutual-fund churning scheme, even though the scheme was already under fire from the SEC; in this instance part of his blindness may have to do with the fact that Continental had just finished muscling everyone in its home office to cough up $100 or more apiece for Sparkman's 1972 campaign.

Wilbur Mills, the Arkansas Democrat, is particularly vulnerable to outside pressure because until 1975 he was the chairman of the Ways and Means Committee, which writes most tax and financial legislation for the country, and he still remains one of the few to understand the labyrinthine complexities of the tax laws. But no circumspection for him. In a brazen attempt to see who his corporate friends were, Mills made a nominal bid for the Presidency in 1972 which hadn't the least hope of getting him anywhere near the White House but was very useful in raising some $493,000 for his incidental needs. An even $100,000 of that came from Ross Perot's Electronic Data Systems in Dallas, which is in the business of computerizing health-insurance programs for various state governments and was concerned with legislation then in Mills's committee which could send EDS a multimillion-dollar windfall; the congressman's Rimian response: "No one's found anything wrong with it." Another $50,000 or so came from oil and energy companies—including an illegal $15,000 corporate handout from the Gulf Oil Company, the knowing acceptance of which is a crime—and Mills, who has always favored the oil industry in writing the nation's tax laws, this time responded by burying "windfall-profits" proposals and oil-depletion limitations so deep in the legislative morass that it couldn't even get through either the 1973 or the 1974 session. Still another $185,000 or so was given to Mills by dairy and agribusiness interests—again including at least $75,000 of illegal corporate funds from the much-tainted Associated Milk Producers, Inc., of San Antonio —and it so happened that Mills was the leading champion in Congress for higher milk prices. Finally, the largest individual donation came from Dick Riddell, a Washington lobbyist who worked for several large shoe-manufacturing companies, and it came just after Mills had intervened with the IRS and persuaded it to give up its extensive investigations of the shoe-manufacturing industry. Again, the complacent Mills tried to defend this interference as "one of his functions" as co-chairman of the Joint Committee on Taxation, but he seems not to have read that part of the Constitution where it suggests that the duty of Congress is simply to write the laws, not carry them out.

Corruption is all relative, to be sure. But the blatant accrual of $493,000 from special interests for whom special favors are done can hardly be considered anything else. Yet the good people of Arkansas don't seem to see it that way: they have elected him eighteen consecutive times.

Barry Goldwater, the Arizona senator, is less a political power in the Congress than a moral power, and as such might be expected to have the cleanest skirts in the Senate. However, Goldwater seems not to have made very clear moral distinctions at the start of his career, for he has acknowledged being friends with Gus Greenbaum, who just happened to be the king of organized crime in Arizona at the time. Greenbaum had established himself in Phoenix in the late 1920s and was in charge of a lucrative wire service for organized crime in the 1930s and '40s, a fact well enough known to the police of Phoenix, if not the future senator, when they raided Greenbaum's operation in the late 1940s. Greenbaum then shifted operations to Las Vegas, where for ten years he ran the Flamingo and Riviera hotels for Meyer Lansky and was a prominent companion of underworld biggies, a fact again well enough known to the American public, if not the future senator, through the Kefauver hearings in 1950. Even while senator, Barry Goldwater (along with his brother Robert) was a frequent patron of the Vegas casinos during the Greenbaum years—particularly Lansky's Flamingo Hotel—though Barry seems to have curtailed his gaming around 1958, at about the same time that his friend Gus was found in his Phoenix home, his throat slashed by a butcher knife, the victim of a gangland slaying that remains unsolved to this day. Despite all this, when this lurid history became a public issue during Goldwater's 1964 campaign, the senator refused to acknowledge any impropriety and asserted that he had "no apologies to make." And as if to show that the Greenbaum association was no fluke, Goldwater also admitted knowing one Willie Bioff, a convicted labor extortionist out of the 1940s; and not only did he know Bioff, travel publicly with him, and fly him around in his own private plane, but he acknowledged that Bioff served as a "labor adviser" and had donated money to his 1952 campaign. This cozy association came to an end in 1954, when Bioff, who had ratted on his former Hollywood friends to federal prosecutors, was blown up by a bomb planted in his pickup truck at his Phoenix ranch.

If it be argued, however, that the sins of his friends should not be heaped upon Goldwater, what about the sins of his brother? Does the pontificating senator, arbitrator of moral rectitude, have no responsibility for the fact that his brother is a charter member of San Diego's Rancho La Costa, where he himself has visited, or for the fact that his brother's Arrowhead Ranch in Arizona employs between 100 and 150 illegal Mexican laborers, at $1.05 an hour, while the ranch makes a million dollars a year ($1,164,766 in 1971)? Or does that, too, require "no apologies"?

John McClellan of Arkansas, who has achieved his greatest fame by righteously going after labor unions he presumed to be crooked and left-wing groups he presumed to be subversive, might well save some of his saintly zeal for his own province. Throughout his entire career he has never taken a single action which effectively interfered with the illegal but well-known gambling empire run by Owney "Killer" Madden and his organized-crime crew in Hot Springs, Arkansas, a few hours' drive from McClellan's home; the empire was disturbed by Arkansas Governor Winthrop Rockefeller in the late 1960s—could it be that even *transplanted* yankees have a different moral code?—

but without the slightest help from the senior senator. Nor has McClellan ever taken a single action that would clean up the electoral practices of his state, notorious even in the South for corruption and chicanery, apparently condoning the judgment of one academician who has noted that among the citizens of Arkansas "revelations of law-breaking in this field provoke more public amusement than public indignation."

McClellan's torpor can be shattered, however, when it comes to the affairs of banks. For virtually all of his thirty-odd years in the Senate, he has been one of the largest shareholders and a director of the First National Bank of Little Rock and simultaneously one of the most faithful champions of the banking industry. One example of his high-minded service was his outraged campaign against an effort by the Treasury Department to license additional national banks during the 1960s, thus cutting into the monopolies of existing banks, and it turned out that the three charters he was particularly anxious to squelch had been asked for by groups in Little Rock, Arkansas. Such is his power that he managed to halt the licensing and, for a time at least, preserve his neat little banking hegemony down home.

The sorry list could go on, through most of the Rim delegations. . . . Florida Congressman Sam Gibbons is an unabashed champion of industries whose companies retain his law firm in Tampa. . . . North Carolina Democrat Richardson Preyer, who enjoys a small fortune because his family owns the company that makes Vicks drug products, openly admits that "my one big conflict of interest is chemicals and I'm on the public health [sub]committee," but he hasn't done anything about it. . . . Republican Congressman Bob Wilson of San Diego so openly abused his congressional franking privilege for private political mailings that he was hauled into court in 1972 and found guilty—but the judge dismissed the case because the custom was "practiced by nearly every other Congressman in the United States". . . . Nevada Senator Howard Cannon, who as chairman of the Rules Committee sat in judgment on Nelson Rockefeller's qualifications to be Vice-President, is cozy enough with the gamblers who own the casinos on the Las Vegas Strip to be able to say, "I flatter myself I know every one of them," and in the past he had no qualms about having testimonial dinners at the Flamingo Hotel while it was owned by front men for Meyer Lansky. . . . The recently deposed Democratic chairman of the House Agriculture Committee, W. R. Poage of Texas, and the Republican ranking member, Charles Teague of California, both happen to have vast agribusiness interests: the former in a large cotton estate to which agricultural subsidies have regularly been paid, the latter in his family's lemon plantation, the largest in the country. . . . Arizona Representative Sam Steiger in 1973 authorized his assistant to place an illegal bugging device in a San Diego hotel in order to overhear a couple of race-track operators suspected of connections with organized crime—but what he wanted the illegal information for is not quite clear, since Steiger himself has been accused of having connections with organized crime. . . . Senator Joseph Montoya of New Mexico, one of the moralizers on the Ervin committee, laundered campaign gifts in 1970 through dummy Washington committees to avoid reporting them publicly in New Mexico—and for three years denied that he knew about such gifts; the reports that he *did* file were submitted illegally with forged signatures. . . . Oklahoma Senator Henry Bellmon, who owns a giant ranch in northern Oklahoma, has always been a friend of the farmer—as, for example, when he pushed through a bill allowing federal land banks to increase the size of their low-cost loans on farm land—and then turned around and got a loan of no less than $475,000 from the local land bank office; but then Bellmon has always been a rather shrewd financial man—he managed to pay only $24,000 in state *and* federal taxes over an eleven-year period. . . . James Eastland, who is in charge of the Senate Judiciary Committee, has been named in court papers as the recipient of a $50,000 payoff from oilionaire Nelson Bunker Hunt for helping to try to squelch a federal investigation into various Hunt shenanigans in Texas; Eastland denies taking the cash but has acknowledged the impropriety of intervening in the case not once but three different times, all the way up to the Justice Department which his committee is supposed to be overseeing. . . . Republican James Collins of Texas was involved in a kickback scheme a few years ago which resulted in a conviction for his top aide and a four-year-long investigation by the Justice Department, but he himself escaped indictment at the last minute through the intervention of Attorney General William Saxbe. . . . Even the Speaker of the House,

Oklahoma's Carl Albert, a man who for months was first in line to succeed to the Presidency, has not elevated himself above his culture: pressured by an Oklahoma electronics firm, he forced the Small Business Administration into a gross violation of federal regulations in granting no less than $4 million worth of contracts to the firm, bailing it out of a threatened bankruptcy. . . . And one could go on.

However unsavory, it is only rarely that malfeasance of this kind becomes grounds for official congressional inquiries or outright criminal action, since neither prosecutors nor juries nor least of all the congressional establishment want to open up the nation's highest legislative body to charges of honest-to-God illegality. From time to time, however, due to unforeseen lapses or insufficiently politicized juries, federal legislators are involved in full-scale scandals and occasionally even tried or convicted. In the last thirty years, 23 representatives have been connected with serious criminal acts of one kind or another, 7 of them from the Southern Rim, which is statistically about normal; during that time 8 senators have been so tainted, 5 of them from the Southern Rim, which is far above the norm. The record of senatorial impropriety is fulsome: Mississippi's Theodore Bilbo was found by a Senate committee in 1947 to be guilty of illegal dealings with war contractors; Florida's George Smathers was named by a Senate committee as one of the business partners in Bobby Baker's illegal shenanigans, the only politician so identified; California's George Murphy admitted receiving at least $20,000 a year and other perquisites from Patrick Frawley's Technicolor Corporation while passing on legislation of interest to both the rabid rightist and his corporation; Florida's Edward Gurney was indicted for a bribery and kickback scheme netting him a $233,000 slush fund; and Louisiana's Russell Long, as we have seen, had an indictment voted against him and recommended twice for his part in the House Office Building scandal. Interestingly, only two of these senatorial scandals resulted in outright criminal charges, and Gurney achieved the distinction of being the first sitting senator to be indicted on serious criminal charges since 1924.

The absolute brazenness of the Gurney case, as outlined in the federal indictment, says something about the way the cowboy political mind must work. According to the government,

Gurney sat down one day in December 1970 with two officials of the Florida office of HUD, two ranking officials of the Florida Republican Party, and two of his close assistants—political people, all—and coolly hatched a scheme to go around forcing Florida real-estate developers to kick in to a private Gurney treasure chest if they wanted any special treatment out of HUD in the way of all-important federal mortgage insurance and housing contracts. For more than two years, apparently, this extortionist scheme operated without a hitch, piling up some $400,000, according to one of the participants, with at least thirty-nine Florida real-estate people going right along with the illegality until 1973, when one bold soul protested and the *Miami Herald* began the investigation that eventually blew the case open. Was Gurney repentant? Absurd. He admitted that he may have been "careless" and "unobserving," and he admitted that he got a good deal of unexpected money in 1972 when he wasn't even running for office, and he admitted that he didn't ever report that money as he was legally required to—but still, in his eyes, those clear gray eyes so familiar to the nation during the Ervin hearings, he was guilty of "no wrongdoing." No wonder that it was this man who was the Ervin committee's prime defender of Richard Nixon.

An uncanny premonition out of the past. "The political dilemma was as clear in 1870 as it was likely to be in 1970," wrote Henry Adams as he surveyed the Washington of a century ago. "The system of 1789 had broken down, and with it the eighteenth-century fabric of *a priori*, or moral, principles." As was true of the previous great period of swift and chaotic growth in the late nineteenth century, so it is true of this one in the mid-twentieth century, and the end point is, as Adams noted, a Washington of "endless corruption." For Adams, the window was Crédit Mobilier and the robber-baron mentality; for us, the window is Watergate.

VI

A small coda. What can one make of the fact that organized crime bears all the characteristics of the cowboy political style?

Insofar as the kingpins of organized crime are known to have political views, they coincide remarkably with the more retrograde conservatives of the Southern Rim. Like many Rimsters, they are interested in minimizing federal interference in local affairs, and it doesn't matter if it's the Justice Department's voting registrar or the IRS's tax investigator. Like many Rimsters, they have become fiercely anti-Communist, for reasons ranging all the way from bitterness over Castro's elimination of the gambling casinos to identification with minorities in the Soviet Union; Meyer Lansky sounds just like Strom Thurmond on the subject of Vietnam, according to one of his friends a few years ago: "He thinks we should go in there and blow Hanoi to pieces. He's really disgusted with all these demonstrations against the war." Like many Rimsters, they have an abiding distaste for the liberal types who want to change the way things are run, for the people who want to clean up the gambling towns and numbers rackets are usually the same people who want to clean up the legislatures and city councils. And like many Rimsters, especially the self-made millionaires, they tend to equate riches with patriotism; as one federal agent put it after a long time investigating organized crime:

> A lot of your mob chiefs are fierce conservatives. They're the guys who came to this country with nothing and who did very well here, who found this a land of plenty. So, in the right-wing sense of the word, they're quite the ardent patriots.

Which may be why Meyer Lansky pulled every string he knew to get his son Paul into West Point.

Organized crime is also notoriously racist. Not only are the various mobs organized almost exclusively on ethnic grounds—Italians, Jewish, Irish—and consciously kept that way, but they have been continuously hostile to the black and Puerto Rican underlings who try to rise through the ranks: "A black man's got a better chance of being elected mayor of Selma, Alabama," a black hoodlum complains, "than of making it into the big money with the mob." And when the mobs moved into the Southern Rim, they were quick to conform to local racist customs, as for example in Las Vegas (according to one exposé of that city):

> The poor whites from Texas, Louisiana, Florida and other points south moved into the state with their gambling devices and bootlegged money and took over not only the gambling but the social and political life of the state as well. They were thugs and thieves and murderers, but they were white, and segregation set in overnight. When the eastern and northern gangsters arrived they were quick to protect the *status quo*. They didn't want any Nigrahs upsetting their high-rolling southern gentlemen, who had more oil wells than the gangsters had slot machines.

Organized crime found it advantageous, too, to make alliances with the white power structure wherever possible, and more often than not the gangsters were willing to be called upon in the days of violent resistance to keep the schools and restaurants undefiled, in return for which, of course, the white power structure was expected to do the same at the local casino. There's less of the rough stuff these days in the South, but gangland has proved very adaptable: when the California grape and lettuce growers and their Teamster allies wanted to use muscle against the Chicano farm workers, they simply applied to the Southern California crime lords and easily got the hoods they needed to carry on some of the most brutal union-busting since the old days on the New York waterfront.

About the affinity of organized crime with repression, little needs to be said, repression clearly being the base of the whole enterprise in the first place—repression of the junkies, gamblers, johns, borrowers, and misfits, of the flunkies and the underlings in the mobs, of the police and politicians who interfere, of the citizens who don't go along or somehow get in the way. No movie, nor a score of them, can convey the utter brutality of which organized crime is capable in grasping its own way and ordering its own house.

About the corruption of organized crime, a simple redundancy, nothing needs to be said. About the corruption of *politics* by organized crime, however, a few things must be said. For one, syndicate crime in recent years seems to have developed the same attraction to the politics of the Southern Rim that it has displayed for the business of the Southern Rim. Part of the explanation for this is simple: money, and the fact that organized crime had it and many cowboy politicians did not. As one of Carlos Marcello's henchmen has put it:

> You have to remember that when Carlos and I were starting out in the rackets just about the only money available for political campaigns in Louisiana and other Southern states was rackets money. They were poor states. There were no "fat cats" around to finance political campaigns. If a guy wanted to run for any important office, the only place he could get any money from was us.
>
> So we got control of the political machinery. We picked the candidates; we paid for their campaigns; we paid them off; we told them what to do. We even provided the poll-watchers and vote-counters. It didn't really matter how many votes a candidate got. What counted was how many votes we tallied for him.

Texas was one of the places where such a system worked very well during the 1940s and '50s, mostly under the direction of Jack "Big Fix" Halfen, who operated gambling rackets out of Houston said to be worth more than $20 million a year in profits. Texas was by no means a poor state in those days, but the racketeers were happy to join the oilmen and the real-estate developers in donating to trustworthy politicians, and Halfen was among the happiest; a former U.S. attorney who eventually went after Halfen describes him as "a payoff man of unbelievably large proportions." Among the worthy officials who benefited from Halfen's criminal largesse were said to be Houston Sheriff Neal Polk, Houston Congressman Albert Thomas, and, according to Halfen himself, Lyndon Baines Johnson, for whom, he said, he was "a prime financial contributor and political supporter." Johnson never owned up to taking rackets money, though there is no doubt he was a close friend of Halfen's, and later, when Halfen was sent to prison, it was the parole board under President Lyndon Johnson which unexpectedly let him off before half his term was up. (On the other hand, Johnson never did feel much aversion to gangsters: he let his protégé Bobby Baker, a man he "loved like his own son," hang around with every piece of filth in the world of organized crime for a half-dozen years and never seemed to mind a bit.)

California is another state where the connections between organized crime and politics have been marked, dating from the heyday of Artie Samish, the lobbyist who represented organized crime's interest in the state so well that he became known as "the unelected governor of California" before being bustled off to jail for tax evasion. At least three known powers in the state Democratic Party in the last few years have had criminal backgrounds or connections: John "Jake the Barber" Factor, who is a product of the Capone mob, successively a stock swindler, a mail-fraud convict, a Las Vegas gambler, and a perjurer, nowadays passes himself off as a legitimate Los Angeles businessman and is a regular, sizable contributor to Democratic politicians; Paul Ziffrin, who was a one-time protégé of Chicago boss Jake Arvey and a business partner of a Chicago gangster wiped out in a gangland slaying, has been a Democratic national committeeman (he resigned in the face of unfavorable publicity about his background) and the chairman of Edmund Muskie's Southern California campaign committee in 1972; and Ben Swig, who has been a partner in California real estate with a criminal who had a police record in three different states and was known to be making investments for the Chicago mob. And those who know the insides of California politics say that this is only the merest scratch on the surface.

But the most notorious convergence between organized crime and politics, and until quite recently the most ominous, is that which centered on the Presidency of Richard Nixon.

It is perhaps not important that so many of Nixon's friends have connections with the underworld: Arnholt Smith, whose banking empire was intertwined with the gambling business of John Alessio and other criminals; Bebe Rebozo, who owns a bank which has been the repository of stolen stock, who has invested in a Bahamas gambling company, and who is repeatedly reported to be mixed up in Meyer Lansky's cash-laundering operations; Walter Annenberg, whose fortune is based on his father's wire-service operation for organized crime and who was indicted with his father in 1939 in connection with these underworld ties; James Crosby, head of Resorts International, which owns a Bahamas casino which has employed Lansky henchmen and has ties to the Lansky syndicate.

It is somewhat more important that so many of the people Nixon put into positions of power had connections with organized crime: Murray Chotiner, who became a White House counsel, had been a lawyer for scores of West Coast crime figures and for Philadelphia mobster Marco Reginelli; Frank Fitzsimmons, the head of the Teamsters who was appointed to Nixon's Pay Board, has shared in most of the slimy deals between the Teamsters Pension Fund and organized crime, is a frequent companion of mobsters at the La Costa Country Club, and was overheard by the FBI in 1973 arranging an illegal kickback scheme with a series of big-time California and Chicago Mafiosi; William Safire, who became a Nixon speechwriter and adviser after a long career as a PR agent, during which he worked, along with certain unsavory friends of Meyer Lansky, for Bahamian gambling interests, including the Lucayan Beach Hotel, home of the Lansky-controlled Lucayan Beach Casino; Peter Brennan, who was appointed Secretary of Labor, had previously been a union chief in New York City's totally corrupt construction industry, where he was a friend and associate of a convicted extortioner, a convicted bookmaker, an indicted extortioner. and various other associates of organized crime; Frederick LaRue, the Mississippi oilman who was attached to the White House as all-around hatchet man from 1969 to 1972, had previously sold his family business to, and thereupon received annual salaries and generous loans from, a Texas swindler with a record of repeated Mafia dealings.

But most important of all is that Nixon's own career indicates repeated contacts with the shadow world of gambling syndicates, operators, and organized crime's Southern Rim wheeler-dealing. Right at the beginning of his career, during either his 1948 or 1950 campaign, according to California gangster Mickey Cohen, Nixon spoke to and raised $25,000 at a banquet attended by Los Angeles and Las Vegas hoodlums invited by Murray Chotiner, and despite later denials it strains

credulity to think that he didn't know with whom he was breaking bread. Several times in the late 1940s Nixon visited Florida
and went yachting or fishing with Chubby Wofford, of Miami
Beach's fancy Wofford Hotel, a mob-controlled establishment
owned by various New York and Cleveland gangsters and
named by Estes Kefauver in 1950 as one of the three centers of
organized crime in south Florida. In 1952, when Lansky was
consolidating his hold on organized crime's gambling empire in
Cuba and young Senator Nixon was putting together a slush
fund so that he could make ends meet, Nixon visited a Havana
casino owned by gangster Norman Rothman in the company of
the California businessman who managed that fund (Dana
Smith) and who dropped at least $4,200 at the tables. In 1959,
he allowed one-time California hood Frank Vitali, "once involved in the biggest bootlegging conspiracy on the West Coast,"
according to investigators, to accompany him on the plane
during his famous visit to Russia to insult Khrushchev. In 1962,
Nixon paid the first of many visits to the Bahamas, during the
period that Lansky and friends were trying to establish a toe-
hold there, and he showed up at the opening of the Nassau Bay
Club casino in 1967 and the Paradise Island casino in 1968,
both times as an honored guest. In 1963, he was named in a
Miami police report which claimed that Bebe Rebozo's Florida
laundromat was actually operating a *bolita* (numbers) operation and theorized that Rebozo was "fronting in this operation
for ex-Vice President Nixon"; the charge was never proved. In
1966 and 1967, Nixon bought stock in a Florida real-estate
company with $65,000 borrowed from Rebozo and his pals and
$100,000 from a bank which had as a director Max Orovitz, a
business associate of a number of organized crime's finest, a
man on the payroll of a Bahamas casino, a henchman of Meyer
Lansky throughout the 1960s, and later a convicted stock
manipulator. In 1967, Nixon was named by a convicted bookmaker and Lansky frontman Max Courtney, in sworn testimony
delivered to the Royal Commission of Inquiry into Bahamian
gambling, as among his most important customers—a charge
that Nixon never denied. In 1967 also, Nixon bought two lots
on Key Biscayne from a man the Secret Service later found so
"unsavory" that they wouldn't even let the President hang

around him, and who in turn had bought the property from a company widely thought to be a real-estate front for Lansky; this real-estate purchase was so odious that Nixon went to unusual lengths to conceal it.

During his Presidential tenure, Nixon's overt connections to the world of organized crime, if any, remained well hidden; no doubt the organization of his own malefactors took up most of his time. But there were a number of acts of commission and omission that suggest he had not forgotten his felonious friends and that he may even have been in their debt. The fact that his 1972 commutation let mobster Angelo "Gyp" DeCarlo out of prison to head his New Jersey mob for another year before his death is smelly but not really so significant, nor was his acquiescence in the early release from prison of Calvin Kovens, a real-estate operator and Florida Teamster official who had been sent up for a Pension Fund fraud. But the commutation of the sentence against Jimmy Hoffa, about whose criminal dealings over two decades no half-wit could be unaware, smacked of something more ominous; it may have been part of a deal with Frank Fitzsimmons in return for the Teamsters' endorsement of his 1972 election, but since Fitzsimmons had no earthly reason to want to see his predecessor and rival out of jail, the possibility is left open that it was a more sinister kind of payoff—perhaps, according to a report said to have been drawn up by Dun and Bradstreet, repayment for Teamster laundering of Mafia money used to buy the San Clemente estate in 1969. Similar possibilities are suggested, too, by the fact that under Nixon the Justice Department killed various criminal prosecutions and investigations of organized-crime figures—among them mob lawyer Morris Shenker, New Jersey Mafioso Daniel Gagliardi, and the California mobsters who were cooking up deals with the Teamsters—and it so bollixed a routine wiretapping authorization in a case against some six hundred organized crime figures in Florida that the whole thing was thrown out of court and the men went free. Taken together with the extraordinarily inefficient "war" on organized crime, the abrupt firing of mob-busting U.S. Attorney Robert Morgenthau in 1969, the penetration by organized crime into Vietnam and the Southeast Asian drug traffic roughly coincident with the Nixon Presidency, and the award of funds from the Small Business Administration to companies owned by organized crime in New York, Chicago, and New Orleans, it all suggests that something more than a coincidence is at work here.

At the very minimum, it seems clear, Richard Nixon did not have a moral sense sufficient to steer him clear of repeated contacts with people in and around organized crime, nor a moral calibrator sufficient to keep him from appointing some very dubious characters to high posts in his Administration. At the maximum, it is possible that Richard Nixon was one more of the large number of politicians in this country who have been bought or cajoled into the service of the ends of organized crime.

By comparison, even Richard Kleindienst begins to look good.

5

The Cowboy Conquest

Politics does not make strange bedfellows; it only seems that way to those who have not been following the courtship.

The bedfellows who surrounded Richard Nixon during his six years in the Presidency, the ones who helped him shape his policies and guided his thinking, those whose interests he held most dear and whose purposes he was most constrained to serve, were, inevitably, those who had wooed Richard Nixon throughout his life and were only too happy to share his Presidential bed. They were the bland and tanned young gophers out of Southern California, the public-relations executives and hustling lawyers from the mid-century boom cities, the "self-made" millionaires of Key Biscayne and Newport Beach and Houston and the Bahamas, the cost-plus defense and technology contractors, the new-money oilionaires, the real-estate manipulators, the ranchers and agribusinessmen, the growth-area entrepreneurs and politicians. In short, they were the movers and shapers of the Southern Rim.

The Nixon Presidency was the culmination of cowboy influence in American affairs, the climax of the thirty-year period of increasing political power. In big ways and little, in conscious ways and not, the Nixon Administration strove to consolidate the influence of the new forces of the land, to shove aside the older, settled forces of the Northeast, to enact laws, create policies, enforce rules, appoint politicians, establish budgets, that would give the cowboys an equal space on the national stage. For almost six years—and in certain lingering ways for much longer than that—the cowboy thrust was supremely successful: Nixon and his Rimsters put their mark upon the ways of the nation, remade Washington at least partially in their own image, maneuvered the Congress to shape their kinds of legislation, led or manipulated public opinion in support of their policies, and in general, insofar as it is within the power of any single Administration, directed the country to their purposes. It is only a symbol of all this, but too obvious to be overlooked, that Nixon chose to establish his two vacation "White Houses" outside of Washington in San Clemente, California, and Key Biscayne, Florida—the precise terminals of the Southern Rim.

I

It has often been said that Richard Nixon was a man without a home, a "rootless" figure, without a "stamp of place," undefined by geography, lacking the unmistakable regional imprints of his two immediate predecessors. But that is impossible, of course—it is asking us to believe that the first twenty-eight years of his life did not exist, that he was somehow deprived of the cultural imprints of childhood and adolescence. The fact is that Nixon bore very clearly the stamp of place, only the place was Southern California, and *that* was rootless and ill-defined, a mercurial, restless society. "To understand Nixon fully," writes Bruce Mazlish, the historian who has probed deeper into his psyche than any outsider, "one would need carefully to analyze the turbulent currents of California life, values, and politics."

The Southern California that was Richard Nixon's "place" was very much a part of the frontier tradition, not more than a few years away from the end of the actual gun-totin' shoot-'em-up era. There was still ingrained in it the frontier virtues of hard work, perseverance, dedication; the frontier spirit of manifest destiny and of triumph over lesser breeds; the frontier culture of ruggedness, *machismo*, a scorn of book-learnin' and the sissified polish of the East; the frontier identification with the small town and hostility to the large city in particular, urbanity in general; the frontier custom of individualism, praising the self-made and damning the government-run; the frontier ethic of pragmatism, what works, over moralism, what's right. But the frontier tradition could never hold still, and when there was no more frontier for it to go to, when the Pacific Ocean became the last insuperable barrier, it began to double back on itself, creating the contradictions that beleaguer the mid-century California soul. Movement became more important than direction, everything was kept in a state of flux, always in motion—the ideas, values, people, political parties, soon enough the innumerable cars—as if invisible new frontiers had to be constructed where the real one had to end. Change became more important than stability, nothing was immutable, everything could be tried and tested, the world was open to the new—and true tradition had to wither, established values fall, coherent communities disintegrate. The "American Dream" took precedence over American reality, with the fierce pursuit of success, or at least of the trappings of success, and a sense that what counts most is the appearance, the image, the surface, that life is a matter of roles, "scenarios," public relations, for which culture there is no higher testament than Hollywood itself. Old ways gave place to new, but nervously so, breeding the bewilderment and uncertainty that made the area prey to any holistic dogma of religion or of government, most notably the virulent superpatriotism and the hysterical anti-Communism that became the hallmark of its mid-century politics. And ultimately in this doubling-back, insecurities—of self, of job, of purpose—became etched upon the persona, absorbed into the community, accepted into political life.

It was, inevitably, this California culture that began the shaping of Richard Nixon, and in it can be found the characteristics, filtered, obviously, through his own particular circumstances, that were to guide so much of his life. The obsession with movement, for example—there was always in Nixon's mind that train he listened to as a child ("He hears the train go by at night and dreams of faraway places he would like to go," as he put it in his 1968 acceptance speech), and it is no surprise that he traveled more than any other President in the nation's history, continually moving his entourage to San Clemente or

Key Biscayne or picking up to go to one summit conference or another . . . the need for combat, for testing—hence the compulsive campaigning that has measured his entire adult life, the preoccupation with *getting* elected rather than *being* elected ("When you have won one battle is the time you should step up your effort to win another") . . . the dependence upon pragmatism—as witnessed by the lack of ethics that characterized his entire public life, as demonstrated by his response to John Dean's suggestion of hush money for the Watergate burglars: "It is wrong, it won't work" . . . the mercurial nature of his moods and his policies—as if, in the words of Theodore White, "the changing unsettled society of Southern California in which he grew up had imparted to him some of its own essential uncertainty" . . . the insecurity that leads to suspicions and hatreds—or, as the *Wall Street Journal* put it once, "an enemy syndrome within him—a deep conviction that he stands almost alone against a hostile world" . . . the concern for appearances and images—from his acting successes in high school to his "scenarios" in the White House, this was a man guided by his *persona* rather than his *self*, and in office quite naturally substituted pomp for authority, publicity for legitimacy, public relations for public support. . . .

But the evidence is, of course, everywhere throughout the man's life: he carried with him a California heritage, as indelible as a language, from his childhood to his Presidency.

Richard Nixon's parents had both come to California in pursuit of the American Dream—Frank Nixon for the material success that always seemed to elude him back East, Hannah Milhous and her family for the isolation in which to practice their unorthodox religion—and they impressed both aspects of this dream upon young Richard. Very little of the success came the Nixons' way, actually—a fact which Nixon mentioned with some bitterness in his farewell speech—but they kept at it, all of the children being required to work in the family grocery store in Whittier, and it was made clear to all of them that they were expected to rise up the ladder: "My mother and father had this devotion: the thing they lived for was the five of us—they wanted us to have a better chance than they did." Religion, somewhat easier to attain, was also important in young Richard's life, but it was a religion very much in the Southern Rim fundamentalist mold, a combination of his father's hell-fire Methodism and his mother's West Coast brand of Quakerism (much closer to the boisterous Baptism of, say, Billy Graham than the pacifistic piety of William Penn), and it even included a revival-meeting "commitment to Christ" while he was in high school.

Through the course of his education Richard Nixon learned at least one thing: for him nose-to-the-grindstone labor and eye-on-the-prize perseverance would have to make up for the intellectual and imaginative brilliance which he lacked. It was this drive which took him through high school and on to Whittier College, a tiny Quaker school in his hometown, this drive which led him to run continually in student elections, even to go out for the football team with the full knowledge that, as his friends put it, "Dick had two left feet"—and to *stay* on the football team when he became the twelfth man on an eleven-man squad. After graduation Nixon set his sights on law school, with some prescient sense that lawyers are truly the aristocracy of America, but since he had neither the money nor the schooling to go for the big schools, he had to wait until someone came to him; luckily Duke University had just started a law school and was giving away scholarships with some alacrity and very little appraisal, so Nixon went to the other end of the Southern Rim for three years, and again a single-mindedness and what his classmates described as "an iron butt" got him through. Diploma in hand, Nixon joined two other classmates on a trip to New York to find jobs with Establishmentarian law firms— "they applied at practically all the well-known law offices"—but though his friends were offered jobs, the awkward provincial from California was not, and the rejection by the heart of the Eastern Establishment must have been a painful reinforcement of his Rimian preconceptions about the wicked East.

Returning then to Whittier, at the time beginning to be swallowed up by Los Angeles, Nixon put in long hours at a backwater firm where he handled divorces and drunks, opened a "branch office" in a desk in a nearby city, joined every civic club around (and usually ran for president), gave speeches wherever and whenever asked, and even helped found a small food-processing plant that tried (without success) to package

frozen orange juice—the whole thing representing a bitch-
goddess lust and an absorption with *movement* at any cost, in
search of a career, a fortune, a self. When World War II came
along, Nixon for some reason chose to try another run at the
Northeastern citadel, this time signing up for a stint with the
Office of Price Administration in Washington, but after a year
of it he became, in his words, "greatly disillusioned about bureaucracy and about what the government could do" and re-
acted strongly to what he called "the old, violent New Deal
crowd" around him; his boss of the time recalls that "Nixon
was uncomfortable among the liberals, the Eastern law-school
graduates, the Jews he rubbed shoulders with on the job. . . .
Because he lacked sophistication and the big-city graces, he
never quite fit in." That experience, too, a failure, Nixon up and
joined the Navy—he didn't have to, being a Quaker, but there
was nothing else beckoning—and eventually was posted to the
South Pacific, where he apparently made a good deal of money
from poker and an improvised hamburger stand before being
returned to Washington for the last few months of the war.

Notable during these years, in addition to other characteristics of restlessness and uncertainty, was a certain carelessness
about moral principles which set oddly with the surface pietism
and religiosity of the young man. At Whittier College, for example, a good Quaker place, dancing was outlawed as un-Chris-
tian barbarism, but Nixon knew that most of the students
wanted it on campus, and so when he ran for student-body
president he made the acceptance of dancing on campus his
major plank, against his own, his mother's, and his college's
principles. (He won: ominous portent.) At Duke Law School,
though he was in competition with only twenty-two other students and was a relentless grind anyway, he broke into the
dean's office to find out what his grades were. As a young
lawyer, arguing his very first case in court, he filed a fraudulent
affidavit to cover up his mishandling of the case, prompting the
judge involved to threaten disbarment and question whether
Nixon had "the ethical qualifications to practice law in the state
of California." And in his South Pacific naval career, though
fully aware that gambling was abhorrent to Quaker principles
and his fundamentalist family, he seemed not to be troubled in
the least in taking up poker, not for fun, not to pass the time,

but for the express purpose of making money; and as to the hamburger stand that proved so successful, no one seems to have satisfactorily explained where all the supplies came from, since Nixon's tiny unit had no PX and no ready access to food except from the regular mess, which, needless to say, was not supposed to be in the business of supporting private enterprise.

Nixon's postwar political career shows more of the same, the combination of single-minded drive, relentless motion, inner uncertainty, superficial composure, and two traits that were to be absolutely embedded in the Nixon personality: an ingrown Rimian antipathy to the Northeast and a self-serving immorality in political campaigning, both of which guided his entire life.

The anti-yankee character that infuses so much of the Southern Rim was particularly strong in Nixon—darkened in him by a certain enviousness, an almost mythic jealousy—and it was developed still further by a political vocation built upon a running battle against one or another figure with roots in the Eastern Establishment. Part of this, to be sure, was a result of the adversarian nature of the cowboy culture, its constant sense of competition with the world back East, but a greater part had to do with the fact that anyone in pursuit of power at Nixon's historical moment would inevitably have had to contend with the long-standing controllers of the power, so predominantly of the Northeast.

The "enemies list" in Nixon's career is studded with various wise men and women out of the East: Jerry Voorhis, Kansas-born, with an old, established family and an Ivy League education; Helen Gahagan Douglas, a fashionable and elegant Easterner, married to a suave New York Jew; Dean Acheson and Adlai Stevenson, personifications of the sophisticated, somewhat snobbish world of high politics, well-born, intellectual, too, and monied; Nelson Rockefeller, John Kennedy, Larry O'Brien, John Lindsay, Edmund Muskie, Bobby Kennedy, all scions and darlings of the Northeast; Daniel Ellsberg, the Berrigan brothers, Leonard Woodcock, John Gardner, Howard Stein, Edward Kennedy, Ralph Nader, Katharine Graham, the whole crowd of critics that cried from the Eastern Establishmentarian battlements. (On the *actual* enemies list— the 490 names that John Dean was ordered to give to the IRS for investigation and harassment—exactly 60 percent of the targets were from the Northeast, only 30 percent from the Southern Rim, and just 5 percent from Rim states other than California.) And especially Alger Hiss, the man who made Richard Nixon's reputation at the start, the man that kept coming back to Richard Nixon's mind at the end: here was the very symbol of yankeedom, of aristocratic birth, graduate of Johns Hopkins and Harvard Law School, trained State Department diplomat, New York foundation executive, tall and slim, smooth, easy, courteous, "impressive to everyone in the room," as even Nixon admitted. For Nixon, as he wrote in *Six Crises*, Alger Hiss was

> the symbol of a considerable number of perfectly loyal citizens whose theaters of operation are the nation's mass media and universities, its scholarly foundations, and its government bureaucracies. . . . They are of a mind-set, as doctrinaire as those on the extreme right, which makes them singularly vulnerable to the Communist popular front appeal under the banner of social justice. . . . As soon as the Hiss case broke and well before a bill of particulars was even available, much less open to close critical analysis, they leaped to the defense of Alger Hiss—and to a counterattack of unparalleled venom and irrational fury on his accusers.

And Richard Nixon never—literally never—forgot this ignominy.

Nor, indeed, was he allowed much time to forget. At every juncture, this cowboy challenger came up against one form of the yankee Establishment or other, and it mattered not a whit which party was represented. When he fashioned the only bill in his entire congressional career ever to bear his name—the 1948 Mundt-Nixon bill to register and jail Communists—the Northeastern Democrats led a predictable campaign against its clumsiness and unconstitutionality, but they were joined by almost the whole Northeastern Republican crowd, led by a vociferous Thomas Dewey, which marshaled editorial and congressional opinion against the measure and handily succeeded in burying it. When Nixon was campaigning for the Vice-Presidency and the notorious slush-fund story broke (appropriately, in the *New*

York Post), it was the yankee contingent around Eisenhower which immediately urged that Nixon be dumped and the yankee Republican newspaper, the *New York Herald Tribune*, that called for his resignation, humiliations that must have been as a branding iron to a raw wound; only Nixon's shrewd end-run appeal to the *non*-Establishmentarian, *non*-Eastern party leaders at the Republican National Committee saved him then, and the lesson was not lost. And when Nixon's association with such low-roaders as Joe McCarthy and such high-rollers as Murray Chotiner tempted Eisenhower to dump the Vice-President before the 1956 elections, it was the yankee wing of the Republican Party (Lucius Clay, Paul Hoffman, Sherman Adams) and what columnist David Lawrence called "a 'left wing' coterie in New York City" that tried to precipitate the fall; again, the attempt was thwarted only because Nixon very quietly and successfully rounded up a majority of the grass-roots delegates to the 1956 convention and had them publicly announce their support.

Given all this, it is hardly surprising that Nixon was confirmed in his early antipathy to the world of the Eastern Establishment. Somewhat more surprising, though, is his affinity with political immorality, evidenced in a record rather above the norm even for a nation that has not always concerned itself with the proprieties of its polity. Put quite simply, each of his campaigns, and there were eight of them in all, was marked by one or another kind of shadiness, illegality, subterfuge, or improbity.

In 1946, the race for Congress with which Nixon began his career, he smeared his opponent Jerry Voorhis with the lie (which he *knew* to be a flat-out lie) that Voorhis was endorsed by a Communist-lining labor group, then repeated it in false advertisements and slanderous speeches, enjoying such success with these Red-scare tactics that he made them a part of his permanent repertory. In the 1948 race for Congress, thanks to the madhouse world of California politics where a candidate may file for *both* parties' primaries, Nixon deceitfully passed himself off as a Democrat in the Democratic primary—a postcard mailing to "Dear Fellow Democrats" with a big picture of Nixon—and a Republican in the Republican primary, and won both endorsements and an easy return trip to Washington. In the 1950 race for the Senate against Helen Douglas, his techniques now refined, Nixon openly accused her of following the "Communist line" (again a lie, which he knew to be such), smeared her with false advertising and a "pink sheet" purporting to show her Communist voting record, brought in friend Joseph McCarthy for an endorsement visit, used—or at least did not repudiate—the anti-Semitic campaign services of Gerald L. K. Smith and his crew, took unusually large contributions (between $1- and $2-*million*) from rich Southern California interests plus an improper $5,000 from the Republican Campaign Committee, and won an easy victory. (He was later to say of that offensive performance, "I'm sorry about that episode. I was a very young man." He was in fact thirty-seven years old, an age when most people are presumed to have grown out of their amoral stage.)

In 1952, selected as Vice-President on the Eisenhower ticket because kingmaker Tom Dewey wanted the balance of a Californian, Nixon was caught up in the scandal over the $18,235 slush fund from a Southern California oil–defense–real-estate cabal, money that he had in fact used for down payments on his Washington home and in return for which he cheerfully intervened with federal agencies on his friends' behalf; but with all the artifice he had developed over the years, plus some small help from his little dog Checkers, Nixon was able to turn back the storm and somehow escape totally any penalties for not only having fraudulently disguised the slush-fund bank account but having failed to report this little windfall on his income tax, both of which are punishable offenses. In 1956, pursuing an image as the "new" Nixon, he calculatedly avoided most of the gutter-sniping of the past but still had time to accuse Adlai Stevenson of "playing dangerous politics with American security" and Harry Truman of "taking the low road"—only everyday slander for him; and it was sometime during that fall that he arranged a secret and laundered $205,000 loan from Howard Hughes to his brother Donald, secured by property worth a bare $52,000—a highly unethical, possibly illegal, arrangement between the nation's tenth largest defense contractor and the nation's Vice-President, which ended up by leaving the Nixon family a cool $150,000 richer when Donald defaulted on the loan a few months later. (The Department of Justice under

Kennedy later investigated this whole deal under campaign financing, bribery, and tax statutes, but, though claiming a case, decided not to prosecute for fear that it would look like part of a political vendetta.) In 1960, making his own bid for the Presidency, Nixon showed the depths of his deceit: for politically cosmetic reasons alone he chose to take and repeatedly defend a position on a central issue of the campaign—U.S. relations with Cuba—which was totally contrary to the one he believed in (he himself later confessed it to be "exactly the opposite of the truth"), thus contorting himself into what a Nixon biographer has called "one of the most incredible acts of double dealing ever confessed to by a man in public life."

For his 1962 campaign for governor of California, Nixon devised, planned, financed, and carried out a scheme that managed to combine Red-baiting, fraud, lies, *and* election illegalities. He concocted a spurious "Committee for the Preservation of the Democratic Party in California" which looked like a legitimate Democratic organization but was really paid for and operated by the Nixon campaign, and whose sole function was to manufacture and spread Nixonian libel about the *real* Democratic Party among the voters and newspapers of California; when the Democrats halted the proceedings by taking the issue to court, the judge found that the fraudulent scheme was "reviewed, amended and finally approved by Mr. Nixon personally," that the phony committee had violated two sections of the California elections code, and that the Nixon organization was to be fined and enjoined against such a fraud again. Unfortunately, this particular court case and assignment of guilt was almost totally overlooked, since no one expected to have Richard Nixon to kick around again after his California defeat, and by the next time Nixon surfaced, it had been all but forgotten. A mistake, too, for during the 1968 campaign Nixon showed himself capable of continuing—even refining—his dubious ways: he organized a gutter-level law-'n'-order smear of Attorney General Ramsey Clark which was in part fraudulent (and he *knew* it to be so); he inaugurated the deal with Howard Hughes that eventuated in the illegal $100,000 campaign gift through Bebe Rebozo; he hired at least one undercover operative, John Caulfield, later famous for his various programs of surveillance, sabotage, and snooping on behalf of the Nixon White House; and he almost certainly played some part in the efforts of his old ally and campaign official Anna Chennault in her underhanded attempt to sabotage the Paris peace talks in the week before the election, the stroke that pollster Louis Harris reckons by itself swung the vote in Nixon's favor.

By this time there was only a thin line to cross to arrive at the campaign of 1972, for which Nixon was able to combine the most successful immoralities and illegalities of all those that had gone before, producing without question the most unlawful, illegitimate, malefactory, scandal-ridden, dirt-laden campaign in American history to date, involving, at a minimum, burglary, bribery, fraud, conspiracy, kidnapping, obstruction of justice, perjury, blackmail, illegal fund-raising, assault, mail fraud, and forgery.

It is an extraordinary record, and sad: the triumph of vice over virtue, means over ends, manipulation over morality, Sammy Glick over Uncle Sam. It simply goes to prove that America is a land where the lowest, most common man can become President. And he did.

II

The last great conquest in Richard Nixon's life, the consummation of his restlessness, his drivenness, his adversarianism, was his ascension to the Presidency of the United States. On January 20, 1969, Nixon took his oath of office and began the six-year period that marked the high point of cowboy political power to date. Slowly, daily, steadily, though not always consciously, checked only occasionally by superior forces on his flanks or the accidents of history, Nixon sought to advance the interests and consolidate the supremacy of the Southern Rim in American life. The people around him—those closest to his heart or ear, those he appointed to his staffs and executive posts, those whose interests he sought to serve, the campaign supporters and Congressional confederates, the friends and allies of his Presidency—were to a degree unusual in American history from a single geographic area, and that area was the Southern Rim.

That bears examining. Let us turn first to the friends and

intimates who counseled and comforted him in his Presidency, then to the benefactors who made that office possible, lastly to the official family who guided him throughout its tenure.

It is not true, as it was sometimes said in Washington, that all of Richard Nixon's friends would fit into one of those golf carts he used to ride in at San Clemente and there'd still be room left over for Bob Haldeman's movie camera and a box of flag pins. But the circle of intimates for this most private, distrustful person was indeed never very wide, and the remarkable thing is the number of Southern Rimsters who were a part of it, who were indeed the closest of all to the President.

A number of Nixon's companions date from his earliest days in California: Jack Drown, a magazine distributor in Southern California, whose wife was always quite close to Pat Nixon; Gaylord Parkinson, a Los Angeles physician and Republican politico; Roger Johnson, a California lawyer who also had been close to Nixon's parents. Others became close during the early campaigns: Murray Chotiner, the Los Angeles lawyer and adviser in Nixon's first campaigns; C. Arnholt Smith, the San Diego banker and early fund-raiser; Herb Klein, newspaperman in the Copley organization and periodic press spokesman; Earl C. Adams, senior partner of the Los Angeles law firm which Nixon joined after his 1962 California defeat; Paul Keyes, a Hollywood TV producer and occasional media adviser. It is perhaps not surprising that all of these people were from California, since that was Nixon's stomping ground, but it is remarkable that once Nixon came onto the national stage his friends also tended to come from the same area—and if not California, then Florida: Robert Finch, a Los Angeles lawyer and upcoming Republican politician; Herbert Kalmbach, the Newport Beach lawyer and real-estate operator who joined up with Nixon in 1962 and had become his personal attorney by the late 1960s; Ray Arbuthnot, a California agribusinessman; George Smathers, the Florida Democratic senator whose Red-baiting campaign style Nixon adopted and whose wheeler-dealing operations Nixon admired; and Charles G. "Bebe" Rebozo, the Florida businessman who befriended Nixon early in his career and remained his closest and most enduring friend. After moving to New York, Nixon widened his circle of friends somewhat: William Rogers, an upstate New Yorker who had been a colleague in the Eisenhower Administration; John Mitchell, his law partner; Robert Abplanalp, the aerosol-top manufacturer who built a fortune from his Yonkers factory; and Donald Kendall, a West Coast boy who had made good as the head of Pepsico in New York—but even then, it is remarkable that all of these men were born to less-than-affluent families, all were straight-ahead self-made men without frills or furbelows, all were decidedly nonpatrician, up-from-under types. Finally, from the pinnacle of the Presidency, when he could pick and choose his companions from anywhere in the nation, Nixon tended to take to his bosom the mostly flashy types from the Southern Rim: California actors like John Wayne and Bob Hope, Los Angeles (later Washington) football coach George Allen, North Carolina evangelist Billy Graham, and Texas machinator John Connally.

Now not all of these people had equal access to the private Nixon, not all were consulted equally. But they were all seen to be friends, and a person's friends have some influence over a person's thought and actions, and in Nixon's case, since the friends were so few, their influence was comparatively greater. It wasn't that Nixon would take Jack Drown's word on foreign policy, no matter how many times he invited him to state dinners for visiting royalty, or George Allen's advice on nuclear strategy, no matter how many times he chatted with him after Sunday football games. But Nixon was inordinately impressed by men who were visibly successful and he tended to listen to them with a rare dependency on all manner of topics. Herb Klein, though in real life nothing but a third-rate gopher in an autocrat's newspaper chain, was regarded by Nixon for years as something of an oracle on matters of publicity, even elevated to the Administration's "communications czar" on the thought (inaccurate, as it turned out) that he knew something about the nation's media. Billy Graham, a button-down revivalist, was elevated in Nixon's eyes to the status of a philosopher, allowed to give advice on recalcitrant youth and the morality of poverty that was apparently taken quite seriously by the President. John Mitchell, a bright enough man, no doubt, but an electoral ignoramus whose bullheadedness almost lost the 1968 campaign, was seen by Nixon as an unusually savvy politician worthy of being followed through a vast series of disasters (from Hayns-worth–Carswell to Watergate) without reproach. Even Bebe Rebozo, whose qualifications for contributing to national affairs are absolutely nil, was repeatedly consulted by Nixon on matters of high policy, encouraged to give advice and suggestions to members of the inner team, and included even in behind-the-scenes chicanery (for example, the receipt of White House reports on the surveillance of Teddy Kennedy); Nixon apparently believed in all seriousness, as speechwriter Patrick Buchanan recounted it, that "Bebe's a self-made man and very often such a man is a great deal more in touch with the thinking of a vast majority of Americans than those silver spoon boys. Bebe's an ideal sounding board for the President."

It is remarkable that nowhere among the publicly known friends of Nixon is a woman, nowhere a black; nowhere is there a novelist or a painter, not even a teacher or a dentist. None are from Ivy League colleges, none from the echelons of Eastern finance, none from Eastern political circles. All live in the world of big money—mostly *new* big money—all are politically very conservative (even Finch, though his contrast to Nixon got him a liberal reputation). Most disturbing of all, though logical enough now in the hindsight of Watergate, an unusually high percentage of them have had the taint, and sometimes the full stigma, of scandal upon them, have been, to an unusual degree, guilty of improprieties in business, a disregard for the public trust, a general lack of ethical sophistication, or in some cases direct association with crime.

To cite just a few examples.

Herbert Kalmbach was, not to put too fine a point on it, Nixon's bagman for a whole series of illegal operations. He was in charge of at least $1 million in secret funds left over from the 1968 campaign, which he dispersed at the whim of the White House for political operations, legal and otherwise. He was the conduit for the $100,000 in illegal campaign funds the Associated Milk Producers used in trying to buy political influence in 1969. He paid $130,000 to Anthony Ulasewicz and John Caulfield for their illegal snooping and surveillance from 1969 on (and knowingly helped them to get fraudulent credit cards); and he paid $45,000 to Donald Segretti for his illegal campaign sabotage activities in 1971 and '72. He ran an illegal $12 million campaign operation—the "townhouse project"—during the 1970 campaign, secretly dispensing by himself some $4 million in hidden funds to favored White House candidates (a crime to which he subsequently pleaded guilty), and personally made $400,000 in hush-hush payments for the operation against George Wallace in the Alabama primary that year. He then went on, apparently addicted by this time, to raise more than $10 million for Nixon's 1972 campaign, much of it in illegal corporate gifts which he did nothing to refuse, some of it going outright to buy prestigious ambassadorships (another crime to which he pleaded guilty). His law firm in Newport Beach handled both the somewhat dubious $1.4 million deal by which Nixon bought his San Clemente house and the unquestionably illegal deal by which Nixon tried to get a $576,000 tax break on his Vice-Presidential papers. And he was the bagman for the Watergate cover-up attempt in the summer of 1972, dealing out some $220,000 or so through bizarre and Bondian methods to buy the silence of the Watergate burglars.

Murray Chotiner was a man as slimy in his own career as he was in Nixon's. His connections with organized crime, for example, were extensive and protracted. Between 1949 and 1952 he handled no fewer than 221 gambler-bookmaker cases for the Los Angeles underworld; he was named by gangster Mickey Cohen as the one who arranged the testimonial dinner for Nixon in an early California campaign; he served as a lawyer for Philadelphia mobster Marco Reginelli, who was about to be deported for a criminal career including everything from larceny to moral turpitude, and he successfully intervened with the Justice Department—specifically, with Rex Collings, a Californian who had been appointed on the recommendation of Richard Nixon—to have the order rescinded; he was said by a henchman of Carlos Marcello's to have demanded $200,000 for a deal, which eventually fell through, to get the Eisenhower Administration to drop its deportation order against the New Orleans Mafia chief; he was alleged (but never proved) to have channeled $875,000 to Nixon's 1972 campaign from the Teamsters and certain Las Vegas gambling interests; he was the Teamsters' man in the White House both in their unsuccessful attempts to reverse the testimony which sent Jimmy Hoffa to jail and in their successful efforts to get him out ("Frankly,"

Chotiner acknowledged, "I'm proud of it"). His other shady dealings included extensive influence-peddling activities in Washington, which led to his appearance in 1956 before the Senate Rackets Committee investigating his role as attorney for a convicted clothing racketeer; his participation in the illegal campaign activities in Nixon's 1962 race for governor of California; his planting of two agents, posing as reporters, to spy on the campaigns of various Democratic Presidential candidates in 1971 and '72, for which he paid some $44,000; and his unrelenting efforts in 1971 and '72 on behalf of the Associated Milk Producers, including channeling illegal funds from AMPI to the Nixon campaign.

Then there are the friends whose sorry records are by now familiar: C. Arnholt Smith and his bank dealings, John Connally and his oil and milk affairs, George Smathers and his involvement with Bobby Baker, Walter Annenberg and his connection with the underworld's racing wire, James Crosby and his Mafia-tainted Paradise Island Casino. And those who have been exposed in the glare of Watergate: Mitchell and his cover-up chicanery, Abplanalp and his questionable real-estate deals at San Clemente and Key Biscayne. And there are still other minor figures who claim Nixon's friendship: Sanford Bronstein, head of a Florida hospital that Nixon dedicated with much effusiveness, who was sent to jail when it turned out he had looted the place for $525,000; Elmer Bobst, a man Nixon has often called his "honorary father," who tried to influence John Mitchell with a $100,000 campaign gift in return for, as he put it, "a more favorable attitude on the part of the tops" with regard to an FTC case he had an interest in; Roy Ash, a Nixon intimate from the 1960s and his powerful budget director from 1972 on, who has been involved in suspect land deals with the government and investigated by the SEC for stock manipulation, and whose Litton Industries conglomerate has been accused of "possible criminal activity" by the Government Accounting Office and found guilty of fraud and theft in evading customs duties by a California court.

And then there is Bebe Rebozo.

Bebe Rebozo, the inscrutable man who over the years has been the closest man of all to Nixon, who has been with him on the nights when he celebrated his election victories and on the days when he sat despondent over Watergate, who has drunk with him, fished with him, brooded with him, driven with him, who has been the only outsider at many of the Nixon family gatherings, who advised him and dealt for him, who has shared many of his most intimate moments for more than fifteen years, who has been, according to one Nixon friend, "the only person Nixon really trusts," and, according to Julie Nixon Eisenhower, "the most wonderful friend my father could ever ask for"—this Rebozo is the most revealing friend of all.

Like Nixon, Rebozo is a marvelously representative cowboy type. He was born into relative poverty in the city of Tampa, long before Florida became a boom area. Through a loan from the father of his high-school classmate, George Smathers, he acquired a gas station in the Miami area and at the outbreak of World War II expanded into the tire-recapping business. His reputation in Miami today is of one who worked in the gray areas of the law during the Office of Price Administration's controls on recapping—and it is a fact that he got a loan from a friend who happened to be on the local OPA tire board, a clear violation of OPA regulations—but no charges were ever brought and he was successful enough to end up as the largest recapper in South Florida by the late 1940s. Sometime around then, Rebozo met Richard Nixon on one of the latter's trips to Miami, and the two seem to have hit it off from the start: both the same age, both quiet, withdrawn, shallow, and humorless, both conservative small-town boys in awe of money, both operators lusting after success, both part of the Southern Rim milieu.

During the 1950s, Rebozo expanded his operations into real estate and financial loans, and in 1964 he established the Key Biscayne National Bank, the only bank on the prosperous island of Key Biscayne, of which he is president and whose first savings-account customer was Nixon. This bank in 1968 was the repository of some $300,000 worth of stolen stocks taken and channeled to the bank by organized-crime figures, upon which Rebozo issued only a $195,000 loan, and to a complete stranger whose name was not even on the stocks, and from which Rebozo presumably made a handsome profit when he decided to cash them in—an operation that smells a good deal like laundering. Rebozo has said that he had no idea the stocks were stolen, but it is known that before he sold them he was visited by an FBI agent who asked about the stocks, that the insurance company issued a circular to every bank in the country listing the stocks as stolen, and that before he sold at least the last third an insurance investigator even came to his office and told him they were stolen. Moreover, Rebozo has indicated that he knew something was fishy about the stocks because he said he called Richard Nixon's brother Donald and Resorts International president James Crosby to ask about them—though why he should have called *those* two particular sources remains mysterious.*

Rebozo's little bank has also been the target of prosecutorial interest for two other operations. First, the bank is known to be the depository of a slush fund that was operated by Rebozo at Nixon's whim. So far, at least $190,000 has been traced to the fund—$100,000 of it from billionaire recluse Howard Hughes, and $50,000 from Florida-based supermarket operator A. D. Davis—but according to Nixon's own statements on the White House tapes there may be more than $300,000 there in all, and some reports have figured it at more than $1 million. Money from this fund was laundered in several bank accounts and secretly used, among other things, to pay Caulfield and Ulasewicz for White House spying operations, to decorate and improve Nixon's Key Biscayne houses, to buy jewelry for Pat Nixon, and to pay for Nixon's personal expenses —and according to Herbert Kalmbach it was also said to have been given to Nixon's brothers, Donald and Edward, to Nixon's secretary, Rose Mary Woods, and to "unnamed others"; according to Nixon himself, in the privacy of his Oval Office, it

---

* Rebozo's bank was sued by the insurance company for the issuer of the stock in a case that went to trial on January 24, 1972, before U.S. District Court Judge James L. King. King, who had been appointed by Nixon, happens to have had an interesting banking background himself: in 1964 he was a director of the Miami National Bank, along with Meyer Lansky's front man Lou Poller and James Hoffa's front man Arthur Desser, during which time it was used, as court cases have proven, as a conduit for skim money passing from Las Vegas to organized-crime accounts in Swiss banks. King decided the case in favor of Rebozo in 1972, it was appealed and returned to him, and he ruled for a second time in Rebozo's favor in 1974.

was used "for the purpose of getting things out" and helping people "who have contributed money over the contributing years."

Second, the Rebozo bank has been under investigation as part of a skimming operation from James Crosby's Paradise Island Casino, accused of playing a role in the laundering of money either for the Cosmos Bank in Switzerland, in which Crosby is said to have an interest, or for domestic political ventures, presumably Nixon's, in which people want to remain anonymous. Supporting these suspicions are several items of fact: Resorts International, James Crosby, and his chief "consultant," Seymour Alter, have accounts in Rebozo's bank; Alter has visited the bank, according to sworn testimony, "on numerous occasions with large amounts of cash brought in from the Bahamas"; Alter has been admitted into the bank after hours, according to the bank's former vice-president, in order to convert large amounts of bills, and he has also obtained at least five different loans from the bank, another way of laundering funny money; Alter has admitted visiting the Presidential compound on Key Biscayne "four or five times" to visit Rebozo, unusual access for an international gambler; and the Joint Congressional Committee on Taxation, according to columnist Jack Anderson, has "traced a curious cash flow" from the Rebozo bank along a trail that "leads to Switzerland." All this a very odd performance for a quiet suburban bank.

But Rebozo's nefarious affairs have not been confined just to his little bank. During the 1960s, Rebozo, though a big businessman by any standards, managed to get a series of guaranteed loans out of the Small Business Administration, a trick which may have been accomplished because of his friendship with George Smathers (who had been on the Senate Small Business Committee and who wrote to the SBA to help ease Rebozo's path) or because the chief Miami officer of the SBA just happened to be a close friend of Rebozo's and a stockholder in his bank. This, coupled with the fact that Rebozo never fully disclosed his business dealings during any of his applications to the SBA, led the Long Island paper *Newsday*, after a series of careful investigations, to denounce the SBA for "wheeling and dealing . . . on Rebozo's behalf," and it led Wright Patman, chairman of the House Banking Committee, to accuse the SBA publicly of wrongdoing in making Rebozo a "preferred customer."

It doesn't stop there. With one of the SBA grants, Rebozo built a shopping center in Miami, and to do the construction for him, at a nice guaranteed sum of $674,000, he could find no better contractor than Alfredo "Big Al" Polizzi, who just happened to be an infamous underworld figure, a convicted tax evader, smuggler, and black marketeer, a crony of Meyer Lansky's and California Mafioso Frank Milano, and who had been named by the Federal Bureau of Narcotics, just four years before this shopping-center windfall, as "one of the most influential members of the underworld in the United States." But then Rebozo never did mind much what sorts of fellows he did business with: as the manager of this fancy new project he selected Edgardo Buttari, who happened to have been a henchman of Cuban dictator Fulgencio Batista, and as tenants he chose Manuel Artime, the military commander at the Bay of Pigs invasion and later the conduit for hush money for the White House to the Cuban-American Watergate burglars, and two other Cuban exiles who were subsequently convicted for their parts in a massive cocaine-smuggling ring in Florida. Rebozo's *own* store was said by the Miami police to house an illegal *bolita* (numbers) operation.

Nor there, either. Rebozo, real-estate intriguer, was a partner during the 1960s in a real-estate company with Donald Berg, who happened to be an acknowledged friend of at least one known associate of Meyer Lansky's and a man with such a shady background that after Nixon became President the Secret Service asked him to stop eating at Berg's Key Biscayne restaurant. This unsavoriness, however, did not prevent Rebozo from bringing Nixon in on a real-estate deal with Berg's company for land along the southern side of Key Biscayne—land which, investigation has now established, had been owned for twenty years by various fronts of organized crime and Fulgencio Batista. This is the sort of affair which led *Newsday* to conclude, simply and sorrowfully, "The deals made by Bebe Rebozo . . . have tarnished the Presidency."

It is upon reflection on all this—Bebe Rebozo side by side with Richard Nixon—that one thinks of Henry Adams's aphorism: "Friendship needs a certain parallelism of life."

Another way to gauge the importance of the Southern Rimsters in the Nixon Presidency is to see how many of them were responsible for the money that put him there.

Naturally many of the benefactors of Nixon's career were Californians. For his initial campaigns he depended most on executives from Union Oil, Standard Oil of California, Bank of America, on Arnholt Smith, Howard Hughes, Los Angeles–based representatives of Chiang Kai-shek, and on real-estate, defense, and leisure interests based in his home district. The famous 1952 slush fund gives some indication of who supported Nixon—21 percent of the donors were in real estate and construction, 19 percent oil, 12 percent defense, 12 percent agribusiness, 8 percent leisure, 5 percent technology—leading the *Sacramento Bee* to complain, "The man who the people of the sovereign state of California believed was actually representing them is the pet and protégé of a special interest group of rich Southern Californians." And perhaps not only Southern Californians, either: according to Drew Pearson, a Texan reported to him in the 1950s that "an untold amount of oil money has been behind Nixon for some time."

Information on Nixon's subsequent national campaigns is sketchy at best—the old California-Texas sources seem to stick with him, but a lot of Eastern money comes in too, and there's no way to tell the proportions—but the 1972 campaign has provided the best look yet at campaign giving, thanks to a modified law that went into effect in April 1972 and to several lawsuits that pried open some of the books. That information indicates beyond a doubt that cowboy financing played a greater part in 1972 than in any other Presidential election in history and that the major source of Nixon's campaign money—and therefore the interests Nixon presumably sought to serve as President—came from the six industrial pillars of the Southern Rim economy.

Which is not to deny the importance of those traditional sources of campaign capital: the bankers of New York, the industrialists of Chicago, the coal, steel, railroad, automobile interests of the Northeast, the old and monied yankee families. They still play a prominent role in Republican fund-raising, and the fact that they have great wealth accumulated over generations, traditions of public participation, and a long heritage of buying into political influence means that their financial clout is never to be discounted. However, with each passing campaign these traditional fat-cats were playing a smaller role. Yes, look at the lists of big donors to Nixon's 1972 campaign, and you will find the Rockefellers, the Mellons, the Phippses, the Fords, but you will also find Henry Salvatori of Los Angeles, Toddie Lee Wynne of Dallas, Anthony Rossi of Miami, and Martin Seretean of Atlanta, in no one's *Social Register*, and they turn out to be giving just as much.

There are several varying lists of the kinds of interests which were most prominent among the Nixon benefactors in 1972, but they all suggest more or less the same thing: those giving most, and expecting most in return, come from the oil, defense, technology, real-estate, leisure, agribusiness, and textile industries. According to the Nixon Finance Committee's own "industry-by-industry program," for example—and it is important as an indication of how the Administration *saw* business support, though the list does not include many corporations that saw more to gain by giving individually—the largest donors were:

Textiles and carpets	$975,000
Pharmaceuticals	$885,000
Oil	$809,600
Investment banking	$690,812
Trucking	$674,504
Automobile manufacturing	$353,900
Real estate	$334,059
Insurance	$319,000
Agribusiness	$209,457

That is, roughly 60 percent of the total industry donations came from industries associated primarily with the Southern Rim. According to the yankees' own Common Cause, which was most diligent in digging into Nixon's financial supporters, the main industries giving during the period of secret (and therefore heavy) fund-raising were—

Financial	$4.5 million
Oil and gas	$1.4 million
Drugs	$1.1 million
Real estate	$1.0 million

—and the registered industry campaign committees gave in this proportion:

Agribusiness	$100,000
Real estate–construction	$ 78,000
Aerospace	$ 35,000
Banking	$ 34,000
Securities	$ 30,000
Railroads	$ 15,000

And calculations based on the published lists of major donors from the Nixon Finance Committee and other sources, estimating the total amounts given between 1970 and 1972 by both individuals and corporations, indicate these approximate contributions:

Oil	$6.1 million
Real estate–construction	$3.8 million
Defense	$3.1 million
Insurance	$2.2 million
Agribusiness and food	$1.8 million
Manufacturing	$1.7 million
Banking and investments	$1.5 million
Leisure	$1.4 million
Textiles	$1.0 million

Again, the interests associated with the cowboy pillars make up close to 75 percent of the total.

These are imperfect indications only, it must be repeated, and, of course, there are many Southern banking interests and California manufacturing companies, just as there are many yankee defense interests and Northern construction companies, so the picture is by no means as clear as the figures might seduce one into believing. Nonetheless, a broad pattern seems clear enough: put simply, the financial interests of the Southern Rim played a significant, in fact a predominant, role in the financial support of Richard Nixon.

Examining campaign finances from a geographical rather than an industrial point of view suggests the same thing. According to the President's campaign committee at its final reckoning,

$19.9 million out of its total of $60.2 million was solicited before public disclosure became necessary, and this was the period in which the largest gifts, particularly the fat-cat gifts, were made; also according to the best reconstruction of the campaign committee's lists, people based in the Southern Rim contributed no less than $8.9 million—or *45 percent*—of that. That is an amazing figure, when you stop to think that the area contains only 35 percent of the nation's population, 30 percent of its states, that it has grown in a major way only in the last generation and that its economic base has been shaped only in the last thirty years.

The importance of these large cowboy contributors can be seen by a brief look at the moneys which were flung around by the most prominent of them (note, too, the industries in which they seem to congregate):

Roger Milliken	$363,000	S. Carolina	textiles
Walter T. Duncan*	$305,000*	Texas	oil/real estate
Sam Schulman	$262,000	California	conglomerates
Howard Hughes	$250,000	Nevada	leisure
Milledge Hart, Thomas Marquez	$224,000	Texas	technology
C. Arnholt Smith	$200,000*	California	banking/real estate
Francis Cappeart	$174,000	Mississippi	agribusiness
E. W. Brown	$150,000	Texas	shipbuilding/agribusiness
Thomas V. Jones	$150,000*	California	defense
Jules Stein	$118,000	California	leisure
Robert Allen	$114,000*	Texas	mining/chemicals
Leonard Firestone	$113,000	California	manufacturing
Sam Wyly	$112,000	Texas	technology
Martin Seretean	$108,000	Georgia	textiles
John and Charles Williams	$105,000	Oklahoma	oil
Christian de Guigne	$102,000	California	drugs

* Money returned by the Finance Committee under legal pressure.

Richard Kleberg	$100,000	Texas	agribusiness/real estate
John Moran	$100,000	Texas	banking
Henry Salvatori	$100,000	California	oil/defense
Eugene Barwick	$100,000	Georgia	textiles
Anthony Rossi	$100,000	Florida	agribusiness
W. W. Keeler	$100,000*	Oklahoma	oil
George Brown	$100,000	Texas	construction
Armand Hammer	$100,000	California	oil

Does the money matter? Does a large donation really mean influence? Does all this concentrated wealth affect things in Washington? Well, Nixon's men certainly thought it did. Speaking of the men they tapped to be chief fund-raisers in each industry, the Finance Committee fund-raisers wrote, "We are also going to have to do what we can to help our industry chairmen with problems of their industry and see to it that they get proper attention from the administration. Only in this way will they become convinced that our relationship is not 'a one-way street.'" George Spater, the chairman of the board of American Airlines, who was hit for $100,000 by Herbert Kalmbach, certainly thought so: "There were two aspects: would you get something if you gave it, or would you be prevented from getting something if you didn't give it." Miami real-estate operator John J. Priestes thought so too: about to be banned from government-supported housing programs for his previous shady dealings, he got together a quick $25,000 for chief fund-raiser Maurice Stans and was told, according to his testimony, "I will make a call and see what we can do. If we cannot do anything for you, we will return the money." And so did the large carpet manufacturers of the South—Seretean and Barwick among them—who met secretly with Maurice Stans to protest a proposed Department of Commerce flammability test, sent along a million or so to reelect the President, and then found a few weeks later that the test was to be scrapped.

But nowhere is the impact of the Southern Rim more evident in the Nixon Presidency than in his appointments.

Now, Nixon did not have very many ideas of what to do upon becoming President—it was *getting* there, after all, that he had concentrated on—but one thing he was quite clear about: he was going to take over the city of Washington, get rid of all the top-ranking Democrats and New Dealers and Eastern Establishmentarian collaborators, install his own people in the departments and bureaus, and make the federal government his own instrument—and he would do it, too, he vowed, a lot faster and more successfully than Dwight Eisenhower did sixteen years before. For a variety of reasons—the entrenchment of the civil service, the limitations on Presidential patronage, the lack of available talent—Nixon was not able to accomplish that dream, but the remarkable thing is the extent to which his assault was successful. A New York writer, concerned with the decline of influence by the yankee WASPs in the government, noted:

> This decline has really taken place not in New York but in Washington, where the vast and clanking mechanisms of the federal government are distasteful to the True Wasp. . . . In the late sixties the True Wasps began to leave the Capitol to its Byzantine excesses. The heyday of the Stimsons, Harrimans, and Achesons was palpably over, and a Southern accent had actually become an asset.

There was by no means an end to yankee influence, nor was Nixon even deceived into thinking so, but there was a vast increase in the proportion of cowboy influence, greater even than in the Johnson days.

Richard Nixon and his close associates preferred to have people in the White House and at the departments who reflected their general philosophy and who had the same rough standards of morality and politics, who could be counted on to carry out Nixonian orders without complaint and who made loyalty to the President a primary virtue—and such people, more often than not, were from the Southern Rim. Of course there were exceptions—George Shultz, for example, a New York–born and Eastern-educated professor brought in from the University of Chicago, proved to be a willing Nixon tool through a half-dozen executive jobs, and though not once did he have his way on any policy recommendations, not once did he rise up in protest; contrariwise, Robert Finch, as thoroughbred a Southern Californian as Nixon himself, proved very ill-adapted to following the Nixon line and found himself farther and farther removed from influence and finally was forced to resign. Still, for the most part, like attracts like, and those born in a particular culture tend to associate with their fellows: so it was with Nixon and his intimate coteries.

The sheer numbers are impressive enough:

Cabinet. For his top Cabinet appointments—secretaries and undersecretaries of the departments, plus other advisers given Cabinet rank—Nixon chose fifty-four people in all, twenty-four of them from the Southern Rim, twenty-one from the Northeast, five from elsewhere, and four with mixed cowboy-yankee backgrounds. That might at first seem to suggest a rough Southern-Eastern balance in the Cabinet, but even so, it represented an enormous increase in cowboy influence, almost double the Johnson record, and it is somewhat misweighted by the number of short-term yankee appointments. A better indication of Nixon's preferences is the make-up of his Cabinet at the height of his rule in early 1973, after he had settled in for his crowning years but before the Watergate reaction came along: of his top twenty-three Cabinet-rank appointments at that time, thirteen were from the Southern Rim (Roy Ash, Anne Armstrong, Kenneth Rush, William Clements, Richard Kleindienst, Joseph Sneed, John Whitaker, J. Phil Campbell, Frederick Dent, Rocco Siciliano, Caspar Weinberger, Floyd Hyde, Claude Brinegar), only nine from the Northeast (William Rogers, Henry Kissinger, George Shultz, William Simon, Elliot Richardson, Earl Butz, Peter Brennan, James Lynn, Frank Carlucci), and two others from points in between (Rogers Morton, Egil Krogh).

Independent agencies. Similarly, of the sixty-four people whom Nixon named to the top positions at the major independent agencies (regulatory commissions, alphabet boards like AEC and NASA, etc.), twenty-six came from the Southern Rim, twenty-one from the Northeast, eleven from elsewhere, and six had mixed backgrounds; of the thirty-four people selected for the six regulatory agencies, perhaps the most important positions outside the Cabinet, fourteen were Rimsters, eleven Northeasterners, and nine were from other regions. Consistently, therefore, Richard Nixon was choosing about 40 percent of his agency appointees from the Southern Rim, about 30 percent from the Northeast—a relative switch from the days of his predecessors.

Supreme Court. Fortuitously finding himself in the rare position of being able to fill no fewer than four positions to the Supreme Court, Nixon resolutely refused to name anyone from the Northeast, apparently being unable to find any yankee jurist with sufficient qualifications. Of Nixon's six nominations for these four seats (since he found himself also in the rare position of having two nominees refused by the Senate), three came from the Southern Rim—Clement Haynsworth from South Carolina, Harrold Carswell from Florida, and William Rehnquist from Arizona—and one other—Lewis Powell—came from Virginia and was in fact named to the unofficial "Southern seat" on the Court; for the other two selections Nixon chose safe and conservative judges from Minnesota.

White House staff. No appointments, not even the Court positions, were more important to the Nixon Presidency than the top positions at the White House itself. Here the cowboy influence, predictably, was even sharper: of the thirty-seven appointments above the level of special assistant—the high-level Presidential aides and political operatives, in other words —which Nixon made during his six-year tenure, twenty-two went to people from the Southern Rim, thirteen to Northeasterners, two from elsewhere. At any given time, even after the Watergate purges and the increase in yankee influence, there was roughly a two-to-one ratio of cowboys to yankees at the upper level of the White House staff.

Moreover, the dimensions of the White House staff under the direction of this crew were absolutely unprecedented. In 1939, when the Executive Office was first established, there were 570 employees, in 1972, 5,895—a growth of more than 1,000 percent in little more than thirty years; in 1940 Franklin Roosevelt had a staff in the White House itself of 45 people, in 1973 Richard Nixon had 567; in 1940 the White House had four separate operating units, none of which rivaled the departments, in 1973 it had twenty units, including several (the Office of Management and Budget, the Domestic Council, the National Security Council) with autonomous authority unmatched anywhere in the federal government.

But numbers are only numbers, and the simple recital of percentages does not indicate the true extent of the cowboy assault. For it was Richard Nixon's design to draw away as much power as possible from the other branches of the government, where mediating influences were greatest, into his own small circle within the White House, where cowboy dominance was unrivaled. And to a significant extent he succeeded: the configuration of power in the Nixon Administration was roughly a spiral whose central point was situated somewhere between the Presidential desk in the Oval Office and the "operations" desk in Bob Haldeman's room a hundred feet away, and which radiated thence through the west wing of the White House and the Executive Office Building next door, out to the boards and agencies and departments, and finally to the wider reaches of the federal bureaucracy. Those at the center of this spiral—Bob Haldeman, Roy Ash, and John Ehrlichman particularly—unelected and mostly unrecognized, exerted more influence than a passel or two of officials elsewhere, and their relative anonymity did not lessen their relative authority. Not even the much-publicized department secretaries carried the weight of the Nixon insiders: "The Nixon cabinet, for the most part," said John Dean after three years on the inside, "was totally controllable by the White House staff." Nor were the agency appointments any more independent: upon their nomination Haldeman would send each a "loyalty package" with a memo alerting them to their "responsibility" as good Nixon men to guard against "having his policies sabotaged by holdovers in the bureaucracy," an admonition that one nominee described as amounting to: "Brother, you may think you're being appointed to an independent agency, but don't think for a minute that you're independent." It was, according to the *New York Times* man covering the Presidency, "the greatest concentration of power within the White House in modern times, and the greatest concentration within the White House in the hands of a few."

These happy few, whatever else you might say about them, were people very much in the Nixon image. Efficient, loyal, hard-working, bland, and conservative, most of them trained either in the law or in public relations, they had none of them taken the elective route to power but they all shared the general cowboy perspective of their commander-in-chief. Like Nixon, they viewed Washington with hostility, as a place too dominated by liberals and Northeasterners, shot through with leftover New Dealers who (as Ehrlichman put it) were conducting "a kind of internal guerrilla warfare against the President," a place where the yankee taint was everywhere—in the Georgetown cocktail parties, the cloakrooms of Congress, the black-run City Hall, the Establishment-oriented law firms, the universities and news-papers, the lower and middle levels of the civil service—and had everywhere to be avoided. Like Nixon, they were loners, tight and private people, incapable of small talk ("We are so goddam square," Haldeman once admitted), putting in prodigious workdays of fourteen and sixteen hours, rarely socializing and even then still on the job; John Dean, an outsider who almost made it into the circle, recalls:

> I already knew about their clubbishness, of course, but I wasn't invited to *join* the club for some time after I became a member of the staff, and I did very little socializing with them even after I was a member of the club, so to speak. I socialized with them just enough to know that their idea of a good time was talking shop together, *playing* at playing tennis and talking more shop. That wasn't my idea of a good time.

Like Nixon, they viewed politics as a war in which all weapons were fair—including "dirty tricks," or what many of them had known at the University of California as "ratfucking"—and they saw themselves as embattled saviors, an attitude of zeal that, as the 1972 campaign bore witness, often slipped into antinomianism. Like Nixon, they were more absorbed in imagery than in substance, scenarios than truth, more interested in process than in product, movement than goal, more concerned with success than with rightness.

And like Nixon, they were products of the Southern Rim: Bob Haldeman, chief of staff, from an old Southern California family, graduate of UCLA, manager of a Los Angeles advertising firm; John Ehrlichman, first counsel and then domestic affairs assistant, born in Tacoma but brought up in Southern California, graduate of Santa Monica High School, UCLA, and Stanford Law School, product of the California bar, then a real-estate lawyer in Seattle; Ronald Ziegler, press secretary, born in Kentucky and a migrant to California, graduate of USC, for six years a Haldeman lieutenant in the advertising business; Alexander Butterfield, administrative assistant, born in Pensacola, Florida, brought up in Coronado, California, graduate of UCLA, an Air Force pilot until joining the White House staff in 1968; Dwight Chapin, appointments secretary, born and raised in California, graduate of USC, another Haldeman protégé in advertising, Nixon campaign aide from 1962 on; Harry Dent, political operative, from Columbia, South Carolina, graduate of Presbyterian College (Clinton) and George Washington Law School, political aide to Strom Thurmond from 1955 to 1968, Southern strategist in the 1968 campaign; Jeb Stuart Magruder, special assistant, brought up on Staten Island and graduated from Williams College, but who married a Californian, settled in California, called himself a Californian, and ran two Santa Monica cosmetics firms; Frederick Malek, personnel chief, born in Illinois, graduated from West Point, but a management consultant in Los Angeles throughout the 1960s, and principal owner of a South Carolina manufacturing company; Frederick LaRue, political operative, born in Texas, brought up in Mississippi, inheritor of a multimillion-dollar oil company, Goldwater supporter and Republican bigwig in Mississippi; plus a variety of other, lesser Southern California gophers answering Haldeman's call, including Gordon Strachan, Bart Porter, Bruce Kehrli, Lawrence Higby, Tim Elbourne, Robert Scalia, John Whitaker, enough of them to be called a "California Mafia"; plus still other White House luminaries outside the Haldeman chain of command, people like Robert Finch (the California politician, in the White House after his Cabinet stretch), Herbert Klein (California news hack, in charge of White House communications), Bryce Harlow (Oklahoma-born, a Washington lobbyist and Nixon's first appointee, head of congressional relations), William Timmons (Tennessee, Harlow's successor in the White House), Lyn Nofziger (a California adman and politico, also in congressional relations), Charles "Bud" Wilkinson (Oklahoma, special consultant and "youth expert"), Dean Burch (Arizona, lawyer and Goldwater aide, special consultant after a stretch at the FCC), Edward Morgan (Arizona, deputy counsel and tax finagler), Richard Moore (yankee by birth, but a California TV executive for twenty years, White House elder statesman), J. Fred Buzhardt (South Carolina) and Charles Alan Wright (Texas), the lawyers called in for the Watergate defense, Anne Armstrong (Texas, White House counselor), and, always flitting in and out, Murray Chotiner (the California lawyer and Washington lobbyist, private adviser).

An extraordinary phenomenon this: as if the shy, private, awkward person at the top, uncomfortable with strangers, wanted to replicate himself throughout his own hierarchy.

The supremacy of Bob Haldeman in all of this should not go without underscoring: he was "almost the other President," according to his friend Alexander Butterfield, "I can't emphasize that enough." Like the President himself, he was pure Southern California—if anything, purer. His family settled in the Los Angeles region in the early years of the century, his grandfather made a fortune in construction supplies and helped to found a right-wing organization called the Better American Foundation in the 1920s, and his father continued both the financial and the political traditions. Haldeman, though it is put about that he has a "genius-level" IQ, betrayed little sign of it in his schooling, getting Ds in grade school, learning hardly more than discipline in military school, performing only a little above average both at USC, where he spent two years, and at UCLA, where he graduated with a B.S. in business administration in 1948; his college career was marked by his friendship with later colleagues John Ehrlichman and Alexander Butterfield, his obsession with anti-Communism (he led an unsuccessful campaign to get "Reds" off the school paper), and his use of shady tactics in campus elections. After graduation he joined the advertising firm of J. Walter Thompson, and for the next twenty years that's where he stayed, working his way up to become vice-president and manager of the Los Angeles office, learning from this, the only professional experience in his life, the not inconsiderable ability to sell inferior goods in deceptive packages. With such a talent it was inevitable that Haldeman would turn to the political world, and during various leaves of absence he joined up with the rising political career of Richard Nixon. He worked in the 1956 and 1960 campaigns as an advance man, was successful enough to be picked as campaign manager for the 1962 governor's race in California (where he helped Nixon conduct the fraudulent postcard-mailing scheme—and, appropriately, its cover-up), and then joined the 1968 campaign as tour director and chief administrator.

Installed in the White House, he proved to be fully as private as the President himself, fully as imperious (though a good deal sterner), and fully as Rimian in his politics. He was, for example, quite fanatic about dissent: he went into rages about campus demonstrators, he ordered John Dean to use "any means, legal or illegal" to keep demonstrators away from the President, he authorized the various instruments of repression put out by the White House during those years, and he went so far as to accuse critics—mere critics, mind you—of the Vietnam War of "consciously aiding and abetting the enemy of the United States." He was proudly superpatriotic, and is credited with originating the idea of putting American flags in the White House lapels; despite his criminality, he was arrogantly moralistic, a Christian Scientist who neither smoked nor drank nor tolerated it, and was the one who started the Sunday-morning prayer breakfasts in the White House; he was zealously anti-Communistic, attracted to Nixon originally by the Hiss case, and according to inside accounts actually believed that foreign Communist money was going to support not only the antiwar protesters but also the campaign of George McGovern, for which he ordered the White House, the FBI, and the CIA to find proof. And he had an abiding hatred of the Eastern Establishment, its political leaders in both parties, its cultural figures, its reporters; in one of his rare public speeches he told a California audience, with intentional hyperbole but perfect seriousness, that "somewhere in the jungle labyrinth of Manhattan Island, there is a secret nerve center where, every Sunday afternoon, an enormously powerful group of men gather to decide what the Eastern Establishment media line . . . will be."

Bob Haldeman gave Nixon privacy, time, and order, the

three things he most desperately wanted, and in return Nixon gave him power.* It was Haldeman who assembled and directed the White House staff, grooming such an unlikely figure as Ziegler and propelling him toward a position of real influence, installing Ehrlichman close to the President and seeing that he was given responsibility over domestic policy ("He *made* Ehrlichman," according to John Dean), plucking the promising young men out of the Southern Rim, testing them in his White House crucible, and then spreading them out over the Administration bureaucracy. It was he who guarded the Presidential gates, screened the visitors ("even John Mitchell comes through me"), censored the memos, made the appointments. It was he who ran the meetings of the topmost staff (Ash, Kissinger, Ehrlichman, Shultz, Ziegler, Timmons) at 8:45 every morning and it was in his office—a signal to Washington status-watchers —that they were held. It was he who decided who should go and when: he saw to it that Secret Service chief Robert Taylor was fired for insubordination (to Haldeman, of course, not Nixon), eased out Pat Moynihan for after-hours drinking and friendship with liberals, demoted Richard Helms and Peter Peterson for socializing with Democrats, shunted Arthur Burns off to the Federal Reserve for insufficient obeisance, froze Mel-

---

* Even Henry Kissinger, despite his prodigious efforts and much coddling from the press, was never a rival to Haldeman in terms of power. In the first place, the Haldeman *apparat* never quite trusted this undoubted patron of the yankee Establishment (Harvard, Council on Foreign Relations, Rockefeller adviser), and though Nixon himself clearly found something attractive in the up-from-under poor-boy-who-made-good, Kissinger was never allowed much freedom of action in the White House or much influence outside his own personal staff. Moreover, he always had Nixon looking over his shoulder—Nixon for some reason prided himself on his management of foreign affairs and insisted on complete authority in setting policy in this area; William Safire, who spent five years in the White House, goes so far as to say that Kissinger was little more than a stooge for Nixon, "a student of President Nixon's foreign policy ideas," a "tool in Nixon's idea of solving the war in Vietnam." In addition, Kissinger, like everyone else in the government, had to relate to Nixon through the Haldeman filter, and there were times when Haldeman would simply freeze him out, whether for his own prestige or on orders from Nixon is unclear; at any rate, Kissinger is known to have complained frequently about his treatment: "A week ago he was on his knees, and now I can't even get past Haldeman."

vin Laird out of inner White House councils for chumminess with Capitol Hill, kicked Robert Dole out of the Republican National Committee for lack of pliancy—to name only the most prominent cases; not coincidentally all but one were Northeasterners. It was he who ran the 1972 campaign ("Haldeman issues the political directives, approves campaign contracts, receives political reports and coordinates campaign activities," Jack Anderson reported. "Those on the inside say he is the most powerful man in the 1972 campaign, second only to the President himself") and who was responsible for planning most of the White House's Watergatery, including the investigation of CBS newsman Daniel Schorr, the audits of *Newsday* reporters, the enemies list, the Huston Plan, the Segretti operation, and the secret $350,000 sabotage fund. It was he, and he alone, who met with the President for four or five hours a day, who presented the "options," framed the tactics, announced the decisions, and implemented the plans. And it was he who, perhaps as much as Nixon himself, set the actual policies, established the fundamental strategies, of the Presidency: "There is no policy," staffer Ken Clawson said once, "he doesn't have a hand in, somehow." Probably that hand was even more than he needed: the White House transcripts show time and again that all it took was one finger, around which the President could very neatly be wrapped:

> P: And I think you should tell—would you tell him about the Magruder?
>
> H: Nope.
>
> P: No, I guess not. . . . I think with Bill, though, you could tell him, don't you think?
>
> H: Nope. I don't think I should. In the first place, I am not supposed to know. . . .
>
> P: I see. You're right.

III

Predict the policies of a cowboy President. He would support those groups he saw as congenial to the Southern Rim— the Far Right, suburban political establishments, police forces, the hinterland radio and television stations, the new-money culture, the Southern wing of the Democratic Party, conservatives generally. He would attack, possibly even attempt to subvert, those interests he saw as supportive of the Eastern Establishment—the yankee press, the universities, the federal bureaucracy, the Left, the liberal wing of the Democratic Party. He would follow the general tenets of the Right, promoting big business, limiting social welfare, strengthening state and local government, encouraging bellicosity and superpatriotism. He would promote the well-being of the white majority to the detriment of the nonwhite minorities, particularly urban blacks, and hold in check measures to desegregate schools and open voting opportunities. He would be intolerant, perhaps even fanatic, about dissent and political confrontation, as ruthless as possible about its suppression. He would shape the economy to assist the industrial pillars of the Southern Rim—defense, oil, and agribusiness probably most of all—and turn government favors (tax breaks, import controls, federal contracts) toward particular firms in the South and West as far as possible. And he would direct a foreign policy to mesh with both the political and economic spirit of the Southern Rim, providing enough force to sustain the balance of power and enough leniency to open new markets for the new money, and particularly to protect and enlarge the development of military, technical, agricultural, and petroleum markets abroad. He would, in short, enact a Cowboy Strategy.

Such a President was Richard Nixon.

The Cowboy Strategy was much more than the Southern Strategy, although it certainly included that. It went beyond just catering to the segregationist tastes of the Old South—it embraced all of the ideas that would appeal to the full Southern Rim, old and new, as well as those constituencies outside that geographic axis (certain new-money suburbs, for example) which mirrored its economic and political characteristics. It went beyond simply winning over the Wallace voters to the Republican camp—it catered to all of the interests of the Southern Rim, seeking to build a "new majority" that could entrench itself in American life. The Cowboy Strategy informed every aspect—domestic, economic, and foreign—of Nixon's Presidency.

DOMESTIC POLICY

Grateful to the South for both his nomination and his election, and reminded of this regularly by Strom Thurmond on the Senate floor and Harry Dent in the White House councils, Nixon was careful to choose as the first demonstration of his Cowboy Strategy that part which the press isolated and dubbed "the Southern Strategy." Nixon decreed that whatever the South might perceive as detrimental was to be eliminated if possible, camouflaged if necessary, that the decisions of governmental agencies should not provoke major Southern powers, and that the condition of the Afro-American population was not to receive significant federal concern. Lest anyone around him mistake his intention, he went so far as to issue an order for Bob Haldeman to ensure that no official anywhere in his Administration was at any time for any reason to make a statement that might upset and antagonize the South.

Nixon, of course, was not able to fulfill all the elaborate wishes of the Southern mossback crowd to turn the clock back to 1953, or perhaps 1853, but he certainly did what he could. He made every effort to reduce funds for school desegregation (from $1 billion to $75 million, for example, in the 1974 budget) and to block enforcement of integration laws, even sending Justice Department lawyers down to sue for the suspension of court-ordered school integration in Mississippi—the first time that the government had brought a case not to *enforce* but to *postpone* such rulings. He spoke out against "instant integration," called Justice Department enforcement teams "vigilante squads," repeatedly denounced "forced bussing" to achieve integration. He tried to sabotage the Voting Rights Act, cutting the funds for Justice Department lawyers in that area, reducing the target states from Johnson's inadequate five to a laughable two, and deciding by executive fiat that all challenges to existing voting laws would have to be decided by protracted lawsuits rather than Justice Department intervention. He fired a series of upper-level bureaucrats who refused to go along with all his foot-dragging schemes, and shunted aside Cabinet officials like Robert Finch and George Romney who displayed any nagging sense of responsibility toward American minorities. And he established an unblemished record for ignoring *all* the reports of the U.S. Civil Rights Commission criticizing the Administration for its abysmal performance, fired its chairman when he tried to gain public support, and then refused to appoint another person in hopes that the whole thing might just go away.

But nothing endeared Nixon more to the Southern Rim, and revealed better his cowboy core, than the Haynsworth-Carswell Supreme Court battles. Only eight months after taking office, Nixon found himself in the happy position of being able to pick a Supreme Court Associate Justice and lost no time in ordering Attorney General John Mitchell to find him a Southerner—a white, male, conservative, middle-aged Southerner. Mitchell came up with Clement Haynsworth, a circuit judge in Greenville, South Carolina, who seemed to fit the bill, and Nixon sent his name with great pride along to the Senate for confirmation. Alas for Nixon, not only did the yankee forces of the Senate look with disdain upon this selection, they also found out that Haynsworth had a strikingly segregationist record as a judge and a total lack of judicial morality, having repeatedly decided cases before him involving companies in which he owned stock—almost always in favor of those companies. After a few painful weeks, the Senate rejected the nomination, with the Southern Rim standing firm behind it but most of the Northeast, including even the Republican leadership, ranked solidly against it—and Richard Nixon went through the roof. He stormed to anyone within earshot, pounded his desk in rage, castigated in vicious terms the liberal press, organized labor, sell-out Republicans, and the North in general. The Evans-and-Novak reporting team, with sources close to the Oval Office, wrote: "Aides who had not seen him raise his voice in anger during ten months in the White House, facing both blunders by aides and attacks from enemies with a bland equanimity, were amazed at the emotion that Haynsworth's rejection aroused in him."

And not simply anger—stubbornness, too: Nixon vowed to find *another* Southerner and nominate *him*. ("You know," one White House staffer said upon hearing this, "the President really *believes* in that Southern Strategy—more than he believes in anything else.") This time he reached to Florida, where he found G. Harrold Carswell, a federal appeals judge whose record was totally undistinguished, whose decisions were so egregious that three out of every five of them were overturned by higher courts, and whose reputation was far more solid as a good judge of wine than of laws—but he was, by God, white, male, conservative, and Southern. Nixon sent the nomination to the Senate in January 1970, still so outraged that he also sent along a letter warning the assembly to bow to "the Constitutional responsibility of the President to appoint members of the Court"—forgetting, during this first outright assertion of royalty, that the President could only *nominate,* not appoint. Once again the Northern liberals, led by Indiana's Birch Bayh, dug into the candidate's record, once again they found the law in ordure: Carswell had an unbroken history of hostility to black defendants and lawyers, was a member of a segregated country club, lived in a covenantly segregated neighborhood, and was on record, some years before, as having announced his "firm, vigorous belief in the principles of white supremacy" and "segregation of the races." No amount of arm-twisting, cajoling, declaiming could amass Senate support for this one, either, and once again the nomination was rejected—the first time since the Presidency of Grover Cleveland that a President had suffered the indignity of two successive judicial rejections by the Senate.

Richard Nixon was near apoplexy. Never before had his visceral hatred of the yankees been so acute. Evans and Novak again were privy to his mood: "He was agitated, his mind seemingly off the subject, and several times he digressed to make slighting remarks about the eastern part of the United States and about the intellectuals. The only decent places left in the United States, he said, were the South and the West." He raged a bit, then calmed, and called in Harry Dent for a conference, and then suddenly sent word that he wanted an instant press conference. White-faced and tense, his hands gripping hard at the press-room podium, Nixon let loose:

With yesterday's action, the Senate has said that no Southern Federal appellate judge who believes in a strict interpretation of the Constitution can be elevated to the Supreme Court. As long as the Senate is constituted the way it is today, I will not nominate another Southerner and let him be subjected to the kind of malicious character assassination accorded both Judges Haynsworth and Carswell. . . .

I understand the bitter feeling of millions of Americans who live in the South about the act of regional discrimination that took place in the Senate yesterday. They have my assurance that the day will come when men like Judges Carswell and Haynsworth can and will sit on the High Court.

It was an extraordinary display of Presidential temper, and though it instantly demolished Nixon's relations with Capitol Hill it just as immediately solidified his reputation in the South: far be it from the region which has celebrated Pickett's Charge to hold the Presidential defeat in anything but admiration.*

If any further proof were needed, North or South, of Nixon's dedication to the Cowboy Strategy it was soon provided by a succession of directives and Nixon-backed laws which went directly to reverse the federal government's forty-year-old commitment to black progress. Most important, Nixon cut welfare funds and stiffened eligibility requirements, tried to gut both the Legal Services Administration and the Community Action Projects, ended or reduced federal funding of urban renewal, manpower training, low-income housing, community health services, and ghetto education programs. The predictable effect: the minimal economic gains enjoyed by blacks in the 1960s as a result of Kennedy-initiated programs were reversed during the 1970s by Nixon-initiated policies (family earnings down, numbers under the poverty level up, etc.). And when, somehow, yankee adviser Pat Moynihan talked Nixon into the actual introduction of a sweeping "Family Assistance Program" that would provide "income maintenance" for America's poor, a long step toward a real welfare system, cooler cowboy heads managed to add on to it a system of "work requirements" so odious and unworkable that the whole thing collapsed and fell soon into legislative limbo. No one misread the Nixon performance, least of all those who suffered most: Bishop Stephen Spottswood, chairman of the NAACP board, denounced the federal government for its open hostility to black progress "for

* After much agonizing, Nixon finally named Harry A. Blackmun, from Minnesota, to this Supreme Court seat, and wrought his revenge later by nominating a conservative Virginian and a Far Right Arizonan to two other vacancies.

the first time since Woodrow Wilson"; and James Farmer, a black civil-rights leader co-opted into Nixon sycophancy, finally was forced to admit, albeit delicately, that the Afro-American community felt "the Administration is not on their side."

Compared to what Nixon actually meted out to blacks, "benign neglect"—that famous principle he had embraced in 1970—seemed positively cornucopian.

But just as the Cowboy Strategy was not directed solely at the South, so the victims were not found solely in the black communities. Central to Nixon's design was a sweeping attack on the welfare state in general—in fact, nothing less than the piecemeal repeal of the New Deal, which was intended in its broadest sense to satisfy the cowboy constituency (and the Nixon philosophy) opposed to grand federal programs, to "handouts," and to liberal notions about social obligations to the victims of society. Hence it was the poor in general (two-thirds of whom are white) who suffered under the Nixon schema, and the weak, and the young, and the uneducated.

Callous it seems, but the proof was abundant, from the beginning of his Presidency to the end. Nixon advocated, and in most cases got enacted, *reductions* in the free-milk program for schoolchildren, public employment for the able-bodied jobless, rent supplements for the rural poor, summer job funds for teen-agers, mental-health centers for the indigent. He desiccated and finally killed the Office of Economic Opportunity (the basic instrument of the old "war on poverty"), the Community Relations Service, the Economic Development Administration, and the Model Cities Program. He jiggered the public housing program so that most of its units were priced beyond the range of the poor, and when that seemed too expensive, managed to freeze most of the funds in the whole federal low-cost housing program. All this, mind you, while the plight of the poor was demonstrably growing worse: the share of the national income going to poor and middle-income families, which had been slowly rising from 1950 to 1968, began to decline during the Nixon years for the first time, as something like $10 billion a year was transferred out of the hands of the lowest three-fifths of the population to the richest three-fifths. A high-level academic report presented to the Senate in the middle of 1973 said it simply: "The needy in this country are hungrier and poorer than they were when Nixon took office."

In place of welfare programs—"a monstrous consuming outrage" according to the 1974 State of the Union address—Nixon offered as the cornerstone of his domestic policy a program called revenue sharing. The idea, dear to the hearts of rightists everywhere, was to take no less than $30 billion away from the federal government and deliver it into the hands of state and city authorities across the land, for them to do with as they pleased. It represented an extraordinary breakthrough for the power structures of the Southern Rim states and cities: they had an immense new source of wealth, so great that every single state in the Southern Rim posted surplus budgets in 1974, with Texas and California the highest in the nation, while only three Northeastern states (New York, Ohio, and Illinois) escaped major budget deficits. Moreover, they could dispense this vast new treasure without any interference from the pointy-headed bureaucrats in Washington; they could use it for programs *they* held important (police, sanitation, salaries) instead of those favored by the bleeding-heart liberals (welfare, housing, education), and they didn't have to create new and unpopular taxes for it (most Southern Rim states have no income tax). "Nixon has changed the whole context of the argument on national priorities," a spokesman for the U.S. Conference of Mayors said after revenue sharing went through. "You don't hear many mayors any more talking about helping poor minorities." Indeed, as one private survey determined in 1974, only 2 percent of the new money was going for social spending, while 75 percent went for police and sanitation, the rest for tax relief and municipal salaries. And imagine the plight of a place like St. Louis County, Missouri, which, like many of the Rim suburbs, already had all the police and garbagemen they could use—it had to spend its $757,000 from the government on a new golf course.

And the Cowboy Strategy didn't stop there. Central to its thesis was the enlargement of the police powers for the state and their use in the suppression of dissent—the very program, after all, upon which Nixon had based his 1968 campaign and through which he won so much Southern Rim support. Hence, as we have already observed, he was concerned to mount a crusade of repression the likes of which this country had never experienced. The machinery he developed for repression of domestic dissent was immense, powerful, vicious, and in good part illegal, involving the CIA, the FBI, the IRS, the NSA, the Defense Department, the Justice Department, the White House plumbers and private police, and it was used to assist and condone the police murders of campus protesters, the unlawful arrests of antiwar demonstrators, the collecting of secret files, the illicit surveillance and harassment of hundreds and thousands of political dissidents, and the draconian laws and intimidating lawsuits against student and Left organizations, leading antiwar activists, the Catholic Left, Vietnam veterans, American Indian fighters, draft resisters, flag burners, marijuana smokers, and others offensive to the cowboy ethic. Moreover, so inherent a part of the Nixon Administration was it that there seemed to be no qualms about using this same kind of machinery to stifle dissent throughout the entire political spectrum and even to cripple and subvert the opposition party in the 1972 election. The Watergate operations were reprehensible, to be sure, but they were not inconsistent with the theoretical underpinnings of Nixon's Cowboy Strategy.

At the same time that Nixon used federal machinery, mostly illegal and mostly secret, to destroy the Left and liberal forces in opposition to him, he was also using federal machinery, mostly legal and mostly open, to attack other bastions of yankee power—or what he crudely assumed were bastions of yankee power. The liberal universities, for example: Nixon cut and impounded university funds for liberal arts, libraries, and scientific research, eliminated most grants for graduate education (down from 51,500 to 6,600 in the Nixon years), and reordered government priorities away from private universities (heavily concentrated in the Northeast, the Ivy League most notable among them) and toward public universities (where Southern Rim enrollment is overwhelmingly concentrated); Columbia University President William McGill said gloomily of the Nixon strategy: "I believe it forecasts very hard days ahead for major [read: liberal] institutions." The egghead academics, too, "the professors [who] don't know anything" in Mitchell's angry phrase: Nixon walled off the White House from all but a few troglodytic professors (Sidney Hook, Irving Kristol, Edward Banfield), abolished all the federal advisory committees (such as the President's Science Advisory Committee) that might have independent or liberal participants, and cut or eliminated federally funded professorial grants in practically every discipline. The big Northern cities as well: in addition to cutting support for their massive welfare bills, Nixon repeatedly fought against any use of highway taxes for mass transit in the Northeast, managed to scuttle a House bill that would have opened up $20 billion to rescue decaying mass-transit systems (25 percent of which would have gone to New York City), and cut or abolished the urban renewal, model cities, and subsidized housing programs that were so vital to the older cities; as *New York Times* analyst John Herbers put it simply, Nixon ended "the Federal commitment to urban development programs enacted by Democratic Presidents in the last four decades."

And the liberal media—*especially* the liberal media. Probably no other nettle stung Nixon, and his supporters throughout the Rim, more than this one; as speechwriter William Safire later wrote, "In all the world of 'us-against-them,' the press was the quintessential 'them' " for Nixon. Reflecting part of the antidemocratic current of the Southern Rim, Nixon always detested the idea of a noisy and irreverent press in general, the Eastern press in particular, especially its refusal to be obeisant to constituted authority and its presentation of the uncomfortable, the unfamiliar, and the unpalatable. But during his term of office this predisposition developed into a positively feverish hatred for the liberal press, so predominantly yankee: the three television networks based in New York City, the national magazines with headquarters along the "Bos-Wash" corridor, the newspaper giants like the *New York Times* and the *Washington Post*. This made up what Nixon himself called "the Eastern Establishment media," which he seriously saw as being (as he wrote in a personal memo to his staff) "on the side of amnesty, pot, abortion, confiscation of wealth (unless it is theirs), massive increases in welfare, unilateral disarmament, reduction of their defenses, and surrender in Vietnam."

Containment and subversion of the liberal media was the full-time occupation, from the first Nixon Inaugural right through to his resignation, of at least fifteen high-level members of the White House staff and Lord knows how many subordinates. The Nixon team tried public browbeating (Vice-President Agnew's recurrent speeches against "effete" reporting and "instant analysis," mixed with threats of using the FCC's licensing power against radio and television stations), private bullying (Herb Klein's and Dean Burch's midnight phone calls to network executives, Charles Colson's desk-pounding confrontations), overt censorship (prior restraint of the *New York Times* and *Washington Post* from publishing the Pentagon Papers, FCC action against "drug-orientated" records and "topless" radio programs), bureaucratic pressure (establishment of a White House Office of Telecommunications Policy, which, its director said, had "no qualms about seeming to influence" the FCC and other agencies to keep the press in line), punitive legislation (Administration-proposed laws to prevent the free coverage of public figures, to establish an Official Secrets Act against reporters who use leaked information, to divest networks of their wholly owned stations), illegal entrapment (wiretaps on reporters' phones, FBI checks and harassment, IRS investigations), and legal intimidation (more than thirty subpoenas for reporters' notes and films, the filing of antitrust action against the three major networks, the encouragement of challenges to local TV and radio license-holders). Most successful of all, the Nixon people managed to remake the nation's Public Broadcasting System—"that left-wing taxpayer-subsidized network" in Buchanan's words—first by placing their own ideologues in charge and then by pushing through a reorganization scheme in 1971 that passed effective control (and money) from the New York and Washington headquarters to the regional stations, not only encouraging more programming of interest to the general cowboy population but also establishing a veto power over program ideas offered by the Eastern network managers.

All that amounted to what the *New York Times,* understandably alarmed, called "a persistent and well-calculated effort to intimidate, discredit and legally curb the press," or what *New Yorker* analyst Richard Harris quite soberly concluded was "the most severe attack since John Adams' Administration" upon the freedom of the press. And it had its effect, frighteningly so: the networks bent and sometimes buckled ("They are damned nervous and scared," reported Chuck Colson to Bob Haldeman, and "anxious to prove they are 'good guys' "); controversial shows were canceled or left unfunded; newspapers chose to curtail their investigative reporting; local radio and TV stations hewed to careful political lines; reporters were shifted from controversial beats; stories that might have caused official displeasure were left undone (CBS News President Richard Salant: "The tendency is to say, 'Oh well, this isn't the ideal one to fight, so let's let this one go' "); independent authors and academic scholars gave up or redesigned projects where confidentiality could not be guaranteed. Had it not been for the backlash of Watergate, indeed, one shudders to think what "four more years" might have produced.

ECONOMIC POLICY

When it came to his economic policy, Nixon was the very personification of the cowboy, embodying all the contradictions of the breed. He favored private laissez-faire growth but also government mothering and support of such industries as defense and agriculture; he was against higher taxation but in favor of tax breaks and shelters for the wealthy; he wanted the federal budget cut and balanced but was unstinting in support of the industries which fed at the federal trough; he supported the forces of a free market but favored import controls to protect beleaguered industries; he wanted loose money policies for continued business expansion but tight policies to control runaway inflation; he approved of high prices (and profits) for management but wanted to cut the wages of labor so it could not afford them. Such contradictions in a Texas oil baron or a Blimpian Florida realtor are mostly laughable; in a President they spell disaster.

For his first two years in office Nixon sought, mostly without ever setting it as a basic policy or really learning any hard economics, to guide the country as near as possible into the laissez-faire, free-market economy that the Southern Rim had always proclaimed: no containment of the galloping inflation brought on by the Vietnam War, no wage or price guidelines (much less controls), no "jawboning" or "browbeating" of gouging unions or greedy corporations, no "rate-fixing" for the stock market or "wide-sweeping" regulation powers, no interference with the stock market, no fiddling with the money supply. All of the instruments which had been developed since the Roosevelt years to guide. and control the economy would be ignored: let free enterprise prevail! Richard Nixon really *believed* in Adam Smith. Born in California and having shared in its easy prosperity, seeing what he thought was the American Dream in his own life, how could he have done otherwise?

But, of course, the free-enterprise economy had long since ceased to exist, and the forces that operated in the American marketplace in the 1960s and 1970s, the product in so many ways of the cowboy heritage of the previous two decades, did not behave in the jejune manner that Nixon's simplicities had taught him to expect. The powerful *concentrates* that had become the hallmark of American capitalism—the giant multinational corporations, the conglomerates, the monopolies, the government-supported industries—simply did not bend to the normal "free market" pressures, nor to the laws of supply-and-demand. Monopoly corporations do not have to lower prices when there is less demand, and in fact there is very little to keep them from raising prices; far-flung multinationals can play one national division off against the other and ignore local pressures almost endlessly; horizontal conglomerates can absorb a loss over here by making a gain over there, rarely having to bow to demand pressures that might affect a single-line business; government-sustained corporations are guaranteed supply, demand, price, and profits by the taxpayer and can completely ignore the consumer. Hence a laissez-faire President will automatically be frustrated in any attempts to set a smooth economy, since on the one hand, concentrates far beyond the control of the market are working, steadily, imperviously, to raise their prices, increase their profits, and accumulate their fortunes—and that will inevitably make for inflation; while on the other hand, smaller businesses in the interstices of all that are being forced, steadily, painfully, to hold their prices, limit their profits, cancel their orders, and trim their staffs—and that will inevitably make for recession. Such, for the first time in the nation's modern history, did Richard Nixon reap: inflation and recession both at the same time.

Nixon, it is clear from his advisers' testimony, knew nothing about economics, but he did know something about politics, or at least the crudest form of politics: winning elections. And when the sorry results of the 1970 elections came in, when it became clear that his laissez-faire inflation-recession was turning the voters against the Republicans, Nixon realized that he had to do *something* to pave the way for 1972. To go all out on the recession side was, obviously, politically disastrous—in fact, Nixon always said it was Eisenhower's 1960 recession that cost him the Presidency the first time around—and the inevitable alternative was to support the inflation side and let Growth take care of everything. But that would mean a bit of government spending and some government support of business —therefore, scrap laissez-faire, install commandez-faire.

So in 1971 the nation saw an astounding turnaround—or what would have been astounding in a President more guided by conviction than convenience. In January of that year Nixon presented a budget which, contrary to all the "fiscal responsibility" he had been talking about for twenty years, ordained a government deficit of $11.6 billion, which actually ended up at $21.1 billion, easily the largest to date in American history, and which fed so much new money into the economy that inflation was unavoidable. To oversee this cowboy budget Nixon brought in John Connally as Secretary of the Treasury, a thoroughly political cowboy, to sell his thoroughly political economic policy with all his honeyed charm, first to the Congress and then to the people; most Washingtonians were surprised at the appointment, but they had not been watching Nixon's growing disenchantment with a series of yankee financial men, Burns, Kennedy, Mayo, McCracken. Then in August, breaking every economic promise he had ever made, Nixon inaugurated a wage and price freeze and across-the-board government control of the economy—a program which, despite its apparent even-handedness, was actually designed to let American business go rampant (profits were uncontrolled and businesses were allowed to pass along all their costs in price increases: the wholesale price index skyrocketed from a 4 percent to a 28 percent annual rate), to hold American labor in check ("The idea of the freeze and Phase II was to zap labor," according to a member of the government Pay Board, "and we did": wages plummeted from a 13 percent annual increase to just over 5 percent), and to make the economy sufficiently rosy by the early fall of 1972 to assure Nixon's reelection. Accompanying this, in order to disguise the effects and give the illusion of increased purchasing power, Nixon arranged the formal devaluation of the dollar— his "most magnificent monetary agreement in the history of the world"—in December 1971. And finally, in early 1972, Nixon engineered an expansion of government spending and a loosening of the money supply so that there would be more cash around in the months before the election.

The whole performance was extraordinary: a total transformation of Nixon-Scrooge into Nixon-Cowboy. John Kenneth Galbraith noted that it was "as if Mayor Lindsay of New York had not only declared street-walking legal but the highest form of municipal service."

And in a sense it worked. Nixon, at any rate, was reelected. But it was not long before the house of cards began to topple: inflation was soaring, but recession did not stop; the concentrates were having their finest years, but wages were falling and unemployment increasing. Above all, the artificial inflation and the devaluation only disguised the underlying problem of the American economy, apparently unrecognized even by the Nixon advisers, that the whole imperial arrangement that had sustained the United States at least since World War II was coming unstuck. The failure of U.S. might in Vietnam—made evident at last by the pullout in early 1973—and military impotence elsewhere in the world, the rise of Europe (particularly Germany) and Japan as rivals for the world's resources and the American market, the battering of the dollar in world money exchanges and the successive devaluations, the growing nationalism and success of liberation armies in much of the Third World, and the new uppityness of resource-producing countries (particularly the Middle Eastern oil nations)—all these signaled an end to American economic hegemony in the world as the 1970s began. It would have posed a serious crisis for the United States at any time, but another President might have been able to see it and cushion the blows; Nixon hadn't a clue as to what was going on—obviously the notion that American power was not foreordained to rule the world forever had never occurred to him—and therefore had no way to deal with it.

America proceeded blithely on its way into the worst economic disaster it had faced since the 1930s.

However, there are disasters and disasters. The rocky course of the American economy, and the fact that at the end it very nearly left the road, does not mean that there were not some parts of it that operated very well indeed, sometimes spectacularly so.

Those that operated best during the Nixon years tended to be the industries associated with the Southern Rim, particularly the ones most dependent upon the beneficence of the federal government. It would be an exaggeration to say that the Cowboy Strategy meant a license for each Rimian industry to print money in the denominations and quantities it saw fit, but it certainly did mean the tilting of the government in their direction where possible. To wit:

Defense. "The first concern of the new Administration, as of the last, was still the care and feeding of the war machine," I. F. Stone remarked with his usual bluntness when Nixon presented his first budget in 1969, and yet even he could not have imagined just how assiduously that concern was to be exercised. For four years Nixon managed to continue the Vietnam War, at a total cost of perhaps $25 billion a year, and after the ceasefire was signed, the troops withdrawn, and the "Nixon Doctrine" of entrenchment fully in the works, he actually contrived to *increase* the defense budget, leaving office with it pegged at some $95 billion, $15 billion more than when he came in; moreover, thanks to provisions which Nixon built into the defense budget, it will almost automatically swell to an astounding $142 billion by 1980. Nor is that Nixon's only military legacy: he also enormously expanded the Johnson program of selling U.S. military hardware overseas, an operation that netted the defense industry $22.3 billion during the Nixon years; he began the negotiations that led to the occupation of the island of Diego Garcia and the opening up of the Indian Ocean to the American military; and he achieved what the *New York Times* called a "major relaxation of civilian control of the military" and a concomitant dominance of military people in the Pentagon that was certain to fatten the procurement payrolls in coming years.

And thanks to Nixon policies, Southern Rim defense contractors stood at the head of the line for practically every major contract. The B-1 bomber project, inaugurated with $2 billion in research and development and expected to cost $18 billion before 1983 (Senator William Proxmire calls it "a public work project for the aerospace industry"), was awarded to Rockwell Aviation's California division, with subcontracts in California, Oklahoma, Arizona, Washington, Kansas, and Ohio. The Trident submarine, a $15–20 billion project pushed through by Nixon despite the fact that the Polaris submarine system works just fine, goes to the benefit chiefly of Lockheed plants in California and Georgia and General Dynamics shipyards in Connecticut. The YF-16 fighter plane, starting out with a $4 billion price tag that is expected to increase to $15 billion, was awarded to General Dynamics's vast plant in Forth Worth, with subcontracts in Florida and Connecticut. The supersophisticated F-15 plane, an initial $10 billion package, was given to McDonnell Douglas's California plants. And even when the Rim defense firms weren't getting new contracts, they could still get new monies; in one of the most extraordinary examples of government-business coziness since the days of cross-country railroads, the Nixon Administration pushed through a $1 billion bail-out for the Lockheed Company in 1971, for no other reason than that it was on the verge of bankruptcy—yes, and that it was very important to the California economy.

That's pretty good for care and feeding.

Oil. Only the most unobservant denizen of a desert isle far from the normal trade routes could have been unaware of the incredible boon to the oil industry brought about by the Nixon Administration in the 1970s.

For a start, it seems apparent in hindsight that one of the major reasons for prolonging the Vietnam War, despite its social and financial costs and military futility, was to secure the offshore oil fields in the South China Sea for the American oil firms that had staked out claims there. (And remember that in this area, unlike the Middle Eastern fields developed by the older internationals, the newer Rim companies were participating heavily.) Major explorations were not begun until late 1968, the significant finds not confirmed until early 1969, so it was not until the start of the Nixon era that anyone realized just how large the stake would be—but when it became clear that it would be "one of the biggest booms in the industry's history," according to *Petroleum Engineer*, it wasn't long before the industry was making plans to lay out $35 billion in exploration alone for the following decade. It does not take much imagination to realize how far Nixon would go to protect this kind of investment, particularly since it would seem to be in the national as well as the private interest to develop and secure a new, rich, enormous, safe, offshore, defensible oil area to rival that of the troublesome Middle East.

Whether or not the Vietnam cease-fire meant the recognition of a failure or postponement of this policy, it was not until then that the oil industry began its orchestration of the "energy crisis," a maneuver that managed to increase oil profits by no less than 146 percent during Nixon's second term. In this convenient windfall, they were assisted at practically every turn by the beneficent Nixon Administration, all of whose agencies —several bureaus of the Interior Department, the Federal Power Commission, the Nixon-created Federal Energy Administration—were coaxed and cajoled to get comfortably in bed with the oil industry, to which the industry, it should be added, made no rebuff. In the six years of Nixon's tenure, the Federal Power Commission approved increases of more than 300 percent in the price of some natural gas and removed all price restrictions on other supplies, a bonus expected to amount to more than $500 billion in all. Administration decisions during the single year before Nixon's downfall increased the price of oil, according to a Library of Congress analysis, by no less than $11.5 billion; government concurrence during the same period allowed companies unilaterally to increase the price of oil, according to Senator Phillip Hart, by $35.5 billion.

But that was just the start. Even more important in the long run was the Nixon Administration's decision in 1973 to launch an ambitious Project Independence, the best thing to happen to the domestic petroleum industry since the East Texas boom. A crash program aimed at making America self-sufficient in energy by the 1980s, Project Independence was designed to pump a total of $10 billion into energy programs between 1975 and 1980, encourage domestic drilling, expand Gulf and Pacific ports, and open up ten million acres of Gulf and Atlantic offshore oil fields. During the same period, the Nixon Administration brought enormous and eventually successful pressure on the Congress to approve the long-stalled Alaska Pipeline, a petroleum bonanza even if an environmental calamity, to the particular benefit of California's Atlantic-Richfield and Britain's British Petroleum, the senior partners of the oil consortium, with Phillips (Oklahoma), Union (California—a longtime Nixon friend), Mobil (New York–Texas), and Amerada Hess (New Jersey), and of Los Angeles's Fluor Corporation, the pipeline construction contractors. And at every opportunity the Nixon Administration was there to veto, shelve, kill, or blunt environmental restrictions on oil refineries, superports, strip-mining controls, competitive solar and geothermal research, windfall-profits taxes, and large cuts in the oil-depletion allowance, while at the same time standing ready to support, initiate, or lobby for petroleum price increases, decontrol of natural gas from wellhead to consumer, exploitation of government oil-shale lands, and "double-dipping" by oil refineries.

All that considered, it seems a wonder that the oil companies managed to come up with so parsimonious a sum—a mere $6.1 million—in their donations to the 1972 Nixon campaign.

Agribusiness. "Grain farmers," reported *Time* magazine in late 1974, "have been doing better than any single part of the U.S. economy outside of the oil industry," and it might have added fruit farmers, livestock farmers, chicken farmers, dairy farmers, and vegetable farmers, too, because the farm industry has, with only a few minor dips, been consistently enjoying boom years during the Nixon era. Farm exports have increased from $6.2 billion in 1968 to an exceptional $21.3 billion in 1974, an impressive 350 percent increase even discounting the dollar devaluations. Farm profits have gone from under $16 billion at the start of Nixon's tenure to $32 billion in 1973 and $27 billion in 1974. And, as any shopper knows, food prices have gone up by 46 percent in the Nixon years, greater than any commodity except—you guessed it—oil.

To be sure, Nixon did not achieve this contemporary Canaan all by himself, but his Administration certainly did all it could. Nixon religiously fought for agricultural subsidies until they were no longer needed, paying the highest prices in history, some $4 billion over the market rate, then just as religiously fought for their removal. He created and pushed through the 1974 "beefdoggle" bill providing $2 billion in credits to the livestock industry, ensured that agricultural products were immune from wage-price controls, allowed beef packers to ignore antitrust regulations, pressed for greater private exploitation of government timber lands, and opened up the Mexican border to allow a vast increase in immigrant labor. But nothing that Nixon did for agribusiness surpassed his engineering of two of the most noisome deals in the history of the Presidency: the grain deal with Russia and the milk deal with Texas.

The grain deal was arranged by Nixon during his visit to the Soviet Union in the summer of 1972, when he opened up $750 million of U.S. credit for Russian trade in order to cement good relations with Russia just before the 1972 Presidential elections. The Russians promptly came to the United States and spent a lot of the money buying up American grain—including a quarter of the total wheat crop—at ridiculously cheap prices, so depleting the American grain supplies that supply-and-demand pressures soon forced up the prices of grain commodities for Americans by 300 to 400 percent. The beneficiaries of all this, besides the reelected President and the recouping Russians: the six top American grain dealers (the biggest based in New York, Minnesota, and Tennessee), who were given $300 million in Agriculture Department subsidies to put the deal through; the grain farmers, particularly in the Southern Rim, who missed the short-term windfall but enjoyed a long-term bonanza as the price of wheat went from $1.63 to $4.50 a bushel while the government kept paying out some $475 million in subsidies besides; and the Gulf port docks and shippers—Houston, Galveston, New Orleans, Mobile, and Pascagoula—which handled the largest commodity shipments in their history and kept busy at it for more than a year.

The milk deal involved a catalogue of criminality that has still to be completed, but what is of primary interest here is its contribution to the health and welfare of the Southern Rim (and Border State) dairy farmer. For a mere $632,000 or so, wisely invested in Richard Nixon, three of the largest dairy cooperatives—Associated Milk Producers, Inc. (AMPI), of San Antonio, Texas; Mid-American Dairies, of Springfield, Missouri; and Dairymen, Inc., of Louisville, Kentucky—shared in a dividend amounting to close to $2 billion. Legal hairsplitters are still debating whether it was this money alone that sparked the deal or whether Nixon was simply looking after his Rimian interests ("because they're dairy farmers," as Nixon said on one tape, "the whole damn Middle America"), but the fact remains that after the milk money started to flow in, Nixon agreed to two enormous increases in federal price supports, the imposition of four broad tariff quotas to protect domestic dairy products, and the burial of an IRS investigation of AMPI which had led to criminal suits being prepared in the Justice Department. Milk, it seems, was nearly as precious to Nixon as oil.

Technology. It must have pained Richard Nixon to preside over the temporary reduction of the American space program in the late 1960s, considering how close he felt to the technology industry. Still, he was not without his resources. Working largely with his left hand, while his right was demonstrating all his budget economies, he managed to get new funding for NASA in the early 1970s and to pave the way for a sharp new expansion of space activity for the later 1970s which will bring the level—and the profits—back to the record years of the Johnson Administration. Among the moondoggles are the ambitious Apollo program, part of a joint Soviet-American manned mission, the Viking project for unmanned landings on Mars, and a half-dozen communications-satellite launchings. Most far-reaching of all, Nixon also pushed through the space-lab–space-shuttle program, a multibillion-dollar scheme (starting at $50 billion, expected to go to $200 billion) that started off very nicely indeed with the first award of $2.6 billion to the Rockwell aerospace divisions in California and Oklahoma (over the Grumman Corporation of New York) and promises to bring employment back to peak levels in the NASA headquarters in Houston, the Marshall Space Center in Alabama, and the launching site at Cape Canaveral, Florida.* At the same time, the Nixon Administration encouraged the aircraft business in its penetration of foreign markets, creating a rapid expansion

* That used to be known as Cape Kennedy back in the emotional days following the President's assassination. As sobriety returned, however, and an awareness of the alien nature of yankee names set in, the city fathers voted to resurrect the old name, native to the soil.

in its commercial sales and record exports of $8.2 billion by 1975, a gain of some 50 percent over the 1972 level.

Compared to that, it was only peanuts, but it was still nice to know that Nixon had time for a couple of his friends: in 1970 HEW awarded a $100 million contract to Ross Perot's EDS company in Dallas, with a nifty codicil allowing the firm 100 percent profits, according to the House Intergovernmental Relations hearings; and in 1974 the Federal Energy Administration awarded its chief information-processing contract to a technology firm controlled by the Murchison brothers of Dallas, thereby neatly giving them access to all the reports of their oil-business competitors.

Real estate. Although there is no question that by the end of the Nixon era the housing industry was in serious trouble, there is no question, either, that real estate—and land development and construction—enjoyed its greatest boom period during those years also. Part of the impetus came from the Johnson-sponsored Housing Act of 1968, for which Nixon could take no credit, and part from the home-building associated with any boom period, for which Nixon can take some credit. But part of it came from specific Nixon policies for which he gets *all* the credit. It was under his aegis that real-estate trusts (REITs) were established by banks and investment firms as a means of cashing in on the real-estate boom, and thanks to him that they were allowed to be tax-free. It was due to Nixon, aware of the coming downturn in housing starts, that the government's 1973 tax package included tax incentives for home mortgages and that the 1974 economic program included an extraordinary $10.3 billion Housing Act providing for easier mortgages and expanded community development. It was thanks to Nixon that the Environmental Protection Agency halted all of its attempts to control private development of land and agreed to turn over land-use enforcement to state agencies, generally much more amenable to pressure from local developers. And it was largely the intervention of the Nixon Administration, coupled with powerful pressure on many Southern Rim congressmen, that led to the unexpected defeat of the stringent land-use bill in the House of Representatives in 1974 ("They pulled the rug out from under this bill," Democratic Majority Leader Tip O'Neill complained afterward). If the real-estate people weren't enjoying unalloyed prosperity, you couldn't say it was because Nixon wasn't trying.

Leisure. Here again, the efforts of the Nixon Administration were somewhat disappointing, largely because the management of the energy panic took top priority and that militated against the vacation-time travel and the low-cost air transportation that mean so much to the tourism part of the leisure industry. Nevertheless, the industry as a whole just kept right on expanding during the entire Nixon period, with total leisure spending rising by about 10 percent *every year*, the entertainment business enjoying its best period since the early 1960s, and the sports boom expanding so fast that it even overextended itself by 1975.

Nixon's main contributions in this area were in the protection of lucrative TV and radio franchises and the expansion of the Hollywood movie industry. It was White House pressure on the FCC, often quite blatant, that led the federal agency to vote as official policy the preservation of most TV licenses from challenges by dissident (and usually more liberal) community groups. The White House in 1972 also sought to get Congress to pass a bill extending the duration of these licenses from three to five years, removing all public-service requirements from the station owners, and putting the onus for proving the truth of challenge claims on the claimants themselves. For the movie industry, Nixon arranged a series of economic benefits, including various tax breaks, favored treatment by the Export-Import Bank, and special provisions in the Administration's investment credit bill, and he tried to limit the amount of rerun programming that the yankee networks were allowed to do, in the hope that cowboy movie companies would be used to fill the gaps with original films. The Hollywood doyens were appropriately grateful: some $575,000 in large contributions found its way into Nixon's 1972 campaign.

The Nixon largesse could be demonstrated elsewhere—the trucking industry, for example, and textiles, domestic air carriers, savings and loan banks, conglomerates, all of which are associated primarily with the Southern Rim—but the pattern is already quite clear enough. A cowboy President with cowboy financing cannot help bowing toward cowboy financial interests.

FOREIGN POLICY

The pattern of Richard Nixon's foreign policy was set early in 1969 at a meeting of the National Security Council staff in the west wing of the White House. The new President made very clear to the men assembled that he himself was going to be the boss of the country's foreign policy—domestic policy can run by itself, as he used to say, but foreign policy needs a Presidential hand—and that he would be using Henry Kissinger, head of the NSC staff, rather than William Rogers, Secretary of State, as his right-hand man. Then he launched into a furious assault on the State Department and its handling of foreign policy, an attitude he no doubt carried with him from his McCarthyite days, and finally declared that it was going to be the President's own staff in the White House that would take charge of foreign policy in the new Administration, not those "striped-pants faggots" in the State Department.

His audience was stunned, as well it might be, but it was privileged at least to be given such a revealing portrait of the Nixon mind and its attitude toward American foreign policy: Nixon saw himself as the great international wheeler-dealer, he intended to build up his own bureaucracy whose loyalty and obeisance he could always check, and he would be giving no power to the snobbish Eastern Ivy Leaguers he imagined infested Foggy Bottom. That was the first indication, but it would not be the last, that the Cowboy Strategy operated just as much in foreign as in domestic affairs.

Take Vietnam. As tragic as it seems, there is little doubt that Richard Nixon prosecuted that war for four years and several million lives, in spite of the fact that he knew he could not prevail, because he did not want to do anything that looked like acknowledging the humiliation of American defeat—thus losing him the support of the superpatriots of the Southern Rim and threatening his reelection in 1972. Cowboy Strategy called for the elaborate machismo of military might to disguise the awful truths that America's Army could not fight, its money could not triumph, its power could not conquer. Cowboy Strategy meant accompanying every demonstration of peace-seeking with massive demonstrations of warfare—hence the saturation bombing of Hanoi just before the visit to Peking, the mining of

Haiphong before the summit meeting in Moscow, the Christmas bombing of Hanoi before the final cease-fire. Cowboy Strategy meant postponing the final defeat until after the 1972 elections and then accompanying it with such elaborate shenanigans around homecoming soldiers and released prisoners of war that it could be given, at least in receptive quarters of the Southern Rim, the guise of victory. Cowboy Strategy meant pumping enough money and materiel into South Vietnam to support Thieu even after the cease-fire, following Kissinger's oft-stated goal that there should be "a 'decent interval'—two to three years—between the withdrawal of U.S. troops and a Communist takeover in Vietnam."

Dean Acheson, a wily yankee, with antennae carefully tuned toward Nixon's strategy, perceived all this in the last weeks before his death. As recounted by fellow yankee Emmet John Hughes, he laid bare the Nixon "rationale" for the protracted war:

> The essence of this rationale argued that the nation's reactionary right would rise in wrath against a hasty retreat, and the disengagement therefore had to be artfully "staged" to blur the truth and avoid the backlash. . . . "Kissinger sums up White House motivation in one pithy phrase," the former Secretary of State explained. "He says we must at all costs avoid *an orgy of recrimination*." . . . Thousands of Americans [were] killed during four years of a military withdrawal staged to appease militant patriots and to protect the President's political right flank.

It was because of this prolongation that the first serious cracks began to show themselves in the wall of support which the business community and its followers had erected before 1968. Both Northeastern and Southern Rim capitalists, of course, wanted to keep Southeast Asia open for the American empire, and both therefore hoped to pacify Vietnam. But there were certain costs that the yankee community wanted to avoid, and as the balance of payments grew steadily worse, as inflation kept mounting, as the social dislocations at home became ever sharper, and as the futility of the operation grew more apparent, more and deeper cracks appeared, more Wall Street businessmen joined the ranks of the polite dissenters. Nixon, ever the politician, sought to keep the revolt from growing by his détente visits to Russia and China and his staged announcement that "peace is at hand" just before the 1972 elections, and that was enough—along with the business world's antipathy to George McGovern—to put almost the entire capitalist spectrum in the Republican camp in 1972. But this early sign of a split in the business ranks should have been a clear signal that the Cowboy Strategy was playing too fast and loose with the yankee vision and that perilous times were ahead.

Nor was Vietnam the only evidence of the fabricated bellicosity of this strategy. Nixon continually delighted in rattling his nuclear weaponry—remember it was he who described himself to the Pope as the most powerful man in the world, and made it sound like a threat—and in reminding less fortified nations (India, for example, the Middle East, Japan) that they were at the mercy of American might. Even his posture with the Soviet Union, though it could unbend for occasional treaties which Nixon saw as being in American interests, was arrogant and pugnacious, born of the essentially Cold War attitude (which he shared with the Metternichian Kissinger) that global diplomacy was a perpetual power struggle which always necessitated a show of strength and a presumption of treachery. Hence, to prove to Russia more than anyone else that America was not a pitiful, helpless giant: the vehement prosecution of the Vietnam War, the mobilization of troops after the Soviet-backed invasion of Jordan, the abandonment of SALT talks after their political purpose had been served, the recurrent deployment of American fleets, and the military alert during the Yom Kippur war. As literary critic Alfred Kazin has put it in his romantic way:

> The drives, the "battle" that Nixon proudly says is "always with me," the necessity to obliterate an opponent rather than to persuade him, the computerized, militarized football-stadium language that vindictively brings all loyalties down to the "team" as the corporate ego in which a man may find his necessary virility, the lack of any cultural ties outside the overwhelming monoliths of American power—these are the "operabilities" behind Nixon's *Mein Kampf*,

born of mid-century American toughness and drive and planetary megalomania fascinated by and envious of Soviet ruthlessness. Bit by bit our old scruples have been eroded by a new value system that recognizes no truth that is not part of what is "operable."

After the settlement of Vietnam, the linchpin of Nixon's cowboy foreign policy became the economic penetration of foreign markets, most especially for cowboy interests. The Nixon Administration poured millions of dollars into the Middle East, sent its CIA operatives as ambassadors to Iran and Lebanon, and expended enormous diplomatic energy for a cease-fire, all in order to protect the long-range interests of the oil internationals, old and new. It let the traditional alliances with Europe fall into a shambles, earning the enmity of virtually every government on the Continent, while it concentrated instead on openings to the Pacific (China, Southeast Asia) and the Caribbean, especially for the new overseas operations of technical and aerospace runaway plants. It badgered Japan to get better protection for the textile industry, nurtured Russia to get better markets for the agribusiness sector, coddled Greece for the protection of shipping and oil interests, and cultivated the Middle East for its reinvestments of "petrodollars" into American real estate, banking, and defense products.

But above all, the Nixon Administration finally got America caught up with the rest of the world in its relations—especially its trade relations—with Russia and China. True, the détente with Russia and the opening to China seemed to be a dangerous defilement of the Cowboy Strategy—and indeed both stirred up considerable passion among the Far Right in the United States—but in fact they were both carefully, almost surgically, limited to the establishment of markets and investments to the benefit of American, especially cowboy, capital. Not at any point did they threaten any of the interests that the cowboy ideology held dear: despite the arms agreements with Russia, there was no limitation whatsoever in the production of weaponry or the relative superiority of American power; despite normalization with China, there was no withdrawal from Southeast Asian or Pacific military posts except in Vietnam. Ultimately it seemed that most cowboys agreed with the businessman in a cartoon of the time who argued, "They may be athe-istic Red Chinese Communists, but I can't help thinking that there's 800 million potential consumers over there."

The reason for the American penetration of these new markets was put with disarming frankness by Alfred Went-worth, head of the Chase Manhattan Bank office that opened up in Moscow in 1973, a yankee who certainly understood cowboy principles: "The Soviet Union"—he should have added China as well—"is the last great undeveloped market for the U.S." Certainly yankee businesses could take advantage of those markets—Nixon, after all, was never one to deny opportunities to American business of any stripe—but the importance of opening them up under the Nixon aegis is that the cowboy industries could share in the bonanza as well, and, insofar as their success depended on government favors, could generally count on being given the larger shares. Particularly important this when it is remembered that in an earlier era, before the cowboy challenge had been mounted, yankee firms swarmed all over Europe, developing hegemonic markets that outsiders could not break—but here at last in Asia and Russia was a chance for the newcomers.

Trade with China was only in its infancy when its Ameri-can midwife was forced from office in 1974, but even so the preeminent role of the Southern Rim was clear enough. Cotton exports had reached the point where the United States stood as China's largest foreign supplier, enjoying annual sales of nearly $400,000, and the State Department expected them soon to amount to "as much as a quarter of the U.S. cotton crop"; tobacco sales, though insignificant in total world-wide trade, started off at some $150,000 a year and seemed encouraging enough to cause several Carolina plants to reorient part of their operations toward this market; fertilizer plants, a product of the Rim's agribusiness know-how, were eagerly sought by China for its vast agriculture, with the first $70 million factory scheduled to be built by a Texas firm; and total contracts from the Chinese for the American construction industry, according to an Ameri-can official, stood at no less than $1 billion by 1973. An indica-tion of the cowboy clout here was the composition of the execu-tive board of the high-level business council formed in 1973 with American government backing "to promote American

trade with China": seven of them were certifiable yankees—
David Rockefeller of Chase Manhattan, Donald Kendall of
Pepsico, and the like—but they were outnumbered by the ten
bona-fide cowboys, ranging from David Packard of Hewlett-
Packard to Anthony Bryan of Texas's Cameron Iron Works.
That just would not have happened ten years before.

Trade with Russia has, of course, been far greater in volume and sales—about $9 billion per year through the 1970s—
but the same pattern emerges there, too. To be sure, there have
been hundreds of firms outside the Southern Rim which have
taken advantage of the new relaxations of the Nixon era and
moved in with everything at their disposal; the Karmaz truck
complex, for example, put together by Chase Manhattan Bank
in 1972, is almost totally a yankee enterprise, and a $270 mil-
lion one at that. At the same time, however, a whole range of
new corporations, some not even in business when the West
European market opened up after World War II, were quick to
embrace this new opportunity for overseas expansion and for a
slice of the potentially multibillion-dollar Russian market. Cook
Industries, the Memphis grain dealer, has been the beneficiary
of some $20 million worth of the grain trading with the Soviet
Union; Dresser Industries of Dallas had done $27.5 million
worth of business by the middle of 1974 and confidently predicted quadrupling of its volume within a few years; Texas
Industries, Cameron Iron, and M. F. Kellog, three diverse
Texas businesses, all won contracts for sales to or plants in the
Soviet Union in the 1970–73 period; and Occidental Petroleum
of California has signed an enormous $20 billion fertilizer deal
with the Soviet Union involving the construction of a 1,500-
mile pipeline, the shipment of Florida phosphates, and the development of ammonia plants over the next ten years.

And still the plum of the whole Soviet-American détente
has yet to fall. So far the Russians have indicated willingness to
go ahead with two massive natural-gas schemes, one piping gas
to Black and Barents Sea ports, the other to the Pacific—both
of which are to be constructed and operated by cowboy con-
sortiums. The Black-Barents scheme would be operated by El
Paso Natural Gas (Texas) and Occidental Petroleum (California), and would be constructed by Bechtel (California) and
Williams Brothers (Oklahoma)—the size of that deal is esti-

mated to be around $10 billion just to start with; the Pacific operation would be operated by Tenneco and Texas Eastern Transmission, would be built by Brown & Root (all Texas)— and that would have an initial cost of $15 billion. Everything has been held up on the American side, and not even Nixon's pressure was able to force Congress into the trade agreement guaranteeing these investments in the Russian wastelands; still, since the ultimate product—natural gas—is badly needed in the American economy, one of the two schemes is almost certain to be approved.

Look at that: and without any striped-pants faggots, either.

In retrospect, it may be that Nixon's greatest contributions will in fact have been in the area of foreign affairs, though not for the reasons ("a generation of peace") he predicted. If the end to American imperial hegemony over the world is supplanted by a new penetration of the markets in *both* semi-developed (Russia) and developing (China) countries, if "neo-imperialist" arrangements are in fact struck allowing a non-national kind of exploitation of world resources, and if upstart American industries are placed in a strong position in the fight for these considerable treasures, then the Cowboy Strategy will have achieved its most lasting effect in the transformation of American foreign policy.

Quite clearly, for good or ill, the Nixon Administration was one of the most important in the history of the American republic. It began a process of rearranging priorities that had been settled, or so it was thought, for the previous half-century at least. It was the embodiment of new power, new money, new influence, new dynamism. It attempted to establish a new structure for the American Presidency, a new reordering of the American economy, a new design for American power. And it did so with a brashness, an imperiousness, a *force*, that eventually betrayed it into bestirring its rivals into action.

6

The Yankee Counterattack

In March 1973, about the time that the whole long process of the cowboy challenge seemed to have culminated in the invincible power of the Nixon Presidency, John Herbers, who had been covering the White House for the *New York Times*, wrote a series of front-page articles on "Richard Nixon's use of the power of the Presidency and its effects on the Government and the national life."

"Richard M. Nixon," Herbers began, "in what he achieved in his first term and what he has undertaken in his second, is attempting an expansion of Presidential powers that could have more impact on the national Government than that of any President since Franklin D. Roosevelt." Ominous enough that, but it was spelled out in detail for almost every area of American life:

> There is concern in both parties of Congress that the constitutional system is giving way to Presidential Government without checks. . . .
>
> Nixon is using his office to reverse some aspects of a trend that has been under way since the nineteen-thirties—the growth of the national Government as the chief instrument

for public policy and services. . . . The President and his men are dismantling programs built by four decades of Democratic government. . . .

What is at stake is whether Congress survives as a strong and effective branch of the Government and whether more power continues to accumulate in the Presidency without accompanying restraints and means of accountability to the public. . . .

He had gone further than any modern President in trying to shape the bureaucracy to conform to both the style and purposes of the President. . . . If Mr. Nixon succeeds, in the opinion of some Government experts, he may well set a precedent that will shape the future of the Presidency. . . .

He has undertaken to make fundamental changes in what kind of schools people attend, what kind of cities and communities they live in, what kind of news they watch on television and read in the papers, what taxes they pay and to whom, what system of justice they live under, what their employment and income opportunities will be. . . .

And, Herbers concluded, "with almost four years remaining in office and with a landslide victory behind him, Mr. Nixon is seeking to consolidate his gains, make new initiatives in shaping the national life and leave a legacy for his successor that would be difficult to reverse."

It was a frightening series, designedly so, and it was like a clarion call throughout the yankee Establishment.

Now it would be Machiavellian to suggest that the Herbers articles did in fact set off the yankee counterattack all by themselves, even though the *Times* and its leading reporters normally share the same general outlook as the yankee powers. But it would be Coolidgean to think that the dangers which Herbers was pointing to had not been recognized by other people in the land over the preceding four years and that many of those in the yankee power structure were not deeply worried about exactly these aspects of the Presidency at exactly this time. What Herbers seemed to be saying, what any careful watcher of the national scene might be realizing, is that the Nixon Presidency was

in fact succeeding in implanting many of the goals of the Cowboy Strategy upon America, and that this might have quite
ominous consequences for those whose purposes would not be
served thereby.

And it is a fact that within a month of the Herbers articles,
L. Patrick Gray began spilling his knowledge of the Watergate
cover-up to the Senate Judiciary Committee (until its chairman,
Mississippi's James Eastland, called it off); James McCord
wrote his letter to Judge John Sirica confessing that "political
pressure" had been put on him and the other Watergate burglars
and that they had committed perjury during their trial to protect higher-ups; John Dean, the White House counsel who
seemed to know just what had been going on in the Oval Office,
agreed to talk both to the U.S. attorneys and the staff of the
Watergate committee; the Watergate committee decided to end
secret testimony and take its hearings to the public; and a federal grand jury was empaneled in Washington and began taking
testimony on the Watergate burglary and the political conspiracy behind it. Within a month, in other words, Watergate,
which up to then had been something between a third-rate burglary and a vicuña-coat scandal, suddenly began to unravel with
great rapidity to reveal the corruption at the very core of the
Nixon Administration.*

---

* It is intriguing to speculate, as many have done, that all of this may
have been more than accidental. Is it possible, for example, that the
CIA, which has always been a yankee power center, Ivy League types
particularly welcome, was reeling under a series of Nixonian measures
which had downgraded its status in the intelligence hierarchy, involved
it in wholesale and illegal domestic spying, purged some fifteen hundred
of its top officers and attempted to make it into a weapon for the political
ends of the White House—and, either out of simple bureaucratic chau-
vinism or something more sinister, decided to react? Is it possible that
when several of its "former" operatives, including James McCord and
E. Howard Hunt, plus one informant still on its payroll, Eugenio Martinez,
became involved in a plot that, if exposed, would prove highly embar-
rassing to Nixon, the CIA decided the job should be bungled (and on
two successive days) with the hope of getting caught? And when even
that didn't produce the full-scale scandal that was wanted, that pressure
was put upon the twenty-year CIA man, James McCord, to write the
letter that finally blew the cover-up apart? Is it even possible that a
wider conspiracy was at work, an entangled affair that might have involved the Rockefeller interests in New York, the yankee bastions in

It is doubtful that anyone at that time could have imagined that any kind of pressure would make Nixon actually resign his office, since that had never happened before in the history of the republic. Nor was it necessary. All that was wanted was to hold the man in check, modify his policies, prevent that rapid and wholesale rejiggering of the society that he was in the process of, and surely that could happen without any such drastic step as resignation or impeachment. Few could have imagined—none did, publicly—in the early days of 1973 what the country would go through by the late days of 1974.

I

The yankee counterattack was not a *thing* but a *process*, not a plan but an eventuality. To talk of a "counterattack" is not to pretend that there was something calculated and controlled, decided upon in the board rooms of General Motors or Chase Manhattan, the fulfillment of a plan craftily hatched by Nelson Rockefeller, Henry Ford, and the staff of the Council on Foreign Relations; it describes, rather, a very slow and inchoate process, a *response*, very real to be sure, but amorphous, unregulated, unplanned, moving like an amoeba without sure purpose or direction although quite capable of absorbing any new thing that comes along and of making it serve its needs. If there was anything conscious about it, it took the shape only of a *New York Times* editorial inveighing against "lawlessness in high places" and the "subversion of free and orderly government," or a liberal congressional group seeking to upset the White House budget cuts and impoundments, or Common Cause trying to open up the books of the reelection committee in the name of campaign finance reforms, or a Rockefeller Foundation report that the economy under Nixon was in such bad shape that new men and new ideas had better take over his economic

Washington like the CIA and the Justice Department bureaucracy, and certain individuals in the Administration righteously fearful of Nixon's increasing power (for example, whoever became the *Washington Post*'s chief informant under the nickname "Deep Throat")? All this is certainly possible—though, so far, unprovable—but not *necessary* in the demonstration that yankee power stood somewhere behind the Watergate reaction.

counseling before there was a collapse, or a Yankelovich survey warning that people were being set loose from their previous political moorings and ideological assumptions. The drift, in other words, was clear enough, and the goal, but no single person or group of persons programmed its course. Power struggles on such a broad battlefield as a nation are never crude.

The process that culminated in the Nixon resignation began some time back in the 1960s, a reaction to the manner in which Lyndon Johnson presided over the prosecution of a pointless war and the containment of the black rebellion, both of which had produced a great disaffection among much of the American population—and not the blacks and poor and young alone—and in the later stages a serious disruption of the American system. One by one, segments of the yankee structure began to assert their opposition: the prestige professoriate, the big-city newspapers, the liberal politicians, the non-construction unions, the Jewish intelligentsia, the big Democratic money, even some among the stockbrokers and investment bankers. Nor did anything seem to get better with the advent of Richard Nixon: the war went on, the disruptions continued, the economy continued its inflation, and it seemed that the use of repression would only become more blatant and ugly, hence more disruptive still. In fact, if anything, the Presidency of Richard Nixon seemed to be moving in worse directions, with more bombings in Vietnam, greater havoc at home (especially after Cambodia and Kent State), a growing disregard for Congress, a devalued dollar and still-continuing inflation-recession, the hint of serious scandals (ITT, My Lai), the downgrading of European alliances and the United Nations, and increasing attacks on liberals, students, draft resisters, university administrators, welfare workers, union leaders, the Catholic Left, television networks, and the Eastern press. Slowly the yankee voices became louder: a few senators like Charles Goodell and Birch Bayh and Vance Hartke and eventually even Jacob Javits got around to opposing the war; the *New York Times* finally accepted the idea of an all-out withdrawal; AFL-CIO head George Meany allowed as how the war economy was not so beneficial to the working population; Edmund Muskie traveled the country with attacks on the war, the wage freeze, the welfare cuts, and seemed to be gathering certain popular support.

When the 1972 campaigns came along, the yankee counterattack was temporarily stymied—George McGovern was insufficient both as Establishmentarian and as imaginable President—so it had to be content with the reelection of Richard Nixon and the desperate hope that the Russian and Chinese détentes, the announcement that "peace is at hand" in Vietnam, the containment of inflation, and the played-down campaign rhetoric were all signals of change and reform.

But it did not take long for that hope to be shattered. Riding the crest of his overwhelming (and fraudulently rigged—but who knew it at the time?) election victory, Richard Nixon immediately made it clear that he was out to remake the country with a vengeance, quite plainly planning to accomplish in his last four years—with a large mandate, four years of experience, a developed system of White House rule, a loyal or subdued team at the upper levels of the Administration, and a refined notion of how the Cowboy Strategy should operate—nothing less than a reordering of American government and power. In private interviews, in his Inaugural speech, in his messages to Congress, Nixon left no doubt that a new era was dawning, and that a strong President was going to see it through.

Perhaps no aspect of the Nixon regime, as it grew out of the first term and as it was shaped for the second, was more disturbing to the countervailing forces in the country as its development of what Arthur Schlesinger was to call "the Imperial Presidency." True enough, the pattern began with Franklin Roosevelt and was enlarged by every succeeding President, but it was not until Lyndon Johnson, and then even more with Richard Nixon, that the Presidency became a world unto itself, effectively free from most influences of public, press, party, or politics. As John Ehrlichman said so proudly in a television interview at the start of the second term, "He is the only elected officer elected by all the people of the United States, unlike the Senators and the Congressmen." But . . . isn't that one-man rule? "Sure, that's what the President of the United States is." To which the yankee avant-garde replied, in the words of I. F. Stone that same month, "The real problem, as the coming weeks will make clear, is not just to disengage America from Southeast Asia but from the increasingly one-man rule of Richard Nixon."

From his reelection on, it was evident that Nixon did not intend to be limited in any way by the theoretically coequal legislative branch of government. When he did not like the laws that Congress sent to him, he vetoed them (at least forty times by 1974), and bent enough arms to make sure that they stayed vetoed; when he did not like the programs passed, he impounded the funds (at least $18 billion worth) despite the fact that the courts continually found this to be illegal; when he wanted to make international deals, he did so by Executive Agreement rather than treaty, so that the Senate would have no say; when he wanted to plaster North Vietnam with bombs, he did so, and when he wanted to sign a cease-fire, he did that, both without consulting friend or foe upon the Hill; when he wanted to bomb Cambodia, he bypassed both the Pentagon and the Congress and unleashed a secret war; when he wanted to disband a program, he simply abolished the agency or board in charge by Executive Order, regardless of whether (as in the case of OEO, for example) this was forbidden by law; when he wanted to devalue the currency without letting Congress know, he went right ahead and did so by executive action without the slightest heed to the specific provision against this in the law; when he wanted to frustrate congressional investigations into his doings (as with the Fitzgerald and ITT cases before Watergate), he simply pulled the blanket of executive privilege around the entire executive branch; and when Congress, poor Congress, just asked politely for a chance to borrow some time on a couple of the Administration's computers to run through a few computations on welfare grants, he refused even that, giving no reason. Even Senator Javits, normally a fawning Nixon supporter and not a notable firebrand, was prompted to public complaint early in 1973: "We are now in the midst of a grave and domestic constitutional crisis brought on by the Administration's unilateral efforts to reorder our domestic priorities. This crisis covers every aspect of legislation pending in the Congress or which may be proposed." Now when a Republican senator says things like that, you know that there are strong forces beginning to gather.

At the same time it was also clear that Nixon was prepared to dismantle the federal system that had been so carefully strung together to build the liberal consensus, the ideological assumptions that had become standard for the "enlightened" academic and corporate world over the previous forty years. He was *really* going to gut the welfare system—that wasn't just talk for his more conservative followers; he was *really* going to do away with programs for the poor, grants for the blacks, scholarships for the students, funds for the teenagers, aid for the cities. If anything had been learned in the days since 1929, it would seem to have been that governmental support for the most depressed and hostile elements of the society was absolutely essential for social control and at least a modicum of social peace— and surely the "Great Society" programs of Lyndon Johnson made that self-evident. And yet here was a man prepared to discard not only the Great Society programs, meager as they were, but many of the other welfare programs that had their roots as far back as the depression of the 1930s. Even the crustiest Wall Street Blimp could see the folly, the enormous danger, in all of that. "The real issue," as the archly Bostonian *Christian Science Monitor* saw it, "is whether Richard Nixon's new-old social philosophy—the 'work ethic'—shall displace the social philosophy of the New Deal in the whole approach of government to the problems of the U.S."

Moreover, Nixon was also abusing the other traditions that had become fairly well established over the previous half-century when, under yankee control, the methods of the modern liberal state were refined. He had mounted an attack, for example, on the freedom of the press—intimidation, prior censorship, regulatory threats—that already had gone beyond anything even his high-handed predecessor had tried to do, and was bidding fair to go even farther, what with his Office of Telecommunications Policy, his politicization of the FCC, and his prosecution of Daniel Ellsberg. He had quite openly chosen to make the hallowed Supreme Court into an instrument of his own policy, selecting not distinguished jurists but people who would follow his own political line and publicly whip-lashing those who did not, and before the next four years was over, would certainly have a majority on the court. He had used the government's repressive powers more fully than anyone before him and, even before all the details of the White House plumbers and the Huston Plan came out, voices from quite sedate and conservative quarters were warning against the coming "garrison state" and the movement "into an era of repression." Worse still, as every passing day bore evidence, he had not confined his repressive techniques to radicals and dissidents alone, but had actually attempted to use them upon one of the two accepted political parties—a direct assault upon the very political contrivance itself by which the oligarchy of the nation has always sought to retain control and maintain the social order. In short, Nixon did not seem to have the requisite respect for the constitutional and political arrangements of the land: "Even in wartime," Massachusetts historian Henry Steele Commager noted as Nixon's second term began, "there was no such broad-gauged and wide-fronted assault on the integrity of the constitutional system as we now have."

Finally, it was clear that Nixon had no idea of how to handle the economy, apart from general policies that seemed to favor such industries as agribusiness and oil, and that he might run the country into a serious depression before "four more years" were up.

Now, in times of great prosperity and expanding empire, factionalism among economic interests is subdued and no one much cares about Presidential prerogatives, but in times of sharp adversity and declining empire, all the rivalries are exacerbated and great contentions emerge about political control: this principle is known as Fagin's Law, colloquially expressed as, "In good times, grab and grin, in hard times, fights begin." As America's imperial influence had diminished, therefore, the fights had begun among the contending factions, specifically taking shape in a competition between yankee and cowboy economic interests. That rivalry took many forms, but basically it stemmed from two ways of reading the economy: the cowboys (to make a broad generalization) tended to be more concerned with inflation that saps too much strength from the upper part of the economy and particularly the purchasing power of the government, since their industries are so heavily dependent upon government favors; the yankees (to make another) are more concerned with recession that saps too much strength from the lower part of the economy and particularly the purchasing power of the consumer, since their industries, the basic manufacturing businesses, are so heavily dependent upon the consumer market. Beyond that, of course, there were specific differences: the cowboys tended to favor trade with Pacific, Latin American, and Caribbean nations, and were less concerned with the traditional relations with Europe; the yankees, with long European trading ties, tended to emphasize Atlantic and Mediterranean markets and placed relatively less emphasis upon Asian ones, with the partial exception of Japan; the cowboys naturally tended to favor the general development of the Southern Rim, the yankees the welfare of the Northeast.

As Nixon's second term got under way, the formal acknowledgment of the diminution of empire was made with the signing of the cease-fire and the withdrawal of the American Army from Vietnam—and this on top of all the other policies, bungled or betrayed, that seemed effective only in driving the country closer to peril. By loosening the ties with Europe and driving France from the Atlantic alliance, Nixon had lessened the chance that there could be any serious economic bulwark to stand up to a new Third World challenge—as, for example, the looming attempt by the oil-producing countries of the Middle East to restructure the petroleum market and increase their prices. By moving hither and yon with federal policies—first no controls, then a freeze, then controls, then guidelines, first fighting inflation, then recession, then neither—he had baffled the corporate world and the consumer alike, and still found no programs that could last for more than a few months. And by making economic policy dance to a political tune, he had taken away all the flexibility which his economic ministers so badly needed, prevented them from reacting quickly to fiscal and market currents, and cut them off from many academic and a number of Wall Street economic experts. Clearly things were growing desperate: the *Washington Post*'s financial editor complained of "no firm hand on the controls," a stock-exchange principal moaned of "the gloom that envelops the stock market," Federal Reserve chairman Arthur Burns confessed that the government "lacks either the knowledge or the competence to make good on the promises that it holds out to people."

The process that was the yankee counterattack, then, grew inexorably, a conglomeration of many attitudes on many political, social, and economic fronts. It had no thought of deposing Nixon, nor would it want to—instability, after all, is not desirable in the smooth running of things—but it did hope, by force of its high academic credentials, or overwhelming media voice, or persuasive politicians, or *somehow* to get Nixon to change his policies, come off his high Southwestern horse, play a simple mainstream game.

But Nixon was not listening. For the first few months imperious, then petulant and blustering over the Watergate stories, he seemed to pay hardly any attention to the growing counterattack. Congress was treated to more end runs and "executive privilege" smoke screens; attacks on the media increased, with the President himself crying "Unfair" and "Scandalous"; the economy was given no guidance whatsoever; foreign policy was permitted to collapse; another devaluation was slipped in, unconstitutionally; and the impoundings, the vetoes, the dismantlings went on.

And so the pressures continued. The media, particularly the Eastern press and particularly the *Washington Post*, the *New York Times*, and *Newsweek*, gave intense clamorous attention to the growing Watergate story, pressing, pressing, pressing, sensing that there was a weakness there in this unwanted President, that enough of the story would soon come out to embarrass him totally, humble him, cripple him, reform him, bring him into line: and it did not have to be a conscious decision by Woodward and Bernstein, even by Ben Bradlee or Katharine Graham, only a received and general feeling that in the pursuit, the relentless pursuit, of *this* story, having given a couple of suburban police reporters their head, then backing them up with an ever-larger crew of sharp, investigative journalists, the national interests would be served. The Congress, especially through its Watergate Committee, made the stakes higher still, beginning a series of well-publicized, and for a while televised, hearings, that slowly laid out a story of corruption, sabotage, cover-up, and scandal that the nation almost could not believe, finally fixing "Watergate" in the national mind as something more than just "a third-rate burglary," something more than just dirty politics as usual. The effect here, of course, was blunted, since the inquiry was inevitably in the hands of the Southern Rimsters who guide the Senate establishment—five of the seven committee members were Rimsters, including the chairman and vice chairman—but that didn't really matter, since on the Hill all that was wanted was a redressing of the balance between the two branches and not a full-scale attack on the President. Naturally, too, the "citizens' lobbies," like Ralph Nader's Eastern-financed legal and study projects, and John Gardner's Rockefeller-backed Common Cause, both of which had begun worrying the Watergate bone in the previous year, now set tenaciously to work to pick it clean, forcing various Nixon crews into court and opening up their crooked books to public inspection. Union leaders joined in, too, even those who had, under Meany's cantankerous direction, sat out the election only a few months before, and before many months were over the AFL-CIO had developed a nineteen-point impeachment indictment and devoted itself all-out to an impeachment campaign aiming—so the labor columnists said—at a substitute like Elliot Richardson or Nelson Rockefeller. The academic world, to no one's surprise, kept up its drumbeat throughout, and perhaps the loudest when the idea of impeachment began to surface; the liberal professoriate—Arthur Schlesinger, Henry Steele Commager, James MacGregor Burns, Richard Neustadt, Raoul Berger, and dozens more—could hardly find enough people to print all their letters, columns, articles, essays, books, pamphlets, paperbacks, and even textbooks. Parts of the judiciary cooperated, too, more out of a sense of wanting to reestablish the prestige of the law than any desire to clip the Nixonian wings, but obviously with a sense that the executive branch had indeed been guilty of humbug and hoodwink before Watergate and during; and when Judge Sirica later on implied that he was more interested in getting to the "T-R-U-T-H truth" than meting out justice, he showed himself perfectly a part of the counterattack spirit.

Even the federal machinery itself was finally forced to participate. Under siege as never before, Nixon in May bowed to the demands to get rid of the tainted Richard Kleindienst as Attorney General and he replaced him with Elliot Richardson, presumably the perfect compromise—Richardson was as Brahminic as a Bostonian could be, but he had also served Nixon in two previous high-level posts and been found a loyal and pliant servant. Richardson, however, was out in the open now and sensed that the winds were blowing out of the Northeast, for he chose as a special prosecutor for the whole Watergate investigation what could only be regarded as a genuine viper for the Nixonian bosom: Archibald Cox, of prestigious yankee credentials (St. Paul's, Harvard, and Harvard Law), a Boston lawyer and Harvard Law professor, Solicitor General under John Kennedy, a Democrat and thorough Establishmentarian. Within weeks Cox had established an office in Washington, stocked it with a clutch of young lawyers who had worked with or for the Kennedys in the past, agreed upon friendly cooperation with the press, and set to work with real ambition to uncover everything that might possibly bring discredit upon Nixon and his Administration. And, it did not take long to discover, there was a lot.

And so, all in all, the pressure during the early months of 1973 was absolutely relentless. And because it was also so successful in uncovering one scandal, one crime, after another —the enemies list, the Vesco contribution, the Huston Plan, the milk scandal, the Stans fund-raising, the Mitchell intelligence plans, the Segretti sabotage, the Kalmbach payoffs, the Agnew bribe-taking, the Hughes-Rebozo gift, the White House plumbers, the Nixon cover-ups, the Nixon hush money, the Nixon tax-chiseling, the Nixon tapes, the Nixon lies, the Nixon bribery—it was irresistible.

II

But it *was* resisted.

By temperament and training, Nixon was a battler—in fact, as we have seen, for him the battle was all-important, and furthermore he had been quite successful throughout his life at battling in the face of adversity and somehow managing to come out on top. Why shouldn't that work now? If he managed to find the dirty trick to smear and defeat Jerry Voorhis, if he just happened to come up with the Hiss typewriter hours before potential disgrace, if his smarmy, blustering attack got him out of the slush-fund scandal, if his elaborate PR mask managed to win him the nomination and election, and if his intricate multi-million-dollar scheming managed to secure his reelection, then surely *something* would be serviceable this time. After all, this is a President of the United States they're going after, and he's the most powerful man in the world, and he's got to be able to find the strategies (stonewalling, stroking, public relations, executive privilege, national security) and the people (lawyers, accomplices, fall guys, flaks) to get him out of this one.

Nixon threw up every defense he knew, and in this moment of highest crisis he depended most upon those he felt shared his vision and his aspirations, even his disregard for moral niceties, generally those from the Southern Rim. When Richardson brought in Cox, Nixon brought in J. Fred Buzhardt, a South Carolina lawyer of undistinguished credentials but known to be loyal and conservative and for eight years an aide to Senator Strom Thurmond; from then right through the finish, it was Buzhardt who ran the whole Nixon defense, who controlled and listened to the White House tapes, who selected staff, and who (with Nixon himself and aide Leonard Garment) shaped the strategies. Around him, Buzhardt built a Rimian legal team, including Charles Alan Wright, from the University of Texas Law School; Samuel Powers, Jr., a Miami lawyer; and a crew of young men, not an Ivy Leaguer in the bunch, whom the *Wall Street Journal* described as being in "a Nixonian mold." And even, later on, when Boston attorney James St. Clair was brought in for window dressing to deceive and deflect the yankee intensity, he always played the willing barrister to Buzhardt's solicitor.

Then when Nixon was facing demands to give over the White House tapes, he suddenly developed a "compromise" by which he would edit the things himself—fairly, of course—and have Mississippi Senator John Stennis—"Judge Stennis" to Nixon—decide whether the transcriptions were full and accurate, an arrangement acquiesced in by two other Southern gentlemen, Sam Ervin and Howard Baker. (The tissue-paper obviousness of that deceit eventually created an outcry and congressional opposition that forced Ervin and Baker to recant and Nixon to take a different tack.) And when the storm broke over Nixon's tax payments—$789 on an income of more than $200,000, for example—he thought it wise to try to bypass the Congress's Joint Committee on Taxation, known to have a lot of dedicated yankee types on its staff, and generously offered instead to have the whole matter turned over to Arkansas's Wilbur Mills, with Russell Long standing by, for them to decide whether there had been any impropriety. (No dice on that one, either: the rest of the Congress wouldn't stand for it.)

And when, ultimately, Nixon's back was against the wall —when Cox was probing into his funny-money transactions with Bebe Rebozo and investigating the persistent rumors about laundered money and Swiss bank accounts—he took the drastic step of simply firing Cox and replacing him with a more tractable prosecutor, Houston millionaire lawyer and Johnson-Connally buddy, Leon Jaworski. It may have been the single greatest error of his final two years, for it brought about the resignations of two other yankee respectables as well (Attorney General Richardson and Deputy Attorney General William Ruckelshaus); it was an open admission that the investigations were coming too close to home; and it ignited a firestorm of protest throughout most of the country, reaching even into parts of the Southern Rim. But for Nixon it seemed to be worth it, for in Jaworski he found—if not exactly a subservient lackey, which he never expected—a man who had a rough identity with Richard Nixon and a lifelong attachment to exactly the same interests (particularly Texas oil, banking, real estate, and agribusiness) and who could be expected to be as minimal a prosecutor as possible. Nixon was not disappointed. In the year that Jaworski spent on the job, he accomplished only two acts of substance, suing for the White House tapes and indicting five Nixon subordinates on the cover-up of Watergate, both of which cases he won. But he did not allow the indictment of Nixon that his own grand jury wanted, he did not even indict Nixon after he had become a private citizen, though he knew him to be guilty, and he did not challenge the unconstitutional Ford pardon in court; he refused to hand over White House tapes to the impeachment inquiry going on in Congress and then refused to issue the final report required of him by statute; he permitted the whole crew of Nixon criminals to get off with copped pleas and minimal sentences (Kleindienst was even allowed to pretend he hadn't testified in the case where he had committed perjury!), and he let the big corporate campaign givers get off without a single jail sentence. And he either squelched or refused to prosecute the ongoing investigations into the whole ITT bribery case (that was so outrageous it caused three staff members to resign in protest), the mysterious but deliberate 18½-minute tape erasure, the sale of ambassadorships to big campaign contributors, the role of Nixon in falsification of his tax returns, the illegal wiretapping in and by the White House, the role of the Justice Department in the cover-up, the use of government agencies against political enemies, the $100,000 Hughes-Rebozo and $50,000 Davis loans in Rebozo's bank, the illegal repressionary tactics of the FBI, the CIA, the Justice Department, and the Army under Nixon's direction, the final disposition of the millions of dollars in secret funds under White House control—and even, sitting at the very core of it all, the question of *who had ordered the June 1972 Watergate burglaries and why*. Well, he didn't get to be one of the biggest and sharpest lawyers in Texas, indeed in all of the Southern Rim, for nothing. Nixon knew what he was doing.

But, alas for the cowboy White House, even all this wasn't enough. The counterattack had too many components to it now, too many disparate interests, to be shunted aside with legal or appointive maneuvers, the famous Nixon stonewalling. All Nixon's efforts notwithstanding, the firing of Cox, and the guilt implied thereby, was the kick that dislodged the pebble that permitted the rock of impeachment to roll.

It was in the face of all this, during what were to be his final ten months in office, that Nixon devoted himself with single-minded zeal to the cultivation of Southern Rim support, the encouragement of Southern Rim passions, the courting of Southern Rim politicians.

It is extraordinary that from the time of the Cox firings to the time of his resignation, Nixon flew twice around the world and dozens of times around the country without setting foot in the Northeast but twice—once in Chicago, once in Caribou, Maine, on the way home from Moscow—while he visited every state in the Southern Rim except New Mexico and the Carolinas, some of them several times. Extraordinary, but not mysterious. Under pressure, like some dictator under siege rushing to the air force to protect him from the army, Nixon made a calculated bid to his cowboy constituency for the support that would keep him in office. He went to Georgia and Tennessee to gain pledges from Republican groups, to Huntsville, Alabama, to receive the plaudits of George Wallace ("God bless you, Mr. President, you're among friends here"), to Phoenix to prove his popularity to Barry Goldwater, to New Orleans to receive the cheers of the Veterans of Foreign Wars, to Nashville to prove that he loved country music, to Jackson, Houston, Stillwater, Los Angeles, Miami, Orlando, San Clemente, and Key Biscayne.

And the response was everything Nixon could have wanted. While the television newscasts and the Northeastern papers were laying bare the scandals, while support among Republicans and Democrats elsewhere seemed slowly to be eroding, Nixon could count on the Southern Rim to provide him with the cheering crowds and the friendly banners, the ads and committees and letters and petitions of support. Consistently the polls showed that in the Southern Rim the President's popularity was higher than anywhere else in the country, and not much diminished, either, from what it had been in 1972. Consistently the letters-to-the-editor sections in national publications were sprinkled with encomiums from the Southwest and the Southeast, of which this one, appearing in the enemy columns of the *New York Times*, is only the most succinct:

To the Editor:

We voted for President Nixon, we support him and we shall vote against and use our influence against any member of the Congress who votes for impeachment. We have lost all confidence in the national news media, printed and electronic, which for diabolical reasons wish to destroy the United States of America.

Mr. and Mrs. Edwin A. Morrison
Dallas, April 29, 1974

Consistently the advertisements trumpeting Nixon support appeared in the newspapers of the Southern Rim—even antediluvian Hamilton Fish, Sr., one of the rare New Yorkers to go to battle for the President, bid for support in the pages of three papers, the *Arizona Daily Star*, the *Dallas Morning News*, and the *Fort Lauderdale News*—or were paid for by Southern Rim groups:

HANG IN THERE, PRESIDENT NIXON! YOU'RE IN GOOD COM-
PANY—*you have just tied the record of* ABRAHAM LINCOLN
for receiving unjust accusations, outright slurs and insults,
slander and defamation—and few seem to have come to
your defense.

The Whittier, California, Area Committee for Fairness
to the President, Earl B. Myer, Treasurer

Consistently the larger citizens' groups formed to support
Nixon were based in the Southern Rim (Houston, San Francisco, Tampa, Whittier, Shreveport, New Orleans, Dallas, Los
Angeles, Charlotte, Roswell, Atlanta, Oklahoma City, Phoenix)
or, as in the case of Rabbi Baruch Korff's much-publicized
group in Providence, drew considerable numbers of their supporters and contributions from the Southern Rim. Consistently
the reporters who went into the Southern Rim for reaction
stories met unabating support for Nixon, undiluted hatred for
the Northeastern press: "We support and sympathize with the
President because we Southerners have been on the receiving
end so long ourselves" (South Carolina). "There's hardly anyone here who does not feel like the damn Democrats are ruining
this country" (California). "He's done so much for the country,
like ending the war. He's had a lot of trouble just like we've had
plenty of it in the South" (Mississippi). "He's one of the greatest men of the century and no evidence whatever has been
produced to blemish that fact" (California). "People down here
say, 'But he's the President.' Southerners are used to having an
authority figure" (Alabama). "I don't believe anything they
say, and I don't care anyway. I'm behind him 100 percent"
(New Mexico). "Nixon, he's the President. He's there. Right or
wrong, he's there. This may be something inherent in the Southern person, I don't know" (Mississippi). "This is Nixon territory" (Arizona). "Night after night on television, they harp on
it. Day after day, the papers hit it. I think there's a conspiracy
to get us" (Georgia). "I'm sick of what I'm reading in the
papers,/ I'm tired of all that trash on TV,/ Stand up and cheer
for Richard Nixon" (Tennessee). "The media are just looking
for bad things to say about our President" (Alabama). "I'm
living proof that the Southern strategy is alive and doing well.

We like Nixon down here. He's the only President in a long time who paid any attention to us. He dared to come South" (Mississippi).

One purpose for the lathering of such support, of course, was to give evidence of a countervailing force to the yankee counterattack; another, simply to give confidence and sustenance to a man who, as he went about lying to the land, must have needed that desperately. But probably the overriding purpose was to convince the Southern Rim representatives in Congress—and as things grew darker, particularly the thirty Southern Rim senators necessary to stave off an impeachment conviction—that their backing of Nixon was not only possible but politically advantageous.

Nixon lavished a good deal of attention on Congress as the Ninety-third session went along, unbending considerably from his imperial pose of just a few months before. He gradually modified his stands on impoundments, met more often with congressional delegations, provided access to Administration officials and information that had been blocked off; he was still the first to blame Congress at any news conference for failures of national policy—Cambodia, energy, inflation—but he no longer defied its rulings or ignored its laws (except, to be sure, the ones that tore down his Watergate defenses). And of course, being tarnished now and under the pressure of the counterattack, there was much less he could do to control the Hill; he had to sit by, angry but compliant, as the Congress passed the war-powers-limitation bill (and over his veto), forced him to end his Cambodian bombing, voted to retain OEO, established its own rival budget office, reformed campaign spending, and provided greater access to federal records.

There was no mystery about Nixon's congressional strategy: "The conservative minority in the Senate—largely Democrats from the South and Republicans from the West—is considered crucial to the President," reporter Herbers concluded early in 1974. The word went out from the White House—carried especially by Arizonan Dean Burch, who gave up his FCC job to handle congressional stroking for Nixon, and Tennessean William Timmons, the long-time congressional liaison—that Nixon meant to be very conciliatory with those whose votes he could count on: he supported the Eastland chicken-farmer fowl-play bill, a Havasupai Indian bill dear to Arizona Senators Goldwater and Fannin, and a sugar-price-support bill pushed by Southern senators, while he acted against the land-use measure, a consumer-protection bill, mass-transit subsidies, and various welfare legislation, all of which had gained conservative opposition, and he vetoed a bill forcing oil companies to roll back their prices. A red carpet was suddenly unrolled from the White House, having been in storage a long time, and soon congresspeople who had not been inside the gates for years on end were being treated to private breakfasts in the upstairs dining rooms, personal audiences in the Oval Office, dinner cruises on the Presidential yacht *Sequoia*. Partisan concerns were all forgotten, Democrats were as welcome as Republicans, all that mattered was that they all be good conservative fellows, preferably from the Southern Rim: a May *Sequoia* trip, for example, full of fine wines and much Presidential attention, was taken by eleven congressmen, five Democrats (from Texas, Mississippi, Louisiana, Florida, and Virginia), six Republicans (from Alabama, California, Tennessee, Illinois, and two from New York, the last three thrown in because they were superconservatives with influence in the House). . . . John Sparkman was given a Presidential plane to fly home in from Paris. . . . Russell Long was granted a rare ninety-minute chat with Nixon. . . . A chosen group of senators invited in for a strategy talk—"the most important of them all," according to conservative columnist William S. White—was confined to Eastland, Stennis, Long, McClellan, Sparkman, Allen, and Byrd. . . . And on it went.

And it might have worked, it just might have worked. Right until the end, the Nixon head-counters figured they would have the votes in the Senate to forestall conviction: at least 22 of the 30 Rim senators (two from Alabama, Tennessee, Mississippi, Oklahoma, South Carolina, Arizona, Georgia, and Louisiana, one each from New Mexico, Texas, Nevada, Arkansas, North Carolina, and Florida), who would provide fully 65 percent of the necessary 34 votes, plus 4 other Western senators (from Idaho, Utah, Wyoming, and Colorado), 3 Border State senators (Virginia and Kentucky), and 5 others from the rest of the nation. That gives as good an idea as anything of the identity between Richard Nixon and the Southern Rim.

III

But the resistance—instead of the accommodation that would probably have kept Nixon in office—had produced a counterforce, like the pull of quicksand which increases the more one struggles.

Haldeman and Ehrlichman had to be thrown to the sharks, an absolutely debilitating blow to Nixon, and Henry Kissinger and General Alexander Haig (a Pennsylvanian with a peripatetic Army career and a Kissinger underling in the White House) gravitated toward the power vacuum. The House Judiciary Committee, under the direction of New Jersey Congressman Peter Rodino, began its deliberate impeachment proceedings, picking for its special counsels John Doar of New York, an old friend and colleague of Bobby Kennedy's, and Albert Jenner of Illinois, a lawyer long enlisted in liberal causes. Major congressional figures from the Northeast, including Representative John Anderson of Illinois, chairman of the House Republican Conference, Senator James Buckley of New York, a leading conservative voice, and Senator Edward Brooke of Massachusetts, the only black man in the upper house, called outright for Nixon's resignation. The Joint Committee on Taxation announced that, in effect, Nixon had committed fraud in the preparation of his income taxes and had to hand over an additional $475,431 in back taxes and interest. The House Government Operations Committee, headed by California's Chet Holifield but with 19 of its 40 members from the Northeast, unanimously decided that Nixon had spent $17.1 million on the care and improvement of his Key Biscayne and San Clemente homes, at least part of it for simple creature comforts that should have come out of his own pocket.

And in the middle of it all, a Rockefeller ally operating as a U.S. attorney in Maryland brought a federal case against Vice-President Spiro Agnew, charging him with having accepted more than $100,000 in bribes and kickbacks from Maryland real-estate and construction operators between 1967 and 1973:

after much plea-bargaining and pussy-footing, Agnew finally pleaded *nolo contendere* to a minor tax-evasion charge in October 1973 and was let off without a jail sentence. He was, however, forced to give up the Vice-Presidency, and suddenly the playbook for the yankee counterattack was written: a new Vice-President who was close—or at least amenable—to the Eastern Establishment, increasing pressure upon Nixon to resign, and a painless takeover of the nation's highest office without shot being fired or vote cast.

It is quite clear that Richard Nixon wanted to nominate John Connally as his new Vice-President (Melvin Laird, called in for consultations, subsequently reported: "I knew that Mr. Nixon favored John Connally for the job")—Connally the swaggering, confident, arrogant Texan, the strongest force in Nixon's earlier Cabinet, the man whom he had almost named to replace Agnew on the 1972 ticket and was known to favor for the 1976 one, the cowboy who most closely shared his outlook. But Connally was certain to provoke a bitter fight in the Congress when it came time for confirmation, since he had been head of Democrats for Nixon in 1972 and actually switched over to the Republican Party in 1973, an apostasy whose direction would alienate Democrats and whose recentness would alienate Republicans—and *another* bitter fight was the last thing Nixon needed now. There was someone, though, who could get through Congress in a breeze, without causing any more fights and headlines . . . someone who was both conservative and, as far as was known, clean . . . someone whose most notable characteristics were a dog-on-the-grave loyalty and a putty-in-the-hands malleability . . . and, above all, someone who was acceptable to all of the Northeastern critics, in and out of Congress, in fact had been championed most by Melvin Laird and Hugh Scott . . . and that was the congressman from Michigan, Jerry Ford. Nominated and confirmed almost without a hitch, Gerald R. Ford became Vice-President on December 6, 1973.

Gerald Ford certainly seemed to be the sort of person that would stand Nixon in good stead. His whole life was one of *secondness*: he grew up with a second father, was named a junior and called "Junie" throughout childhood, he was a second-rate scholar and played second-string on the Michigan football team, he became an assistant football coach at Yale for the junior varsity before deciding upon a law career, and then was an assistant navigator and lieutenant commander in the Navy. Elected to the lower house of Congress in 1948, and for thirteen successive terms thereafter, he was a professional supporter and attendant, a second-in-waiting, there to do the bidding of the leadership without question, and when he himself became the House Republican leader—on a program of "constructive alternatives"—he was always in the shadow not only of the Democratic Speakers of the House, who held the majority, but also of the Senate Republican leadership. In his twenty-five years in the House he performed only two notable feats, both in service to Richard Nixon: the first an admittedly foolhardy attempt to impeach Justice William Douglas, the second an unprincipled attempt to squelch the House Banking Committee's investigation of the Watergate affair before the 1972 election.

What more logical man, then, for *Vice*-President? Yet Nixon reckoned without seeing what kind of culture Gerald Ford stemmed from, what went into him. Grand Rapids is a long way from Manhattan—well, not all that long, not even as long as Texas is wide—but it is still very much yankee country: it is an old city, settled by New Englanders, New Yorkers, and immigrant Dutch Calvinists in the eighteenth century; it has a straight manufacturing-belt economy based on furniture production, fabricated metal products, and metal-working machinery; its politics have always been conservative but not reactionary (it was the hometown of Senator Arthur Vandenberg, one of the main American architects of the UN) and with enough Calvinism to keep them reasonably clean. Ford himself, moreover, was a product of the University of Michigan and the Yale Law School—not a *distinguished* product, mind you, but those were institutions very much in the heart of the Establishmentarian academy and had to have had their effect on the young man. While in the East he had been familiar enough with the ways of New York City to have kept company with a Manhattan model and become a partner in the fledgling Conover model agency, and he eventually married a woman who had been a dancer in the Martha Graham troupe in New York. This was not, then, simply a camouflaged cowboy, a Northern doughface, for all his conservatism and subservience. Kept as a second, he would be no problem, except that his loyalty batteries would have to be recharged from time to time; give him a chance on his own, however, or even let him smell such a chance, and every indication was that he would be something quite different from what Richard Nixon expected.

Besides which, Richard Nixon was not the only person who had an influence upon Ford as a Vice-President. The most powerful forces working upon this most malleable soul, while Nixon was preoccupied with his own concerns, were almost exclusively people of yankee backgrounds. Those closest to the new Vice-President, on his staff and at his side, were Philip Buchen, a lifetime Michigander and a lawyer from Grand Rapids; L. William Seidman, also born and bred in Grand Rapids and a millionaire accountant there; John O. Marsh, a former congressman from northern Virginia; and Robert Hartmann, who had grown up in New York and California, had worked for the *Los Angeles Times*, and had spent the last twenty years in Washington as reporter and aide to Jerry Ford. Those most intimate with Ford, friends and confidants and advisers, were William G. Whyte, Chicago born and bred and a top lobbyist in Washington for U.S. Steel for twenty-two years, Rodney Markley, Jr., born in Michigan and chief lobbyist for the Ford Motor Company in Washington for twenty-five years, and Bryce Harlow, the Oklahoma-born lobbyist for Procter & Gamble who had been in and out of the White House during the past five years. And those most influential upon Ford's thinking, such as it was, were Donald Rumsfeld, a former Illinois congressman who had bounced around the Nixon Administration before being sent off as Ambassador to NATO; Senator Robert Griffin, the Michigan Republican Party Whip who had helped Ford become Minority Leader in 1965; Charles Goodell, a former New York congressman and senator; William Scranton, the patrician former governor of Pennsylvania; and John Byrnes and Melvin Laird, both former congressmen from Wisconsin. Not, be it noted (with the exception of Harlow), a true Rimster in the lot. Indeed, the whole collegium shows a most remarkable identity of backgrounds in the same part of the country, of careers devoted almost entirely to politics, and of political philosophies that seem to fit roughly into the description that Gerald Ford once gave in summing up his own beliefs: "I would say I am a moderate on domestic issues, a conservative in fiscal affairs, and a dyed-in-the-wool internationalist in foreign affairs."

There is one other person to whom these attributes are more or less applicable: Nelson Rockefeller. Now Nelson Rockefeller himself does not yet figure as a force behind Gerald Ford—but there are shadows of him cast over many of the people Ford is closest to: Goodell, a loyal Rockefeller man for a dozen years, appointed by Rockefeller to the unexpired Senate term of Bobby Kennedy; Scranton, a leading member of the Eastern cabal of great wealth and the Republican Party, along with Rockefeller; Whyte, the lobbyist (and vice-president) of U.S. Steel, on whose board sit three men who are directors of companies with Rockefeller family members and interests; Laird, Griffin, and Byrnes, all of whom had long political associations with Rockefeller and had taken his part at various times in previous campaign scurrying; and Buchen and Seidman, both of whom had worked regularly in Michigan for George Romney, a man who has always been in the Rockefeller camp (and vice versa: Rockefeller was the prime supporter of Romney's Presidential aspirations in both 1964 and 1968).* And as Ford moved into his Vice-Presidential term, he was repeatedly solicited by men with Rockefeller interests in mind —Jacob Javits, for example, and Hugh Scott, and above all Henry Kissinger, the old Rockefeller friend and aide (and, as it developed later, $50,000 debtor), who was about to marry a woman who was a Rockefeller consultant—Kissinger spent a lot of time flying about the world, true enough, but he seemed to

---

* There are other Rockefeller-Ford connections, too. According to a *New York Times* list (August 19, 1974), Ford's second-level friends include such people as Max Fisher, president of Marathon Oil Company, in which the Rockefeller family has considerable influence and an investment of some $6.5 million; Stark Ritchie, chief general counsel of the oil lobby's American Petroleum Institute, whose business is promoting the fortunes of the oil companies, in which the Rockefeller family is up to its ears, to the tune of at least $326 million; and Leon Parma, head of the Teledyne Corporation, in which Rockefeller personally has invested $150,000 and on whose board sit two people who interlock with Rockefeller family business.

have plenty of time to court the new Vice-President, successfully enough so that by the early months of 1974 it was reported that Ford "has formed an alliance with Secretary of State Henry Kissinger, whom he praises lavishly in his speeches." An alliance . . . guess against whom.

In October 1973, the same month that Gerald Ford was nominated to become Vice-President, rumors began to circulate in Albany that Nelson Rockefeller would shortly resign as governor and prepare his way for a national political role. Two months later Rockefeller did indeed resign, ostensibly to begin an organization called the National Commission on Critical Choices for America, financed originally at $1.5 million and drawing together some forty members of the national—and mostly Northeastern—elite to set out the problems that would face the nation in the immediate years ahead, and, not incidentally, to prepare Rockefeller for a national role in the wake of the Nixon Administration. Gerald Ford was a member of that commission, and a wholehearted one, taking the occasion of every plenary meeting to come to New York and rub shoulders with the academic and political luminaries, announcing himself as "an enthusiastic supporter of Mr. Rockefeller's efforts."

It was in May 1974 that the Ford team began its initial moves toward the takeover of the Presidency. Philip Buchen, Ford's closest friend, began meeting secretly with Nixon aide Clay Whitehead, whom he happened to know from earlier committee duties and whose office was not far from his, discussing ways to accomplish "an orderly transition." At about the same time three of the men just then closest to Nixon in proximity—though perhaps farthest from him in sympathies—began to send quiet messages around Washington that the Nixon Presidency was too impaired to function properly: Henry Kissinger put it about that he felt Watergate was weakening the American position abroad, Alexander Haig allowed to certain sources on the Hill that Nixon was too preoccupied with his defenses to pay attention to the Presidency, and James St. Clair made it known that he had not listened to the crucial White House tapes but that they were said to contain material fatal to Nixon's chances.

Nixon, still attempting to keep the tapes wrapped firmly

about himself, huddled with Ronald Ziegler and Fred Buzhardt, and increasingly too with his daughter Julie, but it was an exercise more of desperation than of confidence. In July, the House Judiciary Committee began debating its impeachment articles, in front of a national television audience, and on July 27 voted 27 to 11 to send to the House its evidence that Richard Nixon had participated in an obstruction of justice sufficient to warrant his impeachment. That same month the Supreme Court, with four of Nixon's own men upon it, declared unanimously that he had to turn over all the White House tapes to the legally constituted bodies that had requested them—and on those tapes, as Nixon knew, was palpable proof of his guilt. Nixon flirted with the idea of defying the Supreme Court, but the game by now was clearly up.

The rest was only details. St. Clair and Haig forced the release of one incriminating tape, after which virtually all support, public and congressional, crumbled. Haig sent word to Senator Griffin that he'd better prepare Ford for a new job, called in Goldwater to give Nixon the sorry head count on the dwindling votes left for his side in the Senate, and went subtly to work to push Nixon over that last step toward resignation. Kissinger told Secretary of Defense James Schlesinger to keep a tight watch on the military and intercept any orders hastily sent to it from the White House, and then, when the pressure was at its most intense, took Nixon aside to tell him that, after all, it would be in the national interest, in the interest of world peace, in the interest of his reputation in history, for him to resign. Nixon cried. That night he broke the news to his family.

Nixon's leaving of the White House was as deceitful and as pathetic as his occupancy of it. To the nation, on television, trying to look Checkers-sincere and almost managing it, Nixon reverted once more to public relations, false patriotism, and adversarianism, and it almost seemed that the man of images had convinced himself of all the lies that he was telling. The next day, also on television but talking then to his Cabinet and aides and full of the smarminess of catharsis, Nixon dug deeper into his real self, into the poor Southern California boy, the battler against establishments, the loner who didn't know how to approach his own staff, the outsider making his way all the way to the top, the "man in the arena," where the battle means more than the goal and the means more than the ends, the poor boy with a father who was just "a common man" and a mother who "will have no books written about her" (even in his moment of tragedy, he couldn't help thinking about John Kennedy and the yankee mythmakers). He read from a diary of Teddy Roosevelt's, totally inappropriate except for one haunting passage that brought tears to the corners of Nixon's eye, which as written was a sentiment of humanity and love for a dead wife but which Nixon characteristically transformed into a sentiment of politics and remorse for a departed Presidency: "And when my heart's dearest died, the light went from my life forever." And he closed with the most telling insight of all, frightening really in its clarity at that moment, a summation of his lifelong battle against the yankee Establishment and what it had ultimately done to him: "Always remember others may hate you, but those who hate you don't win, unless you hate them. And then you destroy yourself."

And then you destroy yourself.

He turned and went out, stiffly, more hunched than usual, to the waiting helicopter, then to the plane that would take him back home, back to the comfort of Southern California.

IV

On Friday, August 9, Gerald Ford became the thirty-eighth President of the United States. The yankee counterattack had won.

Ford might not have been the perfect instrument, but he was nothing if not serviceable, and his malleability enabled skilled hands around him to use him well. He was an open, simple man, and these qualities were subtly emphasized as a subliminal contrast to the man who had just left. He was a conciliator by nature and by trade, a glad-hander, and this too he was encouraged to display, offering a breathing spell, a harmony, a truce between the contending factions of the nation. He was told, and he believed, and he told the nation, that everything was now all right, that the "long national nightmare is over," that Watergate was behind us. He was told, and he believed, and he told the nation, that the system—the system which had enabled one power group to seize the Presidency by sabotage and fraud, let another power group orchestrate a campaign to discredit and enfeeble that Presidency, and finally permitted the discredited and criminal President to select his successor by appointment—was working. He was asked to apply the balm of reassurance upon a jittery land, and he did.

Ford moved slowly to put a new imprint on the Presidency, so as not to make the dislocation too visible, but it was not long before the new yankeefied tone of the Presidency was apparent. Within his first few weeks Ford offered leniency for war resisters and proclaimed an "amnesty program" to bring them home; he gave public support to the Equal Rights Amendment, backed an anti–sex-discrimination law in Congress, and proclaimed Equality Day; he invited black groups and union leaders to the White House and promised both of them greater influence and increased federal help; he issued a signal to the academic community for "a real partnership" and made friendly overtures toward university students; he ordered an "open Presidency," with more access for officials and reporters, promised not to use the IRS and FBI for political purposes, signed a federal protection-of-privacy bill; he resuscitated a dying $11.3 billion transit bill and signed it into law, promised more money for HEW programs, and approved measures for environmental spending; he established new relations with Europe, backed Kissinger's billion-dollar protection plan for Western nations against the oil-producing nations, announced through Kissinger a threat of war against the Middle East if it should tamper too much with the international oil companies. It was only a start, but there was no question whose interests he had in mind, and they were almost exclusively those who had been frozen out of power before.

Lest there be any mistake about it, there were enough protests from the Southern Rim to make it evident. Ronald Reagan, retiring governor of California but still one of the most favored politicians in the cowboy world, let it be known that he and his backers were alarmed at the Ford Presidency and he quietly stepped up plans for his own candidacy in 1976. Several Rim Republicans in the Congress stormed the White House to complain about Ford's "leftward drift," but despite the new openness only a few of them were actually admitted to the Oval Office and even there found their reception only polite. And

Texas Republicans, meeting in Houston in September, passed with enormous applause this ringing resolution:

> RESOLVED, That the Republican Party of Texas make known to President Ford its very deep concern over the direction of the new administration and apparent compromise of basic conservative principles, as expressed in legislation which would enlarge the federal bureaucracy and subvert personal freedom, legislation which reflects goals of the radical-liberal establishment rather than those advanced by conservative spokesmen, amnesty, and the appointment to high public office of individuals whose personal philosophy has previously been rejected by Republicans across the nation.

> FURTHER, That this resolution be forwarded to our new President whom we earnestly desire to support.

Gerald Ford, the eyes of Texas are upon you.

The yankee imprint on the Presidency was also just as obvious in the shifting of personnel. Slowly the Nixon people were eased out: Ziegler was the first to go, accompanying Nixon to San Clemente like some pallbearer-in-waiting, then Buzhardt, Burch, Armstrong, Timmons, Price, Clawson, Moore; even Haig had to go, somehow protected by the press from the full smear of scandal but too close to the past regime to stay, yet instrumental enough in the creation of the present regime to be rewarded with the job of supreme commander of NATO. Next the Cabinet members left: cowboys first, Brinegar, Ash, Dent, Weinberger; then the Nixon team at the Republican National Committee, George Bush and Harry Dent; and finally Jaworski. A "transition team" consisting of Buchen, Seidman, Rumsfeld, Marsh, Scranton, and Morton was brought in to guide the new President; Whyte, Laird, Byrnes, Harlow, Griffin, and Goodell began spending time in the White House; and Hartmann, the abrasive right-hand man, moved over from the Vice-Presidential offices to take charge of the new staff. Into the top Administration positions went more of the same breed: James Lynn, the Cleveland lawyer who had been Housing Secretary under Nixon, took charge of the Budget Office; Edward Levi, president of the University of Chicago, became the Attorney General; William Coleman, Jr., a blue-ribbon Philadelphia lawyer and a black man, took over the Department of Transportation; William Usery, a Chicagoan and long-time Labor Department mediator, was named director of the Federal Mediation and Conciliation Service; and Frank Zarb, a back-office brokerage partner in New York City, became head of the newly important Federal Energy Administration.

And then, Nelson Rockefeller.

The appointment of Rockefeller as the new Vice-President was such a naked demonstration of the yankee counterattack, such blatant evidence of the Eastern Establishment's determination to hold Ford's hand and monopolize his ear, that one wonders why some subtler method was not found. Still, it was after all a logical choice, the man actually wanted the job, no one could say he didn't have the equipment or experience for it, and who but a few unreconstructed Rimsters could really object? In a way, it was even preordained: surround a simple man with the likes of Melvin Laird and Henry Kissinger, old allies of Nelson Rockefeller and persuasive men besides, with Goodell and Scranton, with friends and lobbyists and businessmen who spent their lives in the shadow of the Rockefeller might, and who else would they select? (In fact, according to the right-wing *Human Events*, Ford even approached Rockefeller at one Critical Choices meeting before his accession and said, in effect, "Nelson, you're the one who should be in line for the Presidency.") Furthermore, there was such a drumbeat of support for this choice from the yankee media—the *New York Times* and *Washington Post* fell over themselves to lavish praise upon it, undeterred in the least by the revelations which laid bare a dozen unseemly skeletons in the Rockefeller closet—that it almost seemed that any other selection would be dangerous and divisive.

There was a minor fight, a small struggle by some cowboys, a few conservative Republicans, a disgruntled liberal here and there, several black and radical groups that had not forgotten history. There were those who pointed out that the wedding of one of the nation's most powerful families to one of the nation's most powerful offices could not help but result in massive and repeated conflicts of interest; there were others who

thought it unseemly of this man to have (in essence) bribed
dozens of supposed servants of the people, to have paid no
income taxes on an income of more than $2 million, to have
laundered money to pay for a hatchet job on a campaign rival.
But there was never any doubt that, finally, the man would be
confirmed and sworn in, and on December 19, 1974, just a year
after he set in motion his campaign for power, Nelson Rockefeller became the Vice-President of the United States.

At least in name. In function, he was to be like no other
Vice-President before him: he was to be nothing less than the
regent, the guiding hand behind the throne. Formally he would
be made the "domestic czar," in *Time*'s phrase, authorized to
"formulate plans for allocation of the nation's natural and financial resources," which pretty well takes in everything that
power is based on. But beyond that, he would certainly have a
hand—perhaps several hands—in shaping policies all across the
board, in drawing in the experts to carry them out, in rallying
public and party support for them. And he would have at his
side Henry Kissinger, the "foreign czar," given a totally free
rein by Ford in the setting of international policy, and between
them they would surely be able to enact on a global scale whatever strategies they might concoct. It looked as if Ford was
second again.

With that the yankee counterattack was complete.

V

On December 13, 1974, a sunny Friday in Los Angeles,
the friends and backers of Ronald Reagan gave a party. The
three hosts were all long-time Reagan money men, deeply conservative: Holmes Tuttle, the millionaire car salesman; Justin
Dart, head of Dart Industries, a successful real-estate conglomerate; and Jack Wrather, a Texas-born oilman and television producer. The guests were the cream of the Republican
Right: Asa Call, chairman of the Pacific Mutual Life Insurance
Company; Fred Hartley, the head of Union Oil; Rodney Rood,
an Atlantic Richfield executive; Bob Six, the president of Continental Airlines; Ed Mills, a trucking-company executive; and
Thomas V. Jones, the Northrop head who had given so lavishly (and illegally) to his friend Herbert Kalmbach. And the

guest of honor was Lloyd Bentsen, the Democratic—yes, Democratic—senator from Texas.

In the same month that Rockefeller's ascension signified the climax of the yankee counterattack, the same month that the newly elected liberal Democrats in Congress started their undercutting of the House establishment, this very strange alliance along the Southern Rim was being tenuously joined. It signaled a new regrouping of forces among the cowboys, then at their lowest ebb in months. It suggested, as one of Bentsen's men indicated, that plenty of the big-money Rimians, still alive and kicking, were "looking for someone, regardless of party, that they hope will put the country's economic house in order." And it meant most fundamentally that the consolidation of yankee power was not going to go without challenge. As the *Nation* perceptively observed, "Rockefeller's appointment means that the Eastern Establishment is back in Washington, but not in a dominant position. It has been invited back on new terms."

For, in spite of the undoubted resurgence of the Northeast in national affairs, there was no way for them, even had they wished to, to turn back the clock by thirty years to the era when they were the virtually unchallenged champions of the realm. Cowboy power was simply too well entrenched to permit that— too well entrenched in the economy, in the polity, in the very culture of the land—and neither the loss of the Presidency nor the retrenchment in the Congress meant its demise by any means. And in the wake of a setback here, a disappointment there, it could simply regroup its forces, seek out new allies, gather adjacent sources of power and reassert its position in the national area.

Although the Nixon resignation was without doubt a blow to Southern Rim political power, it was no sockdolager. In the first place, cowboy influence remained fairly well intruded into the federal machinery, far above what it had been before the Johnson–Nixon era, with thousands of anonymous appointees in place even after the luminaries had gone, a number of very powerful Rimsters still at their posts, and people with Rimian interests in certain key positions (the upper reaches of the Federal Energy Administration, for example, where at least 125 former oil company people worked; the regulatory agencies;

the higher military and intelligence levels of the Defense Department). Then, too, as we have seen, the liberal onslaught in
the Congress, shocking though it must have been, did not, after
all, repeal the basic rules of legislative power, and still left intact
most of the centers of Rimian control—battered here, left head-
less there, but with seniority, experience, authority, diligence,
and safe constituencies on their side. Beyond that, in the subtle
configurations of Washington influence, it was of prime importance that for the first time a significant number of law firms
and political lobbies had been established by or staffed with
partisans of the Southern Rim during the cowboy decade—
George Smathers (Florida), Albert Gore (Tennessee), Fred
Harris (Oklahoma), Thomas Kuchel (California), Mike Mon-
roney (Oklahoma), Ross Bass (Tennessee), Page Belcher
(Oklahoma), Charls Walker (Texas), even Richard Kleindienst (Arizona), to name only the most prominent—for one
ripple from centers such as these meant waves throughout the
Washington power structure. Finally, as if by a natural balance
of nature, the people that remained to challenge Ford for the
upcoming elections—and therefore the people around whom
ideas, talent, and influence tended to gravitate, not just for 1976
but for 1980 and beyond—turned out to be almost exclusively
from the Southern Rim.

Quite amazing, really, that there should be such a seesaw
effect. With Nixon in the ascendancy, it was the Northeast
which always managed to cast up both Republican rivals
(Romney, Scranton, Percy, Rockefeller) and Democratic (all
three Kennedy brothers, Muskie, Humphrey, Lindsay, even
Chisholm). With Nixon down and Ford–Rockefeller in the
ascendancy, the Northeast offered neither Republican rivals
(with the possible exception of Elliot Richardson) nor, remarkably, Democratic (Teddy Kennedy took himself out of the running shortly after Ford became President, sooner than anybody
had expected, then Fritz Mondale, upon whom the liberal man-
tle was cast), while the Southern Rim provided almost all of the
challengers. On the Democratic side the lists were almost uni-
formly Rimian—Wallace, Bentsen, Reubin Askew of Florida,
Jimmy Carter of Georgia, Jerry Brown of California, Terry Sanford of North Carolina, Dale Bumpers of Arkansas, Fred Harris
of Oklahoma, Morris Udall of Arizona, Julian Bond of Georgia

—with the only outside candidate being Henry Jackson of Washington; on the Republican side the only challengers on the horizon were Howard Baker, Barry Goldwater, possibly even John Connally, and above all Ronald Reagan, who early on organized finances and supporters for an interparty battle and even offered himself as the savior around whom a third-party conservative movement could be built. What can one make of such a regional swing except that there are true, solid, rooted, regional interests at work? And that Rimian political power remains undiminished, only gathering below the surface in some shifting and incremental mass, seeking to break through wherever the crust is thinnest, the opportunity greatest?

In the turmoil of the economic realm, where death seemed sure enough but you couldn't tell *what* was going to happen to taxes, the Nixon resignation was the final indication that the era of the rapacious cowboy economy was at an end, but it did not mean that the economic structure of the Southern Rim was any the less stable and durable. In a period of retrenchment—a long period, it would seem, and possibly permanent—all parts of the American economy will have to suffer, but certain elements figure to remain solid, and many of them are rooted in the Southern Rim. Energy supplies, for example: the offshore oil fields, especially in the Gulf of Mexico, the further exploration of the New Mexico–Louisiana axis, the tapping of more geothermal energy in California, the development of solar heating in the California-Arizona desert (where the Federal Energy Administration estimates solar energy could theoretically provide "twice the present generation capacity in all of the U.S."), the opening up of the oil-shale fields in the West by domestic oil companies, and the stripping of coal from the Rockies—all this cannot help but be beneficial, perhaps prodigal, for the states of the Southern Rim and the oil companies therein. Or agriculture: the Texas-Oklahoma-Kansas granary-of-the-world and the attendant transportation and shipping systems for the Gulf ports; the soybean belt of the Deep South and the Mississippi Valley, providing now and for the future the primary source of foreign exchange in American trade and, by 1980, the number one crop in the nation; the California and Florida fruit and vegetable zones; the Texas–Oklahoma–New Mexico beef belt (beef consumption, already up by 40 percent over twenty years ago, is expected to increase another 30 to 40 percent over the next decade)—all these areas, too, cannot help but prosper (unless the world gives up eating) in the years ahead. Similarly with other pillars of the Rim: technology can only be more in demand as the nation tries to make its life and businesses—its energy and food production, its mass-transit systems, its cars and construction methods—more efficient and less expensive; defense and aerospace are universally predicted to expand to keep up with the new demand from newly prosperous countries abroad and new budgets at home; the real-estate market, feeling the demographic pull of the 1950s generation reaching house-buying age, is expected to double to three million housing starts by 1980, and if the massive reinvestments of Middle Eastern "petrodollars" in American real estate in 1973–75 are any indication, there will be no lack of capital for the developers; and the leisure industry, which historically has flourished in contracting economies, may have to shift its emphases (from transcontinental touring, for example, to hometown sports facilities), but with the inevitable increase in the population, the diminution of work hours to make employment stretch, and the steady expansion of leisure time, its profitability is assured.

Moreover, the populational shifts upon which much of the Southern Rim's prosperity have been based will certainly continue, and perhaps increase, in the foreseeable future. A mid-decade Census Bureau report indicated that the migrations out of the Northeast and into the Southern Rim—particularly Florida, Arizona, Texas, and California—were continuing apace, and that some Rim states were increasing in both fertility *and* migrations for the first time in years: "Many Southern states, which historically have had net out-migration, are attracting net in-migration, and most Northern industrial states are having moderately heavy out-migration." In some places, it is true, attempts have been made of late to put a limit on the growth rates—St. Petersburg, Florida, actually passed a law, later rescinded, that the last twenty-five thousand people who had settled there would have to pack up and get out—but these have so far been relatively isolated, and their constitutionality is still being tested in the courts; and in a few places the growth rates have declined by themselves—Los Angeles County, for example, suffered a small decrease in population in the early 1970s for the first time in its history—but that has only been a reflection of the growing "shift to exurbia," as the Census people put it, and not a loss to the region as a whole. In short, all of the demographic predictions which pointed to vastly increased populations in the Southern Rim have been matched and in some cases bettered.

Fortunetelling is a game of fools. But whatever projections can be made for the future, as long as there is a future, there can be a few safe assumptions. The period of the first cowboy ascendancy, roughly from 1945 until 1975, will continue to have its effects upon the way this country is run, the culture it creates, the men it casts forward, the policies it crafts. This, the high period of America's imperium, brought forth entire new technologies and industries, new uses of natural and new development of artificial resources, beyond anything seen at any other time in human history, and these have left an ineradicable mark not only upon the nation but upon the world. It developed the national executive into a political institution with military might, which was probably more powerful than any seen before in this land or overseas, and not likely to lose much authority, though no doubt some autocracy, in the years to come; it created a period of unparalleled global dominance and domestic prosperity, with more material comforts than any society has so far known, the effects of which, though the era is diminishing, cannot help being felt in America and throughout the restructuring order of nations.

Perhaps this cowboy era has led the nation too far down the road to self-destruction; perhaps it really will all end in more smog and pollution and overcrowding and gimcrackery, ultimately in decay and collapse and obsolescence and a lingering death, the cities overgrown and with uncontrolled verminations, the factories choked upon their own wastes, the countryside—what's left from the highways and developments—seared with poisons. Perhaps this was the one moment in history for this kind of power to rise, a single, glamorous, calamitous era for the Southern Rim.

But it is not likely. It is far more probable that there will be a period of retrenchment, much as there was after the like period of rampant growth in the last quarter of the nineteenth century when the trust busters and the muckrakers brought a temporary hiatus to yankee rapacity—only this time, with the lessons already learned and the precedents established, it is not likely to last as long. Indeed, it seems most probable, given the populational and economic verities of the Southern Rim, that the forces of the sunbelt will enjoy another period of national resurgence, and not too many years away. Perhaps they will then be more constrained, perhaps ameliorated by time and fertilization, but their basic characteristics are almost certain to be intact.

By their fruits ye shall know them.

Acknowledgments

Acknowledgments and thanks are owed, and gratefully offered, to the following: James Abourezk, Aerospace Research Center, Michael Aiken, Albuquerque National Bank, American Textile Manufacturers Institute, Ruth Apfelbaum, Les Aspin, Associated General Contractors of America, Hugh Aynesworth, Douglas Baker, Donald Barthelme, David Belsky, Tom Bethell, Philip D. Carter, Robert B. Cassell, the Chambers of Commerce of Albuquerque, Atlanta, Dallas, Houston, Little Rock, Los Angeles, Miami, New Orleans, Phoenix, San Diego, San Francisco, and Tulsa, David Chandler, Mae Churchill, Common Cause, Perry Cozzen, Judy and William Domhoff, Jack Donahue, David Dorsen, Robert L. Eames, Jason Epstein, Andrew Flores, Peter Freitag, George H. Gallup, Jr., Georgia Institute of Technology, Chuck Giles, *Great Speckled Bird*, Neil Herring, Carol Hill, Nanci Hollander, John R. Howard, *Iconoclast*, Institute for Southern Studies, Insurance Information Institute, Elizabeth and Robert Kerns, Aaron Kohn, David and Dorothy Leuser, Joani Levine, Liberation News Service, Jim Love, Robert Malina, Manufacturing Chemists Association, Beth Mintz, Robert Morgenthau, John Muir, National Association of Home Builders, National Association of Realtors, Jack Nelson, Lynn

Nesbit, Victor Navasky, New Mexico Clearing House, Doyle Niemann, Carl Oglesby, Doug Porter, Printing Industries of America, Ray Reece, Larry Remer, Howard and Norma Rodman, Howard Rodman, Jr., Florence Ross, Norman Rush, *San Diego Door*, Gertrude Schafer, A.L. and Dorothy Schlesinger, David Schlissel, Diane and Peter Schrag, Maylie and Peter Dale Scott, Robert Sherrill, James Silberman, Robert Silvers, John J. Simon, Edward Sorel, *Southern Exposure*, Anne Sylvester, Texas Independent Producers and Realty Owners, *Texas Observer*, Audrey E. Thomas, Sue Thrasher, Tobacco Institute, University of New Mexico Bureau of Business Research, Urban Policy Research Institute, U.S. Travel Data Center, Valley National Bank, *Vieux Carré Courier, Voice of the Southwest*, Pat Watters, J. Robert White, Margaret Wolf, Bob Zellner, Lee B. Zink; and most especially to Jean Pohoryles.

Acknowledgments, thanks, and much else besides are owed, and lovingly offered, to Faith Sale.

Notes

Abbreviations

Ervin final: "The Final Report of the Select Committee on Presidential Campaign Activities, United States Senate," 6/74

GPO: Government Printing Office, Washington, D.C.

NYP: *New York Post*

NYT: *New York Times*

SA: *Statistical Abstract of the United States*, U.S. Department of Commerce, GPO, annual; 1972 edition unless otherwise noted

WA: *World Almanac*, Newspaper Enterprise Association; 1975 unless otherwise noted

WP: *Washington Post*

WSJ: *Wall Street Journal*

INTRODUCTION

Page 3. Oval Office meeting: *The White House Transcripts*, Bantam, 1974, pp. 93 ff. Gray testimony: ibid., pp. 839–40.

Page 4. "On and on," "They are going": ibid., p. 120 ("a lot of" appears as "not a"). Nixon/Establishment: Generally, Patrick Buchanan, *The New Majority*, Girard Bank (Philadelphia), 1973; Bruce Mazlish, *In Search of Nixon*, Penguin, 1973, esp. pp. 36–45; Richard M. Nixon, *Six Crises*, Doubleday, 1968, esp. Ch. 1,2; William Safire, *Before the Fall*, Doubleday, 1975; *New York*, 1/27/75, pp. 41–50. Theodore White,

The Making of the President 1964, Signet, 1965, esp. Ch. 3; Seymour Martin Lipset and Earl Raab, *Commentary* 9/73; Kevin P. Phillips, *Harper's*, 6/73; *NYT*, 7/18/74, p. 20; and below, Chapter 5.

Page 5. ESTABLISHMENT: Generally, E. Digby Baltzell, *Philadelphia Gentlemen*, Free Press, 1958, *The Protestant Establishment*, Random House, 1964; G. William Domhoff, *Who Rules America?*, Prentice-Hall, 1967, *The Higher Circles*, Vintage, 1971, *Fat Cats and Democrats*, Prentice-Hall, 1972, *The Bohemian Grove*, Harper & Row, 1974, "State and Ruling Class in Corporate America," *Insurgent Sociologist*, Spring 1974; Floyd Hunter, *Top Leadership USA*, California, 1959; Gabriel Kolko, *Wealth and Power in America*, Praeger, 1962; Ferdinand Lundberg, *The Rich and the Super-Rich*, Lyle Stuart, 1968; S. Menshikov, *Millionaires and Managers*, Progress (Moscow), 1969; C. Wright Mills, *The Power Elite*, Oxford, 1956; Victor Perlo, *The Empire of High Finance*, International, 1957; Kevin P. Phillips, *The Emerging Republican Majority*, Arlington House, 1969, Doubleday, 1975; Carroll Quigley, *Tragedy and Hope*, Macmillan, 1966; Arnold M. Rose, *The Power Structure*, Oxford, 1967; Richard Rovere, *The American Establishment*, Harcourt Brace, 1962; *New Directions in Power Structure Research, Insurgent Sociologist*, Spring 1975. Establishment dominance: esp. Mills, Ch. 5, 12; Domhoff, *Who Rules*, Ch. 1, 2, *Higher Circles*, Ch. 5, 6; *Insurgent Sociologist*, Spring 1975, Part III; Gabriel Kolko, *The Triumph of Conservatism*, Free Press, 1963; Ben B. Seligman, *Main Currents in Modern Economics*, Free Press, 1962. 1869–1945: *WA*, p. 748.

Page 6. Republican Party: below, Chapter 3. Tycoons: below, Chapter 2; John Brooks, *The Go-Go Years*, Weybright and Talley, 1973.

Page 7. Sports: below, Chapter 1. Congress: below, Chapter 3. Stock exchanges: SEC annual reports, GPO; *NYT* 3/5/74, p. 43. New cities: *SA* #22. Organized crime: below, Chapter 2. Perot: Brooks, pp. 1–25, 311–47. Democratic Party: below, Chapter 3. *Fortune*: 7/65, 5/75. Cultural centers: William J. Baumol and William G. Bowen, *Performing Arts*, 20th Century Fund, 1966; Joseph Wesley Ziegler, *Regional Theater*, Minnesota, 1975. Personal incomes: Harvey S. Perloff and Vera W. Dodds, "How a Region Grows," Committee for Economic Development, 1963, pp. 60 ff.; "The Wealth of Cities," Council on Municipal Performance, 1974, p. 6; *NYT*, 7/8/74, p. 58, 3/12/75, p. 19; *WSJ*, 12/31/73, p. 1.

Page 8. West Coast: *NYT*, 7/4/73. Federal Reserve: Southeast Banking Corporation, annual report, advertisements, 1973. ACBL: *NYT*, 12/1/74, Magazine, p. 63. Bergdorf: Standard & Poor, 1975, p. 245. Hebrew National: *Texas Giants*, Texas Industrial Commission, 1971, p. 48. Northeast cities: *SA* #23; Arthur M. Louis, *Harper's*, 1/75, p. 67. "Shift of income": *NYT*, 3/12/75, p. 19. Railroads: *WP*, 5/15/74, business section, 3/18/75, p. D9. Conference Board: *WSJ*, 12/31/73, p. 1.

Page 9. Money markets: *NYT* 1/6/74, Sec. 3, p. 59, 9/10/74, p. 53; *WSJ*, 9/25/74, p. 16; *Newsweek*, 5/26/75, p. 64. Wall Street: *NYT*, 7/23/73, p. 1, 1/6/74, business section, p. 57; *WP* 6/3/74, p. D12.

Climatic: e.g., *NYT*, "Forecast" maps for 1974 show 80–60 degree line roughly along 37th parallel 78 percent of the year. Tropical-semitropical: Charles B Hunt, *Physiography of the United States*, W. H. Freeman (San Francisco), 1967. Temperature/sunshine: *SA* #295, 296, 303. Frost: *Goode's World Atlas*, Rand McNally, 1970, p. 63.

Page 10. Migrations: Henry S. Shryock, Jr., *Population Mobility Within the United States*, Chicago, 1964; *Populational Redistribution and Economic Growth, U.S., 1870–1950*, American Philosophical Society (Philadelphia)—C. P. Brainerd and R. A. Easterlin, 1957, and Simon Kuznets and Dorothy Thomas, 1964, esp. 119 ff.; Robert Estall, *Modern Geography of the United States*, Quadrangle, 1972, Ch. 1; Harvey S. Perloff, et al., *Regions, Resources and Economic Growth*, Johns Hopkins, 1960, esp. back matter; Phillips, *Emerging*, op. cit., pp. 190, 392–98, 437–38. Foreign-born: *New Yorker*, 10/22/73, pp. 105–106. Turner: "The Significance of the Frontier in American History," originally, *Proceedings of the 41st Annual Meeting of the State Historical Society of Wisconsin*, 1894, widely reprinted.

Page 11. Confederacy: E. Merton Coulter, *The Confederate States of America, LSU, 1950*. Southern Baptists: Douglas W. Johnson, et al., "Church Membership," Glenmary Research Center (Washington, D.C.), 1973; Phillips, *Mediacracy*, op. cit., p. 126. Southern Rim, similarly marked: *WP*, 12/6/73, p. B1. Virginia: generally, *Encyclopaedia Britannica*. Phillips, *Emerging*, op. cit., pp. 260 ff.

Page 12. California: Robert W. Durrenberger, *California: Its People, Its Problems, Its Prospects, National Press* (Palo Alto), 1971; *SA* #20. Nevada: generally, *Encyclopaedia Britannica*. *Barron's*, 3/24/75, pp. 3 ff. Northeast: Phillips, *Mediacracy*, Part III. Manufacturing: *SA* #1189; "Employment and Earning Statistics," Department of Labor Bulletin, #137–4, 1967. Megalopolis: "Graphic Summary of the 1970 Population Census," GPO, 1973, #6, 11, 24.

Page 13. Murchison-Kirby: *Life*, 4/28/61; *Fortune* 4/61.

Page 14. Oglesby: in regular use in his writings from 1971 on, e.g., *Ramparts*, 10/71, 11/71, 11/72, 11/73, 11/74, 3/75, and periodic columns in the *Boston Phoenix*, 1972–75; he credits Michael Locker, a founder of the North American Congress on Latin America, for its introduction into political dialogue. Boulding: quoted in *NYT*, 12/9/73, Sec. 4. Viorst: *Fall from Grace*, New American Library, 1968, Ch. 4. Domhoff: *Fat Cats and Democrats*, op. cit., Ch. 2. Additional currency: in Sale, *New York Review*, 5/3/73, Arthur Waskow, *WIN*, 7/73, Dick Roberts, *International Socialist Review*, 11/73, Steve Weissman, *Ramparts*, 8/74, and Maja Bjorkman and Daniel Fleming, *Zenit* (Oslo), Vol. 37, 1974. Ford: *NYT*, 8/24/74, p. 1.

1. The Six Pillars: Economic Power

Page 17. Rim GNP: *SA* #519, reckoning personal income at 15–20 percent below GNP (see #515). Comparative GNPs: ibid., #1331.

Cars, telephones, housing, TV, highways: ibid., #891, 1340, 797, 1341, 1155, 1321, 804, 1341, 881.

Page 18. POPULATION. General statistics: *SA* #12, 14 (Southern Rim population, 1940—39.5 million, 1970—71.2, 1975—c. 78.6). Most massive: Edward L. Ullman, in Durrenberger, *California*, op. cit.; *SA* #135. Foreign populations: *SA* #1318. Growth factors: Ullman, and Richard E. Preston, in Durrenberger; Perloff and Dodds, "How a Region Grows," op. cit.; *Population and the American Future*, U.S. Commission on Population Growth and the American Future, GPO, 1972; Peter A. Morrison, "How Population Movements Shape National Growth," 1973, and "Population Movements and the Shape of Urban Growth," 1972, RAND (Santa Monica). Migrations: *SA* #10, 29; Shryock, op cit., esp. tables 8.1, 8.2, 8.16. City growth: *SA* #20, 22; *U.S. News*, 2/22/71, p. 37, 8/31/71, p. 29; "Metropolitan Area Statistics," Bureau of the Census, GPO, 11/71; Ira S. Lowry, "Metropolitan Populations to 1985," RAND, 1964. Recent statistics: *NYT*, 7/25/74, p. 67. 83.7 million: *SA* #14, using Census Bureau series I-C. Demographers: e.g., Ullman, op. cit., Perloff and Dodds, op. cit. Technology shift: Ullman, op. cit.; Estall, *Geography*, op. cit.; Emma Woytinsky, *Profile of the U.S. Economy*, Praeger, 1967, esp. pp. 123, 137, 232, 323, 493, 501.

Page 19. Employment: SA #352, 364, 1183, 1189; Estall, op. cit., pp. 86, 312; Daniel Bell, *The Coming of Post-Industrial Society*, Basic, 1973; "Economic Growth in the United States," 1969, and "Economic Future of City and Suburb," 1970, Committee for Economic Development.

Page 20. WSJ: 10/15/73, p. 1. Assets: *SA* #985. Income: *SA* #988; *U.S. News*, 4/22/75, p. 27. Profits: SA #988, *Time* 12/9/74, p. 32. Exports: *SA* #1285; *NYT*, 12/31/74, p. 37; *WSJ*, 10/9/73, p. 1; "Foreign Agricultural Trade of the U.S.," Department of Agriculture, annual. Farm population: *SA* #967, 968, 972. Income: *U.S. News*, 2/25/74, p. 86. Cotton: *SA* #976, 975.

Page 21. Farm size: *SA* #967. Corporate holdings: SA #972. California: *SA* #974, 977; Peter Barnes, "The Sharing of Land and Resources in America," *New Republic* reprint, 1973. Rim farm size: *SA* #974. More farms, tractors, trucks: *SA* #975, 996 ("Cornbelt" here defined as Census Bureau's "West North Central" region). Market and farm sales: *SA* #977, 975. Farm values: #974.

Page 22. Banks: *NYT*, 10/14/73. Rim production: *SA* #976, 977, 1032. Per capita consumption: *SA* #128; *WP*, 12/28/74, business page. Corporate farmers: William Robbins, *The American Food Scandal*, Morrow, 1974; Barnes, op. cit.; *Financial World*, 1/30/74, p. 35.

Page 23. Tenneco executive: Liberation News Service, agribusiness survey, 2–3/74.

Page 24. Military-industrial growth: Seymour Melman, *Pentagon Capitalism*, McGraw-Hill, 1970, Ch. 1, 2. Defense budget: *SA* #397, 611; *WA*, p. 84; *SANE Quarterly*, 12/73. Outlays to corporations:

"Military Prime Contract Awards," Department of Defense, annually; Melman, pp. 72–79. Foreign GNP: *SA* #1331.

Page 25. Wartime expenditures: calculated from *Southern Exposure* (Atlanta), Summer 1973; Preston, in Durrenberger, op. cit. Bolton: *Defense Purchases and Regional Growth*, Brookings, 1966. Prime contracts shift: "Prime Contract Awards," op. cit.

Page 26. 1970 defense, aerospace, AEC funding: Michael Barone, et al., *The Almanac of American Politics*, Gambit, 1972; *SA* #407. Installations: *Rand McNally Commercial Atlas*, 1972. DOD payrolls: *SA* #407. R&D funds: "Prime Contract Awards," 1968–70, pp. 72–74. California, LA: Barone, pp. 42, 92, 105; *SA* #407; "California Data," Security Pacific National Bank, 4/73, Table 12. Texas: "The Genesis of the Aviation Industry in Northern Texas," Bureau of Business Research, University of Texas, 1958; "Military Payrolls and the Texas Economy," *Texas Business Review*, 3/67. Largest employer: "Employment and Earnings," Bureau of Labor Statistics, 1970; "Prime Contract Awards," op. cit., 1970. New Mexico: Barone, pp. 502–506; "The Economy, 1971," "The Economy, 1972," Bank of New Mexico; *New Mexico Progress*, New Mexico Bankshare Corporation, 1970, p. 18; *New Mexico Review*, 12/70.

Page 27. Navy: *New Mexico Review*, 12/70, p. 7. "You have nice": *Commonweal*, 3/22/74, p. 50. Rim firms: "Prime Contract Awards," op. cit. 1967 figures: ibid., 1962–67, p. 56.

Page 28. 1970 list: "100 Companies Receiving the Largest Dollar Volume," DOD, Directorate for Information Operations, 1970. Subsidiaries: Standard & Poor, *Register of Corporations*, 1975.

Page 29. 86 percent: Melman, *Pentagon*, op. cit., pp. 76–77. $45 billion: Robert J. Gordon, *American Economic Review*, 6/69; *SA* #309; Melman, p. 80.

Page 30. Profits: *WP*, 11/16/73 (Mintz); *NYT*, 5/16/73; *New Republic*, 2/7/70, pp. 23–25. Aerospace expansion: "Aerospace and the U.S. Economy," Aerospace Research Center, Aerospace Industries Association of America (Washington), 1971, pp. 19, 38; *NYT*, 1/5/75, Sec. 3, p. 38. More scientists: *SA* #853, 857; "Aerospace," op. cit., p. 14. Largest R&D: ibid., p. 15. Space program: *SA* #868. Footnote: *NYT*, 5/16/73.

Page 31. 70/55 percent: "Aerospace Indicators," AIAA. Plants and firms: "Aerospace," p. 10. Technology R&D, output: *SA* #848, 518, 1225, 1227 (including electrical machinery, communications, instruments, aircraft transport). Estimates: *Newsweek*, 10/1/73, p. 80; *Fortune*, 11/73, p. 149. Professional/technical employment: "Skills of the Labor Force in California," Crocker National Bank, 1973; Estall, *Modern Geography*, op. cit., p. 331.

Page 32. State government scientists: *SA* #855. Number of scientists: Crocker booklet, op. cit. Federal R&D: *SA* #850. Los Angeles: Crocker, op. cit. Santa Clara: *Fortune*, 6/74, pp. 129 ff.; *WSJ*, 1/2/74, p. 4.

Page 33. Bostonian: *Fortune*, 6/74, p. 130. Udall: *WP*, 1/13/74, Outlook section. Oil/gas consumption: *SA* #820; *NYT*, 12/1/73.

Page 34. Oil fortunes: Lundberg, *The Rich and the Super-Rich*, op. cit., pp. 35 ff., 138 ff. Oil assets: *Fortune* 5/75, p. 210 (oil—$109 billion, automobiles—$40 billion). Texas: James A. Clark and Michel T. Halbouty, *The Last Boom*, Random House, 1972; John Bainbridge, *The Super-Americans*, Doubleday, 1961.

Page 35. Texas and Southern Rim production: *SA* #1095, 1100. Dobie: Bainbridge, op. cit., p. 61. 500-mile radius: *Fortune*, 4/74, pp. 104 ff., 6/74, pp. 158–59; Norman Medvin, *The Energy Cartel*, Vintage, 1974, Ch. 2; *NYT*, 6/2/75, p. 28, USGS 1974 figures. Rockefeller/Mellon/ old oil: James Ridgeway, *The Last Play*, Dutton, 1973; Medvin, op cit.; Lundberg, op. cit., pp. 156 ff., 165 ff., 595 ff.

Page 36. Mobil: Ridgeway, op. cit., pp. 288–92; *Forbes*, 5/15/73, p. 266; *Directory of Texas Manufacturers*, Texas, Bureau of Business Research, 1971. Stock ownership: "Disclosure of Corporate Ownership," Senate Committee on Government Operations, GPO, 3/74, p. 30; *NYT*, 9/24/74, p. 35.

Page 37. New oil: Robert Engler, *The Politics of Oil*, Macmillan, 1961; "The U.S. Oil Industry," AFL-CIO Maritime Trades Department, 10/73; and oil sources above. Liaison Committee: statement to House Ways and Means Committee, 2/74.

Page 38. Occidental: *WSJ*, 8/7/73, 8/13/73, 2/8/74, 9/3/74; *NYT*, 8/13/73; *Fortune*, 7/68; *Atlantic*, 6/75; "The Phony Oil Crisis," *Economist* (London), 7/7/73. *Fortune* quotes: 4/74, p. 194. "We independents": George Mitchell, *TIPRO Reporter* (Austin), Summer 1973, p. 4. Diamond Shamrock: *NYT*, 3/18/75, p. 58.

Page 39. "I can absolutely": *WP*, 1/14/74, p. A3. 700,000 acres: calculated from *Time*, 10/1/73, pp. 85, 95; *NYT*, 9/3/73, p. 1; Nathaniel H. Rogg and Michael Sumichrast, "Background Paper on Postwar Housing in the United States," National Association of Homebuilders (Washington), 10/72, pp. 15–16. Rogers: *Time*, op. cit., p. 80. Oklahoma: *Progressive*, 5/74, p. 19. Real-estate acreage, prices: *Time*, p. 95; "Background Paper," p. 31, 80; *Newsweek*, 7/29/74, p. 62. Miami/Palm Springs: *Time*, p. 85. Homeowners: *SA* #1155.

Page 40. Housing units: "New Private and Public Housing Units Started, 1940–71," and *Economic News Notes*, 1/74, NAHB; *SA* #1155. Construction expenditure: "Background Paper," pp. 58–59. National income figures: *SA* #518 (contract construction and real estate). Regional housing starts: "Background Paper," p. 78; *SA* #1144.

Page 41. New York/Atlanta: "Construction Review," Department of Commerce, GPO, 2/73; *SA* Sec. 33 (slightly variant). Northeast-Southeast: "Background Paper," p. 78. California: *NYT*, 9/3/73, p. 1; Robert C. Fellmeth, et al., *Politics of Land*, Grossman, 1973; *Sierra Club Bulletin*, 1/71. Arizona: *Arizona Daily Star*, 12/26/71; "Arizona Progress," Valley National Bank (Phoenix), 10/74. Sun City: *NYT*, 3/24/74, 7/5/74. New Mexico: "Facts You Should Know About the

Land of Enchantment" and files, New Mexico Central Clearing House (Santa Fe), 1972; *Time*, op. cit., p. 94.

Page 42. Florida: *Time*, op. cit., p. 80; *NYT*, 6/11/73, p. 1, 9/3/73, p. 1, 11/19/73, p. 1. Corporate developers: Anthony Wolff, *Unreal Estate*, Sierra Club, 1974; *Progressive* 5/74; *Ramparts*, 1/72, p. 23. Kasuba: *WSJ*, 12/2/73 (though filing for bankruptcy since, it is still a major builder). Crow: *Fortune*, 11/73, p. 113. Construction giants: ranked by *Engineering News Record*, 4/73, p. 51. Recession/Rim: *Economic News Notes*, NAHB, 11/74, 1/75.

Page 43. Commission: "Destination USA," Report of the National Tourism Resources Review Commission, 6/73, p. 1. Leisure-time expenditures: *SA* #513; *U.S. News*, 2/25/74, p. 34. Income increase: *WP*, 11/20/74, p. D11. Tourism income: "Destination USA," p. 1. Recreation income: *SA* #330, 513; *SA 1974*, #347, 605; *WA*, p. 106.

Page 44. Spectator/participant sports income: *WP*, 2/17/75, p. C1, 3/6/75, D10. Golf/tennis: *SA* #331, *Newsweek*, 7/1/74, p. 44. Rec-V: *Time*, 7/2/72, p. 82. Most space, etc.: *SA* #12, 273, 297, 303, 307, 314, 307, 372, 1253. Tourism industry, by state: *WA*, pp. 673–701; *Arizona Business Bulletin*, 1/74; "The Economy 1972," Bank of New Mexico; *Fortune*, 3/74, p. 59; *Newsweek*, 12/17/73, p. 82. Florida: *NYT*, 12/5/73.

Page 45. Tourism by city: *WP*, 12/9/73, p. K2 (Miami Beach); *Newsweek*, loc. cit. (Vegas); "Total Annual Visitors," New Orleans Chamber of Commerce, 1973; "Inside Phoenix," Phoenix Newspapers, Inc., 1973; *Southern Exposure*, Summer 1973 (Orlando); Tennessee Department of Commerce. Hotels, etc.: *SA* #1253. Disney World: *NYT*, 12/5/73. Theme parks: Sylvia Porter, *NYP*, 5/30/74. Disney revenues: *Fortune*, 6/74. Games: *WSJ*, 6/20/73, p. 1; "Los Angeles: Industrial Center of the West," LA Department of Water & Power, 1971, p. 16.

Page 46. "Pong": *Business Week*, 11/10/73, p. 212. Movie production: "Los Angeles: Communications Center of the West," LA Department of Water & Power, 1969, pp. 12–13; "The Dallas Economy," Dallas Power & Light Company, 1974. Las Vegas: *Parade*, 3/16/75, p. 6. Nashville: *WA*, p. 630; "Communications Center," op. cit., p. 20. Macon: *Newsweek*, 7/8/74, p. 80. Los Angeles: "Communications Center," p. 20. Radio-TV stations: *SA* #801. Motels: *SA* #1257; *Business Week*, 3/30/74, p. 94; *NYT*, 8/26/73, Sec. 3, p. 1.

Page 47. Room construction: *WSJ*, 10/10/74, p. 1; American Hotel and Motel Association, release, 9/74. Sports boom, Rim Franchises: *NYT*, 7/22–27/74, p. 1, 3/31/73, Sec. 5, p. 1, 7/25/74. Dodgers: *NYT*, 9/2/73, Magazine, p. 41. Championship teams: *WA*, pp. 843, 905. Hunt: *NYT*, 1/25/74, p. 1; *WSJ*, 9/12/73. Spray-paint: personal visit. Davidson: *WSJ*, 3/7/74, p. 1, *NYT*, 11/11/73, Sec. 5, p. 1.

Page 48. Golf league: *WSJ*, 3/1/74, p. 17. Coastline: *SA* #272.

Page 49. Ports, 60 percent, Gulf Coast: *SA* #949 (tonnage), 946; *Southern Exposure*, Fall 1974, pp. 5 ff. Airports: *SA* #930; *NYT*, 9/16/73, Magazine, p. 16. Airlines: *NYT*, 4/28/74, Sec. 3, p. 1, 1/20/74,

Sec. 3, p. 2; *Fortune*, 7/74, p. 122. Railroad, bus, truck rankings, figures: *Fortune*, loc. cit. Trucks: *SA* #891, 913. Bank rankings: *American Banker*, 1/31/74; *Fortune*, 7/74, p. 114; Western Bancorporation annual report, 1972; *NYT*, 11/25/73, Sec. 3, p. 7; *Newsfront*, 2–3/74 (by income increase per share).

Page 50. LA areas, LA-SF: "Los Angeles: The Western Commercial Center," LA Chamber of Commerce, 1973. Bank holding companies: Christopher Elias, *The Dollar Barons*, Macmillan, 1973, Ch. 6–9; *Forbes*, 12/15/73. Timber: *SA* #1041, 1042, 1046; *Southern Exposure*, Fall 1974, p. 140.

Page 51. Furniture: *WA*, p. 691. Textile: "Textile Hi-Lights," 9/73, "Jobs, A Profile of Textiles," American Textile Manufacturers Institute (Charlotte); Estall, *Modern Geography*, op. cit., p. 316; *NYT*, 8/5/73, Magazine, p. 10. Burlington: *NYT*, 11/25/73, Sec. 3. Rankings: *Financial World*, 1/30/74, p. 47; *Fortune*, 6 and 7/75. Apparel: "Jobs," op. cit.; "Los Angeles: The Western Commercial Center," op. cit. Petrochemical: "Houston Facts," Houston Chamber of Commerce; *WP*, 5/13/74, p. A1. ITEL: *Fortune*, 3/74, p. 59. Coca-Cola, Reynolds: *Fortune* 500 lists, 6 and 7/75. TI: *Barron's*, 11/13/72. U.S. Leasing: *Fortune*, 11/73, p. 134. Retail Credit: *WP*, 12/19/73. Houston: *WP*, 5/13/74, p. 1; *WA*, 619–20; "Houston Facts" and "Houston," Houston Chamber of Commerce, undated; *Big Town, Big Money*, Cordovan (Houston), 1973; *NYT*, 1/16/72, Sec. 3, p. 1, 4/25/75, p. 32, 5/29/75, p. 24; *Playboy*, 5/75, pp. 105 ff.; personal visit.

Page 52. No zoning laws: *NYT*, 3/6/74, p. 31.

Page 53. Freeway system: e.g., Samuel J. Lefrak, *NYT*, 1/18/74.

2. THE GROWTH CULTURE: ECONOMIC CHARACTER

Page 55. San Diego: *SA* #22; "Population and Housing," San Diego County Planning Department, 7/1/73; "Annual Review of San Diego Business Activity," Union-Tribune Publishing Co., 1973, pp. 4–5, 31–32; "San Diego 1973 Business Survey," SD Chamber of Commerce; "Focus on San Diego County," Bank of America, 1972; Michael Barone, et al., *Almanac*, op. cit., pp. 105, 107–109.

Page 56. *Union*: "Annual Review," p. 31. *Tribune*, manager, *Journal*, Royal Inns, U.S. Financial, National Bank: *WSJ*, 5/7/74, p. 1.

Page 57. Alessio: Ovid Demaris, *Poso del Mundo*, Little, Brown, 1970, pp. 169–217; *Life*, 3/24/72, pp. 30–37; *Ramparts*, 10/73, pp. 34 ff. Donnelley: *NYT*, 9/10/73, p. 1; Wallace Turner, *Gambler's Money*, Houghton Mifflin, 1965, pp. 185–91; California state police intelligence files, author's possession. Wilson: Larry Remer, *San Diego Door*, 3/12–5/14/74. La Costa: Jeff Gerth and Lowell Bergman, *Penthouse*, 1/75; Jim Drinkhall, *Overdrive* (Los Angeles), 6/72–9/72; *Chicago Tribune*, 4/23/71, Sec. II; Walter Sheridan, *The Fall and Rise of Jimmy Hoffa*, Saturday Review Press, 1972, 528–36.

Page 58. "West Coast R&R": *LA Times*, 5/31/73. Smith: *Life*, 3/24/72, p. 28; *Ramparts*, 10/73, pp. 34 ff.; *Nation*, 9/24/73, pp. 268 ff.;

Voice of the Southwest (prev. *Voice of the City*; Phoenix), 8/16/73, 12/13/73; *San Diego Door,* 1972–74 passim; *Business Week,* 11/3/73, p. 28; *NYT,* 5/19/73, p. 1, 6/1/73, p. 1, 9/10/73, p. 1, 10/22/73, p. 49, 11/10/73, p. 39, 11/24/73, p. 37, 6/26/74, p. 1, 7/3/74, p. 1, 3/21/75, p. 38, 4/22/75, p. 57, 4/25/75, p. 26. Footnote: below, pp. 81, 157; Ervin final, pp. 76–78.

Page 60. *Journal: WSJ,* 8/9/73, editorial page. Manufacturing, business, Washington expenditures: *SA* #756, 753, 611. Business income: *NYT* 1/6/74, p. 59; *SA 1973,* #517; subsidies, below, p. 62. New York: *Fortune,* 7/74, pp. 114, 118; T. A. Wise, *Fortune,* 8/68; *Newsweek,* 5/26/75, p. 65. Federal figures: *SA* #611, 506, 674 (and 636), 630; *WA,* pp. 85, 87.

Page 61. 1970 budget: *SA* 611. Rim welfare/employment: *SA* #444, 455, 644.

Page 62. Joint Economic Committee: "The Economics of Federal Subsidy Programs," GPO, 1/11/72; also, Peter Passell and Leonard Ross, *New York Review,* p. 8; *WSJ,* 10/9/74, p. 1; *SA* #318, 320, 618, 619, 880, 954. Regulatory subsidies: Mark J. Green (ed.), *The Monopoly Makers,* Grossman, 1973, p. 24. Defense subsidies: below, p. 63. Footnote: *NYT,* 8/11/73, p. 1; *Ramparts,* 10/71, p. 12; *New Mexico Review,* 3/70, p. 8; Barnes, "The Sharing of Land," op. cit., p. 20.

Page 63. Brookings study: in Barnes, loc. cit. Defense: calculated from Melman, *Pentagon Capitalism,* op. cit., pp. 49, 63 (=$14.7 billion), plus property figures, above, p. 29 (30 years @ $1.3 billion/year). Oil: also, "The U.S. Oil Industry," AFL-CIO, op. cit. Real estate: also, "Background Paper on Postwar Housing," op. cit. Footnote: Joint Economic Committee, op. cit.; AFL-CIO study, op. cit.

Page 64. $19.3 billion: Joint Economics Committee, p. 187.

Page 65. Footnote: the question of ownership/control is variously explored in Paul A. Baran and Paul M. Sweezy, *Monopoly Capital,* Monthly Review, 1968; John K. Galbraith, *The New Industrial State,* Houghton Mifflin, 1971 (rev.); S. Menshikov, *Millionaires and Managers,* Progress (Moscow), 1969; Adolf Berle and Gardiner C. Means, *The Modern Corporation and Private Property,* Macmillan, 1933; Daniel Bell, *The Coming of Post-Industrial Society,* Basic, 1973; Mills, *The Power Elite,* op. cit.; Maurice Zeitlin, *American Journal of Sociology,* 3/74; Robert Fitch and Mary Oppenheimer, "Who Rules the Corporations," *Socialist Revolution* (San Francisco), Vol. I, #4–6 (1970), and discussions, Vol. II, #1, 2, 6; "Commercial Banks and Their Trust Activities," House Banking Committee, 7/8/68; "Disclosure of Corporate Ownership, Committee on Government Operations, 3/4/74. General evidence for the relative importance of corporate over financial power, or managerial over stockholder influence, in Bell, Berle, Galbraith, Baran-Sweezy, Andrew Hacker, *New York Review,* 5/1/75, Melman, *Pentagon Capitalism,* op. cit., Ch. 1, 2; specific instances include all of the evidence on corporate gifts to the 1972 Nixon campaign (Ervin final, Ch. 4, and Books 13, 25), most of the large corporate frauds (see below), Ralph Nader and Mark J. Green, *Corporate Power in America*, Grossman, 1973, Ch. 2, p. 269, and *WSJ*, 9/17/74, p. 1, 4/12/74, p. 24. On the limited role of banks, see *U.S. News*, 3/25/74, p. 70; *Business Week*, 9/15/73, p. 161; *WSJ*, 10/9/73; *WP*, 9/15/73, p. D10. Norton Simon: *WP*, 3/22/74, p. D7.

Page 66. Denenberg: *NYT*, 1/5/75, Sec. 3, p. 3. AMPI: Ervin final, Ch. 5, Ch. 6 (Parts I, II), Ch. 7 (Part I); William A. Dobrovir, et al., *The Offenses of Richard M. Nixon*, Quadrangle, 1973, pp. 60–74; *NYT*, 3/26/74, 8/1/74, 8/2/74, 8/13/74, all p. 1.

Page 68. *LA Times*: 1/3/61. Midwinter Edition. Atlanta executive, Phoenix vice-president: personal interview, 1974. Real-estate operator: Calvin Trillin, *U.S. Journal*, Dutton, 1971, p. 277.

Page 69. California scientist: Neil Morgan, *Westward Tilt*, Random House, 1963, p. 113. Investor stories: *Texas Giants*, Texas Industrial Commission, 1971, pp. 37, 87–92; *Fortune*, 6/74, pp. 134. California executive: ibid., p. 216.

Page 70. Conglomerates: Richard J. Barber, *The American Corporation*, Dutton, 1970; Brooks, *The Go-Go Years*, op. cit.; Seligman, *Main Currents*, op. cit.; Stanley H. Brown, *Ling*, Bantam, 1973; Leslie Waller, *The Swiss Bank Connection*, Signet, 1972, pp. 124–35; editors of *Fortune*, *The Conglomerate Commotion*, Time-Life, 1970; *Fortune*, 10/74, pp. 154 ff.; *Forbes*, 5/15/73, p. 270; *WP*, 10/25/73, p. A40, 12/2/73, p. H1. Thornton quote: Barber, p. 44.

Page 71. Tanzer, *The Sick Society*, Holt, Rinehart & Winston, 1972, p. 57. Barber: op. cit., p. 36.

Page 72. Economic character: generally, Mills, *Power Elite*, op. cit., pp. 343 ff.; Rose, *Power Structure*, op. cit., Ch. 6; Lundberg, *The Rich*, op. cit., Ch. 2, 3, 15.

Page 73. Turner: "The Significance of the Frontier," op. cit. *Frauds*. National Bank: *WSJ*, 10/23/73, p. 1. Four Seasons: *NYT*, 9/19/73, p. 65, 2/28/74, p. 53; *NYP*, 11/19/73, p. 2. Equity Funding: *Playboy*, 4/74, pp. 129 ff.; *WSJ*, 4/9/73, 4/24/73, 3/29/74, all p. 1. Goldstein-Samuelson: *WSJ*, 5/14/73, p. 8, 6/15/73, p. 14, 6/28/73, p. 38, 11/12/73, p. 10. Home-Stake: *WSJ*, 6/26/74, p. 1, 8/29/74, p. 1; *Newsweek*, 7/8/74, pp. 54 ff. BFA: "Conversion of Worthless Securities into Cash," Select Committee on Crime, GPO, 1973. Sharpstown: Sam Kinch, Jr., and Ben Procter, *Texas Under a Cloud*, Jenkins Publishing (Austin), 1972. Commutrix, State Fire, Alabama Equity: Jonathan Kwitny, *The Fountain Pen Conspiracy*, Knopf, 1973, pp. 180–96, 199–207, 68–80. Seabord: *WSJ*, 3/6/74, p. 4; *WP*, 3/3/74, p. A1, 3/6/74, p. A1. Geo-Tek: *WSJ*, 3/25/74, p. 30, 6/18/74, p. 14, 10/17/74, p. 4; *NYT*, 5/18/73, p. 49, 6/18/74, p. 51. Baker: Milton Viorst, *Hustlers and Heroes*, Simon & Schuster, 1971, pp. 117 ff.; Michael Dorman, *Payoff*, Berkley, 1972, pp. 143 ff.

Page 74. Guterma: *WSJ*, 11/15/73, p. 1; Wallace Turner, *Gamblers' Money*, Houghton Mifflin, 1965, passim. Patrick: *WSJ*, 4/3/74, 5/10/73, p. 1. Estes: *NYT*, 4/13/75, p. 35. Lefferdink, et al., Kwitny. "Con Man's Capital": ibid., p. 286.

Page 75. BFA: "Conversion," Select Committee, op. cit., and "Hearings," 12/7/71.

Page 76. Sentence: *WSJ*, 4/19/74. SEC: "Court enforcement actions," SEC *News Digest*, New York Public Library; see also SEC *Annual Reports*. Ponzi: *WSJ*, 7/26/74, p. 1.

Page 77. Illegal donations: "Status Report," Watergate Special Prosecution Force, 2/1/75; *WP*, 1/3/75, p. A22. Slush funds: *NYT*, 10/12/74, p. 1, 3/13/75, p. 1. Bell Telephone: *NYT*, 2/9/75, p. 1, 3/2/75, p. 35; *WP*, 2/23/75, p. A1, 4/2/75, p. A4. Grain-shipping: *NYT*, 5/20–21/75, p. 1, 5/26/75, p. 1, 5/30/75, p. 17, 6/15/75, p. 1. Hunt: *Newsweek*, 3/24/75, p. 26; *NYT* 4/15/75, p. 19; Jack Anderson, *WP*, 1/27/, 1/29, 1/31, 1975; *Parade*, 3/12/75, p. 4. Arizona: *NYT*, 3/30/75, p. 20. Florida, "biggest fraud": *Newsweek*, 5/26/75, p. 69; *NYT*, 5/15/75, p. 32.

Page 78. Land Office: *WSJ*, 1/24/74, p. 32; *Newsweek*, 3/31/75, p. 64. Homebuilding: *NYT*, 1/27/74, p. 1, 7/5/74, p. 1; *WSJ*, 3/29/74, p. 1. Agribusiness: *NYT*, 7/14/73, p. 1, 7/23/74, *NYT*, 4/1/75, p. 49, 5/29/75, p. 39; *Texas Observer*, 1/18/74, 3/15/74; Ervin final, pp. 722–26. Oil: Ovid Demaris, *Dirty Business*, Harper's Magazine Press, 1974, Ch. 3; *WP*, 12/1/74, p. A1, 3/16/75, p. A1, 3/18/75, p. A7; *NYT*, 3/28/74, p. 1, 4/10/74, p. 1, 8/20/74, p. 1, 9/7/74, p. 1, 2/3/75, p. 1, 4/23/75, p. 1, 6/10/75, p. 1; *Newsweek*, 1/6/75, p. 52.

Page 79. Crime: generally, *The History of Violence in America*, report to the National Commission on Violence, Bantam, 1970, Ch. 4, 5, 14, 18. Taft: in Martin R. Haskell and Lewis Yablonsky, *Crime and Delinquency*, Rand McNally, 1974, p. 583. 1970 rates: *SA* #225. City statistics: *New Times*, 5/2/75, pp. 26 ff. Mass murders: Ovid Demaris, *America the Violent*, Cowles, 1970, Ch. 13; *WA*, pp. 809, 917.

Page 80. Assassinations: ibid., p. 814; Demaris, *America*, op. cit., Ch. 11; *History of Violence*, op. cit., pp. 56–60. National Crime Commission: *SA* #233. Pension funds: *Newsweek*, 9/24/73, p. 98; Barber, *Corporation*, op. cit., p. 57. *Times*: 6/30/74, Sec. 3, p. 4.

Page 81. Congress: *NYT*, 8/23/74, p. 1. Teamsters Pension Fund: Jim Drinkhall, *Overdrive* (Los Angeles), a publication of independent truckers, 6/72 through 9/74; Walter Sheridan, *The Fall and Rise of Jimmy Hoffa*, Saturday Review Press, 1972; *Congressional Record*, 11/20/69, pp. 350 ff.; Ed Reid and Ovid Demaris, *The Green Felt Jungle*, Trident, 1963, Ch. 5; Reid, *The Grim Reapers*, Bantam, 1970, Ch. 10, 11. $1.5 billion: *NYT*, 2/29/74, p. 26. Investments: calculated from above sources, and *LA Times*, 11/15/70, 9/20/70; *WSJ*, 2/20/74, p. 6, 6/5/74; *Life*, 9/1–29/67; *Playboy*, 7/74, pp. 214–15; Jeff Gerth, *Penthouse*, 7/74, pp. 43 ff.; *Barron's* 3/24/75, p. 3; Turner, *Gamblers' Money*, op. cit., Ch. 9. Reid: *Reapers*, p. 266.

Page 82. $500 million: *WA*, p. 623. Deming: *Overdrive*, 1/73, p. 88, WSJ 7/20/74, p. 6. Footnote: *Fortune*, 5/65, p. 191; *LA Times*, 9/10/70, Sec. J; Jeff Gerth, *SunDance* (San Francisco), 11–12/72, p. 67.

Page 83. Indictment: *WSJ*, 2/20/74, p. 6. Organized crime investments: *Overdrive*, 6/72, 9/72/ 10/72; *Penthouse*, 1/75; Reid, *Reapers*,

p. 206, *Playboy*, loc. cit. "that outfit": *Overdrive*, 2/74, p. 54. Demaris: *Dirty Business*, p. 332.

Page 84. Lansky: e.g., Hank Messick, *Lansky*, Berkley, 1973, back jacket. $80 billion intake: similar estimates in Gerth, *Penthouse*, 7/74, p. 44, Tris Coffin, *Washington Watch*, 8/1/74; based on *WP*, 4/27/75 p. A6; *Task Force Report: Organized Crime*, and *The Challenge of Crime in a Free Society*, President's Commission on Law Enforcement, GPO, 1967; Michael Dorman, *Payoff*, op. cit., p. 15; *WSJ*, 4/17/74, p. 1; *Barron's*, op. cit.; Demaris, *Poso del Mundo*, Little, Brown, 1970, p. 160; Gail Sheehy, *Hustling*, Dell, 1974. U.S. Steel: average income, *Fortune* 500 lists, 1970–75.

Page 85. Rossides: *NYT*, 3/10/73. Organized crime in the Rim: generally, Messick, *Lansky*, op. cit., Ch. 9–12; Messick, *Syndicate in the Sun*, Macmillan, 1968; Reid, op. cit.; Demaris, *Dirty Business*, op. cit.; David Chandler, *Brothers in Blood*, Dutton, 1975; "Third Interim Report," Kefauver Senate Committee to Investigate Organized Crime, GPO, 1951.

Page 86. Mobsters southward: *Lansky*, pp. 180, 143; *Voice of the Southwest*, 2/28/74, 8/3/72; Reid, *Reapers*, pp. 86, 223. "It was Mob": Richard Hammer, *Playboy*, loc. cit.

Page 87. Kennedy: Sheridan, op. cit., passim; *Lansky*, pp. 7–8. "Dixie Mafia": Aaron M. Kohn, managing director, Metropolitan Crime Commission of New Orleans, interview, 1974. New Mexico: *Voice of the Southwest*, 2/28/74. Miami, New Orleans: Reid, *Reapers*, pp. 102, 156. Counterfeit: *NYT*, 10/29/74.

Page 88. Southern California, Detroit Mafioso: Reid, *Reapers*, pp. 186, 85. Lansky: *Lansky*, pp. 280–81; *NYT* 12/1/69, p. 1. Cohen: *Lansky*, pp. 216, 269; Waller, *Swiss Bank Connection*, op. cit., pp. 36–38; Dorman, *Payoff*, op. cit., p. 148. Narcotics: *NYT*, 6/2/74, 7/7/74, 7/13/74, 1/30/75, 4/21–24/75, p. 1. Tucson: *Penthouse*, 4–75, p. 49. Arizona: 3/30/75, p. 20.

3. FROM RIGHT TO LEFT: POLITICAL POWER

Page 89. Strauss: *WP*, 1/5/75, *Potomac*, p. 6. Bush: *NYP*, 9/7/74, p. 20. Anderson, Shearer: Ferdinand V. Solara, "Key Influences in the American Right," LEA Communications, 1974, from National Information Center, Springfield, Mass.; *NYT*, 9/23/73. Snider: *Newsweek*, 2/18/74, p. 32. Timanus: *WP*, 2/24/74, p. A2. Morrison: *NYT*, 8/13/73. Smith: *NYT*, 7/12/73.

Page 90. Electoral votes' House increase: *SA 1973*, #591, #597. Far Right: generally, Daniel Bell (ed.), *The Radical Right*, Anchor, 1964; Benjamin R. Epstein and Arnold Forster, *The Radical Right*, Vintage, 1967; George Thayer, *The Farther Shores of Politics*, Simon & Schuster, 1967; William W. Turner, *Power on the Right*, Ramparts, 1971; *Group Research Report*, Group Research Inc., Washington, D.C.; *Homefront*, Institute for American Democracy, Washington, D.C.

Page 91. Birch membership: 60,000 in 1962 (Bell, p. 240), either

80,000 (*Newsweek*, 12/6/74, p. 16A) or 100,000 (Solara, p. 41) in 1975. Gallup: Turner, p. 15. Hunt: *WP*, 12/8/74, p. B2.

Page 92. Tunney, congressmen: Barone, *Almanac*, op. cit., pp. 41–43, 45–111. Turner: op. cit., pp. 23, 27. Thayer: original MS, *Farther Shores*; also p. 195. KKK: Turner, Ch. 4; *Newsweek*, 12/16/74, p. 16. Minutemen, offshoots: Turner, Ch. 5, 6; *Ramparts*, 10/73.

Page 93. SAO: ibid. Nazis: Thayer, Ch. 1. National Socialist League: *NS Kampfruf*, Vol. 1, #1–4, 1974. Smith: Thayer, pp. 49 ff.; Trillin, *U.S. Journal*, op. cit., pp. 265 ff. National States Rights, Citizens Councils: Thayer, Ch. 2, 5. Roberts, Hargis: James Morris, *The Preachers*, St. Martin's, 1973; Thayer, Ch. 9; Turner, Ch. 7. Colleges: Turner, pp. 166–67; Robert Sherrill, *Gothic Politics in the Deep South*, Grossman, 1968, pp. 217–31; *Texas Observer*, 1/23/70, quoting "academic." "largest producer": Institute for American Democracy. Other rightists: Thayer, pp. 200–207, Ch. 9; Turner, pp. 142, 101, 172; *U.S. News*, 5/7/73, p. 25; *Pacific Research and World Empire Telegram* (East Palo Alto), 9–10/74.

Page 95. McIntire: Thayer, Ch. 9; *NYT*, 8/19/74, p. 36, 12/28/74, p. 20. Birch: Solara, pp. 32 ff.; Thayer, Ch. 8, pp. 181 ff.; Turner, Ch. 2; Epstein-Forster, Part II. Houston: *Texas Observer*, 11/12/65.

Page 96. "Phoenix," "the strongest," "to concentrate": Epstein-Forster, pp. 197, 196, 152. Liberty Lobby: Solara, pp. 45 ff.; Turner, Ch. 8; *NYT*, 3/9/75; *Homefront*, 10–11/69; Jack Anderson, *WP*, 12/26/73.

Page 97. ACA: editors of the *National Journal*, *Political Brokers*, Liveright, 1972, Ch. 2; *Human Events*, 4/13/74, pp. 336 ff. 1970 elections: *Political Brokers*, pp. 59–61.

Page 98. Radio: *Homefront* pamphlets, "Who's Who on Far Right," 1972, "Our Troubled Air," undated; Thayer, Ch. 7; Epstein-Forster, pp. 6–9.

Page 99. *National Review*: Solara, pp. 15 ff. Birch vs. GOP: Epstein-Forster, Ch. 11; *NYT* 6/1/75, p. 60. Buckley family: Lundberg, *The Rich*, op. cit., pp. 56–61.

Page 100. Financing: Epstein-Forster, p. 3 (and their earlier work, *Danger on the Right*, Random House, 1964, pp. 272–80); Herbert Alexander, *Financing the 1964 Elections*, Citizens Research Foundation (Princeton), 1966. Engler: *The Politics of Oil*, op. cit., p. 361. Individuals: Turner, op. cit.; *Political Brokers*, op. cit., p. 39; Epstein-Forster, pp. 199, 208; Domhoff, *Who Rules*, op. cit., pp. 70, 88; Lewis Chester, et al., *An American Melodrama*, Viking, 1969, pp. 657, 666.

Page 101. Salvatori: Turner, pp. 191–92; *Political Brokers*, p. 39; Thayer, p. 195; *LA Times*, 4/1/73, p. 1. Hunt: Epstein-Forster, passim; Thayer, pp. 149 ff.; Lundberg, *The Rich*, op. cit., pp. 44–51; *WP*, 12/8/74, p. B2; *NYT*, 11/30/74, p. 1, 4/3/75, p. 19. Wallace money: *New York*, 3/17/75, p. 38. Frawley: Turner, Ch. 9 (quote, p. 195); *Homefront*, 9/69; *Nation*, 6/30/62; *Fortune*, 2/66; Standard & Poor, *Register of Corporations*. Footnote: *Texas Observer*, 8/23/68, quoting Group Research.

Page 102. Schwarz: Turner, p. 178. "clearly," Twin Circle: *Homefront* op. cit. Clinics: *Nation*, 12/10/73, pp. 614–15.

Page 103. Murphy: Mark J. Green, et al., *Who Runs Congress?*, 1972, pp. 157–58; Turner, pp. 190–91. IAD: *Homefront*, op. cit., Wallace: generally, Sherrill, *Gothic Politics*, op. cit., Ch. 10; Neal Peirce, *The Deep South States of America*, Norton, 1974, pp. 240–61; Lewis Chester, et al., *An American Melodrama*, op. cit., Ch. 6, 11, 12; Theodore H. White, *The Making of the President 1968*, Pocket Books, 1970, pp. 426–59, and *The Making of the President 1972*, Bantam, 1973, Ch. 4. Alabama rankings: *SA* #194, 579.

Page 104. Wallace quotes: White, *1972*, pp. 121–22; Peirce, pp. 261, 257; Chester, *Melodrama*, p. 283.

Page 105. Moneymen: ibid, pp. 657, 666, 704; Rowland Evans and Robert Novak, *NYP*, 12/15/73, 5/8/74, *WP*, 3/10/75. Staff/workers: Chester, *Melodrama*, pp. 703–704; Sherrill, p. 259; Turner, *Power on the Right*, op. cit., pp. 133, 146, 162, 252; Epstein-Forster, *The Radical Right*, op. cit., pp. 49, 79; *Homefront*, 10–11/69. 1968 election: *SA* #581; White, *1968*, Appendix A.

Page 106. Third party: White, *1968*, pp. 431, 457. "Before it was": Peirce, p. 254. Stop-Wallace: White, *1968*, pp. 450 ff. Votes: ibid., Appendix A. Democrats/Republicans: ibid., pp. 63, 316 ff.; Chester, *Melodrama*, p. 764.

Page 107. Nixon vs. Wallace: Lewis Chester, et al., *Watergate*, Ballantine, 1973, pp. 122–26; Jack Anderson, *NYP*, 11/11/73; *NYP*, 1/24/74, p. 14, 9/21/74; Ervin hearings, Book 2, pp. 1581–82; *Impeachment of Richard M. Nixon* (Final Report of the House Committee on the Judiciary), Viking, 1975, pp. 205–207. Primaries: White, *1972*, pp. 119–23; Peirce, p. 257. Sabotage: Ervin final, pp. 166–71, 173–78. Assassination, Nixon order: Chester, *Watergate*, p. 129; Ervin final, pp. 129–30.

Page 108. Watergate: Ervin final, pp. 27–29. Wallace electorate: from Appendix A, White, *1968*, and White, *1972*. American Party: ibid. Polls: *Newsweek*, 2/18/74, p. 31; *WP*, 11/3/74, p. G2. 55 percent: Louis Harris, *NYP*, 7/1/74, p. 24. Kennedy: *NYT*, 7/5/73, p. 1. Democrats: *NYT*, 3/30/75, 2/11/74, p. 21. Nixon: *NYT*, 2/19/74, p. 1.

Page 109. "We can't win": *Newsweek*, 2/18/74, p. 32. White: *1964*, p. 81. Hess-Broder: *The Republican Establishment*, Harper & Row, 1967, p. 330.

Page 110. Yankee influence in 1960: White, *1960*, pp. 197–99, 264–67, *1964*, pp. 82–89; Leonard Lurie, *The Running of Richard Nixon*, Coward, McCann & Geoghegan, 1972, pp. 254–55. "Munich": White, *1960*, p. 199. Nixon vote: ibid., Appendix A. Texas Republicans: Earl Mazo and Stephen Hess, *Nixon*, Harper & Row, 1968, and reprint, *WSJ*, 5/9/73, editorial page. "For an unbroken," "défi": *1964*, pp. 88, 89.

Page 111. "Western Establishment": *NYT*, 4/7/74, Magazine, p. 56. Eastern Establishment: White, *1964*, pp. 90–111, Ch. 5. "The Easterners": ibid., p. 89.

Page 112. Convention: ibid., Ch. 7. Press defections, Buckleyites: ibid., pp. 398, 381.

Page 113. "Arizona mafia": ibid., pp. 377–80; Hess-Broder, *Establishment*, op. cit., pp. 39–45, 339; Gary Wills, *Nixon Agonistes*, Signet, 1969, pp. 236–37; Chester, *Watergate*, pp. 140–41. Alliances: Hess-Broder, pp. 251, 336–39. Financial base: Alexander, *Financing the 1964 Elections*, op. cit., esp. Appendix A; Domhoff, *Who Rules*, op. cit., pp. 88–90; Hess-Broder, pp. 59, 262. Footnote: White, *1964*, p. 248.

Page 114. "In geographic": in Hess-Broder, p. 59. Goldwater/ Kennedy: White, *1964*, p. 120. Campaign, vote: ibid., Ch. 11, Appendix A, p. 452.

Page 115. Goldwaterites/GOP: Hess-Broder, pp. 39–42, 52–53. 1966: ibid., pp. 331, 343–58, 394; *SA* #585, 588, 592, 593, 594. Nixon in New York: Lurie, *Running*, op. cit., Ch. 24–27; White, *1968*, pp. 51–60; *NYT*, 1/21/68, Magazine, pp. 24 ff.; Rowland Evans and Robert Novak, *Nixon in the White House*, Random House, 1971, p. 22; Gore Vidal, *An Evening with Richard Nixon*, Vintage, 1972, p. 77; White, *Breach of Faith*, Atheneum, 1975, pp. 72–75.

Page 116. "You can be": *NYT*, 1/21/68, p. 83. "surrogate Goldwater": Hess-Broder, p. 19. Nixon pre-convention, Thurmond: ibid., pp. 167–82; White, *1968*, 171–72, 299; Chester, *Melodrama*, pp. 44–48, 253–54, 433–44, 446–48; Wills, *Agonistes*, pp. 239–40.

Page 117. Nixon at Convention: Chester, *Melodrama*, pp. 455–70, 476 ff. Wills: op. cit., p. 244. *Times*: Wills, pp. 254–55.

Page 118. Vice-President: Chester, *Melodrama*, pp. 486–92; Lurie, op. cit., p. 299. "It shows": Chester, p. 482. Campaign staff: White, *1968*, pp. 173–74, 406; Chester, pp. 759, 614; Lurie, pp. 299–300.

Page 119. Finances: White, *1968*, p. 408; Herbert Alexander, *Financing the 1968 Elections*, Citizens Research Foundation, 1971; *Fortune*, 3/70, pp. 104 ff.; *NYT*, 11/13/68, 11/14/68; *Ramparts*, 10/71, p. 16; Morton Mintz and Jerry S. Cohen, *America, Inc.*, Dial, 1971, pp. 120 ff.; Demaris, *Dirty Business*, op. cit., pp. 266–68.

Page 120. Southern Strategy: White, *1968*, 404–405; Chester, *Melodrama*, pp. 626–27, 282–89. Ripon: *Lessons of Victory*, Ripon Society, Dial, 1969, pp. 7, 15. Nixon/Congress vote: White, *1968*, Appendix A; *SA* #579, 586, 588.

Page 121. Phillips: *Emerging Republican Majority*, op. cit., pp. 442–43. 1972 campaign: Ervin final, Ch. 1–4, hearings, Books 1, 2; White, *1972*, pp. 293, 363–66, 369–71, 403, 432–35, and *Breach of Faith*, op. cit., Ch. 4. "November Group": *NYP*, 6/26/73, p. 33. Campaign money: below, Chapter 5.

Page 122. Nixon: White, *1972*, p. 404. Vote: ibid., Appendix A. "Just think": ibid., p. 11.

Page 123. Congress: *SA 1973*, #600, 603. De Vries: *WSJ*, 5/10/73, editorial page.

Page 124. Chart: *SA 1973*, #608; *NYT*, 11/7/74; *Congressional Quarterly*, 1/18/75. RNC: *Facts on File*, 1973, p. 60. Fritchey: *NYP*,

7/26/73. "Southern Mafia": *NYT*, 3/27/73, p. 27. Phillips: quoted by Reston, *NYT*, 4/6/73.

Page 125. Democrats 1972: *SA 1973*, #599, 600, 603, 607. Traditional strength: Phillips, *Emerging*, op. cit.; Barone, *Almanac*, op. cit. Truman: *SA* #579. Democratic growth: Drew Pearson and Jack Anderson, *The Case Against Congress*, Simon & Schuster, 1968, pp. 55, 237, Ch. 5, 11; Domhoff, *Fat Cats*, op. cit.; *Congress and the Nation*, Vols. I, II, *Congressional Quarterly*.

Page 126. 1960: White, *1960*, pp. 172–77, 322, Appendix A. Guarantees: James T. Crown, *Kennedy in Power*, Ballantine, 1962.

Page 127. Assassination: generally, The President's (Warren) Commission, *Report*, GPO, 1964; Mark Lane, *Rush to Judgment*, Holt, 1966; William Manchester, *The Death of a President*, Harper & Row, 1967; Sylvia Meagher, *Accessories After the Fact*, Bobbs-Merrill, 1967; unpublished researches of Peter Dale Scott. Organized crime: Victor Navasky, *Kennedy Justice*, Atheneum, 1971; Sheridan, *Jimmy Hoffa*, op. cit., p. 166; Messick, *Lansky*, op. cit., pp. 7–8, 194–99, 216–17, 221–23, 241, 244; Reid, *Reapers*, op. cit., pp. 161–63 (Marcello quote, p. 162), 133–45; *Real Paper* (Boston), 6/6/73.

Page 128. Foreign policy: generally, Arthur M. Schlesinger, Jr., *A Thousand Days*, Houghton Mifflin, 1965; David Halberstam, *The Best and the Brightest*, Random House, 1972; Richard P. Stebbins, *The United States in World Affairs*, 1963, Harper & Row, 1964. Russia: *NYT*, 6/11/63, p. 1. Asian policy: Edward Weintal and Charles Bartlett, *Facing the Brink*, Scribner's, 1967, p. 71. Hilsman: *To Move a Nation*, Doubleday, 1967, p. 352. Vietnam: *Life*, 8/7/70, p. 51; *Public Papers of the Presidents . . . 1963*, GPO, 1964, pp. 759–60, 828; Scott, in Mark Seldon (ed.), *Remaking Asia*, Pantheon, 1974, p. 98. Cuba: Schlesinger, pp. 833–34; *NYT*, 4/16/63, 10/8/63; William Attwood, *The Reds and the Blacks*, Harper & Row, 1967, pp. 140–46; Stebbins, pp. 279–80; Department of State *Bulletin*, 4/22/63. Footnote: Earl Golz, *Village Voice*, 11/29/73; Ruby's background in *Warren Report*, pp. 369–70, 792–95, 800–802, but see also Lane, esp. Ch. 19, 20, and Commission Exhibits 1184, 1251, 1288, 1321, 1506, 1520, 1697, 1708, 1761, 2980.

Page 129. Arrests: *NYT*, 8/1/63, p. 6, 7/31/63, 10/3/63, p. 8; *Real Paper*, loc. cit. CIA: *Nation*, 12/7/63, p. 11; *New Republic*, 12/11/65, p. 13; *Time*, 6/12/64, p. 47; *NYT*, 8/21/73. "to splinter": Victor Marchetti and John D. Marks, *The CIA and the Cult of Intelligence*, Knopf, 1974, pp. 29–30. McNamara: *NYT*, 11/19/63, p. 11. *Business Week*: 11/23/63, p. 41. Oil: Robert Sherrill, *The Accidental President*, Pyramid, 1968, pp. 125–26. Far Right: Manchester, esp. p. 46; Warren Leslie, *Dallas Public and Private*, Grossman, 1964; *Texas Observer*, 2/1/64; *Warren Report*, pp. 292–99, 404–15.

Page 130. Johnson: *Nation*, 4/6/74, quoting Evelyn Lincoln; Demaris, *Dirty Business*, op. cit., p. 19*n*; Mark J. Green, et al., *Who Runs Congress?*, op. cit., pp. 144–45; Sherrill, *Accidental*, op. cit., pp. 106–108; "TFX Contract Investigation," Committee on Government

Operations, GPO, 1963; Drew Pearson and Jack Anderson, *The Case Against Congress*, op. cit., p. 91. Organized crime: Reid, *Reapers*, op. cit., Ch. 7, 8; Messick, *Lansky*, op. cit. pp. 244–47; *Playboy* 6/74, pp. 175–80. Caribbean policy: ibid.; Lyndon Johnson, *The Vantage Point*, Popular Library, 1971, pp. 182, 184–87, 190–204.

Page 131. Hoffa: Sheridan, op. cit., p. 300. Foreign policy: Halberstam, op. cit.; Schlesinger, op. cit.; Scott, in Selden, op. cit.; Alfred Steinberg, *Sam Johnson's Boy*, Macmillan, 1968, esp. p. 761; "Gulf of Tonkin," GPO, 1968; Tad Szulc, *Esquire*, 1/74; Marchetti-Marks, *CIA*, op. cit., pp. 30–31, 122–23, 303, 112–14, 244; *NYT*, 11/24/63, p. 1. Corporate response: *WP*, 1/6/74, Dow-Jones chart; *NYT*, 2/12/64, p. 11; *WSJ*, 4/29/63, p. 4; "Prime Defense Contracts," etc., above, Chapter 1.

Page 132. Oil: Sherrill, *Accidental*, op. cit., pp. 120, 126–28, and *Ramparts*, 1/67, pp. 35 ff.; Mark J. Green, et al., *The Closed Enterprise System*, Bantam, 1972, p. 287. Far Right: Warren Commission Hearings, 5 H 34, 37; Epstein-Forster, *The Radical Right*, op. cit., p. 88. Footnote: Additional evidence of FBI-CIA duplicity and Oswald's agentry, Peter Dale Scott, *Ramparts*, 11/73; NYT, 2/23/75, p. 32; *WP*, 11/22/74, p. A3; *New York Review*, 4/3/75, p. 24.

Page 133. Johnson: Sherrill, *Accidental*, op. cit., p. 109. TFX: I. F. Stone, *New York Review*, 3/11/71.

Page 134. Baker: *WP*, 1/9/74, p. A1; Martin and Susan Tolchin, *To the Victor* . . . , Vintage, 1971, pp. 247–48; William Turner, *Hoover's FBI*, Sherbourne (Los Angeles), 1970, p. 185; Pearson-Anderson, *Congress*, op. cit., p. 352. "The President," Johnson: *Look*, 12/16/69, p. 53.

Page 135. Johnson: generally, Sherrill, *Accidental*, op. cit.; Halberstam, op. cit., pp. 302 ff.; I. F. Stone, *In a Time of Torment*, Random House, 1967; White, *1964*, op. cit. Halberstam: op. cit. p. 435. Appointees/advisers: Charles Roberts, *LBJ's Inner Circle*, Delacorte, 1965; "Congress and the Nation, 1965–68," *Congressional Quarterly*, 1969; Tolchins, op. cit., p. 259; *WA*, pp. 748 ff.; Sherrill, pp. 115, 120–23; *Who's Who in America*, 1970–71.

Page 137. Poverty, R&D: *SA* #549, 844. Defense: above, Chapter 1; Sherrill, pp. 20–21, 179 ff., 195–203, 224–26; I. F. Stone, *New York Review*, 3/11/71, and *Polemics and Prophecies 1967–70*, Vintage, 1972, pp. 170–89; Melman, *Pentagon Capitalism*, op. cit.

Page 138. Consortium: Sherrill, pp. 197–202. Other examples: *SA* #222; Sherrill, pp. 172–74, 81, 199–202; *Mayday* (Washington), 10/18/68; "Congress and the Nation, 1965–68," op. cit., pp. 286–90.

Page 139. Rim money: Domhoff, *Fat Cats*, op. cit., esp. pp. 52–53, 44, 59–60, 77–80, 89; Sherrill, pp. 119–20, 70; Alexander, *Financing* . . . *1964*, and *1968*, op. cit. 1964 election: *SA* #586, 588.

Page 140. 1968 Convention, campaign: White, *1968*, Ch. 9, 10, 11, esp. pp. 415–16, 423–24, 440–41, Appendix C; Chester, et al., *Melodrama*, op. cit., pp. 648–49.

Page 141. Results: White, *1968*, Appendix A, pp. 498–99. Democratic National Committee, McGovern: *National Journal* editors, *Political Brokers*, op. cit., Ch. 9. 1972: White, *1972*, pp. 214–36, 126, 224–25, 134.

Page 142. Money sources: ibid., pp. 54, 375; *Congressional Quarterly*, 4/8/72; *NYT*, 3/30/72, 9/25/74; *Newsweek*, 12/2/74, p. 19. Johnson, et al.: Evans-Novak, *WP*, 9/6/73, *NYT*, 3/13/74.

Page 143. Strauss: *Political Brokers*, op. cit., p. 231; *WP*, 1/5/75, *Potomac*, p. 6; *Nation*, 2/22/75, p. 210; *NYT*, 3/20/75, p. 8. Rim Democrats: e.g., *NYT*, 9/27/74; *Nation*, 4/6/74, 2/22/75, 3/8/75, 5/17/75; Joseph Kraft, *WP*, 10/31/74; David Broder, *WP*, 9/11/74. Wills: *New York Review*, 1/23/75, p. 14.

Page 144. 21 percent: Harris survey, *WP*, 2/12/74. Committees: *Congressional Directory, 1973*, op. cit.; *Congressional Quarterly*, 1/25/75, pp. 210 ff.

Page 145. New Yorkers: *NYT*, 11/10//74. Leadership: *Congressional Quarterly*, loc. cit.

Page 146. Eastland: *Directory*, p. 98; *NYT*, 4/24/74; *WP*, 12/30/73, p. D1. Long: Green, et al., *Who Runs Congress?*, op. cit., pp. 81–83; *WSJ*, 12/18/73, editorial page. Stennis: Neal Peirce, *Deep South*, op. cit., pp. 200–201; *NYT*, 12-27-74. Albert: Green, *Congress*, pp. 88–90; *Time*, 11/5/73, p. 31. Burton: *WP*, 12/1/74, p. A1, 12/3/74, p. A1; Evans-Novak, *WP*, 12/7/74; *NYT*, 12/5/74, p. 1.

Page 147. Waggoner: *Directory*, p. 77; *WSJ*, 4/13/73, p. 1. Goldwater: James Wechsler, *NYP*, 2/6/74; *NYT*, 1/9/74, p. 1. Rogers: *Directory*, p. 40; *Commonweal*, 3/8/74, p. 19. Mills: Green, *Congress*, pp. 71–75; *NYT*, 12/4/74, p. 1; *WP*, 12/5/74, p. 1. Baker: *NYT*, 9/30/73, Magazine, pp. 11 ff. Bartlett: Jack Anderson, *NYP*, 9/20/74; *NYT*, 12/22/73, p. 1. Udall: Barone, *Almanac*, op. cit., p. 27. Sikes: *NYT*, 6/20/75, p. 1. Mann/Wiggens: White, *Breach*, op. cit., p. 14; Mary McGrory, *NYP*, 8/3/74.

Page 148. Seniority: *Directory*, pp. 241–55. Chart: *SA* 1973, #597. 1980 figures based on #15, I-C. Rim power: generally, Pearson-Anderson, *Case Against Congress*, op. cit.; Green, *Congress*, op. cit.; Joseph Clark, *Congress: The Sapless Branch*, Harper & Row, 1964; Barbara Hinckley, *The Seniority System in Congress*, Indiana, 1971, esp. Ch. 3, 5; Sherrill, *Accidental President*, op. cit.

Page 149. Rivers: Pearson-Anderson, *Congress*, pp. 268–78; Barone, *Almanac*, op. cit., p. 739.

Page 150. Oil congressmen: *NYT*, 12/22/73, p. 1; 3/16/74. Colorado River: Tolchins, *To the Victor*, op. cit., pp. 229–30. Eastland/Mississippi: *WP*, 4/21/74, p. A20. Closings: Jack Anderson, *WP*, 5/24/74.

Page 151. Land-use: *WP*, 6/12/74, p. A2. Offshore: *NYT*, 9/20/74, p. 1. Housing: *NYT*, 8/20/74. Ervin: *Congressional Directory*, p. 276; Ervin final.

4. THE THREE Rs: POLITICAL CHARACTER

Page 153. Kleindienst: Richard Harris, *Justice*, Avon, 1970; Ervin hearings, Book 9, pp. 3560 ff.; *Congressional Directory, 1973*, p. 541; *Watergate Hearings*, Viking (*New York Times*), esp. pp. 845 ff.; *Voice of the Southwest*, 2/24/72; *WP*, 5/17/74, p. A29; *New York Review*, 4/6/72, p. 8.

Page 154. Quotes: *Southwest*, op. cit. "somewhat to the right," total ignorance: Harris, op. cit., pp. 102–103. "Genghis Khan," Southern Strategy: White, *1968*, op. cit., pp. 168–69. Anti-Left campaign: Harris, pp. 151–54, 130–31, 151–53; Sale, *SDS*, Random House, 1963, pp. 541–42, 643–45; Ervin final, 144–47.

Page 155. "We had": Harris, p. 153. May Day: Chester, *Watergate*, op. cit., pp. 32–33; Charles Goodell, *Political Prisoners in America*, Random House, 1973, p. 377. "There is": *New York Review*, 7/19/73, p. 13. Operation Intercept: Ervin hearings, p. 4561; Demaris, *Poso del Mundo*, op. cit., pp. 152–53.

Page 156. Southern Strategy: Evans-Novak, *Nixon in the White House*, op. cit., pp. 157, 167, 292; Harris, pp. 158–59. "The new": ibid. Warner-Lambert: Demaris, *Dirty Business*, op. cit., p. 47. Sharp: *NYT*, 10/3/73, p. 30; Kinch-Procter, *Texas Under a Cloud*, op. cit. Steward: *Life*, 3/24/72, pp. 28 ff.

Page 157. ITT: Demaris, *Dirty Business*, pp. 51–64; *WP*, 5/17/74, A1; *NYT*, 11/1/73, p. 1; Anthony Sampson, *The Sovereign State of ITT*, Fawcett, p. 1973, passim. Arizona: *WA*, p. 749. Repression: Goodell, *Political Prisoners*, op. cit., esp. pp. 141, 244–52, 285–96; Noam Chomsky, et al., *Trials of the Resistance*, Vintage, 1970; *NYT*, 7/12/72, 7/13/72, 9/9/73; *WP*, 7/9/72. Teamster investigation: *NYT*, 4/29/73, p. 1, 5/1/73. Shenker: *Life*, 11/10/67, pp. 38 ff.; *LA Times*, 9/20/70, Section J. Senate testimony: *NYT*, 4/10/73, p. 1.

Page 158. Watergate: Chester, *Watergate*, Ch. 14; Ervin final, Ch. 1, Part II, and hearings, Book 3; Barry Sussman, *The Great Coverup*, Signet, 1974, pp. 82–83, 226–27; *NYT*, 3/29/74, 5/1/73. Ervin appearance: hearings, p. 3591, *NYP*, 8/8/73, p. 5. Law practice: *WP*, 3/10/74. ITT: *NYT*, 5/17/74, p. 1; *Impeachment of Richard M. Nixon*, Viking, op. cit., pp. 253–55, 645–46. Hart: *WSJ*, 7/11/74, p. 1; Mary McGrory, *NYP*, 6/10/74.

Page 159. Rim rightism: generally, Bell (ed.), *The Radical Right*, op. cit. Ch. 1, 5, 7, 13, esp. pp. 279–80, 421–39; Mills, *The Power Elite*, op. cit., Ch. 14, p. 151.

Page 160. Riesman: Bell, pp. 142–43. Nouveaux: Bell, pp. 108–13, 336–43, 436–37, 341n.

Page 161. "the discontented," elderly: ibid., pp. 111, 142, 400. Anti-Northeast: ibid., pp. 118–19, 164, 329; Epstein-Forster, *The Radical Right*, op. cit., pp. 80, 93. Viereck: Bell, p. 164. Riesman-Glazer: ibid., p. 118.

Page 162. Gallup: *Public Opinion, 1935–71*, op. cit., pp. 2231 ff.

ERA: *NYT*, 8/24/74, p. 12, 2/25/75; *Texas Observer*, 10/15/74; *Facts on File*, 1973, p. 145.

Page 163. Congressional issues: *NYT*, 7/21/74, 4/11/74, 6/16/74, 9/18/74, p. 31, 10/11/73, *Time*, 8/26/74, p. 52; Key votes: *Congressional Quarterly; NYT*, on days after dates.

Page 164. ACA, ASC: *Human Events*, 4/13/74, 10/26/74.

Page 165. ADA: ibid., 4/13/74. Racism: generally, Bell, op. cit., Ch. 1, 5, 6; Peirce, *Deep South*, op. cit.

Page 166. Phillips: *Emerging Republican Majority*, op. cit., p. 437. Progress: Peirce, *Deep South*, op. cit.; John Egerton, *The Americanization of Dixie*, Harper's Magazine Press, 1974.

Page 167. EEOC: *NYT*, 5/6/74. HUD: *HUD Statistical Yearbook*, GPO, complaints for Title VI, 1964, Title VII, 1968. Council on Municipal Performance: *Parade*, 12/8/74, p. 22. Low-income: *SA* #542. Wallace: above, Chapter 3. Arizona: *WP*, 4/21/74, p. A3. New Orleans: Trillin, *U.S. Journal*, op. cit., pp. 155 ff.

Page 168. Chavez: Jacques Levy, *Cesar Chavez*, Norton, 1975. Texas controller: *NYT*, 9/22/73. Far Right: Epstein-Forster, op. cit., pp. 33–40, 45–49, 64–70, 95–106, 111–14, 128–37; Thayer, *Farther Shores*, op. cit., p. 40. "illegals": *Voice of the Southwest*, 1/27/72; *NYT*, 9/15/74, Magazine, p. 24; *Washington Monthly*, 4/73, p. 18. Black students: Sale, *SDS*, op. cit., pp. 640–41. Johnson: Sherrill, *Accidental President*, Ch. 3, 6, esp. pp. 159, 61, 71, 162–63, 167.

Page 169. "I can't be": Gore Vidal, *An Evening with Richard Nixon*, op. cit., p. 82. Nixon: Evans-Novak, *Nixon*, op. cit., Ch. 6; Vidal, pp. 31, 45, 109; *Congressional Record*, 4/25/59; *New York Review*, 8/13/70, pp. 23 ff.; *NYT*, 5/17/74, p. 1, 5/18/74, p. 14; *NYP*, 6/4/74, p. 5.

Page 171. Rim repression: generally, W. J. Cash, *The Mind of the South*, Knopf, 1941; Sherrill, *Gothic Politics in the Deep South*, op. cit.; *The History of Violence in America*, op. cit., Part II, Ch. 14; Richard Hofstadter and Michael Wallace (eds.), *American Violence*, Vintage, 1970; *Kerner Report*, Bantam, 1968, Part II; Richard Slotkin, *Regeneration Through Violence*, Wesleyan, 1974. Irvine: *NYT*, 7/19/74. Coral Springs: visit. Houston: Arthur Bell, *Village Voice*, 8/30/73.

Page 172. Police percent: *SA* #246. Prisons: *SA 1973*, #271, 272, 277.

Page 173. UCLA, Federal Center: *Nation*, 10/5/74, p. 294. Barber: *The Presidential Character*, Prentice-Hall, 1972, p. 12, Ch. 3, Part V. Johnson repression: Goodell, *Political Prisoners*, op. cit.; Paul Cowan, et al., *State Secrets*, Holt, 1974; Chomsky, *Trials*, op. cit.; Sale, *SDS*, op. cit., esp. pp. 347–48, 424, 499–500; *NYT*, 12/22/74, p. 1, 6/11/75, p. 1, 2/3/75, p. 1, 11/17/74; *WP*, 12/29/74, p. 1, 12/7/73, 3/19/74; *WIN* (Rifton, N.Y.), 3/1–15/72; Rockefeller Report on the CIA, 6/75.

Page 174. Nixon repression: Ervin final, Ch. 1, 2, 3; Sale, *SDS*, pp. 541–43, 643–45; *NYT*, 11/15/74, p. 23, 12/1/74, 2/15/74, p. 66; "The Immigration and Naturalization Service and Civil Liberties," ACLU, 1974.

Page 175. Huston Plan: Ervin final, pp. 3–7; *NYT*, 6/7/73, p. 1, 36; *WP*, 6/27/73, p. A20. Never rescinded, continued: *WP*, 6/25/73, p. A1, 6/10/73, p. A1; *NYT*, 6/2/73, p. 1, 10/16/73, p. 1, 6/11/73, p. 1; *NYP*, 5/30/73, p. 5; *Rolling Stone*, 10/10/74, pp. 54 ff. Hunt: 11/14/72 memo to Sirica, Watergate burglary trial. "Tyranny": *NYT*, 6/17/73. "was redolent": *NYT*, 5/25/73. Ervin: *NYP*, 6/1/73, p. 5. Levine: *Nation*, 9/10/73.

Page 176. Southeast Asia: *NYT*, 1/24–25/73; *NYP*, 1/24/73, p. 56; Marchetti and Marks, *CIA*, op. cit., p. 246; *Counterspy* (Washington, D.C.), 5/73; Michael Myerson, International, 1973, pp. 47–49. Shirer: ibid.

Page 178. Congressional additions: *SA* #583. Dallas: *NYT*, 11/24/73; *Texas Observer*, 2/14/75, p. 1.

Page 179. Texas: Kinch-Procter, *Texas Under a Cloud*, op. cit.; *Texas Observer*, 7/2/71, 2/12/71. Florida: *NYT*, 2/5/73, 5/19/73, 5/28/75, 4/28/74, 10/1/74; *WP*, 2/15/75. California: *NYT*, 7/27/74, p. 1, 11/11/73, p. 32.

Page 180. Louisiana: *NYT*, 3/28/75, p. 24. Oklahoma: *NYT*, 3/15/75, 8/5/74, 6/1/73, 3/13/74; *WSJ*, 7/3/74, 6/4/73. Moyers: 11/4/74. Alabama: *New York*, 3/17/75, p. 37. Arizona: *NYT*, 11/11/73. Louisiana: Peirce, *Deep South*, op. cit., p. 69. Georgia: *NYT*, 1/30/75, p. 15; *WP*, 1/6/75, p. 3. Mexican border: *NYT*, 5/21/73, p. 1, 6/12/74, p. 19, 7/15/74, p. 1, 11/24/74, p. 72, 4/27/75, p. 47; *Washington Monthly*, 4/73, p. 16; Demaris, *Poso del Mundo*, op. cit.

Page 181. Impeachments: *Congressional Directory*, 1973, p. 402. Fortas: Demaris, *Dirty Business*, pp. 287, 312–16; Bickel, *New Republic*, 4/26/69, p. 10. California: *WP*, 5/20/73, p. C5. Watergate: Ervin final, Ch. 1–3.

Page 182. Indicted/convicted: Watergate Special Prosecution Force, *Status Report*, 2/1/75. Magruder: *Nation*, 6/8/74, p. 707. Cambodia/ Laos: *Impeachment of Richard Nixon*, Viking, op. cit., pp. 311–16; *NYT*, 7/31/73, 8/21/73, 9/11/73. CIA: *NYT*, 9/8/74; *WIN*, 11/7/74.

Page 183. FHA: Brian D. Boyer, *Cities Destroyed for Cash*, Follett, 1973; *Newsweek*, 5/20/74, p. 86; *WP*, 3/10/74, p. A1. SBA: *NYT*, 11/11/73, 11/15/73, 11/30/73, 12/14/73; *WP*, 11/14/73, 11/19/73. INS: above, p. 180. Hiring/firing: Ervin final, Ch. 3; *WP*, 11/12/74, p. A10; *NYT*, 10/3/74, 10/11/74, 11/24/73. Impoundments: *NYT*, 2/19/75, p. 1, 11/22/73; *NYP*, 8/4/73, p. 23. Emoluments, tax breaks: *Impeachment of Richard Nixon*, Viking, pp. 16–25. "I am suggesting": *New Yorker*, 4/8/74. Jones: Reid-Demaris, *Green Felt Jungle*, op. cit., p. 136.

Page 184. Louisiana: *Atlanta Journal*, 1/23/74; *NYT*, 2/14/74. Arizona: *Phoenix Gazette*, 2/8/74. California: *Parade*, 4/7/74, p. 19. New Mexico: *New Mexico Review*, 3/71.

Page 185. Women's Club: *NYT*, 9/30/73, p. 1, 4/7/74, p. 32. Lincoln Club: *NYT*, 6/19/73. Oilman: *WSJ*, 12/13/73, p. 1. Griffin: Evans-Novak, *NYP*, 9/12/74; *NYP*, 8/17/74, p. 9. Buzhardt: David Broder, *WP*, 3/16/75. Nixon: *NYT* 11/18/73, p. 1.

Page 186. Anderson deal: Sherrill, *Accidental President*, op. cit., pp. 122, 236; *Atlantic*, 7/71, p. 86. 1964 disclosure: *Texas Observer*, 5/1/64; *NYT*, 2/1/71, 2/3/71. Texas Constitution: *Texas Almanac*, annual, *Houston Post*. Contracts: Dugger, op. cit., p. 72. Charters: *Texas Observer*, 4/13/73, p. 7. Jacobsen: *NYT*, 6/25/74, 5/10/74. Bribes: *NYT*, 7/30/74, p. 1. In White House: *New York*, 5/28/73, p. 35; *NYP*, 5/11/73, p. 5.

Page 187. "there isn't": *Newsweek*, 9/24/73, p. 36. Supreme Court: *WP*, 9/12/73, p. A1. Indictment, acquittal: *NYT*, 7/30/74, 4/18/75. Twain: *Following the Equator*, Vol. 1, Ch. 8. Banner: *NYT*, 7/14/73, Op-Ed.

Page 188. 1972 tally: Mark Green, et al., *Who Runs Congress?*, op. cit., pp. 140, 142; *Congressional Quarterly*, 1972, pp. 1635 ff. Bank conflicts: ibid.

Page 189. Kerr: Green, *Congress*, p. 139. Long: ibid., pp. 81–83, 141; *WP*, 9/5/69, p. 34; Pearson-Anderson, *Case Against Congress*, op. cit., pp. 146–47; *SA* #542.

Page 190. Marcello: Sheridan, *Hoffa*, op. cit., p. 408; *Vieux Carré Courier*, 7/27/73, p. 7. Hoffa: Sheridan, pp. 411–83. Indictments: ibid., p. 478; Demaris, *Dirty Business*, op. cit., p. 395. Sparkman: Christopher Elias, *The Dollar Barons*, Macmillan, 1973, pp. 155–61, 344; Common Cause, *1972 Campaign Finances*, op. cit.; Pearson-Anderson, *Congress*, p. 193; Jack Anderson, *WP*, 5/31/73, 6/18/73.

Page 191. Mills: Ervin final, Ch. 7; *WP*, 4/2/74, p. A8, 5/24/74, p. A2; *NYP*, 8/2/74, p. 5; Common Cause, op. cit.; Jack Anderson, *WP*, 2/13/74, 12/19/73; *WSJ*, 8/5/74, p. 2, 6/14/73, p. 1.

Page 192. Goldwater: Reid-Demaris, *Green Felt*, op. cit., pp. 45–47; Michael Dorman, *Payoff*, op. cit., pp. 184–89; Turner, *Gamblers' Money*, op. cit., p. 47; *Penthouse*, 1/75; *Voice of the Southwest*, 1/27/72.

Page 193. McClellan: Messick, *Private Lives of Public Enemies*, Wyden, 1973, pp. 84–88; Dorman, op. cit., pp. 36–38; Peirce, *Deep South*, op. cit., p. 141.

Page 194. "revelations": ibid., p. 153. First National: Pearson-Anderson, *Congress*, op. cit., pp. 195–96. Gibbons: Green, *Congress*, op. cit., pp. 142–43. Preyer: *LA Free Press*, 2/15/74, p. 3. Wilson: *NYT*, 3/2/74. Cannon: Turner, *Gamblers' Money*, op. cit., p. 87.

Page 195. Poage/Teague: Pearson-Anderson, *Congress*, p. 152. Steiger: *NYT*, 6/11/73, p. 1, *Voice of the Southwest*, 8/9/73. Montoya: *WSJ*, 6/28/73, p. 1; *NYP*, 6/29/73; *NYT*, 6/30/73, p. 17. Bellmon: Jack Anderson, *WP*, 10/15/74; *WP*, 10/22/74, p. A10. Eastland: *Newsweek*, 3/24/75, p. 26; Jack Anderson, *WP*, 1/25, 27, 31/75. Collins: ibid., 8/7/74.

Page 196. Albert: ibid., 6/12/74. Criminal acts: *Congress and the Nation*, op. cit., Vol. I, p. 1420; Green, et al., *Congress*, pp. 145–59, 62–64; *NYT*, 10/2/74, p. 1; *NYP*, 7/20/74, p. 6 (includes convictions, indictments, and acquittals, congressional inquiries, sanctions, and floor exposures). Bilbo: *Congress and the Nation*, loc. cit. Smathers: Sherrill, *Gothic Politics*, op. cit., pp. 158–63. Long: above. Gurney: *NYT*,

7/12/74, p. 10, 7/11/74, p. 1, 2/25/75, p. 16, 4/26/75, p. 56, 5/29/75, p. 15, 6/10/75, p. 16.

Page 197. "careless," etc.: *WP*, 5/15/74. Adams: quoted in *Nation*, 8/31/74, p. 136.

Page 198. Lansky: Nicholas Gage, *The Mafia Is Not an Equal Opportunity Employer*, Dell, 1971, p. 63. Agent: ibid. "A black": ibid., p. 140. Racism: ibid., Ch. 7, 8; Messick, *Lansky*, op. cit., pp. 183–85.

Page 199. "The poor": Reid-Demaris, *Green Felt*, op. cit., pp .161–62. Farmworkers: Levy, *Cesar Chavez*, op. cit.; *Overdrive* series, op. cit.

Page 200. Marcello henchman: Dorman, *Payoff*, op. cit., pp. 109–110. Texas/Helfen: ibid., Ch. 7.

Page 201. Baker: above. Samish: Dorman, pp. 213–14; *WP*, 5/20/73, p. C5. Democrats: Demaris, *Dirty Business*, op. cit., p. 420, 328; Turner, *Gamblers' Money*, p. 109; Demaris, *Captive City*, Lyle Stuart, 1969, p. 223. Smith: above, Chapter 2. Rebozo, Annenberg, Crosby, Chotiner: below, Chapter 5.

Page 202. Fitzsimmons: Demaris, *Dirty Business*, pp. 330–37; *Overdrive* series, op. cit.; *Penthouse*, 7/74; *LA Times*, 5/31/73. Safire: *Village Voice*, 10/18/73; *Las Vegas Sun*, 3/21–4/2/71. Brennan: *Village Voice*, 1/25/73, *NYT*, 6/15/72, p. 1. LaRue: *WSJ*, 4/24/74, p. 1, 11/27/74, p. 14; Kwitny, *Fountain Pen*, op. cit. Hoodlum banquet: Pearson-Anderson, *NYP*, 10/31/68, protested by Nixon campaign but never contested.

Page 203. Wofford: Jeff Gerth, *SunDance*, 11–12/72, pp. 32–33. Nixon-Havana: ibid., p. 36; Messick, *Lansky*, op. cit., p. 188; *Penthouse*, 7/74, p. 104. Vitali: Gerth, p. 66. Bahamas: Messick, *Lansky*, pp. 234–45. *Bolita*: Miami police department, 11/13/63, raw file, from P. D. Scott; Orovitz: *Penthouse*, 7/74, p. 106. Courtney: Messick, *Lansky*, p. 235. "unsavory": *Newsday*, "Special Report," issues of 10/6–10/13/71, Part 6; *Penthouse*, 7/74.

Page 204. Real-estate: *Village Voice*, 8/30/73. DeCarlo: Demaris, *Dirty Business*, p. 329; *NYT*, 10/21/73. Kovens: Demaris, op. cit., pp. 337–38; Sheridan, *Hoffa*, op. cit., pp. 369–77. Hoffa: ibid., p. 521. Fitzsimmons: *Overdrive*, 9/72. Dun and Bradstreet: *Real Paper*, in *Iconoclast* (Dallas), 10/19/73. Shenker: *Overdrive*, 7/73, *Penthouse*, 7/74, 3/75. Gagliardi: *WP*, 12/3/73; *Playboy*, 7/74. California mobsters: *NYT*, 4/29/73, p. 1. Wiretapping bollix: *Newsweek*, 5/27/74, p. 75; *NYT*, 1/10/74. Morgenthau: Messick, pp. 268–70. Vietnam: P. D. Scott, *The War Conspiracy*, Bobbs-Merrill, 1972, pp. 191–219; Alfred W. McCoy, *Politics of Heroin in Southeast Asia*, Harper & Row, p. 1972. SBA: *NYT*, 11/16/75, p. 16. and above.

5. The Cowboy Conquest

Page 208. Nixon's biography: James David Barber, *Presidential Character*, op. cit.; Eli Chesen, *President Nixon's Psychiatric Profile*, Wyden, 1973; William Costello, *The Facts about Nixon*, Viking, 1960; Ralph de Toledano, *One Man Alone: Richard Nixon*, Funk & Wagnalls,

1969; Rowland Evans and Robert Novak, *Nixon in the White House*, op. cit., Mark Harris, *Mark the Glove Boy*, Curtis, 1964; Stephen Hess and David Broder: *The Republican Establishment*, op. cit.; Bela Kornitzer, *The Real Nixon*, Rand McNally, 1960; Leonard Lurie, *The Running of Richard Nixon*, op. cit., and *The Impeachment of Richard Nixon*, Berkley, 1973; Frank Mankiewicz, *Perfectly Clear*, Quadrangle, 1973; Bruce Mazlish, *In Search of Nixon*, op. cit.; Earl Mazo and Stephen Hess, *Nixon: A Political Portrait*, Popular Library, 1968; Richard Nixon, *Six Crises*, op. cit.; Gore Vidal, *An Evening with Richard Nixon*, op. cit.; Jerry Voorhis, *The Strange Case of Richard Nixon*, Popular Library, 1973; Theodore White, *The Making of the President—1960, 1964, 1968, 1972*, and *Breach of Faith*, all Atheneum, 1961, 1965, 1969, 1973, 1975; Gary Wills, *Nixon Agonistes*, op. cit.; Jules Witcover, *The Resurrection of Richard Nixon*, Putnam's, 1970. "stamp of place": e.g., Wills, pp. 165, 172–77; Harold J. Abramson, *Columbia Forum*, Winter 1974. Mazlish, p. 42.

Page 209. "He hears": ibid., p. 53.

Page 210. "When you": Nixon, p. 38. "It is wrong": *NYT*, 8/23/73, p. 1; *Impeachment of Richard M. Nixon*, Viking, p. 729. White: *1960*, p. 65. *WSJ*: 5/4/73, editorial page. "My mother": White, *1960*, p. 302.

Page 211. Religion, "commitment": Mazlish, pp. 30–31; Lurie, *Running*, pp. 29–31. Football: Mazo-Hess, pp. 18–19. "they applied": Mazo-Hess: p. 31. Whittier: Lurie, *Running*, pp. 33–35; Costello, pp. 27–28.

Page 212. "greatly": Mazo-Hess, pp. 32–33. "Nixon was": *NYT*, 10/3/73, Magazine. Duke: Jack Anderson, *NYP*, 5/16/73. "the ethical": Harriet Van Horne, *NYP*, 6/6/73. South Pacific: Lurie, *Running*, pp. 39–41; Costello, pp. 30–31.

Page 213. Dean's list: Ervin hearings, Book 24, p. 11675; similar list, *WP*, 12/21/73, p. A10.

Page 214. Hiss: Nixon, Ch. 1; "the symbol": p. 67. Mundt-Nixon: HR 5852, 4/28/48; Lurie, *Running*, pp. 59–60. Dewey/Northeast: Costello, pp. 188–90. Slush fund: *NYP*, 9/18/52; Costello, pp. 104–107, Lurie, *Running*, pp. 125–35.

Page 215. Lawrence: Costello, p. 151. 1946: Voorhis, pp. 11–17, Lurie, *Running*, pp. 48–51; Mankiewicz, pp. 31–45, 1948: ibid., pp. 45–46; Voorhis, p. 17. 1950: ibid., pp. 18–19; Mankiewicz, pp. 47–57; Costello, pp. 60–74, 81–82; Drew Pearson and Jack Anderson, *USA: Second-Class Power?*, Simon & Schuster, 1958, p. 277. "I'm sorry": Costello, p. 74.

Page 216. 1952: ibid., 97–114; Mankiewicz, pp. 62–63. 1956: Costello, p. 163, Voorhis, p. 23; Lurie, *Running*, pp. 266–67; Noah Dietrich, *Howard: The Amazing Mr. Hughes*, Fawcett, 1972, pp. 281–86; *NYT*, 1/23/72.

Page 217. 1960: Lurie, *Running*, pp. 257–59. 1962: Mankiewicz, pp. 65–75; *Village Voice*, 8/16/73; *Nation*, 5/28/73. 1968: Richard Harris, *Justice*, op. cit., pp. 11–12, 22–35, 49–55; Ervin final, 109–19, 931–1075; Demaris, *Dirty Business*, op. cit., pp. 267–69; Mankiewicz,

p. 14, White, 1968, op. cit., pp. 471–74; *Rolling Stone*, 3/13/75, pp. 28 ff.

Page 218. 1972: Ervin final, Ch. 2, 4; William Dobrovir, *The Offenses of Richard Nixon*, op. cit. Inaugural: *WA 1974*, p. 795.

Page 219. Friends: *NYP*, 1/20–24/69; *NYT*, 8/11/74, p. 43; *US News*, 5/7/73, p. 23; biographical sources above.

Page 221. Rebozo: *NYT*, 6/20/74, p. 33, *WP*, 8/1/73. "Bebe's a self-made": *Ladies Home Journal*, 11/73. Kalmbach: Ervin final, pp. 51–60, 110, 161 ff., Ch. 4, esp. pp. 505–510, 589; *WP*, 1/26/74, p. A1; *WSJ*, 2/26/74, p. 5; *NYT*, 5/29/73, p. 1, 2/26/74, p. 1; *Impeachment of Richard M. Nixon*, op. cit., pp. 16–25, 95–98, 144, 457–63.

Page 222. Chotiner: Wills, pp. 80–113; Lurie, *Running*, pp. 113–49; Pearson-Anderson, *USA*, op. cit., pp. 281–83; Sheridan, *Hoffa*, op. cit., pp. 504, 508, 526, 535; Pearson-Anderson, *NYP*, 10/31/68; Ervin final, pp. 633–35, 643–44, 649, 659–68; "Textile Procurement in the Military Services," Senate Rackets Committee, 5/3/56, Vol. 21, pp. 1563–1602; Mankiewicz, p. 70; *NYT*, 5/4/73, 8/29/73, p. 20, 1/28/73, p. 12. 1972 campaign: *Newsweek*, 11/26/73, p. 35; *NYT*, 7/6/73, 1/1/74; Jack Anderson, *WP*, 11/23/73; Demaris, *Dirty Business*, p. 336.

Page 223. Smith: above, Chapter 2. Connally: above, Chapter 4. Annenberg: *WSJ*, 6/28/74, p. 24; *Fortune*, 6/70, p. 91. Crosby: *Las Vegas Sun*, 3/21–4/2/71; *Penthouse*, 7/74; Messick, *Lansky*, pp. 192, 230–35. Mitchell: *NYT*, 1/2/75, p. 1. Abplanalp: *NYT*, 6/1/73, 8/12/73, 4/14/74; *WP*, 12/9/73. Bronstein: *NYT*, 10/12/74, 10/26/74. Bobst: *NYP*, 6/5/74, p. 1. Ash: *NYT*, 12/4/72, 12/24/73, p. 6; *Nation*, 2/26/73; Demaris, *Dirty Business*, pp. 42–44. Rebozo: generally, *Newsday*, "Special Report," 1971, op. cit.; *New York Review*, 5/3/73; Lurie, *Running*, pp. 308–312; Ervin final, pp. 931–1068; *National Observer*, 2/2/74, p. 1; *McCall's*, 7/74, pp. 18–26; *Life*, 7/31/70, pp. 18–27; *NYP*, 1/20/69, p. 37; *Nation*, 11/12/73; *Newsweek*, 4/22/74.

Page 224. "the only": *Life*, loc. cit. "the most": *McCall's*, loc. cit. OPA: *Village Voice*, 8/30/73; Jeff Gerth, *SunDance*, 11–12/72. Nixon meeting: Ervin final, p. 934. Bank: *Newsday*, pp. 16–20; *Newsweek*, loc. cit.; *NYT* 4/4/74; *Village Voice*, 10/4/73; *WP*, 10/25/73, p. A1.

Page 225. Slush fund: Ervin final, Ch. 8; *NYT*, 12/9/74, p. 27; *WP*, 6/7/74, p. A1; *Village Voice*, 11/1/73, 12/20/73. Footnote: ibid., 8/30/73; *NYT*, 12/1/69, p. 42, 11/8/73; *WP*, 10/25/73, p. A15.

Page 226. Skimming: *Village Voice*, 10/4, 10/11, 11/1, 12/20/73; *NYT*, 1/21/74, p. 1, 3/21/74, 11/30/73, p. 1, 12/5/73, p. 22; *Boston Phoenix*, 4/16/74, p. 17; *Miami Herald*, 1/18/74, p. 1; Jack Anderson, *WP*, 3/20/74. SBA loans: *Newsday*, pp. 9–15, 43.

Page 227. Shopping center: ibid., pp. 10–14; *Nation*, 11/12/73, pp. 491–92; Reid, *Reapers*, op. cit., pp. 188, 297–98; Messick, *Private Lives*, pp. 235–40; Miami police report, 11/13/63, op. cit. Berg, real estate: *Newsday*, pp. 40–43; *Penthouse*, 7/74, p. 106; *Village Voice*, 8/30/73. Adams: *The Education*, Ch. 20.

Page 228. Nixon money: above, Chapter 3; Lurie, *Impeachment*, p. 43; Demaris, *Dirty Business*, p. 334; Dietrich, *Howard*, op. cit., pp. 242–43; Costello, pp. 71–72; Voorhis, p. 19. Slush fund: *NYP*, 9/18/52;

NYT, 9/21/52, p. 1, Costello, p. 101. Pearson: Jack Anderson, *NYP*, 12/13/73. 1972 finances: Ervin final, Ch. 4, 5, and hearings, Books 13, 25; Common Cause, *1972 Federal Campaign Finances*, 1974; Herbert Alexander, *Financing the 1972 Elections*, Citizens Research Foundation, 1975.

Page 229. Finance Committee list: Ervin final, p. 549. Common Cause: *WSJ*, 10/1/73.

Page 230. Industry committees: Common Cause, op. cit., Vol. 1, p. x (adjusted to eliminate McGovern donations as listed on pp. 1–227). Published lists: Ervin final, pp. 493–94, 508–510; *Nation*, 2/16/74, pp. 207/210; *NYT*, 1/23/73, 1/31/73, p. 8, 7/12/73, p. 13, 7/15/73, 9/29/73, p. 1, 9/30/73, 10/1/73, p. 26, 2/1/74, 3/17/74, p. 44, 3/20/74, 6/29/74; *WP*, 9/29/73, p. A1, 12/4/73, p. B1, 12/10/73, 2/17/74, p. A1, 9/14/74, p. A6; *NYP*, 5/19/73, p. 24, 7/13/73, 12/29/73, p. 4, 1/2/74, p. 5, 9/21/74, p. 5; *WSJ*, 6/1/73, p. 1, 12/13/73, p. 1, 5/28/74, editorial page; *Texas Observer*, 12/28/73, 7/13/73; *Fortune*, 12/73, pp. 95 ff.; Jack Anderson, *WP*, 1/14/74.

Page 231. $19.9 million: *WP*, 9/29/73, p. A1. Southern Rim percentage, major donors: above lists; *Parade*, 2/17/74; *WP*, 11/25/73, p. A1, 11/26/73, 3/29/74, p. A1, 5/10/74, p. A1; *NYT*, 12/1/73, 4/7/74; 9/1/74, Magazine, p. 12; Jack Anderson, *WP*, 5/2/73, 11/29/73, 12/2/73, 12/7/73, 4/25/74; *New York Review*, 5/3/73.

Page 232. Influence: Ervin final, pp. 550, 450, 447, 525, and hearings, pp. 5334–44; Dobrovir, et al., *The Offenses of Richard M. Nixon*, op. cit., pp. 79–80. Nixon appointments: generally, Evans-Novak, *Nixon in the White House*, op. cit., Ch. 2; White, *1972*, pp. 361–63, 65–68; John Osborne, *The Nixon Watch*, Liveright, 1970, esp. pp. 80, 96–100; Dan Rather and Gary Paul Gates, *The Palace Guard*, Warner, 1975; *NYT*, 5/5/73, p. 1, 6/7/74, p. 1; Ervin final, Ch. 3; Mike Causey, *WP*, 11/26/73, 1/12/74, 7/22/74, 9/20/74.

Page 233. "This decline": Owen Edwards, *New York*, 8/12/74. Shultz: *WSJ*, 5/7/74, editorial page. Finch: White, *1968*, pp. 174–77, *1972*, p. 366.

Page 234. Geographical information on appointments: *Who's Who in America*, 1970–71, 72–73; *Who's Who in American Politics*, 1971–73; *U.S. Government Organization Manual*, 1972–73, 1973–74; *Congressional Quarterly*, "Guide to Current American Government," Spring 1973, "Congress and the Nation," 1964–68 and 1969–72; *Facts on File.; W.A; Congressional Directory*, 1972, 1973, 1974. (Appointment compilations and research by Ruth Apfelbaum, additional research by Peter Freitag and Beth Mintz, SUNY, Stony Brook.)

Page 235. White House staff: see also *The Watergate Hearings*, Viking, 1973, pp. 817 ff.; Michael Myerson, *Watergate*, op. cit. Figures: *WSJ*, 8/23/73, editorial page; *National Journal*, 12/11/71, p. 2447; Gannett News Service, 8/3/73; *WP*, 6/17/74, p. A2 (calculations vary).

Page 236. White House influence: Rather-Gates, op. cit.; *NYT*, 3/6/73, 5/5/73; *WP*, 7/19/73; White, *Breach*, 111, 171, etc. "The Nixon cabinet": *Playboy*, 1/75, p. 78. Loyalty package: Jack Anderson, *NYP*, 9/1/73. "The greatest": *NYT*, 5/6/73, Magazine, p. 104.

Page 237. Ehrlichman: *Watergate Hearings*, Viking, op. cit., p. 503. "We are so": *NYT*, 6/24/74, Magazine, p. 51. Workdays: *Playboy*, op. cit.; *NYT*, 3/21/73, p. 47. "I already": *Playboy*, p. 74. "ratfucking": Carl Bernstein and Bob Woodward, *All the President's Men*, Quartet, pp. 126–28, 132. Biographies: sources above, p. 234; Rather-Gates; White, *Breach; Watergate Hearings*; Woodward-Bernstein; Chester, et al., *Watergate*, op. cit.; Evans-Novak, *Nixon in the White House*; Sussman, *Coverup*; Osborne, *Nixon Watches, Last Nixon Watch.* ALSO: Ehrlichman: *NYP*, 7/24/73, p. 48, 7/28/73, p. 22.

Page 238. Ziegler: *WP*, 2/24/74, *Potomac*, pp. 10 ff. Chapin: *NYP*, 11/30/73. Dent: *WP*, 12/12/74, p. A1. Magruder: Magruder, *An American Life*, Atheneum, 1974; *NYT*, 1/20/73, p. 14, 2/13/74. Malek: Evans-Novak, *NYP*, 8/31/74. LaRue: *WSJ*, 4/24/74, p. 1. Klein: Lurie, *Running*, pp. 180, 245, 299; *WP*, 6/6/73. Harlow: *NYT*, 11/14/68, p. 34. Timmons: *WP*, 5/12/74, p. A1. Nofziger: Broder-Hess, *Republican Establishment*, op. cit., p. 282.

Page 239. Burch: *WP*, 2/16/74. Morgan: *Time*, 11/18/74, p. 35. Moore: Ervin hearings, pp. 1938–2073. Buzhardt: Evans-Novak, *WP*, 12/6/73. Wright: *NYT*, 8/7/73. Armstrong: *Texas Observer*, 1/19/73; *NYT*, 5/30/73, p. 34. Haldeman: *Newsweek*, 3/19/73, p. 24, 6/19/73, p. 27; *NYT*, 5/6/73, Magazine, pp. 39 ff.; Mankiewicz, *Perfectly Clear*, op. cit.; *Village Voice*, 5/2/74; Lurie, *Running*, pp. 312–13; Ervin hearings, pp. 915–19, 2874–77.

Page 240. "consciously aiding": *NYT*, Magazine, op. cit. "somewhere in the jungle": *NYP*, 7/31/73.

Page 241. "He *made*": *Playboy*, 1/75, op. cit. "even John": Lurie, *Running*, p. 312. Staff meetings: *Newsweek*, 6/19/73, p. 26. Footnote: William Safire, *Before the Fall*, Doubleday, 1975, 12/29/74, p. C5; Evans-Novak, *NYP*, 8/24/73; *NYT*, 8/25/74, p. 1.

Page 242. "Haldeman issues": Jack Anderson, *WP*, 8/22/72. Watergatery: Ervin final, pp. 130–50, 160–87, 505–11, 9, 135, 7–12, 132, 3–7, 56; *Impeachment of Richard M. Nixon*, passim. "There is no": *NYT*, Magazine, op. cit., p. 104. "P. And I": *White House Transcripts*, op. cit. p. 416.

Page 244. Domestic policy: in addition to above, p. 208, Alan Gartner, et al., *What Nixon Is Doing to Us*, Harper & Row, 1973; Leon E. Panetta and Peter Gall, *Bring Us Together*, Lippincott, 1971; Reg Murphy and Hal Gulliver, *The Southern Strategy*, Scribner's, 1971. Haldeman order: Evans-Novak, *Nixon*, pp. 152–56. "instant integration," "vigilante": ibid., pp. 156, 174. "forced": *NYT*, 3/24/74, p. 1. Voting Rights: Evans-Novak, pp. 150–51; *NYT*, 12/26/73, Op-Ed; Gartner, op. cit., pp. 86–87. Firings: Evans-Novak, pp. 295, 353–58, 150, 156–69, 358–60, 134; Osborne, *Nixon Watch*, 1971, pp. 183–91.

Page 245. Civil Rights Commission: Harris, *Justice*, op. cit., pp. 209–10; Gartner, pp. 87–88; James Wechsler, *NYP*, 11/14/73. Haynesworth-Carswell: Evans-Novak, pp. 159–72; Osborne, *Nixon Watch*, 1970, p. 114; Murphy and Gulliver, Ch. 6.

Page 246. "He was," "With yesterday's": Evans-Novak, pp. 170–71.

Page 247. Directives/laws: Gartner, pp. 5, 18, 206–12. FAP: Evans-Novak, pp. 230–33; *New Republic*, 7/3/71; Daniel Patrick Moynihan, *The Politics of a Guaranteed Income*, Random House, 1973. Spottswood: Gartner, p. 85. Footnote: *WA*, p. 770.

Page 248. Farmer: Evans-Novak, p. 135. Anti-welfare: Gartner, Ch. 1, 2, 4; *WSJ*, 11/13/73, editorial page; *NYT*, 3/4–7/73, p. 1; *Budget Message*, annual, GPO. National income: John McFall, in *NYT*, 6/9/74.

Page 249. "The needy": *NYT*, 6/20/73, p. 1. Revenue sharing: Gartner, Ch. 1; *NYT*, 6/20/74, p. 28, 8/27/74, p. 1, 12/20/74, p. 19; Sumner M. Rosen (ed.), *Economic Power Failure*, McGraw-Hill, 1975, pp. 224–26. "Nixon has": *NYT*, 3/7/73, p. 22. Private survey: *NYT*, 12/20/74, p. 19. St. Louis: *Time*, 6/4/73, p. 16.

Page 250. Repression: above, Chapter 4. Universities: *NYT*, 3/7/73, p. 1, 3/20/73, 6/17/73, Magazine, 1/16/74, p. 64, 9/4/74, editorial page; *WSJ*, 11/13/73, editorial page; Gartner, pp. 39–40. Mitchell: S. M. Lipset and Earl Raab, *Commentary*, 9/73.

Page 251. Academics: above, and James Reston, *NYT*, 10/11/74; Gartner, pp. 29–40; *NYT*, 12/4/74, letters. Cities: *NYT*, 6/30/73, editorial, 10/12/73, letter, 3/6/74, p. 1, 3/7/74, editorial, 4/16/74, p. 77; *WP*, 1/5/74, p. A1, 3/28/74, 6/17/74, p. A2; *WSJ*, 10/9/73, 7/29/74, editorial page; Gartner, Ch. 4, 6. Herbers: *NYT*, 1/30/73, p. 19. Media: Safire, *Before the Fall*, op. cit., V-5 ("In all," p. 341); Gartner, Ch. 14; Kevin P. Phillips, *Mediacracy*, op. cit., Ch. 2; Voorhis, op. cit., Ch. 14; Patrick Buchanan, *The New Majority*, op. cit., pp. 15 ff.; Network Project (New York), *Notebooks*, 1972–74; Richard Harris, *New Yorker*, 10/1/73. Nixon: Safire, p. 360.

Page 252. Nixon team: *OTP*, Network Project, 1973, p. 4; *Newsweek*, 1/15/73, pp. 42 ff.; *Progressive*, 4/73; *WP*, 5/10/74, B20, 12/3, 12/6/73, editorial page; Sanford Ungar, *The Papers and the Papers*, Dutton, 1972; *New Republic*, 5/5/73; *Broadcasting*, 2/16/70, p. 38, and 4/73, passim; *NYP*, 3/7/74; Harriet Van Horne, *NYP*, 10/10/73; Ervin final, pp. 112, 135–36, 199–200; *NYT*, 1/23/73, p. 28, 2/14/73, 10/15/73, p. 1; *WSJ*, 1/14/74, p. 1; *Impeachment of Richard M. Nixon*, op. cit., pp. 212–20. PBS: *NYT* 5/28/73, 9/29/74, Sec. 2, p. 1; *OTP*, op. cit., pp. 17 ff.; *WP*, 12/6/73, editorial page. *Times*: 3/1/73. Harris: *New Yorker*, 10/1/73, p. 128.

Page 253. Colson: *WP*, 12/3/73. Salant: Gartner, p. 224. Economic policy: Gartner, Ch. 1; Voorhis, Ch. 3–11; Evans-Novak, Ch. 7, 8; Demaris, *Dirty Business*, Ch. 1, 2; Gerald Krefetz, *The Dying Dollar*, Playboy, 1975; Stanley Aronowitz, *Food, Shelter, and the American Dream*, Seabury, 1974; Rosen, *Economic Power Failure*, op. cit.; *Dollars & Sense* (monthly); *WSJ*, 7/22/74, p. 3; *New Republic*, 8/15/70, p. 10; *NYT*, 4/27/75, Magazine, p. 18.

Page 254. *Concentrates*: generally, Richard Barnet and Ronald E.

Muller, *Global Reach*, Simon & Schuster, 1974, Ch. 1, 2, 9, 10; Nader-Green, *Corporate Power in America*, op. cit., Part I; Ira Katznelson and Mark Kesselman, *The Politics of Power*, Harcourt, 1975, Ch. 3, 5.

Page 255. Nixon-Eisenhower: Evans-Novak, p. 179. Turnaround: ibid., pp. 370–401; *NYT*, 12/15/70, p. 1; *WP*, 5/1/74, p. A4 ("The idea," loc. cit.); David Mermelstein (ed.), *The Economic Crisis Reader*, op. cit., pp. 384 ff.; White, *1972*, op. cit.; *Fortune*, 7/74; *NYT*, 8/9/74, p. 45.

Page 256. Galbraith: *WP*, 5/1/74, p. A4.

Page 257. Defense: I. F. Stone, *Polemics and Prophecies, 1967–70*, Vintage, 1972, esp. pp. 169–234. "The first": *New York Review*, 6/5/69, p. 5. Costs: *NYT*, 1/25/73, 1/28, 73, Sec. 3, 4; Kissinger speech, American Society of Newspaper Editors, 5/9/75. Budgets: *NYT*, 1/14/75, p. 1; *WP*, 7/31/74, p. A4; Sanford Gottlieb, *NYT*, 5/20/74. Overseas: *NYT*, 1/26/75, Sec. 4, 4/14/75, p. 1; *Commonweal*, 12/20/74, p. 265. *Times*: 1/22/74.

Page 258. Contractors/projects: *Ramparts*, 7/75, p. 24; Rosen, op. cit., pp. 184–85; *WSJ*, 3/19/74, p. 7; *WP*, 12/22/74, *Outlook*, p. 1; *Washington Watch*, 8/15/74; *New Republic*, 6/9/73, p. 35; *Newsweek*, 1/27/75, p. 49, 4/14/75, p. 70; *NYT*, 12/15/73, p. 1, 3/11/74, p. 43, 6/1/74, p. 1; *SANE Quarterly*, 12/73. Oil-Vietnam: *New Republic*, 3/13/71 (quoting *Petroleum Engineer*); Mark Selden, *Remaking Asia*, op. cit., Ch. 1, 4.

Page 259. "Energy crisis": *WP*, 12/16/74, p. A17, 11/3/74, p. A2; Common Cause circular, 11/74; Robert Sherrill, *Penthouse*, 10/74, pp. 43 ff. (Hart, p. 91); Jack Anderson, *WP*, 10/7/74. Project Independence: *WSJ*, 3/6, 3/7/74, p. 1; *Nation*, 5/2/73, 1/5/74; *Fortune*, 4/74; *NYT*, 11/8/73, p. 1.

Page 260. Alaska: *Nation*, 11/5/73, 6/11/73; *NYT*, 10/14/73, Magazine. Administration: Sherrill, *Penthouse*, 10/74; *WP*, 12/17/74, p. A11; *NYT*, 6/11/74, 10/30/73, editorial page. *Time*: 12/9/74, p. 32. Exports, profits, prices: ibid.; *SA 1973*, #607; *NYT*, 12/31/74; Chester Bowles, *NYT*, 11/8/74. Administration: *New Orleans Times-Picayune*, 10/28/74; *Time*, loc. cit.; Voorhis, Ch. 3; *NYT*, 4/9/74, p. 1, 6/17/74, p. 1; *WP*, 3/27/74, p. A2; *WSJ*, 4/9/74; and above, Chapter 1.

Page 261. Grain deal: James Trager, *Amber Waves of Grain*, Arthur Fields (New York), 1973; *NYT*, 11/25/73, Magazine; *Nation*, 6/25/73, p. 815; *NYT*, 12/5/73, 2/13/74, p. 1, 6/23/74, editorial, 11/10/74, Sec. 3; *WP*, 3/10/74, p. A2. Milk deal: above, p. 66.

Page 262. "because": Ervin final, p. 847. Technology: *SA 1974*, #907; *Budget*, GPO, 1975; *NYT*, 4/2/74, 12/30/74, 15/75, Sec. 3, p. 38, 5/31/75, p. 22, 7/7/75, p. 26; *NYP*, 3/25/74, p. 25.

Page 263. Perot: *NYP*, 5/19/73, p. 24. Murchison: *WP*, 12/21/74, p. A5. Real estate: *NYT*, 6/20/73, p. 28, 8/8/73, 9/29/73, 5/11/74, p. 1, 6/25/74, 8/20/74; *WP*, 6/12/74, p. A2; and above, Chapter 2.

Page 264. Leisure: above, Chapter 2, and pp. 251–52; Jack Anderson, *WP*, 4/30/74.

Page 265. Foreign policy: generally, Gartner, Ch. 15; Voorhis, Ch.

13, Evans-Novak, Ch. 4, Lurie, *Running*, pp. 346–52, 364–74; Rosen, op. cit., pp. 127–38; Barber, *Presidential Character*, op. cit., pp. 417–42; Safire, *Before the Fall*, V-6, VI, X-4, 5. NSC meeting: Jack Anderson, *WP*, 10/18/74. Kissinger: e.g., Lurie, p. 343. Acheson: *Newsweek*, 8/20/73, p. 13. Wall Street: Thomas Powers, *The War at Home*, Grossman, 1973, pp. 197 ff.

Page 267. Spectrum: above, p. 228–31. Pope: Voorhis, p. 202. Kazin: *New York Review*, 12/13/73, p. 23.

Page 268. CIA ambassadors: *Nation*, 6/15/74, p. 745; *Counterspy*, Spring 1975.

Page 269. Wentworth: *WSJ*, 8/8/73, p. 34. China: *NYT*, 3/27/73, 6/1/73, 10/14/74; Edward Neiland and Charles R. Smith, *The Future of the China Market*, Stanford, 1973; *WP*, 3/19/74; *Ramparts*, 10/71, p. 16. Business council: *NYT*, 3/27/73.

Page 270. Russia: *Time*, 6/25/73, pp. 35 ff.; *Newsweek*, 12/2/74, pp. 48 ff.; *NYT*, 2/24/74, Magazine, pp. 11 ff., 3/5/74, 11/10/74, 6/29/74, p. 35; *WSJ*, 5/22/74, p. 5, 6/28/74; *Houston Post*, 2/1/74; *WP*, 11/4/74, p. A1. Plum: *NYT*, 4/13/73, p. 1, 6/9/73, p. 1, 12/12/73, p. 1; *WP*, 7/2/73, p. 1; *Houston Post*, loc. cit.

6. THE YANKEE COUNTERATTACK

Page 273. Herbers: *NYT*, 3/4–7/73, p. 1; also 5/6/73, p. 1, 6/7/74, p. 1.

Page 275. March–April chronology: *Watergate Hearings*, Viking, op. cit., pp. 66 ff.; *Congressional Record*, 5/6/74. Footnote: Carl Oglesby, *Boston Phoenix*, 5/29/73, 6/5/73; *Harper's*, 11/73; *National Review*, 9/14/73; *NYT*, 2/24/73, 3/2/73, p. 1, 4/1/73, p. 1; *US News*, 5/7/73, p. 78; Rockefeller Report on the CIA, GPO, 6/10/75; Watergate: Baker appendix, Ervin final, pp. 1115 ff.

Page 277. Nixon Presidency: above, Chapter 5, esp. pp. 244 ff. Vietnam reaction: generally, Powers, *The War*, op. cit.

Page 278. Schlesinger: *The Imperial Presidency*, Houghton Mifflin, 1974. Ehrlichman: quoted in *Nation*, 2/26/73. Stone: *New York Review*, 1/25/73, p. 13.

Page 279. 40 vetoes: *Congressional Quarterly*, 8/10/74, p. 2192. $18 billion: *NYT*, 11/22/73. Nixon unlimited: Herbers, op. cit. Javits: ibid., 3/5/73, p. 20. Dismantling: ibid., 3/4/73, 3/7/73.

Page 280. *Monitor*: 3/24/73. Abuses: above. "garrison state," "into an era": Voorhis, pp. 249, 263, quoting Henry Steele Commager, Ripon Society.

Page 281. Commager: *NYT*, 3/4/73, p. 47. Fagin's Law: Dickens and Sale, op. cit.

Page 282. Economy, *Post*, Burns: *WP*, 5/16/74, Op-Ed.

Page 284. Rockefeller-Common Cause: *Political Brokers*, op. cit., Ch. 10. Union leaders: *NYP*, 8/30/74, 8/3/73, p. 19; *NYT*, 2/19/74, p. 13, 4/2/74, p. 14. Columnists: e.g., *Human Events*, 11/3/73, quoting Victor Riesel. Academics: e.g., *WP*, 9/16/73, symposium; *NYT*, Op-Ed,

1973, passim. Sirica: quoted by Freedman, *NYT*, 12/14/75, p. 29, Op-Ed. Richardson/Cox: White, *Breach*, op. cit., p. 180; Sussman, *Coverup*, op. cit., Part 8.

Page 286. Legal staff: *NYT*, 4/16/74, 4/21/74, Sec. 4, 11/8/73, p. 1; Sussman, pp. 266–69; White, *Breach*, p. 291; *WSJ*, 7/22/74, p. 1; Joseph Kraft, *WP*, 5/28/74. Stennis: Sussman, pp. 262, 268–73, 280. Taxes, Mills: *WP*, 12/3/73, p. 1, 4/4/74, p. 1; *NYT*, 12/9/73, p. 1; Clayton Fritchey, *NYP*, 3/7/74.

Page 287. Jaworski: *WP*, 11/1/73, p. 1; *NYT*, 11/4/73; *Esquire*, 2/75, pp. 89 ff. Jaworski failures: *NYT*, 1/13/74, editorial, 6/21/74, Op-Ed, 10/14/74, editorial, 10/16/74, Op-Ed, 10/20/74, Sec. 4, 12/29/74, Sec. 4; Nicholas van Hoffman, *NYP*, 6/25/74; *Village Voice*, 5/23/74; *WSJ*, 10/11/74, editorial page.

Page 288. Travel: *NYT* coverage, 10/73–8/74; White, *Breach*, p. 304. Rim visits, response: *NYT*, 11/22/73, p. 1, 3/21/74, p. 33, 5/4/74, p. 1, 4/26/74, p. 1, 6/9/73, p. 1.

Page 289. Wallace: *NYT*, 2/19/74, p. 23. Polls: *WP*, 11/18/73, p. A14, 12/10/73, p. 1; *NYT*, 2/3/74; *NYP*, 5/23/74, p. 18. Morrison letter: *NYT*, 5/4/74. Fish: *NYT*, 8/29/74.

Page 290. "HAND IN": *WP*, 2/19/74. Citizens' groups: *NYT*, 10/31/73, 5/2/74, 5/16/74; *NYP* 3/27/74; stories above, Rim visits. Korff: *NYT*, 4/7/74, 6/10/74, p. 1; *WP*, 6/10/74, p. 1; interview with Othal Brand, general chairman, Washington, D.C., 6/74. Reaction quotes: *NYT*, 12/9/73, 1/20/74, 6/15/74, 6/19/73, 11/22/73, 6/11/74, 3/18/74, 1/13/74; *WP*, 4/26/74, p. A4, 5/17/74.

Page 291. Nixon-Congress: *NYT*, 4/29/74, 6/4/74, p. 1, 7/28/74, p. 1. Congressional actions: *NYT*, 12/22/74, p. 1, 10/6/74, Sec. 4. Herbers: *NYT*, 4/29/74. Burch: *WP*, 2/16/74; White, *Breach*, p. 291.

Page 292. Nixon-conservatives: *NYT*, 4/29/74, 7/8/74, p. 14; *WSJ*, 5/31/74, p. 1; Jack Anderson, *WP*, 6/4/74. Red carpet: Anderson, ibid., *NYP*, 6/3/74; William S. White, *WP*, 11/17/73; *NYT*, 7/8/74, p. 14; *New Orleans Times-Picayune*, 1/27/74, p. 6. Sequoia: *NYT*, 6/4/74, p. 1. Sparkman, Long: Anderson, *NYP*, 6/4/74, 4/29/74. White: loc. cit. Head-counters: e.g., *Newsweek*, 8/12/74, pp. 18 ff.

Page 293. Nixon reactions: White, *Breach*, pp. 219–21, Ch. 9. Judiciary: Jimmy Breslin, *How the Good Guys Finally Won*, Viking, 1975, esp. pp. 95–96, 107–109; *NYT*, 12/21/73, p. 1, 1/8/74, p. 1. Resignation calls: *WP*, 1/22/74, p. A1; *NYT*, 3/20/74, p. 1; *NYP*, 7/24/74, p. 8. Joint Committee: *NYT*, 4/4/74, p. 1. Government Operations: *Impeachment of Richard M. Nixon*, op. cit., pp. 316–18; *NYT*, 3/22/74, 3/23/74. Ally: George Beall, *NYP*, 8/18/73, p. 22; Evans-Novak, *NYP*, 8/11/73. Agnew: *NYT*, 10/11/73, p. 1.

Page 294. Laird: *Parade*, 1/12/75, p. 6. Connally: Evans-Novak, *NYP*, 10/15/73; *NYT*, 4/19/75, p. 15, 10/11/73, p. 1. Ford biography: Bud Vestal, *Jerry Ford Up Close*, Coward, 1974; Jerald F. terHorst, *Gerald Ford and the Future of the Presidency*, Third Press, 1974; John Osborne, *The Last Nixon Watch*, New Republic, 1975; *NYP*, 10/13/73, p. 22, 8/10/74, p. 20; *NYT*, 10/13/73, p. 19, 8/9/74, p. 8, 8/11/74,

Sec. 4, Magazine, 9/15/74; Senate Rules Committee, House Judiciary Committee, "Confirmation of Gerald R. Ford," GPO, hearings 11/74.

Page 295. Douglas: above, and Demaris, *Dirty Business*, op. cit., pp. 309–16. Watergate squelch: above, and *Washington Monthly*, 4/73, 11/74; *NYT*, 5/2/74. Grand Rapids: Vestal, Ch. 5, 8.

Page 296. Ford friends/aides: *NYT*, 8/9/74, p. 4, 8/15/74, p. 10, 8/12/74, p. 1, 8/19/74, p. 1, 8/26/74, p. 1, 9/4/74, p. 28, 9/12/74, 9/25/74, p. 18, 11/17/74, Sec. 3; 12/28/74, p. 1; *WP*, 11/24/74, p. L1, 12/7/74; *WSJ*, 9/26/74, p. 1, 7/10/74, p. 1, *Time* 8/26/74, p. 31; *NYP*, 8/9/74, p. 51, 8/17/74, p. 20, 8/31/74, p. 22.

Page 297. "I would say": *NYT*, 8/9/74, p 9. Goodell: *NYT*, 9/12/74. Scranton: White, *1964*, pp. 108–110. U.S. Steel: *Village Voice*, 12/23/74, p. 42. Rockefeller associations: Hess-Broder, *Republican Establishment*, op. cit.; *White*, 1964. Kissinger: *NYP*, series, 6/3–6/15/74. Footnote: investments, *NYT* 9/24/74, p. 1, 12/4/74, p. 1; *Village Voice*, 12/23/74, p. 3.

Page 298. "has formed": Evans-Novak, *NYP*, 3/14/74. Rockefeller: *NYT*, 8/21/74, p. 1, 12/20/74, p. 17, 8/2/74, p. 25. "an enthusiastic": *NYT*, 8/2/74, p. 25. Initial moves: *NYT*, 8/26/74, p. 1. Nixon aides: *NYT*, 8/11/74, p. 1; White, *Breach*, Ch. 1.

Page 299. Judiciary: *Impeachment of Richard M. Nixon*, op. cit., esp. pp. 15–16. Supreme Court: ibid., p. 183; *NYT*, 7/25/74, p. 1. St. Clair, Haig: White, *Breach*, Ch. 1, *NYT*, 8/18/74, Magazine, p. 6. Kissinger-Schlesinger: *NYT*, 8/24/74, p. 1; *NYP*, 8/28/74, p. 4. Kissinger-Nixon: *NYT*, 8/9/74, p. 1, 8/12/74, p. 1, White, *Breach*, p. 29. Final speech: *NYT*, 8/10/74, p. 4.

Page 300. Ford: NYT, 8/10/74, p. 1.

Page 301. Ford imprint: *NYT*, 8/20/74, p. 1, 9/17/74, p. 1, 8/23/74, 11/14/74, p. 28, 8/23/74, p. 1, 34, 9/1/74, 8/22/74, 8/13/74, p. 1, 9/1/74, p. 1, 8/18/74, p. 34, 1/2/75, p. 26, 11/22/74, p. 1; *WSJ*, 11/22/74, p. 5; *NYT*, 9/4/74; 11/20/74, p. 61, 11/11/74. Reagan: *NYT*, 12/19/74, p. 53; *WP*, 3/24/75, p. A1; *Newsweek*, 3/24/75, pp. 19 ff.; *Human Events*, 12/7/74, 12/14/74. Rim Republicans: Evans-Novak, *WP*, 9/23/74, 8/29/74.

Page 302. Texas: *Texas Observer*, 10/4/74, p. 6. Ford firings, appointments: *Congressional Directory*, 1975; above, p. 296; *WP*, 2/9/75, p. A4, 10/27/74, L1; *NYT*, 12/4/74.

Page 303. Rockefeller: *NYT*, 8/21/74, p. 1. *Human Events*: 10/12/74, by Howard Phillips. Conflicts: *NYT*, 4/28/74, Op-Ed; *WP*, 11/3/74, *Outlook*.

Page 304. Bribes: House-Senate hearings, passim, 10–12/74. Income taxes: ibid.; Safire, *NYT*, 9/26/74. Sworn in: *NYT*, 12/20/74, p. 1. *Time*: 12/9/74; p. 15. Reagan party: *NYT*, 12/18/74, p. 30.

Page 305. Nation: 8/31/74, p. 132. FEA: *WP*, 4/1/74, p. 1.

Page 306. Law firms/lobbies: *WSJ*, 7/23/73, p. 1, 12/29/73, p. 1, 3/8/74, p. 1; Mark J. Green, *Who Runs Congress*, op. cit., pp., 44–45, 141; Mark J. Green, *The Other Government*, Grossman, 1975. Kennedy out: *NYT*, 9/24/74, p. 1. Rim challengers: *NYT*, 9/27/74, p. 37,

12/13/74, p. 1, 3/24/75, p. 1, 12/15/74, 11/24/74, Sec. 4, 11/17/74, Magazine, p. 32; *WP*, 11/4/74, p. A1; Evans-Novak, *NYP*, 8/29/74.

Page 307. Geological Survey: *Fortune*, 6/74, p. 135. FEA: Jack Anderson, *WP*, 10/23/74. Soybean belt: *Southern Exposure*, Fall 1974, pp. 15 ff. Beef consumption: *WP*, 12/28/74.

Page 308. Real-estate starts: *US News*, 1/21/74, p. 7. Population: *NYT*, 7/25/74, p. 67; *National Observer*, 8/3/74. St. Petersburg: *NYT*, 7/28/74, p. 1. Los Angeles: *NYT*, 9/30/73, 6/16/75, p. 1.

Page 310. Fruits: *New Testament*, Matthew, VII, 20.

Index

About the Author

KIRKPATRICK SALE was born in Ithaca, New York, graduated from Cornell University, and has been a writer and editor for more than fifteen years, in this country and abroad. He is the author of the highly acclaimed history of the Students for a Democratic Society, *SDS*, published in 1973, and a work on Africa, *The Land and People of Ghana*. He has also written more than a hundred magazine and newspaper articles for such publications as the *New York Review of Books*, the *New York Times Magazine*, *Harper's*, the *Village Voice*, the *Nation*, the *San Francisco Chronicle*, the *Los Angeles Times*, and *Southern Exposure*. He lives with his wife, an editor, and two daughters, schoolchildren, in New York City.

VINTAGE POLITICAL SCIENCE
AND SOCIAL CRITICISM